AMERICA
WITHOUT A COMPASS

AMERICA
WITHOUT A COMPASS

RAFAEL FERMOSELLE, PH. D.

iUniverse®

AMERICA WITHOUT A COMPASS

iUniverse books may be ordered through booksellers or by contacting:

iUniverse
1663 Liberty Drive
Bloomington, IN 47403
www.iuniverse.com
1-800-Authors (1-800-288-4677)

ISBN: 978-1-4917-8691-8 (sc)
ISBN: 978-1-4917-8692-5 (e)

Library of Congress Control Number: 2016901098

Print information available on the last page.

iUniverse rev. date: 01/21/2016

Americans tried to fix the world and neglected the home front, resulting in failure at both ends. Ignorance became fashionable and opportunistic polymorphous predators, parasites, and false prophets took advantage of the situation. It is hard to believe how far the nation fell into violent interracial melodramas, political mediocrity, incivility, and confusion. There is no agreement on what is good and evil. Everything is relative, ugly and pretty, real and false, right and wrong. American society suffers from a lack of coherence and consistency, and such a heavy burden of illogical non-sense that it can no longer handle all the contradictions. We are unaware of where we are going…

AMERICA WITHOUT A COMPASS

President Abraham Lincoln's "surveying compass" is on the previous page. It is part of the collection of the New Salem State Historical Site in Illinois. The picture was taken by Robert Church under contract with the museum, and he graciously authorized its use in this publication. During preparation of the book we learned that the Illinois State Government decided to shut down all the government museums at the end of September 2015 to reduce the state's operating budget.

TABLE OF CONTENTS

History is the version of past events that people have decided to agree upon.

Napoleon Bonaparte

The greatest historian should also be a great moralist. It is no proof of impartiality to treat wickedness and goodness on the same level.

Theodore Roosevelt

Those who cannot learn from history are doomed to repeat it.

George Santayana

Political extremism involves two prime ingredients: an excessively simple diagnosis of the world's ills, and a conviction that there are identifiable villains back of it all.

John W. Gardner

Two things are infinite: the universe and human stupidity; and I'm not sure about the universe.

Albert Einstein

It is by the goodness of God that in our country we have these three unspeakably precious things, freedom of speech, freedom of conscience, and the prudence never to practice either of them.

Mark Twain

ACNOWLEDGEMENTS

Among the people who most influenced my thinking, reflected in these pages, was University Professor Harold E. Davis (1903-1988), who served as Chairman of the History and Government Departments, and Dean of the College of Arts and Sciences of The American University in Washington, D.C. He mentored me for four years as I completed by M.A. and Ph.D. He was an expert in political and social thought, and author of several books.

Dr. Harold E. Davis
No known restrictions on publication.

SA Gerald T. Grimaldi (1927-2009), the FBI agent who recruited me early in 1968 and supervised my work in COINTELPRO for a couple of years provided me with an opportunity to experience a violent dimension of the 1960s.[1] We became friends and continued in contact until he passed away in 2009. I could never have otherwise understood the direction, length, width, and height of the *counterculture* developing in the 1960s. I had only been associated with the FBI for about three weeks when Dr. Martin Luther King, Jr., was assassinated on 4 April 1968, triggering violent riots. I walked right into the rioting with a young FBI agent, and even entered a liquor store on Irving Street N.W. Washington, D.C. as it was being looted. That evening, I witnessed the incredible spectacle of numerous buildings on fire within a thirty by thirty block area of Washington. From a hill in Arlington, right behind the Iwo Jima Memorial, one could see the night sky red from the fires, and the smell of smoke permeated the city. I did not have to imagine it, I saw Washington burning!

Over the next four years, I attended numerous gatherings where armed revolution and terrorism were discussed, drugs were consumed, and the worse elements of the *counterculture* were displayed. A good number of radical members of the Weather Underground had visited and received training in Cuba, with the aim of overthrowing the U.S.

Government. It was definitely an instructional experience, but without the mentoring provided by Gerry it would have been very difficult to rationalize what I was witnessing: the inability of the government to arrest, try and convict would be Marxist-Leninist revolutionaries and terrorists. He read a considerable portion of this text and offered suggestions, but he passed away in 2009 before I could share the entire manuscript with him.

While completing my Ph.D. dissertation I worked for newly elected Senator Lawton Chiles (D-FL) (1930-1998), who introduced me to several of his Senate colleagues, and gave me an opportunity to learn how business is transacted in the *sanctum sanctorum* of the Capitol.[2] I went to his home early in the morning to teach him Spanish, and then drove him to the Capitol, and along the way briefed him on developments in Latin America, and performed other duties as assigned. I told Senator Chiles that I was working for the FBI, to avoid any potential misunderstandings. I did not want to risk being *blown out of the water* nor have questions raised as to the potential targeting of the Senator by some kind of an undercover operations. He checked me out and thanked me for leveling with him. He joined me in a couple of covert infiltration of anti-war demonstrations after the bombing of the Capitol building by extremists in 1971. He wanted to witness how violent extremists took advantage of demonstrations to wreak havoc in the nation's capital by breaking windows, setting fires, and attacking police officers. Both, Dr. Davis and Senator Chiles represented liberal and progressive philosophies, but with a high doses of sanity and intellectual capacity.

JUL-4 -71

Chiles Gets a Learni

By FRANK MURRAY
Special Writer

WASHINGTON — Although U.S. senators seem never at a loss for words — ready to hold forth on any subject for extended periods — Florida's junior senator, Lawton Chiles, spends the first part of his workday increasing his speaking power.

Rafael Fermoselle, 25, a slight and handsome Cuban refugee who holds a masters degree in Latin American studies, comes to Chiles' Georgetown home at 7:15 a.m. each day to tutor the senator in Spanish.

CHILES ALSO shows interest in politics and history south of the border. He made two trips to Mexico in little more than a month, one to attend the 11th Annual Mexico-U.S. Interparliamentary Conference where he met with Mexico's president. In August, he is going to Brazil and Peru.

On May 20, Chiles delivered a lengthy speech to the Senate, noting the 69th anniversary of Cuban independence and the relationship of that country to his own dating to the time when Cuban militia units fought on the side of the colonies against England in the Revolutionary War. And he [illegible]

SEN. CHILES AND HIS SPANISH TEACHER FERMOSELLE
Pair Chat of World Politics at Capitol

Published picture on 4 July 1971 with Senator Chiles in front of the US Capitol. Times Union, Jacksonville, Florida. No known restrictions on publication.

I learned a lot working for Career Ambassador Terrence A. Todman (1926-2014) when I worked under him while serving as Counselor of the U.S. Embassy in Buenos Aires (1989-1993) during a challenging period of transformation in Argentina.[3] He was an Afro-American patriot and great national asset. We first met at the Department of State while making our rounds of routine visits to government agencies in Washington. When we shared our experiences we realized that we were both being asked what we had done wrong to be assigned to Argentina, which had become a basket case of political and economic mismanagement. President Carlos Saúl Menem had just been elected to office and he had announced his intention to move the country away from failed statist policies by privatizing deficit-ridden utilities and other government owned companies. He had an epiphany about how to achieve progress.

Receiving an award from Ambassador Todman at the US Embassy in Argentina in 1992. No known restrictions on publication.

Ambassador Todman led an effort to be supportive of a left-of-center politician who was trying to be friendly to the U.S. and implement many ideas suggested by American policy makers so as to allow the private sector to become the dynamic force in the economy. The experiment eventually failed, partially due to unrestrained corruption, and partially because the U.S. was not fully prepared to provide support to countries that tried to copy the American model at a time when the Soviet Union was collapsing and it had become eminently clear that Communism does not work.

In writing this book, it was not easy to maintain a degree of detachment and impartiality, which is a typical problem when writing about contemporary issues. I consulted specialists and people with other viewpoints, to maintain objectivity. The failure of public assistance programs and international aid efforts foreshadows even greater problems, as mounting public sector debt undermines America's political, economic, and social systems. A wave of fear about the future is generating a mounting tide of prejudice, xenophobia, and intolerance by extremists. And that is one of the results of extremist generated ideas from the 1960s, which have led to a growing chaotic environment.

I am grateful for the moral support and encouragement provided by friends and colleagues. I am deeply appreciative of the assistance provided by Ambassador Manuel Rocha, who sent me numerous articles on a wide variety of subjects, in addition to his encouragement for my work in putting together this book.[4] Mark Jaworowski helped me to stay on track. My cousin Joaquin M. Fermoselle and my sister-in-law Graciela Argerich assisted me to edit the manuscript. I thank my family and friends for their tolerance through the long process of writing a book of this nature. Errors of fact and interpretation are strictly my own.

PREFACE

It is easy to talk about what you have earned the right to talk about.

Dale Carnegie

The highest expression of loyalty and patriotism is to point out that there are better ways of doing things and healthier ways for a nation to go forward. I do not believe in the concept of "*go along to get along…*" I see an increasing and discouraging lack of purpose and direction in the United States (U.S.). The growth of a vulgar culture since the 1960s resulted in a process of deconstructing the nation, defined as *a people with common historical traditions, identity, culture, language, and unity of purpose that transcend differences in national origin, ethnicity, race or religious convictions.* The American aggregate concept of what constitutes *the will of citizens* is being undermined daily. There are multiple elements to the problem, from the shallow knowledge of Americans about the country's past, to national defense and security misconceptions, economic and fiscal dysfunctions, cultural decadence, and increasing disrespect for law and order. All the internal problems are not only damaging the nation, but are likewise contributing to global chaos.

As a teenager I witnessed how Marxist extremists took control of Cuba and began to dismantle the established order through intimidation, coercion and violence.[5] Without overplaying religious convictions, I saw numerous violations of the basic principles outlined in the *Ten Commandments* all around me. Communists were dishonest, justified lying, stealing, killing, and imposed idol worship of Fidel Castro. I experienced a revolution, the building of a police state, and the destruction of a society. I took an immediate dislike of Communists. Nobody had to tell me about the existence of *inalienable natural rights to life and liberty.* I did not have to read about *natural law theory,* the Magna Carta, the writings of John Locke, Immanuel Kant, Jean-Jacques Rousseau, Thomas Jefferson, George Mason, the American Declaration of Independence, or the 1789 French National Constituent

Assembly's *Déclaration des droits de l'homme et du citoyen,* to understand that the most basic human rights were being violated in Cuba by the Communist revolutionaries.

I was not about to accept being led blindly by individuals who had no respect for others who tried to exercise their right to disagree. The whole idea of *wealth redistribution* and *social engineering,* in practice, does not work. Wealth must be created, but it cannot be usurped! I learned that evil cannot be wished away. After the failure by the Kennedy Administration to provide air cover for the Bay of Pigs landing in April 1961, the possibility of insurrection with American support was gone. I was 15 years old when I was forced to make some difficult choices. I either had to accept living under a dictatorship, being plowed under by the Communists, or leave Cuba and go into exile, without my parents and grandparents, and without knowing if I would ever see them again.

Every book starts with a blank piece of paper… It has taken me over six years to fill about 500 of those blank pages. I have asked myself many times what triggered my commitment to put together this book, but could not come up with a "single detonator." I despise Marxists and Socialists of all brands and persuasions, and loathe all extremists from the far left to the far right, as ultimately, all extremists act alike. I spent several years in clandestine operations infiltrating terrorist groups and/or in a *mano-a-mano* competition with really sleazy characters at both ends of the political spectrum. It is good to have intellectual restlessness and inspirational visionaries, but I have witnessed how good intentions can produce very nasty results, and that happens to be one of the main thrusts of this book. Generally, *social engineering* schemes end up failing and a lot of people get hurt in the process.

I have dealt with dishonest, corrupt, disreputable, and inept characters while serving at five American embassies as a U.S. Foreign Service officer, and as a Department of Defense contractor. I lived in Canada, the Dominican Republic, Mexico, Argentina, The Netherlands, Spain, and Germany, either assigned as an American diplomat or as a government contractor working in support of the Department of Defense and/or the intelligence community (IC). I deployed to Iraq as a contractor with the U.S. Army Human Terrain program. I have visited at least 26 countries. My international experience provided me many opportunities to compare what works and what does not work. Throughout my over 48 years working for Uncle Sam in one capacity or another, I learned a lot and experienced many events that contributed to the conclusions presented in this book. There are many personifications of Satan and his army of evil spirits all over the place. I want to unmask them.

INTRODUCTION

Educate and inform the whole mass of the people... They are the only sure reliance for the preservation of our liberty.

Thomas Jefferson

Americans tried to fix the world while neglecting the home front, and failed at both ends. They live inconsistently, in an absurd self-contradiction frequently forced to choose between unsatisfactory alternatives with fundamentally shaky assumptions. The United States of America has been incredibly resilient, but American society has created such a heavy burden of illogical nonsense that it can no longer handle all the contradictions. The situation resembles the old paradox: *The omnipotent Being that created a stone so heavy that not even the omnipotent Being could lift.*[6] While suffering from a superiority complex (We are #1), Americans no longer know what is right or wrong, and cannot meaningfully address the critical challenges associated with the managing the government, the economy, national defense, education, health care, immigration, or what goes on in the bedroom.

Sisyphus

No known restrictions on publication.

According to a poll conducted by ORC International in May 2014 for CNN Money, most people feel that the so-called *American Dream* is no longer achievable. Young adults between 18 and 34 years of age are particularly negative about the future, with 63% expressing the view that "*the dream*" is unattainable.[7] There have been many periods of economic recession, lasting from a few months to several years, due to multiple causes. Nevertheless, Americans have always exhibited endurance and bounced back. Historically could wake up and turn things around with realistic goals, courage, fortitude, spirituality, and a compass to establish a positive direction. Negativism about the future in 2015 is a departure from the optimism of the past.

The U.S. gradually emerged as a country with a common culture based on Judeo-Christian principles, democratic values, and respect for the rule of law. By the end of WWII in 1945 it was the pre-eminent economic and military power in the world, and regarded as a unique outpost of Western Civilization. After overcoming the challenges of the war the U.S. experienced sustained economic growth and its population flourished during the 1950s. Entrepreneurship steadily drove the economy to new heights. The economy grew by 37%, and median income grew by 30%. About 25% of the population was poor, but there was hope for a way out of deprivation. By 1965 the percentage of poor people had dropped to 15%. The U.S. led the world in labor productivity. Jobs were plentiful, and the size of the middle class steadily expanded year after year.

Through the *Servicemen's Readjustment Act of 1944*, known as the *GI Bill of Rights*, over 7.8 million WWII veterans were able to graduate from college. Veterans were given access to loan guaranties to purchase homes, farms, and start businesses. People were covered by Social Security, millions of workers were covered by employer pension plans, and expected to enjoy a dignified retirement. There was no fear of public sector insolvency, although the seeds for problems that surfaced later on had already been planted. Insufficient attention was paid to the sustainability of new social programs and the expansion of Social Security.

Popular culture became increasingly influenced by broadcast television during the 1950s, and the arrival of new trends in popular music, including Rock and Roll, Electric Blues, and Bebop. TV integrated many aspects of an evolving American culture. The influence of TV, movies and music was reflected in hair styles and clothing. Nevertheless, the young were not influenced by anti-American diatribes and leftist politics. Icons like Elvis Presley respected basic traditions and when drafted he put aside his ducktail haircut and undulating hips to join the U.S. Army like any other young man. Sitcoms such as *I Love Lucy, Father Knows Best*, and *The Honeymooners* presented images of a middle class life within accepted traditional social patterns of the time. They portrayed overly idealistic families.

There was no reference to drug use, violence within the family, or sexual aberrations featured as "*normal,*" or conversations peppered with expletives. A more tolerant society was surfacing, and the direction seemed to be towards a more egalitarian society, i.e. "*equality of mankind,*" particularly in political, economic, and social life. The ratings received by the *I Love Lucy* program, for example, were indicative of progress in terms of diversity.[8] Comedians like Abbot and Costello, Jack Benny, Jackie Gleason, Bob Hope, and Groucho Marx did not have to say four-letter words in every sentence to be funny.

News broadcasters like Walter Cronkite, David Brinkley, Chet Huntley, and Edward R. Murrow, did not engage in extremist diatribes day after day. Although society was challenged as never before through the growth of mass media growth, there was a resurgence of Christianity, as evangelical preachers, such as Billy Graham, used the mass media to proselytize. Broadway musicals did not cause disturbances with shows like *The Sound of Music, South Pacific, Guys and Dolls, Peter Pan, The Music Man*, or *West Side Story* and *Damn Yankees*. Popular vocalists like, Tony Bennet, Frankie Laine, Frank Sinatra, Perry Como, Bing Crosby, Dean Martin, Loretta Lynn and Nat King Cole were not "poster children" for drug use, violence, and sexual deviations, even if they were personally engaging in their own set of *peccadillos*. When Sinatra sang *Come Fly with Me*, the lyrics by Sammy Cahn were not a euphemism for getting "*stoned*" with narcotics.

Sports figures, such as Yogi Berra, Mickey Mantle, Willie Mays, Jackie Robinson, Johnny Unitas, and Bill Russell were good role models. And they were not alone. There was progress in the Civil Rights Movement, with the Supreme Court decision to end segregation in schools and public places in 1954. Segregation and discrimination were heading out, as tolerance and openness were being incorporated into the direction of the country in the 1950s. There were pockets of recalcitrant xenophobic sentiments, but they were slowly heading into the trash can of history. The American vision of the future was positive, with improved educational accomplishments, improving economic conditions, and a more rational interaction between people. Politicians were not exempted from *transgressions*, but there were outstanding figures, such as Presidents Harry S. Truman, Dwight D. Eisenhower, and Senators like Hubert Humphrey, Mike Mansfield, and Everett Dirksen, as well as Supreme Court Justices Earl Warren, Hugo Black, William O. Douglas, and Felix Frankfurter. Young people had plenty of good examples to follow.

In 1957, the murder rate was at the lowest level since 1900, at 4.0% per 100,000 people. In 1960, there were 9,100 murders in the country. By 1969, the number of murders increased to 14,760, and by 1980, the number had climbed to 23,040. A decade later, in 1990, there were 23,440 murders, before the murder rate started to decline. Although civil society was not free of problems in 1958 indeed, the notorious gangsters that emerged during *prohibition* (1920-1933) had been partially, but not totally dismantled. Also, the older Italian organized crime family leaders were either dead, under arrest, or had been deported after WWII. Vito Genovese and associates Gaetano Lucchese and Carlo Gambino were competing with Frank Costello over control of the powerful Salvatore Charlie "Lucky" Luciano organization nicknamed *The Commission*. Luciano had been deported but he hosted in December 1946 a meeting in Havana of major Mob bosses to exercise his authority and reduce internal tensions. Luciano forced Genovese and Cosa Nostra boss Albert Anastasia to shake hands at the meeting in 1946, but in 1957 Costello and Anastasia were both assassinated in New York City. In 1958, Genovese, who had become the most powerful boss in *La Cosa Nostra*, was indicted on narcotics trafficking charges, and given a 15 year sentence the following year. Although organized crime suffered important setbacks these incidents only created the illusion that law enforcement authorities were finally going to prevail. The trend was good, but not good enough.[9]

American dominance in global affairs starting around 1947 was challenged by the Soviet Union in what became known as the "*Cold War*." Americans were defied in multiple fronts. First, in 1948, the Soviets blockaded access to Berlin. The allies – led mostly by the U.S. – airlifted over two million tons of supplies to the city in 270,000 flights, until the Soviets gave up in May 1949. Next, in June 1950 troops from

Communist North Korea staged a surprise invasion of South Korea with the assistance of the Soviets and Chinese Communists. The possibility of using nuclear weapons was considered and rejected. An armistice was finally signed in July 1953, but by then the U.S. had suffered 36,516 dead and 92,134 wounded. A key lesson about not engaging in ground wars in Asia was not learned, as witnessed by the Vietnam War a decade later during the Kennedy and Johnson administrations.

The Soviets continued to sponsor conflicts in Eastern Europe, the Middle East, Cuba, Central and South America, and Vietnam. European Colonial enclaves in Africa became battlegrounds. The two super powers did not engage directly, but used surrogates in proxy wars all over the world in preparation for a possible all-out nuclear war. The Soviets in 1962 pushed the envelope too far in Cuba and brought the world very close to nuclear war, but were forced to back down.

Senator Joseph McCarthy (R-WI)[10] in the 1950s made numerous claims of Communist infiltration, yet despite his recklessness and hysteria there were elements of truth to his assertion that Soviet spies had stolen American nuclear technology. Homophobic attacks added to the despicable tactics used by McCarthy, who exploited fears and dislikes among the population for his own personal gain, reaching the zenith of popular support around January 1954. The Kennedy clan, including future President John F. Kennedy and his brother, Robert F. Kennedy were close associates of Senator McCarthy. However, by the end of 1954, his popularity had plummeted according to Gallup Polls.[11] Republican President Dwight Eisenhower and leaders of both political parties were slow to oppose McCarthy's smear tactics, but eventuality the U.S. Senate by a vote of 67 to 22 censured him for abusing the system with unsubstantiated claims.

As a result of the "*red scare*," Communist sympathizers turned the tables and obtained public support to stop the "*red baiting*," which made it very difficult to combat the potential internal enemies that McCarthy had targeted. He set the stage for Communists and fellow leftists to make inroads into the domestic scene principally due to opposition to the Vietnam War. McCarthy energized domestic leftists by handing them the opportunity to accuse anyone who questioned the drift to the left in the 1960s as engaging in "red baiting." American society was negatively affected by the efforts made by the Soviets and their allies to destabilize the United States..[12] Behind many of the bad things that happened during the 1960s were Soviet handlers and numerous marionettes.

And then, in the mid-1960s, America lost its bearing… The situation resembled the Titanic navigating in the dark waters of the North Atlantic with the passengers and crew unaware of the catastrophe awaiting them. The unintended effects of the exaggerated self-confidence and euphoria of the 1950s, and the mistakes of the 1960s and 1970s, lead to an impending disaster. Part of the problem stems from American irreverence to history. To paraphrase Mark Twain, our national education seems to consist mainly of *what we have unlearned.* As a result, we are not any wiser as a society. The problem is compounded by an irrational and persistent absence of a desire to learn.

A sad example of the prevailing level of ignorance is a National Science Foundation (NSF) survey taken in January 2014, which showed that *one in four Americans is unaware that the earth circles the sun…* Another survey taken about the same time by McCormick Tribune Freedom Museum revealed the dramatic level of ignorance about the Constitution and the Bill of Rights. *Only one in one thousand Americans could list the rights granted by the Constitution to American citizens.*[13] Another study in early 2014 found that Americans are not as technologically savvy as had been previously thought. *About 27% thought that a gigabyte was a South American insect*, 42% linked a *motherboard* to the deck of a cruise ship, and about 11% thought that *HTML* is some kind of a sexually transmitted disease.[14] A series of interviews with students in March 2014 on the campus of The American University in Washington, D.C., revealed that many students do not even know the name of a single U.S. Senator or the number of senators per state.[15]

When you think that you have heard just about every possible example of poor education, you come across something like this. A Transportation Security Administration (TSA) agent at the Orlando International Airport demanded a passport from a resident of the District of Columbia, because *he did not know that the city is part of the*

United States! The TSA agent would not accept Justin Gray's DC driver's license as a valid form of identification because he did not recognize it as the capital of the country, and instead confused Colombia (The country) with our nation's capital. Have Americans become *willfully ignorant* or closed to learning any further?[16]

The rules have changed under a bizarre "*new normal.*" Americans have to redefine how the justice system deals with polymorphous predators, psychopaths, anti-social behavior, violence, and mental disorders. A society has been created in which everything is relative. Everything seems to be the same: right and wrong, ugly and pretty, real and false. Criminals have more rights than their victims, and the actions of some law enforcement can officials often resemble those of criminals. The intoxicating atmosphere of "*relativism*" is nothing but another excuse to disregard right and wrong.

A large segment of society suffers from nihilism. Leftists reject established social conventions, especially morality and religion. Others question objective truth or believe that there is no objective basis for truth. Right-wingers tell great stories, but most of their "talking heads" never were in the military or worked in law enforcement, or intelligence, and many have never even been overseas as tourists. Yet, they pontificate constantly with absurd extremist views without ever personally doing any of the things they want others to do, as for example, going to war. They criticize other societies without ever visiting them. They complain about immigration and offer solutions without understanding the realities of the problem. For example, to talk about creating a path to citizenship for people who are not legally in the country is a bridge too far. There is a requirement to hold a legal resident visa for at least five years to apply for citizenship, and there is a test requirement that includes English language ability, as well as historical knowledge, and a basic understanding of the American Constitution.

Poverty is increasing. Wages are flat. The median income has fallen since 2000. Bigotry, hate crimes, and racism are gaining traction. For all practical purposes, legislation enacted since the 1960s to deal with these transcendental issues has failed to produce the desired results. In 1965 about 15% of the population was below the poverty line, and in 2015, the same is true. Real wages for American workers are stagnant. Thousands of factories have closed or moved overseas, with a resulting huge cumulative trade deficit and increasing level of poverty. Globalization turned out to be poison for the American economy. Consumer electronics, clothing, shoes, telephones, computers, and just about every item commonly found in an American household are imported. China is expected to overtake the size of the US economy in 2016 in large part due to assistance provided by the U.S. since 1973. At the same time, the median household income in the U.S. peaked in 1973 (in inflation-adjusted dollars) and has been declining ever since.

A country that can be energy independent, able to produce all the variety and volume of food needed to feed its people, with all kinds of natural resources and with an infrastructure second to none, has been allowed to decline due to blunder after blunder. Huge sums of money have been wasted in "*nation building*" (however defined), while the American economy has been deconstructed. As a nation, Americans have an aversion to confronting flaws with total honesty. So, they live a comedy, a carnival of dreams, and live off ideas that have no relation to fact. Americans need firmness of mind to address very serious problems. Utopian ideas and legislation enacted since the 1930s must be revised and refocused based on real numbers, actuarial data, and other relevant factors. Redistribution of wealth is not a way to build an economy and reduce poverty. Wealth has to be created, and it cannot be created by threatening to confiscate it from the people that produce it.

One of the most dangerous signs since 2001 has been the growth of *gloom & doom* theories and stupid comparisons with events leading up to the end of historical empires that once ruled the world. We live a climate of unprecedented uncertainty and self-doubt, and the people are starting to believe that the country's best days are in the past. We are honestly sincere and do not feign when we say that the nation stands for freedom, democracy and peace. Our intentions are generally sincere and honest and we want to emphasize truth. So we live in *self-contradicting terms*, or in an illogical and inconsistent political *"dance."* We mix joy and melancholy. As a people, we hear but do not listen. American society has become an *everlasting contradiction*… and that is the rub.

The culture of the country has been taken over by a toxic counterculture. Widespread undesirable behavior has been made fashionable. There is nothing wrong with tolerance and pluralism, except when excesses lead to the creation of *freaks, mutants* and *oddities*. Confusion over right and wrong, a decline in ethics, values, and morals, deviations from traditional standards of behavior, political corruption, constant wars, a failing economy, and high unemployment, can destroy the country. Society does not have to accept the bizarre as the "*new normal*." Considering the country's low voter turnout, we should be cautious about changing Federal laws. We do not have to accept the legalization of dope, or invite the government into the bedroom to rule on what is and what isn't "moral."

A massive deprograming effort is needed to rescue the masses from gigantic con games by demagogues who manage to convince people to follow them with irresponsible promises. Bad ideas can receive dangerous popular support, but that does not change the fact that they are *bad ideas*. Core values are resistant to change, but history is full of examples of how a country's system of values can be hijacked by manipulative predators who are constantly trying to sway public opinion, including politicians, educators, entertainers, interest groups, news media pundits, and false prophets. Somehow, society has to overcome all the enchanting music and manipulations, and put the country back on track. America has to overcome a bad case of allergy to logic, leading to creative destruction.

I – CONSTITUTIONAL ISSUES

> **Do not separate text from historical background. If you do, you will have perverted and subverted the Constitution, which can only end in a distorted, bastardized form of illegitimate government.**
>
> **James Madison**
> **(1751 -1836)**

Political Acrobatic Stunts

After many years of acrobatic stunts by both, the far-right and the far-left, to justify contradictory interpretations of constitutional intent, the nation has moved closer and closer to a socioeconomic and fiscal crisis. Each side interprets the *Declaration of Independence*, the *Constitution*, and the *Bill of Rights* in ways that will justify their particular views, stretching the facts beyond the breaking point. One need not be a constitutional scholar to read about how the Founding Fathers created a system of checks and balances that has lasted over two hundred years and has been copied by other countries.

The Constitution is not perfect, but it was drafted in such a way so as to allow for a process of calibration and any updating over time. The world is changing faster than at previous time in human history, forcing re-evaluation of many aspects of government, including the enactment of a constitutional amendment to require balanced budgets, or a review of the meaning of such things as the right to bear arms or the definition of marriage. However, that is not the same as *making sausage* with a mix of ideas that may or may not be compatible with what the Founding Fathers had in mind. Most Americans do not have more than a very superficial idea of how the country was formed, how the Constitution came about, how the system was designed to work, and how it still functions. Ignorance of constitutional history is very dangerous because it creates conditions that can be exploited by predators, pied pipers and false prophets who can stoke the fires of conflict.

Background to the American Revolution

The American Revolution was led by enlightened individuals, influenced by philosophers of the 17th and 18th centuries, including Isaac Newton (1643-1727), Richard Price (1723-1791), François-Marie Arouet, known as Voltaire (1694-1778), Charles-Louis de Secondât, Baron de La Brède et de Montesquieu (1689-1755), Jean-Jacques Rousseau (1712-1778), Denis Diderot (1713-1784), John Locke (1632-1704), Gabrielle Émilie Le Tonnelier de Breteuil, Marquise du Châte (1706-1749), David Hume (1711-1776), and Adam Smith (1723-1790).[17]

These philosophers advocated republican values, civic duty, patriotism, freedom of religion, religious tolerance, rationalism, civil liberties, freedom of thought and expression, separation of church and state, separation of powers, respect for private property, opposition to arbitrary confiscation of private property by the state, and economic goals such as maintaining a favorable balance of trade. Adam Smith, through his book *An Inquiry into the Nature and Causes of the Wealth of Nations*, published in 1776, was of particular influence on the Founding Fathers, who supported laissez-faire Capitalism and accepted Locke's views that government should not interfere with the distribution of wealth. Similarly to Adam Smith, David Hume held that unequal distribution of property was acceptable and necessary because equality of wealth would destroy the ideas of thrift and industry and result in impoverishment.[18] The American system of government, as it was designed, was based on these economic principles.

Several of the Founding Fathers were Freemasons, including Benjamin Franklin, James Madison, Ethan Allen, John Hancock, Paul Revere, and George Washington. Freemasons believe in liberty, equality, fraternity, and charity. They believe in a Supreme Being and a Great Architect of the Universe, while respecting the particular religious beliefs of their members. The presence of Freemasons among the Founding Fathers was not unique, as many leading 19th century Latin American leaders of different movements to obtain independence from Spain were also Freemasons.

The American Revolution was the first of a series of revolutions against the established order but with an important difference: its' intellectual leaders were educated aristocrats influenced by the ideas of the *Enlightenment*. They did not represent the masses and did not establish mob rule. They did not complain about concentration of wealth in an upper class, question the right to private property, or call for expropriation and redistribution of wealth. They wanted to create a system of government that would be responsive to the electorate, respect basic rights, such as freedom of religion, freedom of thought and expression, and a rational economic and political system. They desired a constitution that could be adjusted and improved over time, with checks and balances, so as to prevent the rise of a dictatorship. This is why the American Revolution succeeded while others failed.

For example, the French Revolution, which was carried out between 1789 and 1799, was a radical and violent revolution of the masses that deteriorated into mob rule under the leadership of radicals calling for an end to absolute monarchy and resulted in punishment of the aristocracy and the clergy for having abused the population. Although many of the ideals of the revolution surfaced from the philosophers of the Enlightenment, somehow these beliefs were replaced by mob rule (proletarian revolution) that began with the assault on the Bastille on the morning of 14 July 1789. The *Declaration of the Rights of Man and of the Citizens* of 1793 sounded great in theory, but in practice, was drowned in blood. Contrary to the American Revolution, the events of 14 July 1789 led to complete anarchy, the *Reign of Terror*, dictatorial rule under Napoleon, and unending wars in Europe.

The guillotine and the reign of terror are more closely associated with the French Revolution than all the idealistic documents that emerged from it. Indeed, well over 16,500 people were executed, including many of the leaders of the revolution and initial instigators of the *Reign of Terror*, including Maximilien Robespierre, Georges Jacques Danton, Pierre Philippeaux, and Camille Desmoulins. Violence generates more violence. Eventually a democratic form of government emerged, but it took over 140 years to materialize. France had to go through repeated upheavals, from the tremendous bleeding that resulted from the Napoleonic wars, additional revolutionary processes in the 19th century, additional bleeding in WWI, and further bloodshed to defeat the occupation by Nazi Germany during WWII. Revolutions are by their very definition, violent episodes, as the French Revolution showed.

The same violent pattern was shared by the Bolshevik Revolution in 1917 in Russia, the Communist Revolution in China, and the Cuban Revolution in 1959. Anytime one faction is out to overthrow the existing social, economic, and political order, blood flows and society goes backward instead of moving forward. The American Revolution presents an important departure from mob rule through revolution. There were no mass executions, and loyalists to the British Empire were not persecuted. Those who elected to leave were able to do so without being chased out of town by a blood thirsty mob.[19]

Legitimacy of Government

The Declaration of Independence introduced a revolutionary concept that contradicted the previously held theory that revolved around the political and religious doctrine that took for granted the so-called "Divine Right of Kings." The American Revolution was not only a political act against the absolute authority of the British monarch, but was also an act against ingrained religious doctrine that held that only God could remove a monarch from his authority. Both Catholics and Protestants justified obedience and submission to the will of monarchs. That concept of absolute power in the hands of a monarch, regardless of any enlightened principles, was no longer acceptable. The age of absolutism was starting to come apart, but it was not yet approaching its' end.

Separation of Church and State and freedom to practice, or not practice, any religion was in the minds of the Founding Fathers, regardless of right-wing extremist efforts to convince the public otherwise. The Founding Fathers held their own basic religious views, particularly the idea that the new nation was *founded under God.*

Articles of Confederation

The Second Continental Congress created a committee to study the form of confederation for the former colonies reconstituted into states. John Dickinson was the principal writer of the Articles of Confederation, which was adopted by Congress in November 1777, after it was debated and amended by the delegates. The state assemblies had to ratify the document. The process of ratification was completed in March of 1781. It is worth noting that, under the Articles of Confederation, the Continental Congress was not granted the power to levy taxes, which created multiple problems because there was no money to pay for normal expenses of government, placing the new confederation on the brink of bankruptcy. Thus, the picture of the Federal Government hanging on the edge of a fiscal cliff over the issue of taxes, as happened late in 2012, is something with deep roots in the American experience.

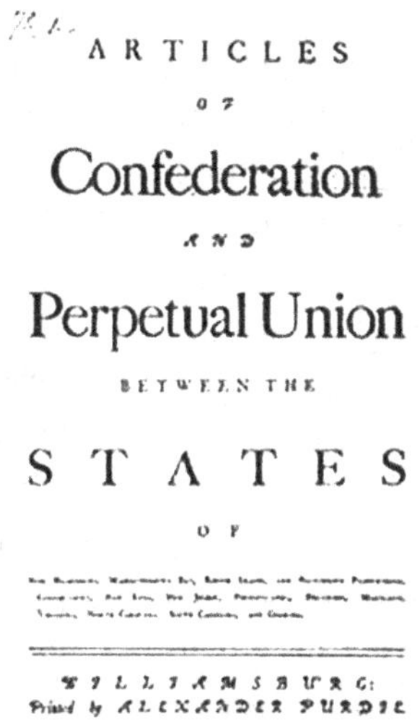

ARTICLES

OF

Confederation

AND

Perpetual Union

BETWEEN THE

STATES

OF

WILLIAMSBURG:

Printed by ALEXANDER PURDIE

While the delegates representing the former colonies were creating the basic documents to build a structure of government, the American War of Independence, known as the American Revolutionary War, went on from 1775 to 1783. What started as a war between the former British colonies in North America and British authorities became a global conflict involving France, the Netherlands, and Spain, taking the side of the Americans. Many Native American tribes sided with the

British against the American colonials seeking independence. What was initially a behind-the-scenes effort to assist the Continental Army with weapons, ammunition, uniforms, military training, food, and funds, changed into open conflict in June 1779, when Spain and France signed the Treaty of Aranjuez, by which France agreed to help Spain battle the British, and Spain agreed to join French efforts to assist the Americans to achieve independence. The Netherlands formally joined the war effort in 1780. Major fighting ceased after the surrender of British troops at Yorktown, Virginia, on 19 October 1781, but the war did not officially come to an end until the signing of the Treaty of Paris in 1783.

Drafting of the Constitution

The Constitution of the United States was drafted in Philadelphia in 1787 and ratified in 1789, replacing the Articles of Confederation. There were two principal points of view about how to organize the government. One faction, the so-called Federalists, proposed proportional representation of the member states based on the size of the population. The Democrat-Republicans held that each member state should have equal representation, without reference to population. Eventually, a compromise was reached taking into account both points of view. Each state would be represented by two members in the Senate, and they would also be proportionally represented in the House of Representatives based on the size of the state population. There would be three branches of government: the Legislative Branch, consisting of the Senate and the House of Representatives, an Executive Branch, comprising the office of the President and the Federal Government agencies managed by the President, and a Judicial Branch, comprising the Supreme Court and other Federal Courts.

POWERS THAT THE CONSTITUTION EXPLICITLY GRANTS TO THE FEDERAL GOVERNMENT

- **Collect taxes**
- **Regulate interstate commerce**
- **Coin money, regulate the currency, set standards or weights and measures**
- **Declare war**
- **Raise and maintain an Army and Navy**

Although not specifically mentioned, the system allowed for checks and balances, as all three branches would work independently, but would also be required to interact with each other to legislate, execute, and adjudicate justice and resolve differences based on the constitutionality of their actions. A series of 85 essays known as the Federalist Papers, written by Alexander Hamilton, John Jay, and James Madison, explained the basic concepts of the system of government outlined in the Constitution; the authors supported the ratification of the Constitution by the states.

The Bill of Rights

The first ten amendments of the Constitution are known as the *Bill of Rights*. Due to differences of opinion over Federal vs. State jurisdiction, the *Bill of Rights* was not included in the Constitution initially, as the Constitutional Convention in 1787 rejected the idea. It was introduced to the 1st Congress in August 1789 by James Madison, who had been elected to the House of Representatives for Virginia. The following month the House approved the Amendments presented by Madison, and passed them to the Senate, and they were adopted as a Joint Congressional Resolution. Three months later, in December 1789, the *Bill of Rights*, as a set of constitutional amendments, was ratified by the states following the process outlined in the Constitution.

Rather than protecting basic human rights, the *Bill of Rights* was perceived by Alexander Hamilton and other Federalists as limiting people's rights to those specifically stated. Jefferson and other Founding Fathers disagreed and did not see the package of amendments as limiting other rights not specifically outlined. To address several areas of concern and to explain how the Constitution would function, Alexander Hamilton, John Jay, and James Hamilton published the *Federalist Papers*, in which they analyzed transcendental issues associated with the Constitution. More than anything else, they addressed the issue of a society's ability to democratically elect representatives who would hopefully exercise "*good governance*" under a republican form of government.[20]

The authors of the *Federalist Papers* explained how the Judicial Branch had the power to review the actions of the Legislative and Executive branches, as well as actions by state governments, with the power to invalidate them if they did not adhere to the terms outlined in the Constitution. The concept of separation and balance of powers was based principally in judicial review. Concepts like separation of powers and judicial review to protect the rights of minorities from the emergence of a tyranny or despotic rule by the majority were new. These important concepts that are imbedded in the Constitution prevent the emergence of mob rule. Sadly, the idea that wealth somehow constitutes a crime has been around for some time.

Under the Constitution, the electorate democratically chooses their representatives, based on majority rule. But the system was also designed to protect the rights of the minority. One of the problems with a democratic process, and majority rule, is that pipe pipers can emerge and stir up the masses through Utopian promises and giveaways.[21] There is always a danger that the concept of *majority rule* can easily translate into *mob rule* if the rights of minorities are not protected.

Federal vs. State Rights

The conflict over state rights and the power of the Federal Government has deep roots going back to the 1790s during the process of ratifying the Constitution. George Washington and Alexander Hamilton interpreted the powers granted by the Constitution to the Federal Government, particularly in financial matters, to be considerably larger than how James Madison and Thomas Jefferson interpreted the intentions of the drafters. The theory of "implied powers" granted to the Federal Government led to considerable conflict between Federalists and Republicans, eventually leading to the enactment of the *Alien and Sedition Acts* in 1798, which allowed for punishment of anyone who voiced or articulated attacks against Congress or the Executive. Those that supported the view of a limited government clashed with those who believed in a strong national government. The roots of secession did not start right before the Civil War, but went all the way back to the first few years after independence. These arguments continue to exist and resurfaced once again after the 2012 elections when groups in Texas and other states refloated the idea of secession from the United States.[22]

Slavery and its' legacy

If slavery is not wrong, nothing is wrong.

Abraham Lincoln
4 April 1864

Not all men were created equal, despite what the *Declaration of Independence* stated. In practice, only property owners were allowed to vote until the 1820s, and many restrictions continued to exist. For example, election by voice vote rather than secret ballots put constraints on elections since voters had to consider potential ramifications due to the way they voted. Democracy was in the hands of the upper classes and did not reflect the will of the masses.[23] The preservation of slavery, despite the language of the *Declaration of Independence* was, without a doubt, the most important contradiction associated with the document. Many of the Founding Fathers were slave owners. The British abolished slavery through the enactment of the *Slavery Abolition Act* of 1833, long before it was abolished in the U.S. and went on to use their Navy to stop the slave trade, intercepting ships at sea carrying slaves from Africa to the Americas to free and return them home.

Behind the argument of State vs. Federal rights was the issue of slavery, which was important to the agricultural economy of the southern states. The northern states had achieved economic development through industrialization, which did not depend on slave labor. The nation was increasingly polarized over the issue through the 1850s, in part through the publication of abolitionist literature, persecution of runaway slaves that fled to "free states" in the north and Canada, and the inclusion of new states into the Union as either free or slave states. Maintaining a balance of free and slave states was the key to maintaining the *status quo*. The debate became increasingly violent, including punching brawls in Congress.

In the general elections of 6 November 1860, Republican candidate Abraham Lincoln was elected President. He shared anti-slavery views with a substantial majority of Members of Congress. Almost immediately, and before President Lincoln could take office, South Carolina and six other states formed the Confederate States of America and began to raise an army. In April 1861, Confederate forces shelled Fort Sumter in South Carolina, as four additional states joined the secessionists. South Carolina, Mississippi, Florida, Alabama, Georgia, Louisiana, Texas, Virginia, Arkansas, Tennessee, and North Carolina, all with agricultural economies dependent on slave labor, claimed that they had a constitutional right to secede, despite the fact that *most southerners did not own slaves.* Most southern whites were poor subsistence farmers. Nevertheless, the prevalent view in the south was: *Negroes are an inferior and dependent race, not equal to whites.* Southerners were willing to fight for their views. At the time, there were about three million slaves in the southern states. The right to secede was not recognized by Congress, and the Confederate states were declared to be in open rebellion.

The Constitution provided the mechanism to make important corrections, such as the abolition of slavery, but the country was divided on economic and transcendental philosophical differences that led to war. At least 350,000 Union and an estimated 250,000 Confederate soldiers died during the Civil War between 1861 and 1865 from combat, disease, and other causes.[24] Key infrastructure and hundreds of towns and cities were destroyed, and the economy of the South was seriously damaged. It would take years to repair and the region continues to suffer from the after-effects of the war over a century after it ended.

There were many economic interests that played a part in the struggle to end slavery. Slavery was a key component of the agricultural economy of the southern states, but it was also linked to the British textile industry that depended on imported cotton to survive. The Civil War came close to becoming an international conflict, had the Confederate forces been successful at the Battle of Antietam in September 1862, after defeating the Union Army in the initial battles of the war.[25] President Lincoln's *Emancipation Proclamation* that same month further pushed the British away from entering the war on the side of the Confederacy.

Despite abolishing slavery in 1833, British economic interests could have put them on the side of slave owners in the Confederacy in direct contradiction to their efforts to abolish the slave trade and slavery beyond their territories.[26] France considered entering the war on the Confederate side, but they were already involved in an invasion of

Mexico, where they set up a puppet government under "Emperor" Maximilian. The carnage and destruction of the Civil War could have been much worse had the conflict become internationalized. Despite considerable opposition from Democrats in Congress and lukewarm support from some Republican Members of Congress, President Lincoln was able to obtain the two-thirds majority needed to enact the 13th Amendment on 31 January 1865.[27]

The idea of a biracial integrated society was absent from the minds of the Founding Fathers as far as historical documents attest. Even after the abolition of slavery, it took another century to enact the Civil Rights Act in 1964. The abolition of slavery did not translate into racial integration or grant the freed slaves the same rights and privileges as their former masters. The Civil Rights Act of 1964 did not automatically sprinkle angel dust over the country to obtain societal change and to make racial discrimination disappear. Racism continues to fester fifty years after the enactment of the Civil Rights Act of 1964.

Wave of reform and revolution

During the period between the end of the Civil War in 1865 and the turn of the century the U.S. experienced an economic revolution with the expansion of the railroads, industry, the discovery of petroleum, the invention of the internal combustion engine, the harnessing of electricity, and the initial work of building an electric grid. Entrepreneurs and inventors made huge fortunes in a short period of time. With the rapid economic expansion came the so-called *Gilded Age*, as a relatively small number of tycoons made huge fortunes, triggering calls for taxing their profits, controlling their power, and redistributing their wealth to the needy. The issue of wealth confiscation and redistribution has been alive for quite a long time.

These magnates included John D. Rockefeller (1839-1937), founder of the Standard Oil Company; financial prodigy Andrew W. Mellon (1855-1937), a leading banker and industrialist; Andrew Carnegie (1835-1919), who led the expansion of the American steel industry and contributed significantly to the expansion of the railroad system; J. P. Morgan a banker who became a key investor in the expansion of the new electric industry, founder of the General Electric Company, and leading investor in the expanding steel industry; Henry Flagler (1830-1913), one of the founders, as well as one of the key thinkers, who led to the growth of the Standard Oil Company and investor in the expansion of the railroads; Cornelius Vanderbilt (1794-1877), operator of steamships and railroad service lines between New York City and Chicago. These demonized men were instrumental in building the United States into world's the leading economy.

Industrial expansion employed thousands of workers, including waves of new immigrants. However, there were abuses, as workers were required to work long hours for low wages that placed them and their families in overcrowded and unhealthy dwelling conditions. Child labor was rampant. The growing working class, led to the creation of labor unions, violent strikes, and deadly confrontations with police and hired goons. Economic expansion was temporarily interrupted by periods of depression in 1873 and again in 1893. Corruption among elected officials became rampant, particularly in large urban centers like New York City and Chicago. The situation brought about a wave of reformers and promoters of social justice who, with popular support, went about addressing many of the new problems caused by the rapid economic expansion and the abuse that the working poor were subjected to.

Legislation was enacted to control abusive practices. The Sherman Antitrust Act of July 1890 was enacted to put an end to activities that were deemed to be contrary to the general well-being of the country. The business community had created corporate trusts to monopolize control of some economic activities, which allowed them to fix prices and keep out competitors. The problem was particularly evident in the nascent petroleum sector, from production through refining, marketing, and pricing of refined petroleum products. The new legislation led to the creation of government regulators, something that was far outside the language of the Constitution. The Constitution allowed for the enactment of legislation to control new circumstances that had not existed when the Founding Fathers wrote it. What started as a small effort to regulate some aspects of the business cycle morphed into a huge bureaucracy with the power to write and enforce regulations outside the electoral process through which the people's representatives are empowered to enact laws deemed necessary for the "public good" (however defined).

Taxes and Regulation of the Economy

Taxation has been, since day one, a key concern for Americans. After all, taxation was the catalyst for the Revolutionary War, and taxes continue to generate a great deal of anxiety. Nevertheless, although governments need revenue to function, taxes have to be perceived as equitable, fair, and impartial. Historically, all the way back to the time of the Pharaohs in Egypt, governments collected taxes from the people. Greeks, Romans, and every civilization have had to deal with the issue. Tax collectors have never been popular, and tax policies have always been considered oppressive. Traditionally, an effort has been made to tax people based on their income, wealth, and ability to pay. There is nothing new about progressive taxes, exempting or demanding lower taxes from the poor, while imposing higher taxes on the wealthy.

In post-revolutionary America, taxes continued to be as controversial as when the British imposed them on the colonies. President George Washington had to mobilize troops to quell anti-excise tax rioting. The so-called Whiskey Rebellion, in 1791, resulted from an effort to impose a tax on distillers. The Federal Government logically needed revenue to function, and a tax on whiskey seemed like the least objectionable, but it was as controversial as every form of taxation that has come about ever since. The Federal Government derived funding primarily from duties on imports until the Civil War. Tariffs later became a tool to protect American industry from foreign competition in the 1820s. However, the practice of levying tariffs hurt some areas of the country more than others. The more industrial Northern states benefitted, as foreign competitors were kept out of the market, while the agricultural economy of the South, which depended more on imports, suffered.

The first attempt to tax income came about during the War of 1812, but before taxes could be collected, the war ended. With the start of the Civil War in 1861, the need for revenue for the war effort was evident. The enactment of income taxes in 1862 was very controversial, leading to its elimination in 1872, only to be revived again in 1894.[28] Starting on or about 1880, the so-called "Progressives" and "Social Reformers," including the Socialist Labor Party and the Populist Party, advocated the enactment of income tax legislation on wealthy people. The US Supreme Court ruled that income tax laws were unconstitutional, particularly because they unfairly taxed the people with the highest incomes. Achieving social justice through taxation of wealth was highly controversial. The issue of proportionality in the way taxes are levied was a concern to the Founding Fathers and language was written into the Constitution to limit the power of government to impose direct taxes on the population.

By the 1890s, the Republican and Democratic parties had become the largest political parties with numerous other smaller parties, generally led by Utopian Socialists attracting a much smaller segment of the electorate. The two majority parties participated in the enactment of legislation to address social ills, such as ending child labor, promoting safety in the workplace, and granting women the right to vote. Republican President Theodore Roosevelt (1901-1909) declared war on wealthy capitalists and took up the fight to break up large companies that manipulated the marketplace to gain monopoly control over some segments of the economy. Both leading political parties participated in the Progressive Movement, each contributing to the enactment of legislation with the goal of improving socio-economic conditions in the country.

President Teddy Roosevelt was instrumental in the enactment of the Sherman Anti-Trust Act to prevent monopolies from controlling important sectors of the economy. He was a leader in enacting legislation to create national parks and protect the environment. Roosevelt was a "social activist" who rescued positive ideas for change, while discarding the most wild and destructive notions of class warfare. Through the enactment of the National Conservation Commission in 1908, Roosevelt earned the title of the "first real environmentalist." Roosevelt expanded the number of government regulators through the enactment of the Meat Inspection Act of 1906 to stop serious mismanagement, unsanitary conditions, and corruption at packing houses, particularly in Chicago, which put the health of consumers in peril. He went on to promote the enactment of the Pure Food and Drug Act of 1906, which expanded Federal control over interstate commerce. Roosevelt's actions led eventually to the creation of the Food and Drug Administration in 1930. Among other things, the 1906 legislation imposed controls over dangerous substances, such as opium, morphine, cocaine, marijuana, and alcohol. The legislation introduced important uniform regulations to stop misbranding of food and medicines.

Another Republican President, William Howard Taft, proposed a two percent Federal income tax on corporations in 1909. The idea of using the tax system to redistribute wealth or to make the upper income bracket pay for most of the cost of running the government would have been inconceivable to the Founding Fathers. To legitimize income taxes, the 16th Amendment to the Constitution was ratified in 1913, granting constitutional legal authority to the Federal Government. During WWII, withholding taxes on wages became the law of the land. The Constitution was drafted to allow for substantive revisions like this.

President Woodrow Wilson (1913-1921), a Democrat, enacted legislation to exercise further control of the economy, including the Clayton Antitrust Act in 1914 to supplement the Sherman Antitrust Act, and established the Federal Trade Commission. The war on anti-competitive practices continued, including requiring companies to inform and obtain approval from the government before they could merge and gain market share and virtual monopoly control over segments of the economy. The legislation also favored labor unions by exempting them from some of the same legal constraints imposed on companies, including peaceful picketing and strikes, as well as the use of boycotts to expand unionized labor.

Under President Wilson, the government established an eight-hour work day for railroad workers through the enactment of the Adamson Act of 1916. Although the legislation was ruled unconstitutional in 1917 by the U.S. Supreme Court, it set a precedent of government support for the struggle of workers and unions to improve labor conditions. The Keating-Owen Act of 1916 prohibited interstate commerce of goods produced in factories by children younger than 14 years old and in mines that employed children younger than 16 years of age. However, once again the U.S. Supreme Court ruled the

Act unconstitutional. The tug-of-war between elected officials and the Judicial Branch over the constitutionality of progressive legislation functioned just like the Founding Fathers had envisioned, by providing a balance between the three branches of government. Change was possible, but it had to be within constitutional boundaries. The system was not designed "to be easy;" rather, it was designed to make people "think" before they acted, particularly when transcendental changes were to be introduced.

Another important legislation enacted in the first years of the 20th Century was the creation of the Federal Reserve System in 1913, which was to function as the Central Bank for the United States. The new institution was to establish monetary policy, something that continues to be questioned. The presidentially appointed Board of Governors of the Federal Reserve Board and the twelve Regional Federal Reserve Banks were to exercise control over policy that some constitutional scholars viewed as something that should be controlled by elected not appointed officials. Nevertheless, the Federal Reserve System has withstood all the questioning and, to this day, controls interest rates, formulates policies aimed at achieving economic stability, and exercising control over the banking system.

Administration after administration continued to introduce new legislation to deal with the challenges of the 20th Century, particularly between WWI and WWII. The military had to be expanded well beyond what the Founding Fathers had envisioned. Legislation was enacted to regulate a larger portion of the economy and to expand the safety net for the elderly, the infirm, the poor, and the unemployed. Republicans and Democrats steadily increased the tax rate for wealthier income earners. President Franklin D. Roosevelt's New Deal brought about the Social Security program, as well as numerous other Utopic well-intentioned programs without proper cost/benefit analysis and adequate ways to keep these programs solvent over time. Elected officials created programs without taking into account actuarial changes, increasing longevity, inflation, and other important factors that should have been considered to ensure the proper funding of government programs into the future.

President Harry S. Truman (1945-1953) was the first to call for national universal medical coverage, triggering a debate that lasted about 20 years until President Lyndon Johnson (1963-1969) created the Medicare and Medicaid programs, which were to become the fastest increasing portion of the entitlement programs and the federal government's budget. The much maligned President Richard Nixon (1969-1974), a "Conservative" Republican, is hard to match in the creation of new programs, from the Minority Business Development Agency (MBDA), an agency placed within the U.S. Department of Commerce, to the Environmental Protection Agency (EPA), and the Consumer Product Safety Commission. Nixon expanded the Medicare and Medicaid programs in 1972 and created the Supplemental Security Income (SSI) program for the elderly and disabled poor.

Under President Ronald Reagan (1981-1989), hospice benefits were added to these programs on a permanent basis in 1986. President George W. Bush further expanded Social Security and Medicare in 2003, with the Medicare Part D program that extended coverage to include prescription drug benefits, but did not include a new revenue stream to pay for it. Democrats and Republicans acted without proper fiduciary responsibility to make sure that entitlement programs were created with appropriate sustainable funding.

As the demands on government increased, from the creation of a safety net for people in need to increased costs for national defense, taxation increased. Nevertheless, additional revenues were used for current operations without regard for future needs, thus creating unfunded liabilities for future generations. Leadership failures and poor planning pushed the country closer and closer to a financial cliff. For some reason, the Founding Fathers did not put limitations on elected officials to force them to be fiscally responsible or mandate that they balance budgets and stop passing debt to future generations. Perhaps it was unimaginable back in 1791 that future leaders would be so inept at handling the affairs of state.

Federalist Paper No. 30, attributed to Alexander Hamilton, deals with the controversial subject of taxation. Considering that taxation by British authorities was the prime mechanism that triggered the

Revolutionary War, the subject continue to be particularly important as the nation neared the so-called "fiscal abyss" after the recession of 2008. Hamilton argued that the Federal Government needs to have the power to raise revenue through taxes to fund its basic constitutional activities, such as national defense. Congress must have the power to write legislation to collect taxes. The supremacy of the Constitution over state governments did not preclude states and local governments from independently raising their own taxes as needed, with the exception of duties on imports and exports. The Constitutional tools to deal with the fiscal challenges are available, but the wisdom to ensure proper fiscal management has not been available.

Within national boundaries, trade was to flow free of any kind of taxes between member states. Hamilton, as well as other Founding Fathers, held the view that it was dangerous to the national economy for states to levy duties, which became one of the principal sources of revenue for the Federal Government for over a century, together with taxes on distilled spirits, tobacco and snuff, refined sugar, and luxury goods, before individual income taxes were introduced in 1862 to pay the costs of the Civil War. Hamilton further explained that in the interest of revenue itself, the government would be prevented from exceeding limits on taxing articles, as it would destroy the market for that article. The idea of introducing an increasing amount of government regulations on many areas of the economy was far from the minds of the Founding Fathers, so the subject was not discussed in the Federalist Papers. Hamilton held that there were two evils that would result from the certain confinement of taxation in the Union - one being the oppression of particular types of industry and the other one being the unequal distribution of the taxes among the states and people. Increasing regulations and environmental taxes on coal, for example, is a case in point. Targeting coal with special regulations and taxes may be great for the environment, but they may be contrary to constitutional intent.

Estate and Inheritance Taxes

A new type of tax on inheritances was introduced in 1866. The concept was not new. There was a precedent dating to 1797 when an inheritance tax was levied temporarily, but was repealed in 1802. The 1866 tax was also repealed in 1872. Under the Revenue Act of 1916, inheritance taxes were once again introduced to cover the costs of WWI, but they were not repealed after the war ended. In 1924, a new "gift" tax was enacted for the purpose of closing a loophole which had allowed individuals to pass money to relatives through gifts in order to avoid inheritance taxes. In 2003, Congress enacted legislation to gradually reduce estate taxes with the goal of repealing them altogether in 2010. However, in 2011, they were brought back under President Barack Obama at a rate of 35 percent over the first $5 million for one individual and $10 million for a couple. Each state has its' own tax legislation covering inheritances.

Redistribution of Wealth

> **Sixty years ago, there were no great fortunes in America, few large fortunes, no poverty. Now there is some poverty... and a greater number of gigantic fortunes than in any other country of the world.**
>
> **James Bryce,**
> **1st Viscount Bryce[29]**
> **(1838 – 1922)**

Redistribution of wealth is *the taking away of property or income from some people to be distributed to others through government policies, such as taxation, welfare, nationalization, confiscation, and related efforts to attain a more "egalitarian" society.*[30] Redistribution of wealth is nowhere to be found in the Declaration of Independence, the minutes of the First and Second Continental Congress, the Constitution, the Bill of Rights, or amendments to the Constitution. The opposite is true, as expressed in the thoughts of several of the Founding Fathers.

John Adams said: "*The moment the idea is admitted into society that property is not as sacred as the laws of God, and that there is not a force of law and public justice to protect it, anarchy and tyranny commence.*" Using the tax system as a tool to redistribute wealth was a concern of Thomas Jefferson, who said: "*To compel a man to furnish funds for the propagation of ideas he disbelieves and abhors is sinful and tyrannical.*"

Benjamin Franklin, who had spent several years in Europe during the Revolutionary War, had witnessed the failure of programs to alleviate the plight of the poor. Instead, he proposed to create opportunities for people to improve their situation, rather than by handouts or redistribution of wealth to the poor. The so-called "American Dream," has its' roots in the idea that everyone in the United States has the chance to achieve *success* and *prosperity*, however defined.

The American Revolution was not like other revolutions, as it was *far from a rebellion of the masses*. The intellectual leaders, including John Adams, Benjamin Franklin, Thomas Jefferson, and James Madison, were educated members of the Colonial upper class. They supported the elimination of dynastic and hereditary monarchies and the creation of government institutions led by people freely elected by property-holding members of the population. They wanted a "balanced" government under a doctrine of separation of powers and a republican form of government. They were *strong supporters of private property rights*.

Many of the most prominent military leaders of the American Revolution, including George Washington, Ethan Allen, Horatio Gates, Nathanael Greene, and John Paul Jones, were members of the upper class. Foreign military commanders of the Continental Army, including the Marquis de Lafayette, Baron Friedrich von Steuben, and Count Casimir Pulaski, were aristocrats and members of the European upper class. Class warfare and redistribution of wealth were not goals of the American Revolution.[31] They were for the most part realistic people who were aware that they could not create an ideal and perfect place for everyone to live in harmony. They were not out to create a fictional *Utopian* country.

There are many aspects to what could be misconstrued as a form of redistribution of wealth from the wealthy to the needy. The concept of "graduated" or "progressive" tax mechanisms, so that the wealthier pay a greater share of the revenues needed to support government operations, has been enforced since the first days of the Republic. There was nothing new about a progressive tax system. As far back as Roman times, taxes were levied based on people's ability to pay. Although progressive systems generally apply to income taxes, the concept extends to other forms of taxation. For example, excise taxes on luxury goods generally apply to wealthy people who can afford them, whereas basic necessities, such as food, are exempted from taxes. The wealthier are taxed at higher rates basically because even after paying a greater share of their income, they continue to have a large amount of disposable funds, whereas the poor barely have enough to cover their most basic needs, such as food and shelter. The Constitution does not specifically describe how taxes should be collected.

Graduated tax systems are not in contradiction to the Constitution. Nevertheless, there are serious concerns about progressive taxation, mainly when a large percentage of people in the lower economic strata are exempted from income taxes and are granted other immunities from taxation. Coupled with government welfare programs, such as food stamps and other handouts, people in the lower economic strata become increasingly dependent on the government. Benjamin Franklin was critical of these types of programs that he witnessed during the time he spent in Europe because *they made the poor dependent on government programs* and over time made them less inclined to find their own solutions to their problems. There is another potentially dangerous side to welfare programs. As the number of people receiving welfare increases, they become a strong voting bloc that will favor the politicians who promise to protect their entitlements to additional welfare. Politicians can take advantage of such a situation by stirring up class warfare and pushing for redistribution of wealth rather than creation of wealth.

Creation of the "Welfare State"

The economic depression that followed the crash of the stock market in 1929 resulted in the election of economic reformers led by President Franklin Delano Roosevelt (1882-1945) in 1932. President Roosevelt created new regulatory agencies, such as the Securities and Exchange Commission and the Federal Deposit Insurance Corporation, to prevent a repeat of many of the problems that led to the 1929 stock market crash and the ensuing economic depression. President Roosevelt created programs that hired millions of unemployed workers to build economic infrastructure, including the Works Progress Administration (WPA) and the National Youth Administration (NYA). Nevertheless, reinvigorating the economy proved to be harder than expected, as it did not really take off until the start of WWII. The legacy of the WPA and NYA in national parks, roads, hydroelectric dams, and other important infrastructure projects, without a doubt has benefitted the national economy but, at the time, only served as a palliative to systemic socio-economic problems that were only partially overcome by the huge investments in the war effort starting in 1942. The WPA and NYA were not truly efforts to redistribute wealth, but programs disguised to deal with an unprecedented economic crisis by offering employment.

In 1935, Congress enacted legislation creating the *Federal Old-Age and Survivors Insurance Trust Fund* to be supported through payroll taxes. It was conceived as a separate account in the U.S. Treasury and assigned to receive the deposit of payroll taxes paid by every worker to cover their retirement when they reached old age, as well as provide a pension to the surviving spouses and children until reaching adulthood. *Social Security Act* amendments passed by Congress in 1939 superseded the initial account established under the *Social Security Act of 1935*. Over the years, additional amendments have been made to the original plan enacted into law in 1935. Social Security rapidly became the largest component of the Federal budget comprising about 21 percent of annual expenditures. From around 53,236 beneficiaries in 1937, the number of beneficiaries increased to around 50,898,244 in 2008. As of 2015, around 11,000 people retired daily, thus increasing exponentially the number of people collecting a Social Security. For many years, there were more people working and contributing to Social Security than retired people collecting benefits, but as the population aged, that situation changed. The income of the Social Security Trust Fund is exceeded by the outlays to pay beneficiaries. This situation is expected to continue into the future as more "baby boomers" retire. The challenges associated with the Social Security will be addressed in more detail in Chapter VI.

The creation of the Social Security program in 1935 was justified without violating Constitutional parameters or the basic design that the Founding Fathers intended for the country. Notwithstanding, if a program is worth creating, then it should be created based on judicious cost/benefit analyses and designing realistic funding mechanisms to sustain them. The problems with Social Security and other welfare programs are not a constitutional issue, but one of *mismanagement.*

The one program that most closely resembles a wealth redistribution plan in the United States is the *Earned Income Tax Credit* (EITC or EIC), which was created by the Tax Reduction Act of 1976.[32] The EITC was designed to help low and moderate income working people through reductions in their income tax liability and through entitlements to refunds beyond what they deducted from their wages through payroll taxes. The EITC is considered to be the largest and most effective anti-poverty program in place.[33] Most families covered by EITC earn considerably less than the maximum income allowed to qualify. A substantial number of members of the armed forces and disabled veterans receive benefits under the program. Based on data derived from the 2009 tax year, about 27 million families and individuals received EITC.

Although right-wing elements may object philosophically to a welfare program like the EITC, considering that a large percentage of enlisted soldiers who risk their lives to defend the country benefit from this program, it is very difficult to argue against the program. The beneficiaries are working lower wage earners, not people who either refuse to work or for whatever reason cannot find suitable employment. Supporters of the EITC point out that the program provides incentives for poor people to go out and work, instead of relying on welfare handouts that create the opposite effect of incentivizing the poor not to work to continue receiving handouts. Even Benjamin Franklin may have supported a program like the EITC, despite his strong views on the subject of wealth redistribution.

According to estimates made by the Wall Street Journal, based on data from the U.S. Bureau of the Census, it is possible that around 49.1 percent of the American population may be receiving some form of government benefit.[34] To put it in perspective, in 1963, only about 30 percent of the population was receiving benefits from government programs. However, they may be receiving benefits from programs like Social Security and unemployment compensation, and Medicaid, which were not designed to function based on anything close to redistribution of wealth, since they were created to be supported by contributions from future beneficiaries, not funded from funds taken from anybody else.[35] Other programs, for example, the Food Stamps program and Section I Housing programs administered by the Department of Housing and Urban Development (HUD) are clearly welfare programs that involve wealth redistribution. It is alarming to see a considerable increase in the percentage of people who receive some type of government benefit, because this trend is unsustainable.

During a general election campaign, as the one in 2012, there is always a lot of *blah, blah, blah* about such topics as "*wealth redistribution*," but in general, the arguments tend to be very shallow on both sides. Time and time again they make references to the Constitution, but are generally engaging in *ad hominem* personal and emotional attacks against opponents instead of presenting solid and logical arguments based on facts.

The Fifth Amendment to the Constitution (part of the Bill of Rights) clearly states that *no person should be deprived of property without due process of law, or private property taken for public use without just compensation*, but it does not say anything about using the tax system to redistribute wealth from the rich to the poor. Taxes are accepted as necessary to pay for the functions of government authorized by the Constitution, but there is nothing explicitly allowing or denying their use for wealth redistribution. Thomas Jefferson held that *Congress has not unlimited powers to provide for the general welfare, but only those specifically enumerated* (in the Constitution)... *If Congress can determine what constitutes the general welfare and can appropriate money for its' advancement, where is the limitation to carrying into execution whatever can be effected by money?*[36] James Madison said: *If Congress can do whatever in their discretion can be done by money, and will promote the general welfare, the government is no longer a limited one possessing enumerated powers, but an indefinite one subject to particular exceptions.*[37] In another thought, Madison added that: *Charity is no part of the legislative duty of the government.*[38]

The Founding Fathers allowed Congress, the Executive, and the Judiciary to have the power to act on just about any issue not specifically enumerated, which means that there is considerable discretion to deal with issues not specifically addressed in the Constitution but not without engaging in exhaustive debate and negotiation. The masses have the power to freely elect their representatives to manage the government and come up with legislation to address just about any issue subject to judicial review.

When close to half the population is sucking the breasts of the state and receiving benefits, there is a clear danger that they will favor politicians that promise to continue and/or expand such benefits, thus placing in danger the rights of the minority of wealthier members of society at the other end of the spectrum. That is how a democratic majority rule can easily turn into mob rule. The American Revolution called for peace, liberty, human rights, democracy and opportunity for all. The inscription in the Statue of Liberty reads: *Give me your tired, your poor, your huddled masses yearning to breathe free...* It does not say anything about confiscating the property of the wealthy to redistribute it to the masses... Benjamin Franklin covered the subject of redistribution of wealth in another famous quote: *When the people find that they can vote themselves money that will herald the end of the republic.*[39]

Basic Constitutional Rights

When fifty six delegates to the First Continental Congress met in Philadelphia on 5 September 1774, one of the first challenges they faced was how to deal with the diversity of religious views. Could they have an invocation without favoring one set of views over another? They opted to accept a combination of diversity, respect, and *tolerance for other people's personal convictions*. The Founding Fathers asked the Reverend Jacob Duché, Rector of Christ Church of Philadelphia to open the 7 September 1774 session with a religious invocation. They set a precedent which continues to the present. For example, on 20 December 2012, a Catholic priest, the Reverend Patrick J. Conroy, S. J. said the Opening Prayer for Members of Congress on a memorable day when Senator Daniel K. Inouye (D-HI), the most senior member of the U.S. Senate, and President Pro-Tempore lay "in state" in the Capitol Rotunda, after serving in the Senate since 1962, when Hawaii was accepted into the Union as the 50th state. The Founding Fathers proved that it was possible for all religious views to coexist while at the same time maintain separation of Church and State.[40]

When the Second Continental Congress met in May 1775, Thomas Jefferson was sent as a delegate from Virginia. Jefferson was instrumental in advocating that the government should be *neutral* - not *secular* - on the question of religion views and *not promote, endorse, or fund any particular religion or religious institutions.* His views were shared by most of the 204 Founding Fathers who participated and signed the *Declaration of Independence*, the *Articles of Confederation*, and the *Constitution.* The majority, about 89 percent, were Episcopalians (~54 %), followed by Presbyterians (~18 %), and Congregationalists (~17 %). The reminder were split between Dutch Reformed Church members, Quakers, Lutherans, Catholics, Huguenots, Unitarians, Methodists, and Calvinists. (There were only two Catholics among the 204 Founding Fathers.) All the others were Protestant, although in many cases their particular denomination is unknown. They not only held strong and conflicting religious views, but also had conflicts within their own religious denominations, as the decisions they made to join the American Revolution in some cases conflicted with some of their most basic religious principles.[41]

Over the years, the issue of religion has come up repeatedly. For example, the Pledge of Allegiance was changed in 1954 by Congress from its original wording written in 1892 by a Christian Socialist preacher, Francis Bellamy (1855-1931), to include "under God" in the pledge.[42] The principal proponents and lobbyists for the change were Catholic members of the Knights of Columbus. President Eisenhower signed the bill into law on 14 June 1954. The pendulum started to swing back in the other direction during the 1960s, and in 1978, as a result of *Lipp v Morris*, the 3rd Circuit of the U.S. Court of Appeals ruled unconstitutional a New Jersey law that required all students to stand during the recitation of the Pledge, and in 2002, the 9th U.C. Circuit Court of Appeals ruled in *Newdow v the U.S. Congress* that the words "*under God*," violated the First Amendment principle of separation of church and state because it endorsed religion. A "stay" on the ruling was issued pending appeals, and Congress and multiple state legislatures passed resolutions condemning the ruling by the 9th Circuit Court.

Whether school children should or should not be forced to recite the Pledge of Alliance was always controversial, but adding "*under God*" made the issue considerably more controversial, particularly as the masses were persuaded to move further and further to the left since the 1960s. At some point, taking into account the direction of the electorate, it naturally will follow that the motto "*In God we trust*" will be forcibly removed from American currency, a practice that was started in 1864. Previously, in 1837, an Act of Congress had prescribed such mottoes in coins and paper currency. It was reversed in another Act of Congress in 1865, and on 12 February 1873, the Coinage Act directed the U.S. Secretary of the Treasury to place the inscription in coinage. In 1956, another Joint Resolution of Congress declared *In God We Trust* to be a national motto to be used in all currency. Surprisingly, there has not been a successful legal challenge.[43]

The important issue of freedom of speech granted by the First Amendment has been challenged over the years. There have always been some extremists around pushing for violent revolution and willing to import foreign ideologies that would result in a chaotic situation and bloodshed. Some veterans of the Revolutionary War were fascinated by the French Revolution and wanted a similar event to take place in America, and a subset wanted to secede from the Union. President Adam's Democratic-Republican Party, strong supporters of Federalism, was concerned about civil war, and enacted legislation to control elements that were stirring up the masses, exercising their constitutional right of free speech. Congress, at the instance of President John Adams, enacted the so-called *Alien and Sedition Acts of 1798* to deal with the extremists, but in the process violated the principle of free speech.

James Madison and then- Vice President Thomas Jefferson opposed the *Alien and Sedition Acts* as unconstitutional. The state legislatures of Virginia and Kentucky passed their own resolutions, calling on other states to oppose Federal encroachment on state rights, and legislation that they deemed in violation of the First Amendment. Some scholars believe that the seeds of the Civil War were planted during the controversy erupting from President Adams' attempts to control dissent and what he considered to be treason.

In 1873, the enactment of the Comstock Act granted the Post Office authority to open and censor mail deemed to be obscene, including information about contraception. But what is the definition of *obscene material*? The Comstock Act opened a dangerous road toward controlling free speech in violation of the First Amendment. The issue of how to define obscenity continued to be part of the debate on what constitutes unprotected speech for decades. In 1964, Supreme Court Justice Potter Stewart unsuccessfully attempted to define *pornography* and *obscenity*. In 1973, the Supreme Court ruled in the case Miller v. California that if an average person applying contemporary community standards finds that a particular work, taken as a whole, appeals to the prurient interest, is patently offensive, and lacks serious literary, artistic, political, or scientific value, then it is not protected by the right of free speech.

Based on these decisions, the Court seems to accept the view that *community standards* can change overtime, and that each community has the constitutional power to decide what is and is not acceptable within the definition of free speech. When these standards are transferred from sexual content to political speech, society is faced with the possibility that pied pipers supported by the far right or the far left could move the masses to extreme views. The task of defining what constitutes intrinsically objectionable material outside the right of free speech is extremely challenging and dangerous.

In 1918, a *Sedition Act* was enacted, targeting individuals and organizations that opposed participation in World War I. The Act was used to go after left-wing activists, including Anarchists, Socialists, and Communists, in part due to fears of a copycat revolution, in line with the Bolshevik Revolution of 1917 in Russia. European immigrants who were militant members of Anarchist, Socialist, and Communist organizations were arrested, prosecuted, and deported using the *Sedition Act*. In 1987, several states enacted legislation banning desecration of the American Flag, but in 1989, the U.S. Supreme Court ruled that it is unconstitutional to restrict the people's right of free speech- including burning or otherwise desecrating the flag. Although these legal actions were directed against sedition from the far-left, similar actions could be taken against people who hold opposing points of view.

The so-called *Alien Registration Act* of 1940, granted powers to the Federal Government to target anyone advocating the overthrow of the government and required that all resident aliens register their location with the government at least once annually.[44] In 1957 the Supreme Court ruled that the *Sedition Act* had gone too far and violated some aspects of the First Amendment. In 1969, the Supreme Court ruled that students could not be punished for wearing armbands in protest of the Vietnam War. The framers of the Constitution were smart enough to protect minority views from majority rule that can become mob rule under the influence of extremists. The concept of *evolving standards* over time can become a positive or negative factor, depending on the subject. On the related questions of freedom of thought and religion, the pendulum has been swinging back and forth for over two hundred years. Society has moved toward more tolerance, but the basic Christian heritage is constantly being challenged by groups that want to strip every link of religion from daily life and take separation of state and religion to extremes. People who demand tolerance for bizarre points of view often want to deny the same level of tolerance and First Amendment rights to people who do not agree with them… and that is the rub!

Right to Bear Arms

The 2nd Amendment to the Constitution was ratified and became law on 15 December 1791. The Supreme Court has interpreted the language of the amendment to mean that American citizens have the right to possess firearms and use them for lawful purposes, such as hunting, self-defense, and to protect their home, without any link to membership in the Armed Forces, the National Guard, or service in a lawful militia.[45] The right to bear arms was not a new concept when the Founding Fathers wrote the Bill of Rights, as British citizens had been granted the right to bear arms by the English Bill of Rights, enacted on 16 December 1689. Since 1791, conditions have changed in many ways, and although the Constitution granted the right to possess firearms, other important factors have come into play that should be evaluated and balanced with constitutional rights.

In a Democracy, there are lots of pressure groups, and people have a right to offer their opinions, debate important issues, and petition elected officials. One of the most heavily debated issues has been the right to own guns. Pressure groups, such as the National Rifle Association (NRA), have a right to petition elected officials to support their point of view regarding the meaning of the 2nd Amendment. Opponents of unregulated ownership of firearms have a constitutional right to present their point of view and petition their elected officials for a more restrictive interpretation of the 2nd Amendment. The process of shaping public opinion is complex and uncertain, as direction can change quickly after significant events that shake up the moral conscience of the nation. Apparently the moral conscience was not shaken up enough by school shootings for the U.S. Senate to pass on 18 April 2013 new legislation to expand background checks for gun purchasers.

A well-regulated militia being necessary to the security of a free state, the right of the people to keep and bear arms shall not be infringed.

2nd Amendment to the Constitution
(As ratified in 1791)

The interpretation of the writers' intent of the 2nd Amendment is one of the most controversial, and persistent issues in American constitutional history. At the time it was written, it was necessary to have weapons for self-defense, as well as for prudent local authorities to have armories and militias for defense. There were serious debates about the rights of states, limitations of power, and jurisdiction of the Federal Government, including the right of member states to secede. Things do not remain static, as society evolves and accepts new concepts and ideas that were far from those on the minds of the Founding Fathers back in 1791. The meaning of "keep and bear arms" outside of an official militia unit, the State National Guard units, or the Federal Armed Forces, can be debated *ad nauseam*. It is all hypothetical, while there are more important issues that need attention, such as how to handle the increasing number of mass killings by deranged people with firearms.

So what?

The Constitution is not perfect, but it was drafted in such a way so as to allow for a process of calibration and updating based on new challenges and new conditions. As Benjamin Franklin put it, "*the Constitution does not guarantee happiness, only the pursuit of it...*" However, the Constitution is the *Schwerpunkt* or "*center of gravity*" for the United States. Thomas Jefferson envisaged the country as a model for Democracy and a beacon of hope and freedom in the world. The political system was designed to prevent any faction, pied piper, false prophet, individual, group, or majority of the masses from becoming so powerful so as to establish a tyranny.

Some Americans believe in a mythological *Golden Age* in a distant past when there was respect for the Constitution, and everyone lived in perfect harmony and achieved the fulfillment of the "American dream." Actually, such a time never existed. There have always been challenges, and there has always been pressure for radical change. The world is changing faster now than at previous times in history, forcing reevaluation of many aspects of government. Rather than referring to a *Golden Age* in the past, we must maintain alive the ideals that point to a better future and fight back against the *counterculture* that wants to derail the nation from its original ideals. Regardless of all kinds of acrobatic stunts that stretch facts regarding constitutional intent, these changing times force reevaluation of many aspects of government. However, wisdom is needed as the Constitution does not prevent the masses and politicians from acting without foresight and objectivity. The Constitution is the compass... but as Americans move away from it they lose direction...

II – NATIONAL SECURITY

> **If we learn anything from that horrible day (9/11/2001), it is that there are evil, maniacal subhuman maggots in the world that have no respect for life.**
>
> **Ted Nugen**[46]

Confronting National Security Threats

There is no consensus or widely accepted definition of what is meant by "*national security*," or how to achieve it. Diplomatic, military, economic and information tools are part of a complex and interrelated system needed to protect the people, the culture, the values, the economy, our national assets, and institutions from internal and external threats. National security depends on multiple sources of strength beyond military might against all types of domestic and foreign enemies. Traditionally, the United States focused on achieving and maintaining military superiority based on a traditional hypothesis of a peer-to-peer conflict with another nation-state. After the collapse of the Soviet Union and the end of the *Cold War* in 1991, the principal national defense focus shifted to defending against asymmetric threats presented by terrorism and rogue states that support trans-national organizations that use terrorism as a strategy of choice. However, the reconstruction of the national security system with a different hypothesis of conflict is still incomplete, as the old hypothesis of a *peer-to-peer* conflict cannot be totally abandoned.

The possibility of a conventional conflict with the Russian Federation, the People's Republic of China (PRC), or any other emerging military power has not gone away simply because we share some of the same threats from Islamic extremists. Both, Russia and the PRC, are dealing with internal Islamic insurgencies, and share the same concerns over asymmetric warfare. The Russian people have been dealing with Islamic terrorism practically since the breakup of the Soviet Union.[47] The PRC is dealing with Uighur Islamic insurgents trying to create a pan-Islamic state in Xinjiang. These insurgents have carried out over 200 acts of terrorism in China in the past few years.[48] Islamic terrorism has become a shared challenge around the world.[49]

When al-Qai'da terrorists attacked the homeland on 9/11/2001, the systems in place to stop such an attack failed. The process of restructuring national security to deal with the increasing threat of terrorism by Islamic extremists was incomplete. Resources were stretched out. Terrorists only have to do things right once. The defenders have to be right all the time. When neophytes were running the show due to the departure of a large number of experienced professionals during the 1990s, the homeland was exposed. After 9/11/2001 thousands of new intelligence experts were formed, but by 2015, thousands had been let go, as the incursion into Iraq ended in 2011, and the U.S. prepared to leave Afghanistan.

There is an American colloquialism that says - *It ain't over till the fat lady sings* – implying that one should not presume to know how an event will end until the situation plays out to its final conclusion. As of December 2015, some American troops had been deployed back to Iraq, as Islamic insurgents had managed to regroup under ISIL, and capture vast areas of the country. Russian troops had been deployed to Syria to take active part in the counterinsurgency. Will the U.S. once again be faced with a shortage of qualified and experienced intelligence assets in the future? It all depends on lessons learned – if any - after 9/11/2001. Competition for areas of influence between the U.S. and its allies and Russia and China on the other side, is increasing, not decreasing. The need for experienced intelligence analysts is increasing exponentially, but it is impossible to create them overnight.

Dealing with Satan's Minions

When I was approached by the FBI in January 1968, I was not even 21 years old. I was asked by two senior special agents if I would be willing to cooperate in a national security investigation. I said yes. I will not go into the details, but essentially I was offered employment, but we had to wait until after my birthday. Then we got down to the particulars. I started my association with the FBI, and within days, I found myself in the middle of the racial riots that broke out after the assassination of Dr. Martin Luther King on 4 April 1968. Rioting broke out in at least 110 cities across the country, with some of the worse in the Capital.

Stokely Carmichael, a foreign troublemaker born in Trinidad-Tobago who had conflicts with Dr. Martin Luther King and the Student Nonviolent Coordinating Committee (SNCC), gathered a crowd at 14th and U Streets in N.W. D.C. and started a violent looting spree soon after news of King's assassination in Memphis was broadcast. The rioting continued into the next day with violent confrontations with police, and escalated from looters breaking store windows to setting them on fire, worsened by the fact that fires could not be put out, because firemen were pelted with rocks and bottles.[50] The city was devastated. It was quite a sad sight. I do not have to imagine Washington burning. I saw the city burning from high ground in Arlington across the Potomac.

Domestic terrorism was a fact of life back in the late 1960s and early 1970s. A group of members of the Students for a Democratic Society (SDS), several of them trained in Cuba by the General Directorate of Intelligence (DGI), formed the Weather Underground (WU).[51] A War Council was held in Flint, Michigan between 27 and 31 December 1969, where plans were finalized to form the WU, and start what they called a *revolutionary war* in the U.S. A Declaration of a *State of War* was released in a communiqué on 21 May 1970, prepared by Bernardine Dohrn and Bill Ayers, among others, as a prelude to a bombing campaign.[52]

There is always some pied piper from the far left or the far right seeking to build Shangri-La through violent means, and civil society has a duty to defend itself from them. I attended SDS meetings starting around June 1968, and witnessed first-hand the direction that the organization was taking. Many of the domestic terrorists of the late 1960s and early 1970s never served a day in jail, because illegal wiretaps and other improper means were used by law enforcement, which made prosecuting them impossible.[53] American society was not serious about administering justice to terrorists and domestic insurgents. There was plenty of evidence of foreign involvement in the training of terrorists who carried out multiple bombings all over the country, including at the Pentagon, the Department of State, the U.S. Capitol, police headquarters in NY, but they got away with it. The FBI knew who they were, tracked them as they planned their attacks, yet they were not arrested and prosecuted.

The Domestic Front is not Peaceful

In addition to external threats, domestic extremists from both ends of the political spectrum, and all kinds of predators, lunatics, nefarious actors and their minions constantly threaten peace and harmony; However, the restraints placed on law enforcement and intelligence organizations in 1976 substantially reduced the ability of these institutions to protect civil society. Year after year, the U.S. comes out in the top 3 to 4 places in the world with the highest incidence of use of improvised explosive devices (IEDs). Hoaxes and actual terrorist attacks using explosives and military weapons make the news practically every day, although most of these events are only covered by the local news media. The national news media covers extraordinarily significant events, such as the 20 July 2012 event in Colorado, when a deranged gunman attacked moviegoers as the latest Batman movie played on the screen, and the Newtown Elementary school massacre in CN, which was carried out by another mentally challenged individual. Nevertheless, most people are unaware of the real level of extremist violence in the country month after month.

These are some examples from a two week period in late August and early September 2012 that did not get much national press coverage. On 21 August, the Brazoria County Courthouse in Texas had to be evacuated after a bomb threat.[54] On the same day, a man in Red Bank, Tennessee was arrested accused of wanting to lob two Molotov cocktails at the local police department headquarters, in retaliation for his girlfriend being arrested for a second DUI since the beginning of 2012.[55] On 23 August the Dodge City, KS, Public Library had to be evacuated as a result of a bomb threat.[56] The following day, a San Francisco, CA, apartment building had to be evacuated and streets closed, while the bomb squad inspected suspicious items.[57]

On 24 August, there was a bomb threat at the Paramus Park Mall, in Paramus, NJ. A note had been left in a dressing room asking for an undisclosed amount of money.[58] Meanwhile, police were making an arrest in Lafayette, Louisiana, linked to a bomb threat in Iberia Parish. The deranged perpetrator had threatened to blow up a bank with a Trident missile![59] In Nogales, AZ, ICE agents discovered 6 grenades and 2,400 pounds of marijuana stashed at a Rio Rico home, and arrested two suspects.[60] On 27 August, police in Hollywood, CA, found explosives while investigating a shooting. While searching a suspect's apartment police found a gun and a prop stick of dynamite.[61] The next day, the bomb squad in Oklahoma City, cleared suspicious items from a house, and in Springfield, MA, police found that a suspicious package thought to contain explosives turned out to be filled with cocaine, while in Torrence, CA, the bomb squad was inspecting another suspicious package found at a PetSmart store.[62]

On 5 September, a 27-year-old woman in St. Charles, MO, was arrested and charged with terrorism after threatening to blow up a building after being fired from her job for insubordination.[63] The next day, a 26-year-old woman was arrested after making bomb threats against the Atlantic Cape Community College in NJ.[64] On 6 September, a Dallas-bound U.S. Airways flight from the Philadelphia International Airport was ordered back after a caller reported to authorities that an explosive liquid was present to cause problems to a passenger. The passenger was arrested and released after it was determined that he had been the victim of a hoax.[65] Apparently the caller was a former girlfriend, who had to face justice for her prank.

Also on 6 September, an IED destroyed a truck parked in front of a home in Holly, MI. Based on a press report this incident was the third time that a vehicle at the same address was targeted with an IED during a two-year period.[66] This incident is not unique. On the same day, federal authorities in Glendale, AZ, released the pictures of a suspected serial bomber, who placed IEDs on three occasions at the same house, twice in July 2011, and in August 2012.[67] Although most threats turn out to be hoaxes, not all of them are. Therefore, it is impossible for law enforcement authorities to intercept previously unknown would-be terrorists and criminals before they strike.

Although many mentally ill and violent-prone individuals come to the attention of school teachers, employers, supervisors, physicians, and people who work in the mental health care system, in many cases they fail to alert law enforcement officials about potential dangers associated with a particular individual. Not all people who hold extremist views of one kind or another join affinity groups to be with people that hold similar views, although the Internet is making it easier for these people to find each other and remain anonymous. That makes it even harder to identify the mentally ill before they strike.[68]

Cults, Militias, and Apocalyptic Sects

Right-wing and xenophobic groups have existed in the U.S. going all the way back to the 19th century, but they have proliferated since the 1970s. These groups should not be confused with Conservative groups, even if, at times, they may look like first cousins. Conservatives generally want to preserve traditional and conventional values, morals, institutions, and customs, and accept the introduction of change "cautiously" so as to maintain social stability. Modern Conservatives are not into unrestrained Capitalism, and accept the need to have government institutions and regulations to protect civil society from criminal action and excesses that undermine Capitalism.[69]

Right wing extremists fall within a very wide definition. Some have neo-populist views that resemble the views of extremists at the other end of the political spectrum. They all hate the Federal Government. Ironically, Anarchists, Communists, Socialists, Fascists, Falangists, and the KKK act like first cousins.[70] They are anti-government and anti-establishment, even if they do not arrive at their views by taking the same path. They want some of the same things and share the same propensity to violence to impose their fanatical views on others. For example, the anti-intellectual "White Supremacists," claim Caucasian racial superiority, but generally could not find the Caucasus on a map, and have no idea of how ethnic groups from the Caucasus look like; furthermore, they don't know that *most Caucasians are Muslims*![71] They hate government, the wealthy, practically all symbols of "the establishment," and share other views with violence-prone Anarchists. Many incidents involving extremists of all political persuasions are intertwined and feed on each other, as anti-establishment lunatics have a great ability to associate things in curious, creative and unusual ways.

For example, Randy Weaver, a blue collar worker, college dropout, and former Army Green Beret, drifted into extreme religious views, which he somehow weaved into anti-government rhetoric. At some point in the late 1980s Weaver moved his family to a secluded rural area of Northern Idaho, where he proposed to protect his family from what he perceived as a corrupted world and the intrusion of the government in his personal affairs. As with other extremists, he had an apocalyptic view of the end of the world nearing, and among other things, decided to home school his four children, gathered a vast assortment of weapons, and joined the White-Supremacist Aryan Nation.

The Secret Service, the ATF, the FBI, and local law enforcement authorities began to get concerned about real or alleged threats against government authorities by Randy Weaver. Informants provided government investigators a mix of good and false information, and Weaver was arrested. Clerical mistakes by court employees regarding a court date were made, which led to a bench warrant for Weaver's arrest. The U.S. Marshals Service was brought in to carry out the arrest. Weaver held up in his cabin in the woods at Ruby Ridge with his family, leading to a long standoff starting in March 1992, which ended in a firefight the following August, during which additional mistakes were made by law enforcement agents.

Numerous violations of the rules governing the use of deadly force were made. Weaver and several family members, including his children, were shot without justification by trigger-happy law enforcement agents. After several investigations, it was determined that government agents committed multiple law violations. Weaver's unarmed 14-year-old son and a house guest were shot dead by U.S. Marshals. Mrs. Weaver, who was holding the couple's 10-month old baby in her arms was shot and killed by an FBI sharpshooter. Weaver himself was shot and wounded. After a ten day ordeal, Weaver surrendered. The Weaver family filed a wrongful death suit, and Randy Weaver was awarded a $100,000 settlement, and his three daughters $1 million each. A house guest was awarded $380,000 by the government as part of a settlement.

Additional tragedies were derived from Ruby Ridge, as the case inspired other lunatics to take action against what they perceived as a dictatorial government. FISA had nothing to do with what happened at Ruby Ridge, but the lack of discipline that surfaced after the death in 1971 of the much-maligned J. Edgar Hoover, the long-time Director of the FBI, had a lot to do with these events. While Hoover ran the FBI these types of wild cowboy operations did not happen. Sure, some criminals back in the 1930s were gunned down, but the Ruby Ridge story was very different than the country-wide chase of Bonny and Clyde.[72] The whole thing was stupid.

The following year, starting in late February 1993, ATF attempted to execute a search warrant at the Branch Davidians compound near Waco, Texas, resulting in a shootout in which four agents and six Branch Davidians were killed. The FBI was called to the scene and a 50-day siege of the site followed, ending in an assault by Federal authorities and a fire that destroyed the compound, resulting in the death of at least 76 people, including around 20 children and at least two pregnant women. About a third of the victims were British nationals. In the European press, coverage of the Waco nightmare contributed to downgrading the U.S. reputation for law and order.

The religious sect was led by Vernon Wayne Howell, known as "David Koresh," born of a teenage unwed mother, victimized through his childhood by convoluted living arrangements, affected by dyslexia, and a high school dropout. Koresh apparently sought answers by joining a series of religious congregations and Bible study groups. Eventually, around 1981, when he was about 22-years old, he joined the Branch Davidians, a dissident group of the Seventh-day Adventist Church. Within a few years, Koresh became a messianic leader of the group claiming a gift of prophecy, leading to internal disputes within the congregation. Koresh was forced out, but by 1985 he had gathered already some 25 followers.

As other pied pipers and messianic leaders have done, Koresh managed to recruit more followers, including foreigners, and moved his sect to Israel. He envisioned that his life would end in martyrdom, and moved back to Waco, Texas, with his followers around 1991. His arrival back to the Branch Davidians compound in Waco resulted in a gunfight between him and a several followers and a group loyal to the leader of the Branch Davidians at the Waco compound and his own followers. Koresh and his followers were charged with attempted murder, but they avoided jail time due to a mistrial.

The Davidians were linked to numerous improprieties and illegal activity, from drug trafficking to murder, child and sexual abuse, and statutory rape, but somehow they were able to continue to exist, as the U.S. legal framework allows for all kinds of wrongdoing if it takes place behind the veil of religion. When the FBI, with the approval of Attorney General Janet Reno decided to act and end the 50-day standoff, they acted based on information of multiple law violations in the compound. In the course of the assault the compound caught fire. Despite allegations that the FBI fired into the burning compound, the government actions were justified. Right-wing and religious fanatics built a mythology around the Waco tragedy, leading to larger tragedies.

The bombing of the Alfred P. Murrah Federal Building in Oklahoma City in 1995, which killed 168 people, illustrates this point. The bombing using an IED was a follow-up to the Ruby Ridge and the Waco tragedies. The principal author of the bombing, Timothy McVeigh, a former U.S Army soldier, claimed that he had been radicalized against the government due to frustration about high taxes, gun control legislation (particularly the Brady Bill enacted after the attempted assassination of President Reagan in 1981), and the Waco and Ruby Ridge tragedies, which he blamed on the Federal Government. McVeigh frequently spoke to friends, co-workers, and acquaintances against these issues, and government encroachment into civil liberties protected by the Constitution. McVeigh was another pied piper in the making, but he did not have the basic qualities to develop a following, except a couple of useful idiots who provided him assistance. The legal system functioned efficiently and McVeigh was sentenced and execute, as compared to other cases that have dragged on for years.

On 10 June 2009, 88-year-old White Supremacist and Holocaust denier James Wenneker von Brunn walked into the Holocaust Memorial Museum in Washington, D.C. and shot and killed a security guard. In a notebook found in his car von Brunn claimed that President Obama was created by Jews, and that his Jew owners tell him what to do. Like other conspiracy theorists and anti-Semitic extremists, he was influenced by the *Protocols of the Learned Elders of Zion*, a fantasy describing a Jewish plot to control non-Jews and control the world. He had been convicted in 1981 by an all-Black jury in the D.C. Superior Court, an experience that fueled his views against Marxist/Liberal/Jews, but he also had other arrests and convictions for drunken driving, and disorderly conduct and gun violations. He served several years in prison for attempted kidnapping, burglary, and assault charges. Security guards returned fire and critically wounded von Brunn.

On 18 February 2010, Andrew J. Stack, III flew his Piper Dakota airplane into an office building in Austin, Texas, that houses the Internal Revenue Service (IRS) and other Federal agencies. Prior to his suicide he had been under audit by the IRS for failure to file income tax reports. In his suicide note Stack called for violent revolt against the government. The incident was followed by considerable commentary against the IRS, including Iowa Congressman Steve King (R-Iowa), who advocated for abolishing the IRS and the creation of a new national sales tax. It is practically impossible to intercept lone wolves before they act, but without an efficient system of informers and robust intelligence program, civil society is exposed to these mentally-challenged individuals.

Enter what I call *The Pied Piper of Hamelin Syndrome*. A *"syndrome"* is a *collection of symptoms* that characterize a specific disease or condition. As in the traditional German folk tale *The Pied Piper of Hamelin*, messianic leaders attract young people that suffer from certain specific conditions that make them susceptible to recruitment. The characteristics of mental weakness of people who tend to follow without questioning produce a pattern that can be easily recognized. They target ***vulnerable*** young people and convince them that they could be part of the solution to the problems affecting the world. They are fed simple answers and not given time to think. *Anyone with a weak mind is an easy recruit.*

The story of the *Pied Piper of Hamelin* was a German attempt to show children the dangers of following people without thinking and without consulting with family and friends. (The advent of Hitler shows that the story of the Pied Piper of Hamelin did not save the Germany from disaster.) Children all over the Western World have heard the story, yet over and over again people continue to make the same mistakes. A charismatic leader like Jim Jones was able to get over 914 people in 1978 to follow him and even convinced them to commit suicide. While most of the other nut cases were right-wing lunatics, Jones could be labeled a left-wing lunatic. Some deranged televangelists try to link tsunamis, hurricanes, earthquakes and even terrorism to the *"End of Times"* described in the Bible.

Every country, every ethnic and religious group can generate evil messianic people. An example worth mentioning is the Jewish right wing, Koch Movement of the late American orthodox Rabbi Meier Kahane. He founded the Jewish Defense League (JDL) in the U.S. and the Koch movement in Israel. His followers were blacklisted as terrorists by the U.S. Government and his party was similarly removed from the Israeli Parliament (Knesset). Among other things, he wanted to create an *orthodox Jewish theocracy* or religious state to run Israel and to *forcefully remove all Palestinian Arabs from Palestine*. He supported *Zionist terrorism*. Interestingly, he worked as an FBI informant in the 1960s infiltrating the Anti-War Movement and other leftist organizations as part of COINTELPRO. He also had connections to organized crime boss Joe Colombo. Eventually he was assassinated in New York City by an Arab terrorist in 1990, with ties to the terrorists who bombed the World Trade Center building in 1993.

What kind of people fall for *Apocalyptic Visionaries?* How did Jim Jones manage to get 914 people to accept *revolutionary suicide* to protest racism and Fascism in 1978? How did David Koresh manage to convince at least 75 followers to accept communal living, a highly regulated and disciplined life, and to gather a huge arsenal of weapons and use them to fight off government agents trying to execute an arrest warrant? How did he manage to convince them to stage some kind of a murder-suicide pact in 1993? How did Luc Jouret, a *New Age* homeopathic doctor manage to recruit people for the *Order of the Solar Temple* and convince them to engage in a murder-suicide pact between 1995 and 1997? How were some people convinced to join the *Heaven's Gate* cult and to commit suicide in 1997, expecting to be picked up by some kind of a spaceship linked to the tail of the Hale-Bopp comet?

There are no easy answers to any of these questions. They illustrate the need to have an effective system of domestic intelligence collection to protect civil society from pied pipers that abuse the freedoms granted by the Constitution for the wrong purpose.

Left-Wing Anti-Establishment Groups

After the demise of the Soviet Union in 1991, the principal catalysts for left-wing activists disappeared, as an assortment of Marxist and Socialists groups became disenchanted. Communism had failed not only in the Soviet Union, but also in Central and Eastern Europe. As a result, many of the radical organizations with roots in the 1960s disappeared or lost their appeal, and the number of activists went way down. Without Soviet sponsorship leftist radicals could not operate as in the 1960s and 1970s. The *Prairie Fire Organizing Committee*, predecessor of the *Weather Underground*, the *Black Panther Party*, the *Symbionese Liberation Army*, and lesser known groups, as the *United Freedom Front*, carried out numerous bombings in the late 1960s and through the 1970s. They had been rolled up by the 1980s, or had ended their operations as ineffectual for achieving their goals.

Some left-wing single-issue groups, such as those espousing environmental causes or the defense of animal rights, continued to exist and grow, and depending on the charismatic leader leading them, they engaged in terrorism as a tool to achieve their goals. Not all of these groups engage in violence, but those that did, caused considerable damage through different forms of terrorism. Eco-terrorists and animal rights activists are believed to have carried out over 2,000 terrorist-like crimes from about 1980 to 2010, based on information derived from DOJ data bases.

The domestic intelligence programs of the 1960s resulted from the growth of a mix of anti-establishment organizations with a mix of Anarchist and Marxist rhetoric that slowly drifted into believing that they could start an armed insurrection in the U.S. The Soviet Union, the Cuban, North Vietnamese, and East German Government, the PRC, and their allies supported, trained, and fomented internal dissent in the U.S. and helped to coordinate and guide the anti-war movement during the Vietnam War. Cuban and Soviet agents handled like marionettes many of the young people who emerged as leaders of the so-called New Left. Although excesses were committed by intelligence and law enforcement organizations, there was ample justification for keeping an eye on these groups. However, when something is worth doing, it is worth doing correctly and within the law. The use of illegal wiretaps and other improper actions to control the terrorists of the 1960s and early 1970s was a mistake. The terrorists got away without prosecution due to improper police practices.

My views are derived from personal experiences. In June 1968, I traveled to the University of Michigan for a national meeting of the Students for a Democratic Society (SDS). At this gathering I personally witnessed how activists who had travelled to Cuba were provided training, and were in turn speaking out in favor of a Communist revolution, and were providing weapons training to a select group of idiots recruited from universities all over the US. I attended similar gatherings in the next two years at Michigan State, the University of Illinois, the University of Texas, Princeton, Yale, and the University of Colorado. Yippies,[73] Hippies, Up-Against-the-Wall-Motherf***ers, Anarchists, several brands of Trotskyites, Maoists, and an assortment of radicals – mostly linked with the Cuban and Vietnamese Communists – and iconoclast Communists who accepted many of the life-style ideas of the different Anarchist groups.[74] They clustered around the Chicago headquarters of the SDS, and clashed with the Maoist and Trotskyites. Eventually, they coalesced around the Revolutionary Youth Movement (RYM) faction, and some decided to go underground to start a revolution under the brand of the Weather Underground (WU), inspired by the lyrics of Bob Dylan's song released in 1965 entitled Subterranean Homesick Blues... *You don't need a weatherman to know which way the wind blows...*[75] At these meetings in 1968 and 1969, workshops were held on sabotage and other forms of terrorism, including ways to turn otherwise peaceful anti-war demonstrations into violent riots. I participated in some of these meetings, so I can attest that it happened. This is not fiction!

New Left groups had emerged from within the U.S. in part due to the widespread opposition to the Vietnam War. However, I learned how some key leaders of the SDS who later formed part of the Weather

Underground maintained contact and received instructions from the North Vietnamese Communist delegation in Paris holding talks with a U.S. delegation headed first by Averell Harriman, and later by Henry Kissinger, and specifically, Madame Nguyeb Thi Binh. Others had visited Cuba and received indoctrination and training by Cuban military and intelligence to start armed revolution in the U.S. I had documents in my hands, and listened to the instructions and discussions, although I was never able to fully penetrate into the *sanctum sanctorum* of the more radical activists that became the cadre for the Weather Underground. One of the reasons is that I was not willing to use drugs or participate in orgies and other activities that served as a tool to keep informers and intelligence operatives away. That was very clever. After the collapse of the Soviet Union and the end of the Cold War in 1991, a lot of information has become available regarding the Soviet participation in promoting dissent in the U.S. back in that period between 1967 and 1971, and how anti-war activists were played like marionettes by Soviet intelligence.

Islamic terrorism in the homeland

The terrorist attacks of 9/11/2001 should not have been a surprise to anyone. One of the first incidents of Islamic terrorism in the U.S. took place on 25 January 1993, when Mir Aimal Kasi, a Pakistani immigrant, opened fire on the occupants of several cars waiting at a stop light to make a left turn into CIA headquarters in Langley, Virginia, killing two and injuring three other employees of the agency. Kasi had entered the U.S. using false papers in 1991, and later procured a fake residency permit. Using money from an inheritance he received in 1989, Kasi invested in a courier business, where he worked as a driver. Despite his false identification papers, he was able to purchase an AK-47 military rifle at a gun shop in Virginia. (This type of data somehow is kept away from the debate about 2nd Amendment rights!) The following day, Kasi returned to Pakistan.

The manhunt launched after the attack led to his arrest by FBI agents in 1997; He was returned to the US, tried and convicted for murder, and finally executed by lethal injection in 2002. The body was repatriated to Pakistan, where he was buried as a local hero in the presence of high-level officials including general officers and the Pakistani Ambassador to the U.S. Instead of lifting his diplomatic agreement or government permission to serve as a foreign representative, Ambassador Ashraf Jehangir Qazi, was allowed to return to his post in Washington, and he later continued his diplomatic career with several UN appointments.[76] This was one of the first signs that our so-called "Pakistani allies" should not be trusted.

A month and a day later, on 26 February 1993, six people were killed and about 1,000 injured when a radical Islamic group consisting of about a dozen people linked to al-Qai'da drove a truck bomb (VBIED) into the North Tower of the World Trade Center building in New York City. Financing was provided through illegal activity in the U.S. and funds provided by Khaled Sheikh Mohammed. The mastermind behind the bombing, Ramzi Yousef, and his group of terrorists were arrested, tried, convicted, and sentenced to prison. Yousef was born in Kuwait and had received training by al-Qai'da in Afghanistan. He flew to the U.S. in September 1992 using a false Iraqi passport, and upon arrival requested political asylum, and was allowed into the country as a parolee until a hearing date to consider his request. Once in the country, he contacted Omar Abdel Rahman, a blind Egyptian Muslim cleric, who arranged for his meeting with the rest of the terrorist cell.

Yousef was able to purchase 1,500 lbs. of urea nitrate and hydrogen gas canisters to construct the improvised explosive device. One of the co-conspirators, El Sayyid Nosair, had been arrested in 1991 for the murder of Rabbi Meir Kahane, but somehow had been able to escape a murder conviction. Yousef drove a rented Ryder van into the World Trade Center. Pieces of the truck were recovered by investigators, leading to finding the vehicle identification number (VIN), the owner of the truck, and who rented it. Some of the members of the terrorist cell were able to escape, after they had been arrested and released by the FBI. Despite having information provided by an informant to the FBI days before the bombing, the terrorists were able to carry out their terrorist plot.[77] Obviously, despite the excellent investigation carried out after the attack, the whole thing could have been prevented, as the FBI had sufficient information through an informant to intercept the terrorists. As in other cases, including the events of 9/11/2001, somehow available intelligence did not get to the right people, or there was a failure to act based on the information available.

On 24 February 1997, a Palestinian immigrant, 69-year old Ali Hassan Abu Kamal, opened fire on tourists visiting the observation deck of the Empire State Building in New York City with a handgun bought in Florida. A Danish tourist was killed, and several tourists from Argentina, France, and Switzerland, in addition to visiting American tourists were wounded. The attack ended when the perpetrator committed suicide. Kamal had entered the U.S. legally a year earlier with a non-immigrant visa. Despite some controversy over his motives, after some time passed it became clear that he carried out the suicidal terrorist act based on his anti-Israeli and anti-American views and his support for the Palestinian cause against Israeli occupation.

Three years later, on 13 October 2000, a synagogue was firebombed in Syracuse, N.Y. Three Palestinian terrorists attacked with incendiary devices another synagogue in the Riverdale neighborhood in New York City, just before the Yom Kippur holiday. One of the Palestinians was arrested and sentenced to fifteen years in jail. Several months earlier, a group of American Black Muslim activists were arrested for plotting to blow up two synagogues in Riverdale, as well as to shoot down military planes flying in or out of the Air National Guard base in Newburgh, N.Y. Using a Pakistani national as an informant, the FBI had penetrated the would-be terrorist group, provided fake explosives, and arrested the four conspirators. Three of the men were African-American, and the fourth was a Haitian immigrant. Three had converted to Islam while in prison. The leader of the group, James Cromitie, had at least 27 prior arrests for minor crimes. The Haitian had a history of schizophrenia, paranoia, and other mental disorders.

Iranian-Sponsored Terrorism

On 11 October 2011, the U.S. Department of Justice announced that two Iranian operatives linked to Iran's Quds Force, a special operations unit of the Islamic Revolutionary Guards Corps (IRGC) were charged with plotting to assassinate the ambassador of Saudi Arabia to the United States and other terrorist attacks to coincide with the hit on the ambassador. One of the men was arrested, but the other managed to escape and was thought to be in Iran. Manssor Arbabsiar and Gholam Shakuri were charged with the attempted assassination, and conspiracy to use a weapon of mass destruction (WMD). Arbabsiar, who was arrested in New York on 29 September, was described as a dual Iranian and U.S. citizen, and a member of the IRGC. He supplied thousands of dollars to finance the plot. The conspiracy may have been discovered by DEA agents in Mexico who intercepted an attempt by the Iranians to contact a Mexican drug trafficking organization (DTO) to obtain their participation in the plot in exchange for $1.5 million. His co-conspirator, Gholam Shakuri, was thought to be in Iran.

Nightmare in Boston

A blueprint for future terrorism played out at about 2:45 p.m. on 15 April 2013, when around 27,000 runners were completing the Boston Marathon. Two improvised explosive devices (IEDs) exploded on Boylston Street placed by brothers Tamerlan Tsamaev and Dzhokhar Tsamaev, two immigrants from the North Caucasus in Russia. They arrived in the U.S. as children, grew up in American culture, but were imperfectly assimilated.[78] Police recovered several unexploded IEDs, and other IEDs were used in a firefight with police in which one of the perpetrators was killed. The other was captured later by police.[79] Thousands of former Islamic insurgents from the N. Caucasus republics fighting for independence from the Russian Federation have gone into exile throughout the world since the 1990s, and they constitute a risk of Islamic terrorism, in alliance with al-Qai'da and other Islamic extremists, or as "lone wolf" terrorists.

Since the start of the first Chechen War after the collapse of the Soviet Union in 1991, the resurgence of nationalism in the North Caucasus has undergone a metamorphosis. At the beginning, the movement was led by nationalist former Soviet military officers who revived the frozen conflict between Turkish tribes from former lands of the Ottoman Empire that were conquered by Tsarist troops in the 19th century, followed by forced internal exile and other forms of cultural, religious, and political repression under the Communists. As Russian military forces defeated Chechen insurgents in the 1990s using extreme tactics, the conflict morphed into an Islamic insurrection under Кавказский Эмират (*Imarat Kavkaz-* IK). The Islamic insurgents retaliated against Russian repressive counterinsurgency tactics against civilians by bombing Russian civilian airlines, rail and metro-rail stations, schools, a theater, the Moscow international airport, and other sites packed with civilians. Nevertheless, although coordinating their operations with al-Qai'da and other Islamic extremists, they did not target American or Western European interests, and from time to time issued statements that their problem is with Russia, not with the West.

After the Boston Bombings, IK issued statements about their non-involvement with the terrorist incident, and reiterated that their fight is against Russia. The possibility of expansion of the conflict from the North Caucasus to other areas, is of very serious concern to the Russian Government. It should also be a concern to other countries where there is a large presence of former Islamic insurgents from the North Caucasus.[80]

The new blueprint for Islamic extremists, particularly al-Qai'da, is to promote individual "lone wolf" and small independent terrorist cell actions. They radicalize Islamic youth through Internet web sites and through radical preachers that cater to frustrated and easily influenced young people. They know that immediately after a terrorist atrocity the international news media and all major networks provide minute-by-minute coverage for days and weeks. The terrorists are seeking "theater" and attention, regardless of how they are cast. They are convinced that God is on their side, and any action against infidels is justified, regardless of who gets hurt, including other innocent Muslims who happen to be victims together with everybody else, simply because they were in the wrong place at the wrong time.

The international news media and "think tanks" have published numerous articles and studies about the presence of Chechen, Dagestanis, Ingushetians, Circassians, and other Islamic militants from the North Caucasus in guerrilla training in Pakistani tribal districts of North and South Waziristan, as well as fighting with al-Qai'da elements against the government in Syria. Hundreds of jihadists have flown from Western Europe and other Muslim countries to join the conflict in

Syria, just as they answered the Jihadist call for help in West Africa and the Sahel. There are 57 majority Muslim countries involving multiple nationalities, ethnicities, races, and skin colors, which makes it very challenging to profile potential Islamic terrorists. They could have Asian features if they are from Indonesia or the Philippines, or look like Western Europeans like the people from the North Caucasus, or African from Nigeria, Somalia, Chad or Mali, or the mixed features of people from Morocco, Tunisia, Algeria, Libya, or Egypt. Profiling of potential Islamic terrorists is practically impossible, as the events in Boston clearly show. Countering the new Islamic terrorist blueprint will have to depend on better intelligence and oversight of social media that is being successfully used to proselytize and plan insurgency and terrorism.

Americans were outraged after another terrorist massacre resulting in 14 people dead and another 17 people wounded, carried out in San Bernardino, CA, on 2 December 2015. Clearly, the intelligence community failed to detect the plot, despite numerous opportunities to pick up critical information before the husband and wife team could strike. The Department of State failed to conduct due diligence before issuing a visa to the Pakistani woman who requested a fiancé visa to travel to the United States to marry an American-born citizen of Pakistani parents. The FBI and other members of the IC failed to detect questionable travel to Saudi Arabia and Pakistan by Syed Farook. Members of the public failed to report suspicious activity to law enforcement. Weapons were obtained using a surrogate "friend," who the system failed to properly investigate when he purchased military-style weapons and ammunition. And to add to the blunders, despite all the hallmarks of terrorism, there was initial denial that the incident was a classical act of Islamic terrorism. And this incident took place within a month of coordinated terrorist attacks in Paris, which resulted in 130 people killed and wounded hundreds. Within the system blinking red, once again Americans were caught with their pants down.

Cyber threats

Since the 1990s cyber threats to national security have been increasing. Rogue states, criminal syndicates, anti-establishment activists, and multiple brands of malicious actors, including state-sponsored intelligence organizations, target soft cyber spots to penetrate public and private networks. Hackers attempt thousands of times daily to break through security walls with increasing sophistication. They probe defenses around the world associated with the management of basic infrastructure, including potable water supplies, gas and electricity networks, metro rail, long line systems, and other elements of a modern society.

Hackers can disrupt the global supply chain, interrupting the normal flow of parts and components to factories, as well as the distribution networks that deliver product from factories and farms to markets around the world. Financial systems are prime targets as criminal elements try to withdraw funds from bank accounts or fraudulently use stolen credit card numbers. Malicious hackers use *phishing* emails with attached infected files or links to infected websites for financial gain, or simply to cause havoc. Criminal elements sell stolen data over the Internet to other criminal organizations that can make fake credit cards to withdraw money from ATMs, or directly from compromised bank accounts. They constantly modify and improve their tactics to take advantage of security vulnerabilities and bypass enhanced security programs. This tug of war is expected to continue into the future and will require an increasing investment in personnel and equipment, as the competition for supremacy in cyber space grows to unpredictable levels. Malicious actors with technical skills can conduct their raids at little cost and using the most basic resources, but defending against them is very costly.

There is another mounting national security problem involving the exfiltration of classified documents from government computer networks. When government secret documents are made public they can put at risk the personal security of informers, agents, Foreign Service officers, and intelligence analysts whose names are listed as either sources or drafters of intelligence assessments. The largest scandal thus far has been the famous WikiLeaks case, involving the release of over 700,000 stolen classified documents, including some that revealed the identities of agents working in several foreign countries.

Julian Assange, an Australian national, founder of WikiLeaks and U.S. Army soldier, Pfc. Bradley Manning, were charged with stealing and publishing secret documents. Manning shares with spies arrested in the past a history of mental instability, including a "gender-identity" problem.[81] He was able to steal the documents due to poor supervision inside a Sensitive Compartmentalized Computer Facility (SCCF) while serving in Iraq. In a classic American tradition, the barn door was locked after the horses had escaped.[82] Sometime around November 2008, DOD barred the use of all computer media, including thumb drives and writable discs, from use in government computers.[83] For several years, thumb drives containing government data were for sale by street vendors in Afghanistan, according to press reports.[84] Inexplicably, Manning was not executed.

The private sector is targeted for downloads of inside information and economic espionage by foreign countries. For example, in July 2010, a People's Republic of China (PRC) national was arrested in Massachusetts by the FBI and charged with misappropriation of trade secrets from Dow AgroSciences, LLC. The Chinese National, who had entered the U.S. with a legal permanent immigrant visa obtained employment with Dow and passed internal company secrets to researchers at a university in the PRC to study, expand, or copy the technology.[85] The indictment explained that the Chinese National had worked at Dow between 2003 and 2005, and had signed an agreement not to disclose internal information. He had published an article without prior authorization from Dow in a journal of the Hunan Normal University (HNU) disclosing proprietary information. The article had listed a bogus grant from the National Natural Science Foundation of China (NSFC) as the funding for the research that had produced the results outlined, when in fact they had been stolen from Dow. According to the indictment, the Chinese National had been seeking a manufacturing facility in the PRC to produce the product to compete with Dow internationally. This was a typical case of industrial espionage, which has increased with the advent of the Internet, which provides an easy tool for information to be accessed and diverted to foreign entities. These incidents are just as damaging to national security as cases of espionage targeting the public sector.

Espionage and traitors

According to the *Old Testament*, disloyalty and deception have been around for a very long time, as for example, the betrayal of King David by his son Absolum, as told in 2 Samuel.[86] In the *New Testament* we have the story of how Judas Iscariot betrayed Jesus.[87] Espionage has also been around for a very long time.[88] America has been faced with betrayal since the Revolutionary War. Continental Army Major General Benedict Arnold, born in 1741 in Norwich, CN and a veteran of the battles of Fort Ticonderoga, Quebec, and Saratoga, NY, sold himself to the British in 1780. The traitor joined the British and fought in their uniform against his own countrymen until the end of the war, and then fled to London. Arnold was one of the first in a long line of betrayers who have caused considerable damage to national security.

Julius and Ethel Rosenberg, both members of the Communist Party, passed nuclear secrets to the Soviets and worked as spies until they were caught, tried and executed in 1953. Another traitor was Navy communications specialist John Anthony Walker, Jr, who spied for the Soviets from 1968 until he was arrested in 1985. Not only did he betray his country, but recruited his son Michael and Navy co-workers to spy for the Soviets. As a result of their betrayal, the Soviets were able to decipher over a million encrypted messages and put in peril national security. The spy ring received thousands of dollars for their espionage activities. Walker was sentenced to life in prison. Inexplicably he was not publicly executed by firing squad.

Aldrich Hazen Ames, a CIA officer, was arrested and convicted for spying for the Soviets after working on and off for the agency since 1957, despite a serious drinking problem and other signs of mental instability, and this led to his selling of documents to the Soviets. His betrayal resulted in in the arrests and executions of CIA agents. [89] After living beyond his means, Ames was finally arrested and sentenced to life in prison in 1994. In 2001, Robert Philip Hanssen, an FBI agent since 1976, was arrested and given a life sentence for selling secrets to the Soviet Union and the Russian Federation for at least eleven years, which resulted in the arrest and execution of agents, informants, and spies working for the U.S. Despite warnings of possible wrongdoing as early as 1991, Hanssen was able to continue spying for another ten years. His betrayal resulted in what has been called the worst intelligence disaster in American history, according to a report issued in March 2002.[90]

Ana Belén Montes, a senior DIA analyst was arrested in 2001 for spying for Communist Cuba after working as a mole at the DIA for Cuban intelligence since1985. At the time of her arrest, Montes was the senior intelligence analyst focusing on Cuba. As in the previous cases, stolen documents passed to Cuba exposed several agents, resulting in their arrest and at least one death of an American Special Operations soldier assigned to Central America. She was sentenced to 25 years in prison to be followed by another five years of probation.

On 25 April 2013, the Justice Department unsealed an indictment Charging Marta Rita Velázquez, a US citizen born in Puerto Rico, with conspiracy to commit espionage, and as the principal recruiter working for Cuban Intelligence (CuIS), who recruited Montes to spy against the U.S.[91] Prior to joining the Defense Intelligence Agency (DIA), where Montes served in the capacity of Desk Officer for Cuba, she had worked at the Department of Justice. After operating as a Cuban spy for many years, she was arrested on 21 September 2001 and charged with Conspiracy to Commit Espionage, and sentenced to 25 years in prison. During the investigation to assess damage caused by Montes, it was revealed that she probably provided the DGI the names of at least four American agents, as well as the location of a special training site in El Salvador, which was attacked by Communist insurgents in 1987.[92] During the attack, at least one American Special Forces soldier was killed by FMLN Communist guerrillas.[93]

As these and many other cases of betrayal and espionage illustrate, national security is always exposed to foreign actors who, for one reason or another, want to penetrate and capture American codes, sensitive technology, and secret documents associated with national defense. Nobody can be trusted, including countries that claim to be "loyal friends," as for example, Israel, which has carried out espionage numerous times to obtain American secrets. Counterintelligence operations are more than justified by numerous historical precedents. In 1997, Jonathan Jay Pollard, a civilian intelligence analyst at the Naval Investigative

Service (NIS), was arrested and given a life sentence for spying for Israel. According to published information, classified information stolen by Pollard and provided to Israel was later traded with the Soviet Union in exchange for increased emigration permits for Jews.[94] As a result of the release of classified information, intelligence agents inside the Soviet Union were compromised. Pollard had been a heavy drug user, and may have shown signs of mental health issues, but despite coming on the radar screen as unstable and unreliable for employment in intelligence, he was not terminated before he could cause damage.

Titanic disaster on 9/11/2011

A commission was established on 27 November 2002 to study the events leading up to the terrorist attacks of 9/11/2001, and a final report was issued on 22 July 2004. Over 1,200 people were interviewed and over 2.5 million government documents were reviewed. The Commission came to the conclusion that the President was not served well by the intelligence community (IC), specifically by the FBI and the CIA. The Commission concluded that the events of 9/11 should not have come as a surprise, since Islamic extremists had given plenty of warning about their intentions to kill Americans indiscriminately and in large numbers, and for months in 2001, the IC had picked up many indicators that something very big was going to take place.

As CIA Director George Tenet put it, "*the system was blinking red.*" Terrorists that had previously been linked by the IC to plans to hijack commercial airplanes were found to have entered the country. The terrorists had numerous vulnerabilities as they moved to carry out their plans, but these were not exploited. "*Across the government, there were failures of imagination, policy, capabilities, and management.*" The most serious weaknesses were found to be in the domestic arena, in part because the FBI "*did not have the capability to link the collective knowledge of agents in the field to national priorities.*" Information collected across the IC was not pooled and shared. The CIA and the FBI did not work jointly to deal with what they perceived as an imminent threat.[95]

With all respect to the Commission members, I have my own views about contributing factors to what happened. After the Watergate scandal in the 1970s, left-wing politicians, particularly Senator Frank F. Church III (1924-1984), went all out to expose and end domestic intelligence and law enforcement programs that had existed for many years, including the FBI's COINTELPRO. Senator Church had made a name for himself opposing the Vietnam War, and by conducting hearings on extra-legal FBI and CIA covert intelligence operations. Congress enacted legislation to reform domestic surveillance of groups that called for the destruction of the country. The 1978 Foreign Intelligence Surveillance Act (FISA)[96] outlawed many intelligence collection practices and made it very difficult for law enforcement and intelligence organizations to investigate, track, and counteract anti-establishment groups regardless of politics or motives.

Excesses of the past, poor coordination of intelligence collection and analysis, coupled with inter-agency friction, resulted in numerous new restrictions on what could and could not be done for the sake of national security. Back in 1978 a Titanic disaster like the one that occurred on 9/11 was not predictable because something like it had never happened before. A mythology of "*American invincibility*" had been erroneously created and promoted as factual.

That same year – in 1978 - the Soviet Union orchestrated a *coup d'état* in Afghanistan that put Communists in power, created the Democratic Republic of Afghanistan (DRA), and started an authoritarian campaign to "modernize" the country by combating ancient Islamic traditions. Men were ordered to shave their beards, women were ordered to stop wearing burqas, mosques were shut down, and anybody who resisted change was either executed or forced to run to the hills.

In February 1979, the American Ambassador to Afghanistan, Adolph Dubs, was kidnapped and killed as Russian and Afghan security forces botched a rescue attempt. The American Embassy in Kabul was reduced to a handful of diplomats from 1979. The pro-Soviet local Communists had their own internal problems, as they fought each other for power. The first President of the DRA only lasted a few months, until his own Prime Minister ordered his assassination to assume the office of President himself. About three months later, he was also assassinated by Russian KGB agents to replace him with another *marionette* more easily controlled.[97] After a year of internal convulsion, the assistance provided to local Communists by Soviet advisors was not sufficient to contain the growing opposition, and Soviet troops invaded Afghanistan in December 1979.

Next door in Iran, another revolution was brewing, as fundamentalist Shia clergy led mass demonstrations starting in September 1978 against the Shah. In January 1979, the Shah went into exile and fundamentalist Ayatollah Ruhollah Khomeini returned from exile, leading to the creation of the Islamic Republic of Iran in April. In November 1979, Islamic militants attacked the American Embassy and took hostage mission employees, demanding that the Shah be returned for trial. By not supporting and encouraging the Shah to use extreme force to wipe out the Islamic extremists, the Carter Administration made a horrible mistake, and the world is suffering for it.

Unleashing the Islamic Behemoth

In July 1979, President Jimmy Carter signed a Presidential Decision Directive (PDD) instructing the CIA to assist the opposition to the Soviets in Afghanistan.[98] The CIA program was denominated Operation Cyclone, and was managed by the Special Activities Division. By 1982, Islamic insurgents controlled about 75 percent of Afghanistan. Another national security directive (NSDD-166) in 1986 instructed the CIA to enter Afghanistan to establish a secret relationship with Afghan *mujahedeen* and provide them with advanced weapons systems to counter Soviet air superiority and armored units. The insurgents were receiving assistance from Pakistan, the UK, Saudi Arabia, Egypt, the US, and even from Communist China (PRC)! Assistance to the insurgents was stepped up after Congressman Charlie Wilson (D-Texas) took a particular interest on the subject and was instrumental in providing Stinger antiaircraft missiles to the insurgents to counter Soviet control of the air. In mid-1987 the Soviets announced their intention to withdraw. After the Soviets left Afghanistan, conditions were deemed to be too dangerous to maintain even a token presence and the American embassy was closed on 30 January 1989. For many years the U.S. did not have eyes and ears in the country, and could not rotate intelligence officers through the embassy to build a cadre officers with knowledge of Afghanistan.

The *mujahedeen* turned into a destructive and out-of-control monster after the Russian troops withdrew in 1989.[99] The government the Soviets left in Kabul supported by a Soviet trained and equipped Afghan military could not control the Islamic insurgency and the country drifted into civil war between 1992 and 1996, when one of the *mujahedeen* factions morphed into the Taliban (meaning religious students). The Taliban, with support from Pakistani intelligence operatives took Kabul and slowly expanded their control to most of the country. The Taliban reversed the Communist efforts to destroy Islam, and retaliated with their own brutal Islamic fundamentalist and intolerant interpretation of Islam. Beards and burkas were back, and anything considered not Islamic was banned.[100] The Islamic insurgency in Afghanistan turned into disease that spread outside the borders of the country and eventually produced the events of 9/11/2001.

America watched as events unfolded throughout the 1990s. Little to nothing was done as Afghanistan drifted into the hands of Islamic extremists, leading up to becoming a sanctuary for al-Qai'da from where the events of 9/11/2001 were put together. The U.S. backed away from neighboring Pakistan during the 1990s, in response to the development of nuclear weapons in competition with India. When the J2 at Joint Staff warned about the growing dangers in Afghanistan, the answer from OSD was that the U.S. did not have any national interests in Afghanistan. During a visit to Afghanistan and Pakistan in January of 2010, Secretary of Defense Robert M. Gates opined that the U.S. had made a *"grave strategic mistake"* by *"largely abandoning Afghanistan"* after the Soviet departure and severing defense ties with Pakistan in the 1990s.[101] The affinity of thoughts attracted the Taliban and a group of former allies in the fight against the Soviets who coalesced around Osama bin Laden to form al-Qai'da. They added the U.S. and other non-Islamic western countries to their list of enemies, and as covered in the previous chapter, they declared war with terrorism as their weapon of choice. American policymakers generally ignored what was going on in that part of the world.

In 1995 Congress chartered a bipartisan Commission to report on the *Roles and Capabilities of the U. S. Intelligence Community* and review its' efficacy and appropriateness. The report was issued on 1 March 1996 under the title 21st Century: *An Appraisal of U.S. Intelligence.*[102] The Commission found that the core missions had remained relatively constant despite a substantial shift in intelligence requirements and priorities since the end of the Cold War in 1991. The report described the *raison d'être* of the IC as providing "accurate and meaningful information and insights to consumers in a form they can use at the time they need them."[103] It pointed out that some consumers of intelligence "*take a jaundiced view of the analytical support they receive. The President and senior cabinet officials appear to be relatively well served, but many decision makers at lower levels find that the intelligence analysis comes up short… and what they receive fails to meet their needs by being too late or too unfocused, or by adding little to what they already know.*" These comments fit well with the multiple failures and lost opportunities to stop the hijackers before they carried out their plans on 9/11/2001. Intelligence efforts were unfocused, uncoordinated, and slow.

The successful attacks of 9/11/2001 cannot be blamed on entirely on the failure to implement recommendations made by the bipartisan Commission on the *Roles and Capabilities of the U. S. Intelligence Community*, or the failure to pay due attention to the monster growing in South West Asia and the Middle East. Lowering the guard created a situation in which it was difficult to protect the nation from enemies representing the entire spectrum of politics and extremist sects. Terrorist and anti-establishment elements come in all colors, persuasions, and ideologies.

Potential peer-to-peer conflicts

When the Soviet Union collapsed in 1991 and several former Soviet republics obtained their independence, Ukraine had a vast arsenals which included about 1,800 nuclear weapons and missile delivery systems. In 1994, the so-called *Memorandum of Budapest* was signed by Ukraine, Russia, the UK, and the U.S., by which the Ukrainians agreed to destroy or give up their nuclear arsenal in an attempt to eliminate the possibility that they may fall into the wrong hands and the potential for proliferation of weapons of mass destruction (WMD). The signatories of the memorandum agreed to respect the *territorial integrity* of the country in exchange for giving up the nukes. Nevertheless, in March 2014 Russia invaded Ukrainian territory and annexed the Crimea. Thousands of Russian troops were sent to the Eastern border of Ukraine, and ethnic Russians on the eastern part of the country with Russian support began to seize government buildings and threatened to secede and join Russia. The promises outlined in the *Memorandum of Budapest* were ignored. The implications for the future were extremely significant. Could other countries really trust the U.S. and other world powers? Should other countries, including India, Iran, Israel, Japan, North Korea, Pakistan, and Saudi Arabia build and maintain their own arsenal of nuclear weapons as a deterrent to foreign invasion? Any future American *hypothesis of conflict* will have to include the potential for escalation of situations like the one that surfaced in Ukraine to an old-fashioned peer-to-peer conflict and a world affected by the proliferation of nuclear and other WMD stockpiles.

The PRC is challenging its neighbors over disputed waters and small islands. In January 2013, a Chinese frigate entered disputed waters with Japan around the Senkaku Islands. A Japanese destroyer confronted the Chinese frigate and both turned on their weapon systems. The PRC is involved in a dispute with Vietnam over contested waters around the Paracel Islands. In May 2014 a Chinese ship rammed and sank a Vietnamese fishing boat near a Chinese oil rig. The incident triggered violent anti-Chinese riots in Vietnam. There have been previous border disputes which resulted in considerable fighting in 1974, 1979, and 1988, which produced thousands of casualties on both sides. Similar disputes exist between the PRC and the Philippines around Hainan and the Spratly Islands, which both countries claim as part of its 200-mile exclusive economic zone. The U.S. has warned the PRC about the territorial claims. The U.S. has repeatedly reassured allies of its commitment to contain Chinese hegemonic desires and naval reach over the region.[104] In the age of asymmetric warfare the U.S. has to continue preparing for the possibility of peer-to-peer conflicts.

So what?

National security is a very complex proposition, which involves defending the country from domestic and foreign enemies. There are *no permanent friends or permanent enemies*, and even our best friends have to be watched. Far right and far left extremists, as well as people who are mentally challenged, surface periodically and endanger civil society and national security. These challenges make it difficult to achieve consensus on a definition of what national security is all about. There are numerous nefarious actors constantly at work seeking vulnerabilities to gain access to American secrets. They identify their targets' obsessions, *peccadillos*, passions, preoccupations, weaknesses, sexual preferences, and manias, to exploit them. Next, they provided temptations, inducements, and turn-ons, to lure them, and use every form of demonic oppression, coercion, and cruelty to keep them under control. The forces of darkness are always at work, and never rest in their efforts to breach our security walls. The news media acts as the *Ministry of Propaganda* for Satan, so the masses don't know what they don't know about the daily battle with diabolical people, systems, and institutions that are devoid of respect for anybody.

On 3 February 2015, Lt. Gen. Vincent R. Stewart (U.S. Marine Corps), Director of the Defense Intelligence Agency (DIA) delivered the annual *Worldwide Threat Assessment* to the House Armed Services Committee. In a summary paragraph he stated:

> *Our challenges range from highly capable, near-peer competitors to empowered individuals, and the concomitant reduction in our own capacity will make those challenges all the more stressing on our defense and intelligence establishments. This strategic environment will be with us for some time, and the threat's increasing scope, volatility, and complexity will be the "new normal."*

These annual comprehensive reports are the result of extensive work of intelligence officers and reviewed by policymakers to summarize the perceived threat level. However, when then DIA Director Admiral Thomas R. Wilson in March 2001 presented a similar report to the Armed Services Committee, he did not mention once the threats presented by Islamic extremist activity in Afghanistan. Five months later we had the 9/11/2001 attacks on the homeland! So much for accuracy…[105] In the 2015 report, General Stewart only used the term "*Islamic*" six times, and only in association with the names of Islamic extremist organizations.[106] "*Muslims,*" "*Islamist,*" "*Muslim extremists*" are not mentioned once! In other words, policy guidance apparently prevented mentioning "Islamic extremists" or any link to the Muslim or Islamic community at large worldwide. We are engaging in the denial of the obvious. Weakened threat analysis due to *political correctness* is very dangerous.

III – THE MIDDLE EAST MINEFIELD

Genesis

It is impossible to understand the Middle East without a historical perspective of the complex relationship between the US and Israel. The U.S. was among the first countries to recognize Israel, but did not take a primary role in supporting the new state. France was the prime source of Israeli weapons from 1947 until the mid-1960s, and the British were a close second, with West Germany in third place. Things began to change after a military *coup d'état* that overthrew Egypt's King Farouk I in 1952. One of the co-conspirators in the *coup d'état*, Gamal Abdel Nasser, led the creation a new supranational Arab nationalist agenda with a secular Socialist overtone. There was not even a hint of Islamic inspiration in Nasser's ideology, which resonated well in Moscow. Nasser was a closet Communist with a blend of nationalism, ideologies that are incompatible, as Communism aims at breaking down nation-states as part of the road to establishing a secular one-world government.[107]

Nasser encouraged insurgents to stage terrorist attacks against Israel from Sinai, and Israel crossed the border in hot pursuit of the attackers. In 1956, Nasser nationalized the Suez Canal creating a community of interests between the UK, France and Israel against Egypt. After numerous provocations, Israel invaded Egypt and French and British troops arrived to support the Israelis and to recapture the Suez Canal, which was of vital economic and strategic interest for them. The Soviets threatened to intervene in support of Egypt. President Eisenhower intervened and forced the French, British and Israeli forces to back off. As a result, the U.S. "bought the problem," and was forced to pick up the support of Israel from the Europeans, while the Soviets established a long-lasting link to the Arabs. Although the numerous conflicts in the Middle East have roots that go back at least 5,000 years, the more recent struggle for supremacy and survival can be traced to the 1956 intervention of the Soviet Union and the United States in the region as part of the *Cold War*.

UN peacekeeping troops were sent to Sinai as a buffer between Israel and Palestinian insurgents groups, and to ensure free navigation for all countries through the canal, except Israel. The entire region then became involved in the *Cold War*, with some Arab neighbors of Israel becoming surrogates for the Soviets, and others becoming US client states, but Israel became the leading U.S. client state. The 1956 incident was the last British attempt to act as if they were still an empire. Nasser became the transnational leader that the Arabs had desperately been seeking. The French were so angered by the U.S. action that they pulled out of full participation in NATO, and eventually lost Algeria, as the Soviets and Egypt increased support to North African nationalists seeking to shed European colonial control.

You break it and it is yours

The old saying, "*you break it, smash it, or crack it, and it is yours,*" worked like a charm. If the French and the British had not been undermined by Eisenhower and U.S. Foreign Policy, they would have continued what they had been doing supporting Israel. The U.S. would not have become practically the sole military supporter of Israel, and perhaps many of the problems that came about afterwards could have been avoided. The Soviets were in no position in 1956 to risk a major war to support Egypt.[108] In 1967, Nasser kicked out the UN peacekeepers from Sinai and the Suez Canal and placed additional restrictions on Israeli shipping, leading to the Six Day War and the Israeli capture of the Sinai and the closure of the canal until 1975. In 1973 Egypt tried to retake the Sinai and the canal, triggering the Yom Kippur War, which Israel survived through massive American replenishment of military equipment. As in 1967, Israel fought successfully a two-front war against Syria and Egypt and their allies.

Who is responsible for injecting the U.S. into the conflict in the Middle East? Was it Secretary of State John Foster Dulles (1953-1959), or President Eisenhower? While Secretary Dulles supported an aggressive stance against Communist advances in Guatemala, Iran, Viet Nam, and elsewhere, he caved in when the Russians threatened to intervene in the conflict between Israel, France, and the UK against Egypt and their Arab and Communist allies. His lack of "brinkmanship" in this conflict allowed the Soviets to exercise considerable influence over the Arab world until 1991.[109] It also married the U.S. to Israel in a way that places unwritten restrictions on the way American Foreign Policy deals with the complicated issues of the Middle East, and gets on the way of truly assisting Israel to achieve peace. It painted a bull's eye on the U.S. for an assortment of Islamic extremist organizations, leading up to the events of 9/11/2001 and the costly interventions in Afghanistan and Iraq.

Ally, collaborator, or accomplice

An ally is a partner, an associate, a friend, a bedfellow, but also a "*collaborator*" or an "accomplice." Just because we have our own definition of ally, it does not mean that others do not focus on "*collaborator*" or "*accomplice*" with completely different connotations, including "*partner in crime.*" Islam has been an enemy of Israel and Jews for 1,300 years, and extremist Muslims regard the U.S. not as an ally, but as an Israeli *partner in crime*. But the problem between Israel and its' neighbors is ancient, going back to Biblical times. Long before Muhammad was born in 570 AD, Jews were fighting over territory with immediate neighbors in Canaan/Israel/Palestine. The territory was overrun by invaders from Assyria, Babylonia, Greece, Persia, Rome, Muslims from the Arabian Peninsula, crusaders from Western Europe, Turkey, and the British Empire. Conflict is endemic to the area, and there are as many versions of right and wrong as history books on the subject, including the Bible.

After WWII, Jews from all over the world migrated to Israel and demanded independence from British rule.[110] The UN proposed the establishment of two states – one Jewish and one Arab. The Jews accepted the proposal and created the independent state of Israel in 1948, but the Arabs turned down the UN proposal. Five Arab armies invaded Israel, but the Jews heroically defended their land and defeated the invaders. Thousands of Palestinian Arabs fled the area into camps in Jordan, Lebanon, Syria, and other Arab countries, always with the hope of returning. Others sold their lands to Israelis and left.

Arab and Palestinian views are radically different from the views of supporters of Israel. Palestinians are representative of various ethnicities and are comprised of both Muslims, and a variety of Christian denominations. Christians side with both Israel and the Palestinians, depending on multiple circumstances and how history treated their own families since 1947. Note that many Palestinian militants, although born to Muslim families, are not practicing Muslims and joined Socialist and Communist inspired organizations. Islamic extremism did not really come about until after the collapse of the Soviet Union in 1991. Before the 1990s, Palestinian extremists had close links to the Soviets, who used them as pawns in the Cold War.

Supporters of the so-called Palestinian cause, claim that in 1947, as Israel became an independent Jewish state, about 85 percent of Palestinians were expelled through fear and atrocities by the Jews from over 700 villages and towns where their ancestors had lived since time immemorial. They do not mention selling their property to Jews, even though some decided to take money offers and run somewhere else. They estimate that some 900,000 Palestinian refugees were forced out into Lebanon, Jordan, Syria, and other Arab countries, and that since 1947, the size of their displaced population has increased to over 4.5 million people, spread over many areas, but with a large presence in Lebanon, Jordan, and Syria.[111] There is no historical record that a Palestinian State ever existed, its borders, its capital, what kind of government it had.

There have been numerous initiatives, to find a permanent solution to the Palestinian-Israeli conflict. Some progress has been made, particularly in the relationship with Egypt and Jordan. However, another source of conflict surfaced after the Iranian Islamic revolution in 1979. Iran started funding and training a new generation of fighters clustered around Hezbollah in Lebanon, as well as making periodic threats to destroy Israel. Thus, the conflict remains in a stalemate, and despite developments that seem to signal some progress, something happens to delay or undermine a permanent solution.

There are only permanent interests

Israeli spies are in American jails for stealing military secrets. Jonathan Pollard was not a unique case.[112] One of the biggest scandals in Washington in the recent past involved Republican lobbyist Jack Abramoff, who was sentenced to five years and ten months in jail in 2006, for tax evasion, fraud, and conspiracy to bribe public officials, leading to the resignation of Members of Congress, and the conviction and sentencing of Congressman Robert Ney to thirty months in prison. Abramoff was a Zionist activist and contributor to extremist groups. Money sent by Abramoff to extremists in Israel was used to purchase camouflage uniforms, night-vision devices, sniper scopes and other items for paramilitary groups who operate outside the law and target Palestinian Arabs to exacerbate the Arab/Israeli conflict. At about the same time that Abramoff was incarcerated, officials of the American Israel Public Affairs Committee (AIPAC) were caught passing secret US Government documents to Israel.

Israelis live surrounded by enemies and cannot depend on promises to protect the integrity of their country. They see how promises made to others, as for example, Ukraine, are not worth the paper they are written on. Why should they trust similar promises? Despite American assurances, the credibility of the US as a partner is increasingly questioned. As the U.S. is perceived as flip-flopping and navigating without direction, even close allies like Israel lose faith on promises of everlasting support and friendship.

Confronting "JIHAD" (داهج)

The terrorist attacks of 9/11/2001 triggered numerous cultural, ideological, legal, philosophical, and political discussions among policymakers with different ideas about what would be an appropriate response. Different options were considered without really understanding what *Jihad* was all about. Fundamental constitutional principles and American ethical values were challenged. The response had to fit within American and international laws and conventions. In addition to basic constitutional constraints, the *War Powers Resolution* of 1973 limited the ability of the Executive Branch to intervene in other countries or employ military power overseas without first consulting and obtaining approval from Congress. The time had come for a review of long-held concepts regarding the role of the U.S. in world affairs. Whatever was done had to withstand the test of domestic and international public opinion.

Despite all the efforts to find an appropriate response, some decisions were made in haste. Part of the problem is that most people know very little about Islam and the difference between law enforcement efforts and carrying out a counterinsurgency operation (COIN). More than anything else, the war against Jihadists is a war of ideas.

Birth of Islam

The Islamic faith started in the 7th century, on or about 622 AD, under the spiritual guide of the Prophet Muhammad (1570-1632), in the Arabian Peninsula. After Muhammad death, his message began to be corrupted and subjected to internal disputes among his followers, even though the core belief in one eternal and absolute God (Allah) continued to be the cornerstone of Islam. The *Quran* (*Koran*), divided into 114 chapters (surah), gathered the *revelations* that Muhammad claimed to have received from God. Islamic law, as outlined in the *Quran*, covers not only issues of faith, but also rules for governance of the state, personal hygiene, dietary laws, family life, and defines crime and punishment. Church and state and the courts are indistinguishable as separate units of a whole.

Prophets claim to provide humanity with a message, or *revelations*, from God. The religious faiths that share a common origin with Abraham have a history of claiming to receive such communications through prophets, starting with the Jewish Faith, to be followed by Christianity and Islam. The *Book of Genesis*, which is the first book of the *Hebrew Bible (Old Testament)*, is where the story of Abraham is first related. Abraham is presented as the person appointed by God to lead his family from Haran, probably Harran, an Assyrian town located in present day Turkey (possibly Iraq), to the land of Canaan, present day Palestine. Abraham is considered the father of Israelites, and is also considered a prophet by Muslims, who also see Jesus Christ as a prophet of Islam. Muslims generally accept all the prophets of the *Bible*, but believe Mohammad to be *the last prophet*.

Jihad was introduced as *the way that God guides a Muslim to achieve personal perfection*, based on the rules outlined in the *Quran*, as well as the collective duty to expand the faith. Since its' inception, jihad has been interpreted as *a duty to expand Islam* over a vast geography through military conquest and by proselytizing non-believers. It was conceived as a "holy war," that fundamentalists have revived to declare war on Western culture and on anything that they perceived as a deviation from Islam. They target other Muslims that disagree with their radical views just as they target infidels (non-believers). Their goal is to establish a world-wide caliphate under a supreme leader to guide Muslims through *the path of faith.*[113]

Islamic Insurgency

What are we fighting and who is the enemy? Convoluted linguistic semantics – *the study of meanings* - are extremely dangerous, because the wrong terminology can disrupt the logic, the circumstances, and the understanding of the challenges presented by Jihad. Is jihad an amorphous global insurgency, or an extremist ideology that happens to use terrorism as a tool to achieve its' goals? One of the consequences of using the wrong terminology is that we chased our tails for a long time because policymakers refused to accept that Jihad is an *insurgency*, ergo *we are fighting an insurgency*, not the tools and the strategy used by the insurgents. Terrorism is a byproduct of insurgency. Terrorism is not an ideology; ergo a "*war on terrorism*" (GWOT) is a serious misnomer.

Is Islam the problem?

The extensive geography of the Islamic world, composed principally by 57 countries with Muslim-majority populations is affected by poor governance, widespread illiteracy, poverty, and general backwardness. This situation contributes to the raise of extremists seeking solutions to the many challenges affecting their lives in religion, mixed with extreme hatred directed at the people and institutions who they believe are responsible for their problems. The foundation of Islam, as outlined in the *Quran*, contains enough ambiguity to provide extremists justification for dishonoring the very sanctity of life.[114] Misinterpretations abound and extremists use them to justify their own ideas, which generally reject anything but the most backward views espoused by extremists who reject anything that looks like a pluralistic society.

In analyzing the current situation it is possible to fall into the trap of "*presentism*," or introducing contemporaneous ideas and perspectives as if they had always been existent in the past. Between the 8th and the 13th centuries there were important Muslim cultural centers, such as Cordoba, Baghdad, Damascus, and Alexandria, which contributing to preserving ancient Greek culture and other key aspects of Western civilization. The *Quran* encouraged Muslims to acquire knowledge. Madrassas provided free education for young people, including women. Somehow what is stated in Surah 20 – Ta-Ha (MAJJA): Verse 114: *"My Lord! Increase me in knowledge,"* was affected, possibly as Islam rejected modernity.[115] Islam contributed to advancement in mathematics, engineering, science, medicine, astronomy, law, and philosophy, despite its' roots in tribal, nomadic, and illiterate Arab culture.

Islamic extremist thought, which feeds 21st Century jihad, stem from three sources: *Deoband*, the *Muslim Brotherhood,* and the Iranian Revolution of 1979. The process on incubation has taken over 200 years. Some scholars trace today's Islamic militancy to *"Deoband*," a town in Uttar Pradesh in India, where Hadhrat Moulana Muhammed Qasim Nanautavi established a *madrassa* or religious school in the 1860s, where he preached a very orthodox form of Islam. The preachers *taught against rationalism, secularism and anything associated with Western culture.*[116] The *madrassa* became the center of anti-British colonialism. Within a few years, the school had produced several hundred graduates who went on to form other religious schools across India and Pakistan. The movement that was ideologically shaped by Deoband eventually helped to inspire the Taliban regime of Afghanistan after the Soviets retreated in 1989, and became closely associated with al-Qai'da, which has its' roots in the war against the Soviet occupiers during the 1980s. Pakistani support for Jihad can be traced to Deoband, and more recently, relationships built during the 1980s associated with the war to push Soviet forces out of the neighborhood.

The second source of extremist Islamic thought has its' roots with Muhammad Ibn Abd al-Wahhab, who in 1744 together with Muhammad Ibn Saud started a strict brand of orthodox Islamic thought in Saudi Arabia, known as the *"Wahhabi"* movement. They declared war against Shiites, Sufis and any other Muslim that did not accept their interpretation of the *Sunna* or *practices of the Prophet Muhammad.* They rejected practically all reforms and practices that had developed over the previous 1,000 years. Among other things, they created a religious police in Saudi Arabia called *mutawi'oon* to enforce their interpretation of Islamic law, and help to maintain the Saudi royal family in power by acting as a political police and persecuting any deviations from Wahhabi standards. Since its' inception, Wahhabism has tried to establish its' predominance *by force*, declaring a Jihad against other Muslims that do not accept their interpretation of Islam.

When the Wahhabi version of Islam developed, Ottoman Turks ruled a large empire that controlled the Middle East.[117] The Wahhabis rebelled against Ottoman rule, while fighting to impose their interpretation of Islam throughout the region. They penetrated Iraq and fought against Shiites, capturing their Holy City of Karbala where they destroyed the tomb of their venerated Imam Husayn in 1801.[118] The following year, they attacked and captured the Holy City of Mecca. The Turks managed to defeat the Wahhabis and regain lost territory, but they were unable to completely subdue their interpretation of Islam. In 1901 the Wahhabis supported a successful rebellion led by Amir Abd al-Aziz al-Saud in Saudi Arabia, establishing a dynasty that started in 1924, right after Turkey lost its' empire at the end of World War I. France and the UK moved in to take pieces of the territory vacated by Turkey. Once in power, the Wahhabis continued their Jihad to impose their rule *by force* and destroy any vestiges of other interpretations of Islam, including the destruction of religious sites and the tombs of venerated Islamic saints by the other Islamic sects. Once they had secured control over Saudi Arabia, they started to send missionaries to proselytize in other parts of the world.

In the 1960s, the Saudi Arabian Wahhabis set up the *Muslim World League* and stepped up their efforts to convert other Muslims to Wahhabism. They built Islamic schools, clinics and mosques throughout the Muslim world, with the financial support of the Saudi Royal House of Saud. Money derived from oil and gas exports fueled the expansion of Wahhabism into Egypt, Indonesia, North and East Africa, Pakistan and as far away as Central Asia. Wahhabism is the basic spiritual philosophy behind the holy war or Jihad, supported by al-Qai'da throughout the world, with the goal of establishing a Pan Islamic state or *caliphate*. They reject any innovation or any deviation from Islamic Law as they believe it was practiced under Prophet Mohammad. They command all Muslims to wage war, supported by numerous calls in the *Quran* and the *Sunna*, as an expression of their devotion for God. The supporters of al-Qai'da have become revolutionaries who threaten all established governments in Muslim countries, including the Saudi regime under the Saud Dynasty, which they do not consider true believers and in bed with the West in general and the U.S. in particular.

The *Muslim Brotherhood* is another extremist school of thought founded in Egypt around 1928, later sprouting to Syria, Jordan and other Muslim countries. Their motto is: *Allah is our God. The Prophet is our leader. The Qur'an is our law. Holy war is our way. To die for Allah is our highest expectation.* Like the Deoband, this organization had roots in anti-British colonialism. After WWII, the British and the French secret services may have used the old pro-Nazi sympathizers of the Muslim Brotherhood to fight against the creation of Israel in 1948. Over the years the movement has grown to include several million people, mostly in Egypt, despite being declared illegal and the members subjected to political persecution, arrest and assassination. After the so-called Egyptian Revolution of 2011-2012, the Muslim Brotherhood was able to take power through democratic elections. On 30 June 2012, Mohamed Morsi Isa El-Ayyat, a prominent leader of the Muslim Brotherhood, became President of Egypt, but was later overthrown by a military *coup d'état,* and condemned to death in 2015 by a military court. Although the organization is not as anti-modernity as the Deoband and the Wahhabis, their political activism has attracted youth who later graduated to more aggressive Islamic organizations.

Violence is not regarded as an aberration, but as an integral part of Islam, rooted in the *Quran* itself. Intolerance for different points of view has historically been endemic with all religions, all of which claim to represent the *ultimate truth*, and a justification for war and violence against people who hold other points of view. Each religion has its' own

Scriptures, subject to contradictory interpretations, and easily hijacked by people who claim to be the "correct" bearer of the message from God. While it is impossible to achieve consensus and pass judgment on Islam, clearly it is used as a justification for numerous heinous crimes, from slavery to violations of basic human rights, including blocking the emancipation of women.

Heinous crimes

> **So take not friends from the ranks of the unbelievers, seize them and kill them wherever ye find them.**
>
> **Surah 4 verse 89**

In October 2012, Islamic extremist linked to the Taliban in Pakistan shot a 14-year-old girl, Malala Youdafzai, because she advocates schooling for girls. Two other young girls were injured, one critically. Emotional rallies were held throughout Pakistan to condemn the heinous crime, and some Islamic religious leaders issued *fatwas* condemning the attack. Nevertheless, the perpetrators were unrepentant and supported their actions based on the Quran, Sharia law, and Islamic history. For them, it was perfectly justified to kill women and children, because the victim promoted what the Taliban perceive as preaching secularism.[119]

As Kamila Shamsie in an article in the British newspaper *The Guardian*, asked rhetorically: *What do you do in the face of an enemy with a pathological hatred of woman?* Secretary of State Hillary Rodham Clinton condemned the shooting and offered support for *"brave young women... who struggle against tradition and culture and even outright hostility, and sometimes violence"* to pursue their rights.[120] However, this shooting was part of a larger challenge to the civilized world involving such things as honor killings, sexual abuse, arranged marriages, and murder, which are engrained in Muslim culture and historical traditions.

The basic problem is that it is extremely difficult to separate actions ingrained in historical traditions and culture, from specific Islamic dogma or historical interpretations of Sharia law. Do only fanatics and extremists engaged in such practices, or is it a cultural problem in addition to a matter of misinterpreting Islamic dogma? Every one of the 57 Muslim majority countries has its' own answer to the question.

In February 2006 Islamic extremists opened fire and killed several students at the Kartilaya School, in Lashkar Gar. In January 2009, the Taliban maimed with acid several girls and female teachers while walking to the Meir Weis Mena School in Kandahar, Afghanistan. In August 2010, the Taliban carried out a poison attack at the Totia high school for girls in Kabul, requiring 46 girls and nine teachers to be treated at a hospital. Several of the students were unconscious for hours.[121] Again, in June 2012, another school in Kabul was attacked with toxic chemicals that were placed in the school's drinking water supply, affecting at least 125 students.[122] The pattern is very clear, regardless of protestations that these extremists do not represent true Islam. American policymakers believe what they want to believe and create their own mythology to support bizarre politics that ignore reality, and then feed it to the public as if people are stupid. (Many Americans are *ignorant*, but they are not necessarily *stupid.*)

Shia Muslims in Iran behave in a similar fashion as Sunni Muslim extremists in other countries. Under their interpretation of Sharia law they execute women and children using stoning and hanging. Adultery and homosexual acts are punishable by death. For example, in September 2011, three men were hanged in Ahvaz for engaging in homosexual acts.[123] Executed women include at least one ten-ten-year old girl and at least thirty two pregnant women. Virgins are raped previous to their execution so that they would not be allowed into heaven according to Shia extremist interpretation of the *Quran.*[124] Homosexual teenagers, some aged 16 or 17, are routinely lashed or otherwise tortured before they are executed by hanging.[125]

Not only do they carry out these practices in Muslim countries, but take them along when they emigrate to Western Europe and the U.S. For example, in February 2009, Muzzammil Hassan, a prominent Muslim in the Buffalo, NY, cut off his wife's head because she dared to file for divorce. In October 2002, Abdullah Yones admitted that he killed his 16-year-old daughter in London by slitting her throat for violations of "the honor code." These cases also take place in other European countries with large Muslim populations. In October 2007, a Belgian court sentenced Tarik Mahmood Sheikh, a Pakistani immigrant, to 25 years in prison, and his wife to 20 years for shooting their daughter for refusing an arranged marriage in a fit of rage. Other members of the family were given prison sentences for conspiring to carry out the killing.[126] The link to Islam is so obvious that one wonders how it can be ignored by policymakers fixated on selling concepts that do not add up.

On 6 July 2013, Islamic insurgents in Nigeria linked to al-Qai'da affiliate Boko Haram attached a government secondary boarding school, set it on fire, and shot at least 30 students and a teacher. Children were burned alive. This attack was part of a series of similar attacks on schools since 2010. Two days before the attack, Islamic insurgents killed a primary school headmaster and his family. On 16 April 2014 over 270 high school girls were kidnapped and in May Boko Haram leader Abubakar Shekau announced that they would be sold into slavery. Politicians can come up with numerous excuses and continue to blame "radical Islamists," but despite their dance around the issue, members of other religious faiths do not engage in these dastardly actions. In February 2015, 21 Christians from Egypt were beheaded in Libya by ISIS. A couple of days later the news media informed the world that at least 45 people had been burned alive in Iraq by ISIS. The perpetrators of these atrocities are violent Islamic fundamentalists who will not stop until they are wiped out. What creates these monsters? Failed and failing states, resentment and reaction to the image of immorality portrayed around the world about America, and a crisis of American moral leadership. One could debate about why these monsters exist, but regardless of why, they have to be wiped out. In Spanish we have an old saying… *Muerto el perro se acabó la rabia!*

ISLAMIC BARBARISM

IRAN:

In October 2013 a young Iranian girl was attack with acid by a young man. As a result of the attack, the girl lost her eyes and one ear. An Islamic court convicted the attacker and sentenced him to have his eyes gouged out and his ears chopped for pouring acid on the girl. Under Islamic law, the judicial system in Iran frequently orders convicts to have their limbs and/or eyes removed or cut off, and public executions are frequent.[127]

NIGERIA

On 6 March 2014, four homosexual men were condemned by a Nigerian Islamic court in Bauchi City to be whipped 15 times publicly plus a year in prison as punishment under the Same Sex Marriage Prohibition Act enacted in January 2014. Homosexuality is considered an evil imported from the West. They could also have been sentenced to death by stoning or lethal injection.[128]

SYRIA

On 29 April 2014, Jihadists (*Islamic State of Iraq and Syri*a) in Syria crucified several Christians at Raqqa Plaza in Malula. Pictures transmitted through YouTube showed a young man and an older man crucified and left in exhibition for people to see. In the predominantly Christian area of Abra, an industrial zone outside of Damascus the Jihadists killed men, women, and children. They chopped heads and then played soccer with them. A pregnant woman was killed and after disemboweling her used the umbilical cord to tie her to a tree.[129]

The current "cycle" of "JIHAD"

During times of universal deceit, telling the truth becomes a revolutionary act

George Orwell

Islamic military expansion has been stopped in the past through significant military defeats. From its' birth in the Arabian Peninsula, Islam invaded Palestine, Syria, Egypt, and North Africa, all the way to the Maghreb, and crossed into the Iberian Peninsula within 100 years. Starting in 718 AD, the people of the Iberian Peninsula fought a long war to defeat Muslim invaders from the Maghreb. The first important victory over the invaders took place in 722 AD, when Christians defeated the Muslims at the Battle of Covadonga, resulting in the consolidation of a Christian enclave in the north of the Iberian Peninsula, followed by about 800 years of intermittent warfare to recapture land and push the invaders back towards the Maghreb. Gaul (present day France) and the rest of Western Europe's fate confronting Islamic invaders was decided ten years later, in 732, at the Battle of Tours (also called Battle of Poitiers) in north-central France.

After having successfully invaded present day Spain, an Islamic army under the command of Abdul Rahman Al Ghafiqi, crossed the Pyrenees and invaded Gaul. They had jihadists from as far away as Yemen and Syria with them. After initial victories, which made them overconfident, they faced the forces of Charles Martel (c.688 – 741), grandfather of Charlemagne, a Frankish political and military leader. The Muslims tried again in 736 to invade Gaul, landing forces at Narbonne. They were again defeated by Charles Martel at Arles and at the River Berre, near Narbonne. After 26 years of conquest, the Battle of Poitiers and the defeats near Narbonne closed what could be the described as the first cycle of jihadist conquest by force into Christendom.

By the XIII century, four Christian kingdoms had come about in the Iberian Peninsula, Castilla, Aragon, Navarra, and Portugal, while the Muslims continued to hold to their own kingdom (Al Andalus) based in Granada, in the southern part of the Iberian Peninsula. With the unification of the Christian kingdoms of Aragon and Castilla, through the marriage of King Ferdinand and Queen Isabella, a new war was launched to liberate the Iberian Peninsula. By 1482, the "*Reconquista*" was underway, with the Christians taking Ronda, Malaga, and finally Granada itself in 1492, when Boabdil, the last Muslim king surrendered. While this final phase of the liberation of the Iberian Peninsula was underway, the Ottoman Turks were pushing the frontiers of Islam into Western Europe, including an attempt to capture Italy in 1480. The second cycle of Islamic expansion was underway, contemporaneous to their defeat in Spain.

The Ottoman Empire was founded in 1453 by Mehmed II, after the capture of Constantinople by Turkish Islamic forces. The Ottoman Empire reached the heights of its power under Suleiman the Magnificent (1494-1566). Under his direction, the Ottoman Turks attacked Central Europe, capturing Belgrade, Rhodes, part of Hungary, and were only stopped with their failure to take Vienna in 1529. Suleiman's armies captured most of the Middle East, and large territories along the Mediterranean, as far away as Algeria and Tunisia, after building several powerful naval fleets, which operated not only in the Mediterranean, but also in the Red Sea and the Persian Gulf.

On 7 October 1571, a combined naval fleet of a coalition of several Catholic countries, including the Republics of Venice and Genoa, the Pope's own naval forces, the kingdoms of Naples, Sicily and Sardinia, led by the Spanish Navy under the command of John of Austria, son of Holy Roman Emperor Charles V (Charles I of Spain), defeated the Ottoman Navy at the Battle of Lepanto. This significant defeat put an end to the Ottoman expansion into Christian lands, which could be described as the end of the second cycle of jihadist efforts to impose their will by force. It was truly a turning point in history.

One significant defeat of Muslim extremists in one battle may not be viable anymore, as the present conflict with jihadists is *a conflict of ideas and cultures*. Unlike the conventional peer-to-peer conventional wars of the past, the present conflict can best be described as *asymmetric* warfare. Military might is an integral component of the solution today as it was in the past. However, tactical COIN operations have to be balanced with other *measures to win the hearts and minds of the masses* and convince them not to help Islamic insurgents. *Jihad is a global insurgency* involving a large number of groups of different sizes, as well as *lone wolves* who act on their own.

The current cycle of Islamic extremist efforts to create a Pan Islamic state is different than the previous cycles. As Governor Romney stated, *we cannot kill our way out of the current mess* as in the previous experience with other cycles of Islamic expansion by force.[130] What is driving the current conflict is a combination of extremist religious convictions together with an increasing number of majority-Muslim failed and failing states, a proliferation of ungoverned spaces, and increasingly challenging economic problems that are further complicated by the destruction caused by civil unrest and war. Even after the killing of Osama bin Laden in May 2011, and the decapitation of al-Qai'da the organization has continued to replace the fallen with a new generation of leaders, and franchised the movement to sub-groups in Somalia, the Maghreb, the Arabian Peninsula, Nigeria, and other territories. In the case of Shi'a Islam, under the leadership of Iran since 1979, the conflict is just as complicated, as it entails a combination of the traditional peer-to-peer conflicts, as well as intervention in internal conflicts in Iraq, Syria, and Lebanon.

Islam is what it is

> **Be who you are and say what you feel because those who mind don't matter and those who matter don't mind**
>
> **Dr. Seuss**

Islam "*is what it is.*"[131] It makes no sense to try to disguise it. After centuries of authoritarian regimes, Islamic culture lacks freedom of thought and expression, tolerance for different points of view, or any form of pluralism. Any deviation from Islamic historical traditions is rejected. Modern points of view that represent a break with classical and traditional forms are rejected. Even after a wave of revolution, the so-called *Arab Spring* (الثورات العربيّة) that started on 18 December 2011 in Tunisia, and spread to Egypt, Libya, Bahrain, Syria, and other Arab countries, what has emerged is a chaotic environment and new forms of repression, not necessarily a catalyst for the introduction of liberal democratic principles. The masses are angry, and they have reason to be angry. About one-fifth of the world population is Muslim, for the most part living in 57 Muslim-majority countries, with the largest populations in Indonesia, Pakistan, Nigeria, Bangladesh, Egypt, Iran, Turkey, Algeria, Afghanistan and Morocco. There are huge differences in historical traditions and cultures, but generally authoritarian regimes and flawed democracies prevail.

There is an internal clash of civilizations between these Muslim countries, with their own concepts of "civilization," widely different cultural and religious traditions, and the non-Muslim world. Each has particular arbitrariness about Islamic religious dogma, different value systems and heritage. They generally share a high misery index, including widespread poverty, relatively young populations suffering from high unemployment, high illiteracy rates, and substantial educational challenges, widespread unhappiness and emotional distress. To forget their misery, they turn to toxic and passionate religion, and blame others for their anguish. Infidels, women, Christians, are convenient targets for butchery. The table that follows illustrates the challenges affecting a sample of Muslim-majority countries.

ECONOMIC AND POLITICAL CHALLENGES
Selected Islamic Countries

Country	Population (Millions) / Median Age	Poverty	Unemployment Youth age 15-24	Literacy Age 15 and over	Failed / Failed State Ranking
Afghanistan	30.4 17.9 years **Significant**	36%	35% **Significant**	28.1% **Significant**	6 **Significant**
Algeria	37.3 28.1 years	23% 2006est.	24% **Significant**	72%	
Bangladesh	161 23.6 years	31.51% 2010est.	5% 2011 est.	56.8%	29
Egypt	83.6 24.6 years	20.5% 2005est.	24.8% **Significant**	72%	31
Indonesia	248.6 28.5 years	12.5% 2011est.	22% 2011 est. **Significant**	90.4%	
Iran	78.8 27.4 years	18.7% 2007est.	23% est. 2011 **Significant**	77%	34
Iraq	31.1 21.1 years **Significant**	25% 2008est.	15% est. 2010 **Significant**	78.2%	9 **Significant**
Libya	5.6 24.8 years	NA	30% est. **Significant**	89.2%	50
Morocco	32.3 27.3 years	15% 2007 Est.	21.9% **Significant**	56.1%	
Pakistan	190.2 21.9 years **Significant**	22.3% 2006est.	5.6% est. 2011	54.9%	13 **Significant**
Syria	22.5 22.3 years **Significant**	11.9% 2006est.	19.1% est. **Significant**	79.6%	23 **Significant**
Tajikistan	7.7 22.9 years **Significant**	53% 2009est. **Significant**	2.2% 2009 Est.	99.7%	46
Tunisia	10.7 30.5 years	3.8% 2005est.	30.7% **Significant**	74.3%	
Turkey	79.7	16.9%	25% est. 2009 **Significant**	87.4%	

Sources: Foreign Policy Magazine & Fund for Peace, 2012 edition of Failed and Failing States; CIA Fact Books 2012; Index Mundi; Note that the situation in Syria as of October 2015 is significantly worse than what these numbers show. The same is true for Libya and Iraq.

So What?

> **Individual Muslims may show splendid qualities, but the influence of the religion paralyses the social development of those who follow it. No stronger retrograde force exists in the world.**
>
> **Winston Churchill (1899)**

Based on key demographics one can assess with high confidence that there will be conflict throughout the Muslim world for the foreseeable future. Populations are increasing, youth unemployment and poverty are high, education is poor, and there are a many failed and failing states among the 57 Muslim majority countries. While the creation of Israel was the primary source of conflict in the Middle East, the raise of fundamentalist Islam is a broader driver for instability. The conflict has expanded from a Middle East problem to a global insurgency that affects 57 Muslim majority countries, as well as countries targeted by Jihadists, from the PRC to the Russian Federation, to Western Europe and the United States of America. The wide diversity of regional conflicts indicates that it will take a long time before extremists can be defeated. The conflict can best be described as a *clash of civilizations* that will not be resolved simply through military force. And that is the primary reason why it is important for Americans to correct direction by addressing internal cultural challenges that have emerged since the 1960s, and the hypocrisy associated with comments about Islam.

IV – THE "LONG WAR"

The belief in the possibility of a short decisive war appears to be one of the most ancient and dangerous of human illusions.

Robert Wilson Lynd[132]
1879-1949

At some point in 2005 the hypothesis of a "long war" began to emerge, but without a clear definition other than some kind of "*epic struggle*" against Muslim extremists hell-bent on creating a supranational Islamic caliphate to replace Western dominance. There is no consensus about the term, because it was a realization that the U.S. was looking forward to many years of conflict. The implications were particularly serious in terms of cost and the strong possibility that the American electorate would not accept having to continue funding an *interminable war*. A parallel realization began to emerge that *the U.S. is not omnipotent*, and that the costs associated with a "*long war*" may be unsustainable. In other words, there are *consequences* that result from every decision regarding going to war. The calamitous consequence is that one has to *pay the piper*.

Left out of that realization of a protracted conflict ahead was an understanding of how Muslim fundamentalists – the *Jihadists* – are trying to delegitimize Western Culture in general and American Culture in particular through their peculiar interpretation of the Koran. We are engaged in a *war of ideas*, a *war of cultures*, and a *struggle for the hearts and minds of the masses*. It is a conflict with numerous surrogates and proxies that generate many asymmetric challenges. The main thrust behind this book is to point out that Americans have to get back on track, and fix deviations from the mainstream ideology of the Founding Fathers. Whoever holds *the moral high ground* will prevail in this conflict.

Afghanistan War

On 26 September 2001, Special Forces led by the CIA went into Afghanistan with the clear purpose of overthrowing the Taliban regime, and capturing or killing al-Qai'da leaders responsible for the terrorist attack of 9/11/2001. Within eight weeks, the Taliban were on the run with their al-Qai'da allies. This successful initial operation with limited but challenging objectives was followed by an ill-defined presence in Afghanistan, other than to continue pursuing the Taliban, al-Qai'da, and other bad actors. There was no memory of what normalcy looked like in Afghanistan before the 1979 Soviet invasion, and the international community did not clearly define how the "*end state*" they were seeking to build in Afghanistan would look like. As Yogi Berra once put it in one of his memorable quotes, *"if you don't know where you are going, you might wind up someplace else."* That is what has happened in Afghanistan since 2001. As the US starts to withdraw, we are still unaware of where we are going, and could easily wind up with a much larger problem. The war in Afghanistan in 2015, is already the longest war ever fought by the United States.

GWOT vs. COIN

When American troops deployed to Afghanistan they had to deal with some convoluted concepts about their mission, which was initially defined as part of the *Global War on Terrorism* (GWOT). As the Taliban regrouped, an insurgency began to form. Military operations shifted to something closer to a classical counterinsurgency operation (COIN). However, until the arrival of Lt. Gen. David Barno in November 2003, the office of the Secretary of Defense (OSD) had for all practical purposes refused to accept that an insurgency was underway in Afghanistan, and military officers had not been allowed to refer to military operations as a COIN. It did not take long for General Barno to figure out that as the new Commander in Afghanistan he was facing an insurgency not GWOT, however defined.

To complicate matters, few officers, including "bird colonels," had experience in COIN. Some senior officers reached into their own pockets to order books on COIN from Books-a-Million, Amazon, and other Internet book vendors. General officers consistently downplayed the ability of the insurgents, calling them *amateurs*. They took issue with strategic analysts in Washington who were warning that the direction of the conflict was going in the wrong way, while the generals could only say *"we are stacking them up like cord wood,"* and did not see the insurgent's *ability to regenerate* and slowly take *control of the momentum* in the fight.

Somehow, the lessons learned in past conflicts – as for example, Vietnam- were lost or were irretrievable. Intelligence analysts working on strategic assessments had to practically start from scratch a methodology to analyze insurgency. (US Marines have a peculiar acronym for describing these types of conditions: FUBAR, which stands for *"f**ed up beyond all recognition/any repair/all reason.)*[133] Starting in late 2003, logistical and tactical support for COIN efforts had to be built from scratch, through the introduction of new tools which included new IT technology, drones, and vehicles with improved armor. There were factors that complicated the way ahead. First, there were few assets with knowledge of the languages and culture of Afghanistan and South West Asia, and second, the more experienced personnel were shifted to prepare for the invasion of Iraq. Afghanistan was put on a back burner, and insufficient resources were committed to an ill-defined undertaking. Military commanders failed to understand that their successes in tactical COIN did not take into account the developing *strategic picture*.

It did not matter how successfully they were stacking up fallen enemies *like* "*cord wood*," if they could continue replacing them with new fighters. Another Yogi Berra famous quote seems appropriate: *"You can see a lot just by observing."* While senior intelligence analysts were conducting strategic analysis to create a "big picture" description of the situation objectively, field commanders failed to understand that the enemy had taken the initiative. While the insurgency could visualize their objective to defeat foreign troops without any reference to time, the international community and American policymakers could not clearly define an achievable "*end state*."

Military commanders underestimated the enemy. For example, in a *Time Magazine* article on 28 March 2005, Major General Eric T.

Olson, Commander of Combined Task Force-76 (OEF) and the 25th Infantry Division, suggested possible troop reductions, and viewed the Taliban as a force in decline. He described the construction and use of IEDs as "amateurish." The IEDs turned out to become the prime enemy weapon and the cause of most casualties for American, NATO and other international troops. Despite a huge investment of billions of dollars through JIEDDO to defeat IEDs, the enemy consistently increased their use year after year, perhaps with diminishing results. ISAF Commander General Dan K. McNeil and CENTCOM J2 Major General John M Custer III in January 2008 were quoted as disagreeing with the strategic analysis by the IC about the direction of the war. As the situation steadily deteriorated, insufficient resources were provided, and then small incremental resources were invested, while continuing to give the conflict in Iraq priority attention. The enemy was given time to regroup and take the offensive, while some American generals were out in *la-la land* with unrealistic expectations.

Nationalizing the war

During the Vietnam conflict, as the U.S. hoped to disengage from the war around 1969, the concept of *Vietnamization* was put forward by the Nixon Administration as a way out. Vietnamese troops were recruited and trained to replace American troops as they returned home. There were two components of the program: First, to train the South Vietnamese military to take over the fighting with the Communists, and second, to work out an agreement with the Soviets and the PRC to avoid more regional conflicts. The policy failed in 1975, as North Vietnamese troops overthrew the South Vietnamese Government. In Afghanistan the Soviets attempted a similar arrangement by building up the Afghan military to take over the fighting against Islamic insurgents as they withdrew after about ten years of fighting the insurgency unsuccessfully. The Soviet-sponsored Afghan Government and the Soviet-trained military collapsed in April 1992, right after the collapse of the Soviet Union the previous year.

The Soviets recruited and trained annually thousands of Afghan soldiers between 1979 and 1989. Despite the challenges associated with training an army with illiterate conscripts, while suffering a high desertion rate and a high number of casualties, the Soviets were able to pull out, but it did not take long for the puppet government they left behind to collapse. External factors, primarily the collapse of the Soviet Union in 1991, and the refusal of the new Russian government to continue providing support, resulted in the overthrow of the Afghan poppet government. The implosion of the Soviet Union in 1991 was due in part to their failures in Afghanistan.

The U.S. and NATO allies started a process of recruiting and training the Afghan National Security Forces (ANSF) in 2002, but despite many annual promises, the targets set did not materialize. They faced similar problems to the ones faced by the Soviets, including the over 90 percent illiteracy rate in Afghanistan. Between 2007 and 2012 the US spent over $200 million on literacy programs for Afghan soldiers, but no more than 50 percent of ANSF members could function at a level of literacy above the first grade. The ANSF, as happened in the past during the Soviet period, suffers from a high level of desertion, which makes it practically impossible to reach the desired level of 352,000 members. A level of attrition of anywhere between 30 and 50 percent made reaching the goal of building an effective Afghan military practically impossible.[134] Contracting out the education of the Afghan soldiers, based on published reports, was a failure, according to NATO and ISAF reports. As a result, once American and NATO troops leave the country, there could be a replay of past experiences with the concept of *nationalizing* similar conflicts where there is an active insurgency.

Until President Barrack Obama and his new national security team picked up management of the war in 2009, there was no clear system to measure progress or lack of progress, which since 2002 had lacked a clear focus. Retired Marine Corps General James Jones, who was appointed National Security Advisor by President Obama, is credited with suggesting new ways to measure performance (MOP) and assess the direction of momentum.[135] Without a clear way to measure performance it is impossible to produce effective decisions to reach objectives. Despite the effort to function with a clear focus, numerous irrelevant and misleading MOPs continued to be pushed out based on improper metrics, and irrelevant statistics.

Afghan Islamic insurgents have been quoted as saying that the international military contingent in Afghanistan may own the clock, but the insurgents own the time. They are in no hurry to win. The U.S. lacks patience and has run out of money to face a conflict without a clear end in sight. U.S. will be pulling out after losing a victory that had already been won in 2001 by mismanaging the situation. The same people who criticize the Obama Administration for announcing the pull out by 2014, failed to provide due attention to the conflict for several years, allowing for the deterioration of the situation and Islamic insurgents to regroup and gain momentum.

So what?

After over a decade of promises by American military commanders, the Afghan military and police do not show signs that they will be able to hold back the insurgents on their own. According to the UN Office of Drugs and Crime, in 2013 the opium crop hit an all-time high of 516,000 acres in 2013, despite a $7.5 billion investment by the U.S. to reduce dependency opium production. And production went up again in 2014. The insurgency is well funded through illicit trade, which is fueling corruption and undermines all efforts to establish good governance. The fall of Afghanistan could produce a larger conflict, as Sunni and Shi'a extremists will fight for supremacy, creating a strong possibility of dragging Iran and Pakistan directly into war that could easily transcend Afghan ill-defined borders.

Clear goals for the intervention in Afghanistan were never outlined. Nobody could remember that "normalcy" looked like before the conflicts that started as far back as the late 1970s, thus it was impossible to set as a goal to take the country back to a stage of *historical normalcy*, however defined. Nobody could clearly outline how a new Afghanistan would look like other than in clichés, general platitudes and flat, dull, and banal statements. Without clear goals and timetables the outcome was predictable. People simply got tired of a never-ending conflict far away from home and with no perceivable interests for the U.S.

From the Report of the Special Inspector General for Afghanistan Reconstruction: Department of State Assistance to Afghanistan - $4 Billion Obligated between 2002 and 2013:

- The Department of State obligated $4 billion for reconstruction in Afghanistan between 2002 and 2013
- A total of 1,874 contracts were awarded to 771 organizations and individuals.
- Nearly 90 percent of the contract awards were to improve governance and the rule of law, support for cultural activities, civil society education, humanitarian assistance, human rights, and economic development.
- Most of the contracts were awarded to DYNCORP, which received at least $2.8 billion in contracts.
- PAE Government Services was the company in second place for contract awards with over $598 million

In January 2003 the *Operational Net Assessment* (ONA) System-of-Systems Analysis (SOSA) team of the Standing Joint Forces Headquarters (Prototype) at Joint Forces Command (JFCOM), was asked to assist BG Steven Hawkins, Commander Joint Task Force IV (Reconstruction of Iraq) at Central Command (CENTCOM). This picture of the team with Gen. Hawkins was taken at McDill Air Force Base, in Tampa, prior to the invasion. Team members: Paul Bowen, Cecil Johnson, Rafael Fermoselle, Mike Terelli, Rick Wilson, BG Hawkins, Dan Larned, Houston Tucker, and Bob Kuth.

Picture was taken using the author's camera and he owns the copyright. No known restrictions on publication.

Coalition Military Fatalities By Year

Year	US	UK	Other	Total
2001	12	0	0	12
2002	49	3	18	70
2003	48	0	10	58
2004	52	1	7	60
2005	99	1	31	131
2006	98	39	54	191
2007	117	42	73	232
2008	155	51	89	295
2009	317	108	96	521
2010	499	103	109	711
2011	418	46	102	566
2012	310	44	48	402
2013	127	9	25	161
2014	~53	~6	~13	~72
TOTAL	**2354**	**452**	**675**	**3482**

Source: http://icasualties.org/oef/

By the end of 2014, the US military and civilian agencies had suffered over 4,000 fatalities, and over 20,500 wounded and injured in combat and non-combat incidents in Afghanistan from October 2001 to 31 December 2012.

The author with fellow members of the April 2008 class of the U.S. Army Human Terrain System, while in training at Ft. Leavenworth, Kansas, prior to deploying to Iraq.

The picture was taken with the author's camera and he owns the copyright. No known restrictions on publication.

Iraq War

> **For too many people—including defense "experts," members of Congress, executive branch officials and ordinary citizens—war has become a kind of videogame or action movie: bloodless, painless and odorless. But my years at the Pentagon left me even more skeptical of systems analysis, computer models, game theories or doctrines that suggest that war is anything other than tragic, inefficient and uncertain.**[136]
>
> **Robert Gates**

The George W. Bush Administration directed the beginning of deliberate planning to invade Iraq early in 2002. Operation Iraqi Freedom (OIF) was planned for over a year, as military assets were moved to staging areas. Considerable resources were dedicated to collect and analyze intelligence on Iraq. Contrary to the expedited actions taken immediately after 9/11/2001 to overthrow the Taliban regime in Afghanistan, there was ample time to prepare for OIF. Yet, policymakers did not pay attention to what the experts were predicting. They selectively ignore factual intelligence, and supported their reckless hawkish views with uncorroborated and faulty intelligence, pushing the President and Congress into what history will record as a big mistake.

While the insurgency that developed in Afghanistan had not been predicted, a number of reports, both within and outside the USG, foretold what surfaced in Iraq after the country was invaded in March 2003, including civil strife. Each insurgency is unique, requiring adaptations of the strategic analysis process, as well as tactical COIN operations.[137] In the Iraqi case, the conflict was a combination of multiple forms of unconventional warfare requiring more complex analysis. Despite numerous intelligence gaps, experienced analysts were able to develop accurate conclusions. Senior policymakers appeared unwilling to accept the implications of assessments of the intelligence community. The IC, however did not predict that the Iraqi episode could turn into a religious conflict fueled by extremists with convoluted interpretations of Islam.

The author in Baghdad, Iraq 13 December 2008

This picture was taken by the foot of the famous *crossed swords* over the parade grounds where Saddam Hussein showed off his military might. Behind me at the helmets of Iranian soldiers killed in the Iran-Iraq War during the 1980s.

The picture was taken with the author's camera. No known restrictions on publication.

Ambassador Paul Bremer, who served as the Administrator for the U.S.-led Coalition Provisional Authority in Iraq, claimed in an interview on 6 January 2006 on NBC Television, that the U.S. did not anticipate the insurgency. The U.S. had conducted secret war games in 1999 entitled *Desert Crossing*, in anticipation of a possible invasion of Iraq.[138] Based on this exercise, it was anticipated that if an invasion was carried out, it would require about 350,000 troops, roughly three more times the number that were used in 2003, and according to some of the "likely scenarios," there was a strong possibility of conflict among ethnic and religious lines, as they bid for power. There were concerns of potential local resistance to a government linked with a foreign invasion, and Iranian tinkering with Iraqi domestic issues.[139] All of this information is in the open domain, not hidden in some top secret government safe. Paul Bremer did not know what he was talking about.

Pre-war warnings disregarded

On 25 May 2007, the Select Committee on Intelligence of the US Senate issued a Report on *Prewar Intelligence Assessments about Postwar Iraq*.[140] The findings of the investigation conducted clearly show that the IC had issued warnings. The report concluded that "*The Intelligence Community assessed prior to the war that establishing a stable democratic government in postwar Iraq would be a long, difficult and probably turbulent challenge.*"The report cited the IC as assessing prior to the war that "*al-Qai'da probably would see an opportunity to accelerate its' operational tempo and increase terrorist attacks during and after a U.S.-Iraq War.*" The Bureau of Intelligence and Research (INR) of the Department of State warned in January 2003 that a well-executed military campaign could be followed by internal conflict.[141]

The CIA predicted in two reports dated February and March 2003 that U.S. Forces would be faced with civil unrest, humanitarian burdens, and lingering military threats, particularly in light of the relatively small number of U.S. military forces assigned to the mission. DIA warned in March 2003 of possible problems and noted intelligence gaps on Iraqi attitudes. It warned of a risk of civil strife following the demise of Saddam Hussein's regime. Ignoring all of these assessments comes close to *criminal neglect* or *criminal intent.*[142]

There were very significant differences between the background knowledge and preparation by the IC before the invasions of Afghanistan and Iraq. There was relatively little knowledge and few people with a background to analyze conditions in Afghanistan as compared to Iraq. The U.S. had been studying the situation in Iraq for as long as twenty years, covering the Iraq-Iran War (1980-1988), and in preparation for the Operation Desert Storm (2 August 1990- 28 February 1991). After the war, the U.S. maintained troops stationed in the region and started Operation Southern Watch, to enforce no-fly zones over southern Iraq. However, despite years focusing on Iraq, because there was no diplomatic relations, there was no Defense Attaché office in country to develop a better understanding of objective conditions and develop Iraqi assets. For many years DIA and CIA simply did not have the benefit of staff in country working out of the American Embassy writing analytical papers.

Secretary of Defense Rumsfeld insisted on conducting military operations with as few units as possible. His views were supported by Gen. Franks as CENTCOM Commander. For example, when Lt. Gen. Wallace requested a temporary halt in his advance towards Bagdad, in part due to unexpected heavy resistance by irregular Iraqi troops, namely Saddam's Fedayeen, he was threatened with dismissal. Lt. Gen. Wallace's assessment was supported by Marine Corps Lt. Gen. James T. Conway, who was experienced in intelligence and COIN operations, and was concerned by potential trouble ahead with irregular forces.[143] General McKiernan, supported Lt. Gen. Wallace's position and defended the decision to slow down the march to Baghdad. Both, Wallace and McKiernan took a lot of heat from their higher ups for being risk averse.[144] This incident was followed by the decision not to deploy the

1st Cavalry Division, a decision which resulted in not having sufficient troops to prevent random acts of violence, looting and destruction of Iraqi assets after the fall of Baghdad. According to a quote attributed to then Acting Chief of Staff of the Army, Gen. Jack Keane, the decision not to deploy the 1st Cavalry was not just an intelligence community failure, but also a failure of senior military leadership.[145]

Multipolar Insurgency

What started as a classic *peer-to-peer war* changed into *irregular warfare* very quickly, characterized by guerrilla operations led by Saddam Hussein supporters, mainly secular Baath Party members, Iraqi nationalists, and former members of the military, against Coalition forces. It is not clear how many insurgents participated in the initial phase of the uprising which ended with the capture of Saddam Hussein on 13 December 2003. Intelligence units operating in Iraq concentrated on looking for WMDs in the first few months of the occupation. With insufficient HUMINT collection capabilities there was limited intelligence to understand how the situation was developing, including the "order of battle" of the insurgency, if indeed there was an insurgency, as multiple groups were issuing conflicting claims for incidents of violence.

An undetermined number of foreign fighters joined Iraqi resistance starting at some point before coalition forces entered Iraq on 20 March 2003.[146] Within a short period of time, guerrilla fighters began to use improvised explosive devices (IEDs), anti-tank grenade-launchers (RPGs), and sabotage operations against the country's infrastructure. By the end of the first conventional phase of the war on or about 1 May 2003, a total of 139 American military personnel had died.

Just about everyone in a position of authority among civilian and military leaders of the Provisional Authority and Coalition forces, as well as IC intelligence analysts, could see the deteriorating environment. The so-called "honeymoon period" after the invasion in which the population had been expected to receive the coalition forces with open arms came to an abrupt halt or never materialized. Murders, looting, vandalism, bombings, and ethnic and religious conflicts surfaced practically overnight, and with the disbanding of the Iraqi military and police institutions, the people who may have been able to assist in controlling the chaotic situation were not available, and in fact, joined the growing insurgency. For the IC and military intelligence units identifying who was behind the growing conflict was a priority, but apparently, second to finding the WMD that constituted the *casus belli* for the war. *They were never found!* Criminal elements took advantage of the chaotic situation for personal gain, and numerous other actors, including foreign jihadists began to arrive to proselytize and link up with local groups interested in fighting against the foreign invaders.

Coalition forces were engaged in what could best be described as *occupation duties.* According to policymakers the situation could not be described as "counterinsurgency," since *there was no insurgency* according to them. By the Geneva Convention, the nation whose forces are in control of an area is the *Occupying Power.* The characterization of the Coalition presence in Iraq as an "*occupation force*" in May 2003 backed into corners key Iraqi leaders who had been cooperating but did not want to be categorized as "*collaborators*" with a foreign occupation.[147] Intelligence analysts were confronted with a debate over semantics, in a highly politicized environment, where *language subtleties had serious potential implications.* Strategic analysis of the situation was immediately affected by controversy over the words used to describe the environment.

CENTCOM had made inadequate preparations to deal with civil strife in a post-invasion environment, in part, because the command was denied the necessary assets by OSD.[148] A team of selected Foreign Service officers to support the CPA was prevented from deploying by OSD- as former CIA Director Tenet put it: "*The State Department team of experts could sit on the runway at Dulles or Andrews Air Force Base, waiting for a lift to Baghdad, until hell froze over.*"[149] Almost from the start, the quality of intelligence and political reporting was poor, due to the shortage of qualified personnel. But the team on the ground was caught in the euphoria and optimism of the first few days after a successful initial military campaign. That atmosphere changed rather quickly over the next months.

As conditions in Iraq continued to deteriorate from 2003 to 2005, the "Iraq Study Group" (ISG) was organized to analyze the situation and come up with a formula for addressing the challenges.[150] The report, which made public in December 2006, stated that there was *no magic formula* for dealing with the problems, and there was no guarantee that any course of action would stop sectarian warfare, growing violence, or a slide towards chaos. The ISG report called for a new political and diplomatic effort and a reassessment of the primary mission of American forces, with the aim of training the Iraqis to take the responsibility for COIN so that the American troops could start moving out of Iraq responsibly.[151]

The ISG assessed that sectarian violence was the principal challenge to stability, and the situation could only be resolved by the Iraqi Government moving forward with national reconciliation. Violence was fed by a Sunni Arab insurgency, Shiite militias and death squads, al Qaeda, and widespread criminality, and the government was not providing basic security or delivering essential services. The IC was *"not doing enough to map the insurgency, dissect it, and understand it on a national and provincial level."*[152] The report called for a greater emphasis on imbedding American troops with Iraqi military units to support their efficiency and help them to take over primary responsibility for combat operations. The ISG suggested that the U.S. should continue to provide intelligence support to the Iraqi forces. The Iraqi Government was to set milestones and adhere to them or the U.S. should reduce its' level of support across the board.[153]

A New Military Doctrine

In January 2007 President Bush announced that General David Petraeus was taking over from Gen. Casey as Commanding General of MNF-I, and tasked with implementing the new doctrine, which consisted in taking back areas from the insurgents, persistent presence in recaptured territory, assigning military units to live among the population to provide them security, relentlessly pursuing the insurgents, stepped up recruitment and training of Iraqi military forces, and integrating the Iraqi Army, police, and local militia into a counterinsurgency force together with MNF-I. In addition, over 20,000 additional troops were assigned to Iraq in order to have sufficient assets to take the war to the enemy.

Prior to 2007, the policy focus was on *troop rotations*, plans to reduce troop presence, handing over the conflict to the Iraqis, and casting "objective condition" in multiple ways while avoiding descriptors like *resistance, civil war,* and *insurgency*. As previously mentioned, Gen. Casey and SECDEF Rumsfeld repeatedly discussed with the press plans to reduce the American footprint in Iraq.[154] That policy was about to change. *Field Manual 3-24 Counterinsurgency* was informed by classical COIN theory based on experience gained in prior conflicts around the world, and summarized as making the population the center of gravity, winning the hearts and minds of the population, and clearing territory, holding it, and building the government's legitimacy by addressing the population's grievances. For intelligence operations, the change in strategy brought about more flexibility in providing accurate, "negative" assessments, to senior officials went a long way to changing the analytical process. The principal change was not in the analytical process, but in a better environment to deliver assessments to clients of intelligence.

Poor Situational Awareness, Wishful Thinking, or What?

To compound the problems resulting from ignoring what the experts had said before the invasion of Iraq, almost immediately after the fall of Baghdad, Gen. Tommy Franks announced in April 2003 the *intention to drawdown the number of soldiers in Iraq* from 175,000 to 30,000 by September.[155]

Gen. Petraeus articulated well his intelligence requirements and the intelligence analysts knew what he wanted. They focused on the insurgency fault lines, and resources were used to expeditiously target them. Intelligence was used to identify and take advantage of enemy mistakes. A concerted effort was made to win the information war against the insurgency. An important change was to unleash what was described as "command and feedback," instead of simply "command and control" (C2).[156] According to this concept, advanced by Gen. James Mattis, co-author of the new *Coin Manual* published in 2007, intelligence results from the decision making of command and feedback, which enhances the ability to adapt to the environment as part of a dynamic process to counteract insurgency as an "adaptive system." The use of a broad spectrum of intelligence disciplines is required to apply this concept of constant evaluation, measurement, and adaptation.[157] Another important change to military operations in Iraq in 2007 was the troop surge, which provided the assets necessary to act on intelligence before it became stale.

It ain't over 'til it's over[158]

A considerable effort was made by DOD to come up with a methodology to assess when an insurgency is over, based on prior experience associated with insurgencies since WWII. At least two studies were carried out by the RAND Corporation's National Defense Research Institute, with funding from DOD. One of the studies, *Money in the Bank: Lessons Learned from Past Counterinsurgency (COIN) Operations* examined a handful of insurgencies to determine tactics, techniques, and procedures used by insurgents and counterinsurgents in an attempt to reach general conclusions. It was not intended to conduct a comprehensive study of insurgency.[159]

Another RAND study sponsored by the U.S. Marine Corps Intelligence Activity (MCIA) and the Defense Intelligence Community, focused on how insurgencies end, based on a study of 89 different insurgencies throughout the world since WWII.[160] The study explored how these insurgencies ended, who is recognized as the victor, and why. According to this study, "*What has been missing is a systematic attempt to identify and meet critical analytical, planning, and operational decision-making needs for global COIN exploring revolutionary progress in information networking. Consequently, U.S. COIN has been as clumsy as the new insurgency has been cunning.*"[161] The primary reason for these efforts was to come up with an accepted methodology to determine what the "*end game*" was in Iraq. Published guides and manuals that predate 9/11/2001, did not address this important issue head on, leaving a gap in doctrine dealing with the analysis of insurgency. However, there is no accepted methodology to deal with this difficult subject. By 2014, it became quite clear that the *end game* is very far away… years away. By mid-2015, it became obvious that Islamic extremists associated with IS had gained momentum, i.e. driving to victory.

Pull out in 2011 and return in 2014

After invading Iraq in 2003, it took five years before the U.S. could sign a Status of Forces Agreement (SOFA) with Iraq. Part of the agreement signed in 2008 by the Bush Administration was that American troops would return home by the end of 2011. This type of agreement granting legal immunities for American troops from local laws is standard procedure with any host government. Discussions for extending the SOFA beyond 2011 for any residual force left in Iraq started right away. However, Iraqi politicians did not cooperate, and as the Obama Administration took office in January 2009, the goal of withdrawing all troops by the end of 2011 picked up support, despite recommendations by senior military leaders that it was important to leave behind a residual force to continue training Iraqi troops. Shi'a extremists continued to oppose signing a new SOFA or extending the existing one signed in 2008. In hindsight, withdrawing all the troops was unwise.

American troops were pulled out of Iraq before the end of December 2011. There was no agreement with Iraq regarding a legal status for any American forces left to continue training the Iraqi military. Within days of the departure of American troops the situation began to deteriorate as Sunni and Shi'a groups traded terrorist bombings. It was unpredictable if somehow all Iraqis would find a way to live with each other, or if the country would break up into three separate entities, one Sunni, one Kurdish, and one Shi'a. As of January 2013, al-Qai'da in Iraq had reconstituted itself, the incidence of terrorism went up, and jihadists freely moved between Iraq and Syria. Conflicts between the Kurds and the Shi'a dominated central government increased. Almost as soon as American troops left, the Shia dominated Iraqi government headed by Prime Minister Nouri al-Maliki started to round up Sunni leaders, and even tried to arrest Vice President Tariq al-Hashimi, who fled the country. All the successful efforts behind *"The Awakening"* to stop the civil war in 2006 and 2007 were destroyed practically overnight and extremists took advantage of the situation.

It did not take long for al-Qai'da to revive their campaign of terror. With the start of the civil war in Syria, Sunni extremists from other countries began to arrive again in Iraq and Syria, and to build the so-called *Islamic State of Iraq and Syria* (ISIS). Throughout 2013 the incidences of violence grew exponentially. At least 7,500 people were killed in a surge of terrorism, including multiple car bombs in front of mosques in Shiite neighborhoods. The number of victims more than doubled the 3,238 number registered in 2012. These numbers do not take into account military and insurgent casualties. Prime Minister Nouri al-Maliki was unable to control the deteriorating situation, and made it worse by his deliberate campaign against Sunni Muslims.

By mid-2014 the government was on the edge of collapse, as jihadists took over the second and third largest cities and prepared to attack Bagdad. The insurgency coalesced behind the *Islamic State in Iraq and Syria* (ISIS), a Sunni/Wahhabi alliance that surfaced in 2004 and formed a close alliance with al-Qai'da. Initially, the ISIS was led by Jordanian-born Abu Musab al-Zarqawi, as the head of *al-Qai'da in Iraq* (AQI), until he was killed by American forces in June 2006. Abu Bakr al-Baghdadi took over leadership of ISIS after being released by the Iraqi Government; he had been arrested by American troops and handed over to Iraq.

After taking over Fallujah, Mosul, and Tikrit, ISIS continued on towards Baghdad in June 2014, killing hundreds of captured Iraqi soldiers and Shi'a Muslims in mass executions. The radicalization and extreme cruelty exhibited in ISIS in Syria and Iraq led to al-Qai'da severing ties with the organization in February 2014. Not even al-Qai'da accepted the extreme violence and terrorism used by ISIS.

In neighboring Syria, the UN estimates that over 150,000 people had already been killed since 2011. The arrival of foreign fighters to participate in both conflicts, and foreign assistance provided to a broad array of factions, complicates the regional environment. The unintended consequences of the intervention in Iraq in 2003, the decision to pull out in 2011, plus the decision to stay out of the conflict in Syria, set the stage to a more complicated regional scenario. Radical Islamists exploited the situation to expand their numbers. Iraq and Syria are failed states with different factions using extreme brutality to gain the upper hand. Despite international community efforts to mediate between insurgents and Syria's President Bashar Assad, there was no progress as of mid-2015.

The Shi'a-dominated government of al-Maliki in Iraq sought military assistance from Iran. Iranian Special Forces were reported in Baghdad in June 2014.[162] Washington policymakers sent an additional 275 soldiers to reinforce the approximately 200 troops already guarding the American Embassy in Baghdad. By the end of 2014, there were over 3,000 American troops once again supporting the government of Iraq with military trainers. The possibility of expanding the role of American troops to participating in direct combat with insurgents increased daily. Future historians will have to evaluate the outcome of the Iraqi adventure. It may take thirty years to properly evaluate what happened, how it happened, and who were the responsible parties for the mess.

So what?

To defeat a religion, you need a religion.

T. S. Eliot[163]

The experience with the handling of Iraq and Afghanistan since 2001 supports the principal argument of this book that *America is navigating without a compass.* Pulling out of Iraq at the end of 2011 may turn out to be a horrible mistake, possibly worse than the original misguided decision to invade the country to overthrow Saddam Hussein and reestablish a democracy that never had existed. The explanatory statements for the invasion turned out to be faulty. The IC presented assessments about conditions that turned out to be accurate, i.e. *the invasion led to considerable civil strife.* Policymakers did not listen to the experts. The syllogism from which the logical conclusion is drawn is that *American foreign policy urgently needs proper direction.* Policymakers need to analyze all possible consequences of their actions *beforehand.*

There are close to 190 different streams of information feeding experienced analysts in the IC, who in turn inform policymakers of their conclusions based on fact. If they are regarded as *Cassandras* by policymakers then all the resources spent on maintaining the best intelligence system in the world is wasted.[164] The hypothesis of a long conflict or "*long war*" that emerged around 2005 has proven to be accurate. As of the middle of 2015 it was evident that we are facing a conflict that is nowhere close to a final resolution despite over a million casualties on all sides.

Americans suffer from Utopian ideals and poor intellectual understanding of religious extremists. There is a tendency to forget or ignore that history is full of religious wars. Americans distort reality and engage in wishful thinking, and believe that they can make other people and cultures in their own image. Despite the warnings by the intelligence community before the invasion of Iraq, and the Russian experience in Afghanistan, the dangers posed by religious conflicts was not given due attention by intelligence analysts, although it is questionable if the policymakers would have paid attention. Americans are taught not to engage in hate speech, and to respect religious creeds regardless of the potential implications. Thomas Jefferson said in a speech to Virginia Baptists in 1808: "*And we have experienced the quiet as well as the comfort which results from leaving everyone to profess freely and openly those principles of religion which are the inductions of his own reason and the serious convictions of his own inquiries.*" Eight years later, in a letter to Mrs. HJ. Harrison Smith in 1816 Jefferson said: "*I never attempted to make a convert, nor wished to change another's creed.*" This type of reasoning is typically American, but *it takes two to tango*. Islamic extremists hold the opposite point of view. They want to impose their degenerate views on others to convert them, or if they do not comply, kill them.

In this conflict the very existence of Western Civilization is threatened. Islamic extremists are willing to fight and die for their convictions. Although T.S. Eliot made his famous remark – "*religion can only be fought with another religion*" – in reference to Communism as a form of "secular religion," his views fit well in the conflict with Islamic extremists.[165] Western society, particularly American culture has been deteriorating since the 1960s, as a counterculture developed that provides Islamic extremists plenty of ammunition to propose their warped religious views as a valid alternative to Western and particularly American immorality and blasphemy. As will be explored later on in this book, the moral incoherence of our time is a key handicap in the long-war against Islamic extremists. We are faced with a war of ideas and convictions, which has to be won like any other counterinsurgency by winning the hearts and minds of the masses, in combination with deadly force.

Coalition Military Fatalities in Iraq by Year

Year	US	UK	Other	Total
2003	486	53	41	580
2004	849	22	35	906
2005	846	23	28	897
2006	823	29	21	873
2007	904	47	10	961
2008	314	4	4	322
2009	149	1	0	150
2010	60	0	0	60
2011	54	0	0	54
2012	1	0	0	1
Total	4486	179	139	4804

Sources: http://www.icasualties.org/Iraq/index.aspx

Congressional Research Service

Operation	US Service Member deaths	DOD Civilian Deaths	US Service Member Wounded in action
Iraqi Freedom OIF	4,412	13	31,949
New Dawn OND	66	0	295
Enduring Freedom OEF	2,346	4	20,037
Inherent Resolver OIR	2	0	0
Total	**6.826**	**17**	**52,281**

V – SNAGS OF WAR

Disorderly drama

Inexorably, a lot of stupid things happen before, during, and after armed conflicts. War by its' very nature is supreme and disorderly drama, chaotic, and costly. In the early days of the wars in Afghanistan and Iraq senior policymakers were delusional, and adopted a mindset of denying the obvious. They failed to pay attention to warnings, refused to accept that things did not go the way they had predicted, and rebuffed suggestions for corrective action until things had reached a level where they could no longer continue living a mythology. Policymakers failed to clearly define the enemy, specific mission goals, and to channel popular support for justice towards contributing to the war effort. Wars are costly, and there is no way to avoid paying for them.

Despite previous irregular warfare experience, the military was not prepared to deal with IEDs and other tactics related to COIN operations. Initial cost estimates proved to be highly inaccurate. Dysfunctions, disorder, lack of transparency, and bizarre decisions led to distress and vulnerabilities that could be easily exploited by the aggressors that attacked the homeland on 9/11/2001. The loss of faith in the ability to achieve victory was critical. As a consequence, Americans are not in the mood to engage in any other foreign conflicts for humanitarian or any other reason, preferring to address their own economic problems. But despite fourteen years of war, we are not anywhere close to the end. The next decade is bound to be more complicated than the period from the millennium to 2015.

False pretenses to start wars

According to *Article One, Section Eight* of the Constitution, the power to declare war rests with Congress, but *there is no specific path to war*. The President is granted the power under the Constitution to repel an attack upon the country without waiting for Congress to authorize going to war.

Claiming that the country was under attack several presidents requested and received from Congress formal declarations of war. Under the *War Powers Resolution of 1973* (50 USC 1541-1548) Congress tried to put an end to questionable past practices and require presidents to obtain consent from Congress before engaging in future wars, or at least notify Congress within 48 hours of the need to repel aggression, accompanied by a formal request to declare war. The law was enacted overriding a veto by President Nixon. In practice, the *War Powers Resolution* has not really changed much if anything.[166] Presidents have always exercised considerable discretion and freedom of judgment to engage the military in conflicts, before and after 1973, although not always with due prudence, which was the reason to enact the *War Powers Resolution* in 1973.

There was ample historical precedent for the start of the Iraq War in 2003 using false pretenses and poor judgment. On 11 May 1846 President James Polk sent a message to Congress asking for a declaration of war on Mexico. Although Congress promptly approved, within a few months the majority of the Members of Congress came to the realization that the war was unprovoked, unnecessary, and unconstitutional. On 20 April 1898 President William McKinley asked for authority from Congress to address the situation in Cuba with the Spanish Government after the sinking of the USS Maine. Congress decided instead to declare war on Spain. Once again, the justification to declare war was false. Let's examine these precedent-setting cases.

Early in the 19th century a concept surfaced to the effect that it was the destiny of the U.S. to expand across all of North America, despite it being rejected by prominent Americans as a form of imperialism. Members of the Democratic Party, as it formed during the 1830s, generally supported what became known as "*Continentalism*" and "*Manifest Destiny*." Later on, the concept transformed into an American mission to promote and export Democracy throughout the world, which further transformed itself to an ill-defined romantic concept of *Nation Building*.[167] However, the root of these ideas was based on a form of imperialism that developed between 1818 and 1850.[168]

In 1836, American settlers in Mexican territory declared the independence of Texas. The "*Texians*" not only fought the Mexican military but they also fought Native Americans over the land, particularly the Comanche, who started moving into Texas from Wyoming, Nebraska, Colorado, Kansas and Oklahoma about the same time as the Spanish arrived in the 16th and 17th centuries. A pivotal event on the Texas secession was the attack by Mexican troops on the Alamo Mission in San Antonio in March 1836, which had been taken over by revolutionaries and an assortment of thugs including James Bowie and David Crockett.[169] All the defenders (about 200) were killed or wounded. Within a month, the Mexican Army was defeated at the Battle of San Jacinto, which for all practical purposes ended Mexican control of Texas. The U.S. recognized the independence of Texas in 1839, together with Belgium, France, the Netherlands, and another independent republic created in the Mexican territory of Yucatan in 1841.

In 1842, the Mexican military was sent into Texas to put down the secessionists. They captured San Antonio, but retreated back to Mexico. The capture of San Antonio and other skirmishes along the Rio Grande caused panic in Texas, leading to a decision to join the U.S. In 1845, the Republic of Texas, was admitted to the Union as the 28th state. The delineation of the border between Mexico and Texas continued unsettled. Many American settlers who had been allowed into Texas by Mexico since the 1820s were from slave states, and they wanted to continue holding slaves, while Mexicans overwhelmingly were opposed to slavery. Acquiring another slave state was an incentive to President James K. Polk, slave owners in the South, and the Democratic Party.[170] Born in North Carolina, he was a former Speaker of the House, and former Governor of Tennessee. Polk was not only a slave owner, but had a reputation for mistreating them through the overseer of his plantation in Tennessee.[171] He was a member of the planter class clinging to the past to preserve its' political and economic power and place in the social order.

President Polk wanted to purchase California and other lands from Mexico, influenced by both, the concept of *Manifest Destiny*, as well as by the economics and politics of slavery. When the negotiations failed, Polk sent troops to the Mexican border in an effort to create an incident or provocation in the still-ill-defined border. Claiming that Mexican troops had attacked and killed American soldiers in American territory, President Polk told Congress that "*war exists*," and asked that war be declared. The House of Representatives passed a bill declaring war by a vote of 174 to 14. In the Senate there was considerable debate about the facts, leading to an effort to strip the bill from the preamble because it stated that Mexico was responsible for the hostilities. Twice motions to strike the preamble failed. Finally, the bill was approved by a vote of 40 to 2, despite the lack of facts to justify the declaration of war.[172]

Future President Abraham Lincoln was elected to Congress in 1846. He immediately took issue with President Polk for starting an unprovoked war, and investigated the details of the alleged attack by Mexico. Contrary to what President Polk had claimed, Lincoln obtained details that the attack took place within Mexican territory and that it was the U.S. Army that was intruding in Mexico. Lincoln, as well as other members of the Whig Party, forerunner of the Republican Party, called the declaration of war against Mexico immoral and linked it to pro-slavery elements.[173] Multiple articles were published in the Whig Party journal, *The American Review*, during 1847 stating that the declaration of war was the result of misleading statements. After a new Congress took over with a Whig Party majority, an effort was made to stop the war, and on 7 December 1847 an amendment was passed by a vote of 85 to 81, censuring President Polk and calling the war unnecessary and unconstitutional.[174] Despite the opposition to the conflict, Congress appropriated funds for the war.

In hindsight, the victory over Mexico produced the desired expansion, and established the foundation for a vast country with significant natural resources. At the start of the war there were only about 6,000 regular troops in the U.S. Army, but the number swelled to over 115,000, and the percentage of casualties was much higher than in any other war ever fought by Americans. About 1.5 percent was killed in combat, and about another 12 percent died of disease and wounds.[175] It has been estimated that the actual casualty rate was as high as 40 percent if the number of veterans that died from war-related health issues were taken into account. At least 9,000 soldiers or about 8 percent deserted during the war.[176]

The cost of the war was well over $100 million, not counting the cost of supporting wounded veterans, and the $15 million paid in compensation to Mexico for the vast territory taken, in addition to the assumption of Mexican sovereign debt to American citizens.[177] In addition, the U.S. agreed to fight a military campaign against Comanche and Apache natives that had been raiding Mexican towns for years, besides protecting other U.S. states and territories. Veteran benefits were paid for the next 80 years. The last surviving veteran, Owen Thomas Edgar, passed away in 1929.[178]

The House of Representatives passed a resolution with the support of future President Abraham Lincoln after the war ended calling the conflict *"a war unnecessarily and unconstitutionally began by the President of the United States."*[179] Lincoln issued this warning in a letter to his former Law partner in Illinois, William H. Herndon:

> *The provision of the Constitution giving the war-making power to Congress was dictated, as I understand it, by the following reasons. Kings had always been involving and impoverishing their people in wars, pretending generally, if not always, that the good of the people was the object. This, our convention understood to be the most oppressive of all Kingly oppressions; and they resolved to so frame the Constitution that no one man should hold the power of bringing this oppression upon us. But your view destroys the whole matter, and places our President where Kings have always stood.*[180]

Another unprovoked conflict started under false pretenses was the declaration of war against Spain in 1898. The events leading to the declaration of war after two explosions that sank the battleship USS Maine in Havana harbor have deep roots going all the way back to the American Revolutionary War. Due to geographic proximity, a very close relationship exists between Cuba and the U.S. There was a large Cuban community living in the U.S., as well as a fairly large number of Americans living in Cuba. American investments in Cuba in 1895 were in excess of $50 million (in 1895 dollars), particularly in sugar production, tobacco, and mining. In this case, President McKinley, as well as Speaker of the House Thomas Brackett Reed, opposed a declaration of war. The President only asked authorization for use of the armed forces, if necessary, to try to return peace to the island, but Congress passed a joint resolution declaring war, due to considerable warmongering by *yellow journalists* riding a wave of indignation for the sinking of the USS Maine,.[181]

The USS Maine was the second new battleship commissioned after a decision to build a powerful Navy, resulting from the writings of Admiral Alfred Thayer Mahan, particularly his book *The Influence of Sea Power Upon History: 1660-1783*, which was published in 1890.[182] His ideas triggered an arms race around the world. As the U.S. tried to commission new ships as fast as possible, using new and unproven technologies, mistakes were made as new armored battleships powered by coal were built. The USS Maine and its' sister battleship USS Texas were poorly designed without due precautions to prevent spontaneous combustion of coal dust. The ammunition storage (magazine) was placed in close proximity to coal storage bunkers, which in the event of a coal dust explosion, a secondary explosion could be ignited in the ammunition storage area.

The USS Maine entered Havana Harbor in January 1898. It was sent to Havana under the disguise of protecting American citizens and economic interests after rioting took place in the city. Three weeks later it suffered two explosions and sank, with the loss of over 266 of the complement of 374 officers and men on 15 February. There was considerable speculation as to what caused the two explosions, but fueled by public opinion and the news media, which supported Cuban patriots fighting for independence from Spain, the blame was hastily placed on a deliberate attack by Spain using a naval mine. A U.S. Navy Board of Inquiry mistakenly attributed the sinking to an external explosion.[183] Before any legitimate investigation could be carried out, President McKinley reluctantly turned the issue over to Congress without formally requesting Congress to declare war. On 11 April President McKinley only asked that he be:

Empowered to take measures to secure a full and final termination of hostilities between the government of Spain and the people of Cuba...

On 25 April 1898, under pressure from public opinion and the work of Hearst and Pulitzer newspapers stirring up anti-Spanish sentiments, Congress declared war, but with an amendment which stated that the U.S. did not have any intention to annex Cuba. Senator Henry M. Teller of Colorado introduced an amendment that read:

> The United States... *hereby disclaims any disposition of intention to exercise sovereignty, jurisdiction, or control over said island except for pacification thereof, and asserts its' determination, when that is accomplished, to leave the government and control of the island to its' people.*[184]

President McKinley was a veteran of the Civil War and not inclined to start a war. He was aware that a Spanish Navy fleet was in Cuban waters, and that the U.S. Navy did not have enough ammunition along the Atlantic seacoast to even fire a salute if it encountered the Spanish at sea.[185] He had inherited a serious economic depression, and his principal goal was to restore prosperity, not going to war. McKinley had been trying for at least a year to persuade Spain to grant independence to Cuba and put an end to the war that had been going on since 1895, with the support of the large Cuban exile community in the U.S., and with the participation of American volunteers, some of whom reached the rank of general officer in the Cuban Army.[186] The diplomatic effort was affected by the appointment of Senator John Sherman as Secretary of State despite declining mental faculties which were compounded by two senior assistants at DOS who were unfamiliar with diplomacy and also affected by health issues.[187] Diplomatic talks were not going anywhere and it was obvious that Spain was willing to do whatever had to be done to maintain control of Cuba. Increasingly harsh military tactics by Spain were widely covered by the American press, which tilted public opinion in favor of military intervention in Cuba. The USS Maine had been sent to Cuba as part of the efforts to bring about peace, and for the purpose of protecting American citizens and economic interests.[188]

A preliminary investigation of the sinking of the USS Maine was completed within a month, but the report had serious flaws. Additional inquiries produced similar conflicting conclusions. Finally, in 1974, Admiral Hayman G. Rickover decided to revisit the incident, using the previous investigations as his starting point.[189] He came to the conclusion that the explosion was not caused by a mine, but by spontaneous combustion of coal dust in the bunker, which had been placed next to the magazine.[190] There was no evidence of an explosion outside, but the design of the ship, with common bulkheads separating the coal bunkers, the type of smokeless coal (anthracite), the close proximity of the ammunition magazine, and other factors caused the explosion inside the ship. The hypothesis which blamed the explosion on a naval mine and Spain did not make any sense. No evidence was ever found tying Spain, Cuban insurgents, or a self-inflicted attack by the U.S. to have a *casus belie* to declare war.

Defining the enemy since 2001

Who is the enemy? Is the enemy terrorism?[191] Groups that use terrorism as a tactic usually have specific goals and objectives and use terrorism as the "equalizer" that allows them to fight much larger forces that enjoy superiority in weapons and equipment. Groups that use terrorism come in all political persuasions, from the far right to the far left. In addition, to round out the roster we have all kinds of religious fanatics. In conventional peer-to-peer conflicts, each side tries to outdo the other with superiority in the number of troops and weapons available to prevail. In asymmetric warfare, groups that resort to terrorism are generally anti-establishment organizations that share some affinities, even when their stated goals differ widely. However, not all organizations that use terrorism are necessarily "enemies" of the United States.

French Resistance (*Maquis, Alliance Réseau, Fer Réseau*) used terrorism during WWII to fight the Nazis, and they were labeled as such by the Germans. *The Maquisards* in particular, composed of Communists, were known for brutal terrorist tactics. The British Special Operations Executive (SOE), as well as the American predecessor of the CIA, Office of Special Operations (OSS) provided assistance to the *Maquis*. SOE and OSS operatives who parachuted into France to assist the Resistance were illegal combatants according to the Geneva Convention of 1929.

Israeli intelligence agents and Jewish paramilitary organizations, including *Haganah, Irgun, Lehi, and Palmach*, used terrorism against British authorities, as well as against Arabs who opposed Jewish national aspirations starting around 1939. The British provided training to *Haganah* during WWII to fight against Nazi targets. Irgun and Lehi carried out terrorism against the British starting in 1946, as part of their insurgency to create the state of Israel. In 1947, during the UN announced partition of Palestine a civil war broke out. Car bombing attacks and IED's were frequently used. Despite the Jewish concept of *Purity of Arms*, war is not a dinner party. Future Israeli Prime Minister Menachem Begin was internationally condemned as a terrorist, but he is considered a national hero in Israel and was always received in state visits to the US and the UK. Where these "freedom fighters," or just terrorists?

Defining the enemy as "terrorists," was just as stupid as calling the legitimate counterattack after 9/11/2001 against al-Qai'da a *Global War on Terrorism* (GWAT). In part due to this misnomer, military leaders conducting tactical operations in Afghanistan and Iraq were confused and disgusted with the limitations placed on them by policymakers who would not let them *call a spade a spade*. The correct description of what they were asked to do was to fight a COIN operation. It took about two years before they were allowed to use the proper terminology. Next, they realized that had very limited knowledge about the subject. A very senior general officer told this author that at one time he went to visit a tactical unit and found that the Colonel commanding the unit and other senior officers had used their own personal credit cards to purchase books from Books-a-Million on counterinsurgency! Several officers meeting with the author at the National Ground Intelligence Center (NGIC) said that they had found themselves in the same predicament while posted to Afghanistan in the initial phase of that conflict.

Consensus lost

Immediately after the terrorist attacks of 9/11 practically the entire population was united in repudiating the Islamic extremists and supported punitive actions. Nevertheless, the Bush Administration and senior policymakers failed to rally the population for an unavoidable "*war of all the people*" against al-Qai'da. There was consensus that terrorist evildoers had to be punished. The citizenry was not given ways to participate in what was conceived as a just war, even though the people were eager to play a role and do something. Instead of providing people venues for sacrificing for the common good, policymakers lowered taxes and used deficit financing to pay for the war.

During previous conflicts, as for example, WWI and WWII, the citizenry was asked to participate in multiple ways in the support of the war effort, as witnessed by numerous posters suggesting ways for everyone to personally contribute to winning the war. The lost opportunity to rally the people by asking for some sacrifices contributed to delinking military operations from the masses and created the opportunity for an anti-war movement to grow. One did not have to go all the way back to WWI to find ways to rally the masses. President Ronald Reagan rallied the people against the "*Evil Empire*," to bring about the end of the Cold War by outperforming the Soviet Union and stopping their plans of achieving world domination through proxy wars and other tricks. If Americans had been asked to pay for the war they would have, and that would have been better than increasing the national debt.

Policymakers failed to maintain the good will and positive attitudes towards the U.S. that was generated by the attacks of 9/11, which produced victims from about 80 different countries who happened to be present at the sites that were attacked. The so-called "coalition of the willing" which included over thirty countries fizzled out through inadequate justification to invade Iraq and by projecting an image of rushing out like an angry mob for revenge, instead of waging a just war for self-defense.[192] When WMDs where not found in Iraq, whatever goodwill existed fizzled out. The primary justification for the war proved to be incorrect. Some people do not understand that *lies have very short legs!*

Not ready for "prime time"

As the hypothesis of conflict changed during the 1990s from the possibility of a *peer-to-peer conflict* with the Soviet Union during the Cold War to dealing with *asymmetric warfare*, the intelligence community was stretched thin, and the mix of weapons systems, equipment, and software became inadequate for the new reality.[193] Basic military transportation hardware was not designed for COIN. The Army and the Marines did not have appropriate armored vehicles like the V-shaped MRAP. DOD had to purchase "*Buffels*" (Buffalo vehicles) in a hurry from South Africa of all places! The HUMVEE, which had replaced the Jeep, was not armored and exposed troops to IED's and other weapons used by insurgents.[194] Nothing was learned from the fact that during the Vietnam War about 33 percent of all casualties were caused by mines and IEDs. The lethal effects of IEDs used by insurgents should have been known and equipment should have been designed for American forces taking this threat into account. Soldiers had to scavenge through dumps to improvise some protection to their vehicles.

A new generation of officers without prior experience (or training) in COIN were placed in command of troops facing insurgencies. Within the intelligence community (IC), the situation was similar. Although there were experienced senior analysts and operatives, despite attrition during the 1990s, at the worker bee level, there was a serious absence of language-capable experienced analysts, coupled with knowledge of tradecraft and Afghanistan and Iraq. There was little clinical understanding of the insurgencies. Policymakers complicated the situation with myopic and distorted views of the root causes of the problems faced by the troops.

Protecting the force vs. protecting the mission

As the insurgencies in Afghanistan and Iraq progressed and an increasing number of IED's were effectively used against Coalition forces, *protecting the force* became the key element of the strategy, instead of concentrating on *protecting the mission*. With very ill-defined missions, it was not clear what needed to be protected. Extending a war to protect *the force* only extends the conflict, and at the end, more casualties result from not concentrating on achieving *the mission*. Obviously, this presupposes that there is a clear mission, and it is questionable if clear goals and objectives were ever stated to define *the mission*.

Nation-building: what is it?

Very often terminology is created and used extensively without ever defining its' meaning and this happens to be the case with the obscure concept of *nation-building*. The purpose of this theory held by some American policymakers seems to be that it is possible to permanently rebuild another country as a mirror image of America, regardless of its' traditions, culture, prevailing religious views, and the desire to be transformed into something that resembles the look and feel of the warped American image portrayed by Hollywood around the world. Reshaping or molding a country into an internal state of harmony, with political stability and a viable economy is not easy, but transforming people who have cultures that differ widely from Western culture is practically impossible. In fact, attempts to achieve Utopia, may delay indigenous efforts to achieve some form of legitimacy, normalcy and a workable system of government that is based on their traditions and culture that reflect how the natives conceive their priorities. The unintended consequences of trying to put a round peg into a square hole produce the opposite rather than the intended effects of nation-building efforts.

Multiple recent examples of American attempts in nation building have not produced immediate viable results or have failed miserably. In 1994, the U.S. led a multinational force to Haiti to "reestablish law and order" and constitutional democracy. (Reestablish what law and order?) Deposed president Aristide was returned to power, and with international assistance water, sanitation, roads and power generation were improved. U.S. forces withdrew in 1996, and were replaced by other peace keepers. Nevertheless, Haiti continued to be extremely poor, and riddled with human rights abuses, corruption, crime, and poor governance. Since then the U.S. and the international community have maintained a presence or gone back to Haiti over and over again.

In 1992, NATO and UN forces intervened in Bosnia-Herzegovina to restore peace.[195] Nevertheless, the civil war continued. In 1995, under the Dayton Peace Agreement, an Implementation Force (IFOR) consisting of over 60,000 NATO troops was setup, but what was initially conceived as a temporary presence, expanded for many years with no end in sight. IFOR became a Stabilization Force (SFOR), which extended well beyond the initial estimates. As of 2015, the region continues to suffer from periodic clashes of ethnic groups, and the European Union (EU) continues to station troops together with NATO and UN technical assistance personnel.

Findings, observations, and best practices

In 2011, General Martin Dempsey, Chairman of the Joint Chiefs of Staff, requested that a study be conducted on lessons learned during the previous decade, since the events of 9/11/2001. The study was carried out by the Joint and Coalition Operational Analysis (JCOA), Joint Staff (J7). The JCOA study reviewed numerous studies conducted since 2003, and synthesized over 400 findings, observations and best practices. Among the key findings *was "the failure to recognize, acknowledge, and accurately define the operational environment, leading to a mismatch between forces, capabilities, missions, and goals."* The JCOA study pointed out that *"interagency coordination was uneven due to inconsistent participation in planning, training, and operations; policy gaps; resources; and differences in organizational culture."*[196]

The JCOA findings did not point out that prior to the invasion of Iraq in 2003, policymakers did not pay attention to what the IC and outside experts were saying, came up with their own narrative about the goals of the mission, without really defining the goals and desired end state, except in platitudes that ignored what the IC was telling them, resulting in inadequate plans and resources devoted to the mission. Similar situations affected the mission in Afghanistan, where inadequate resources were applied at the right time. The JCOA study additionally pointed out that *"establishing and sustaining coalition unity of effort was a challenge due to competing national e, cultures, resources, and policies."*[197] The enemy identified and exploited these fault lines – *remember that we could not even accept that we were facing an insurgency for a long time!* Policymakers kept on talking about GWOT, instead of accepting that we were faced with a classical COIN operation.

"Mercenaries"

The use of "mercenaries" has deep roots going all the way back to the Revolutionary War. When the war started the 13 colonies had only about 64 ships that could be organized into the Continental Navy to face the powerful British Navy. To address the shortfall, *Letters of Marque* were issued to commission "privateers" to support the war effort. Before the war ended somewhere around 1700 privateer ships were commissioned. They captured an estimated 2,280 British ships while sustaining a loss of about 1320 ships. The seamen who sailed these ships represented multiple races and nationalities, and were paid well for their work. While the average earnings for a seaman at the time was around $9 monthly, the privateers made as much as $1,000 per voyage, which could last several months. An estimated 55,000 seamen served, and an estimated 11,000 captured privateers died in British prisons.[198]

Several NATO members have a "foreign volunteer force," including France (French Foreign Legion), the UK (Gurkhas), and Spain (*La Legión*). Although these units are not called mercenaries, to avoid conflict with Article 47 of Protocol I of the Geneva Convention of 1929, they come very close, as they are recruited to fight wars for material compensation. Regardless of the names used, these forces resemble practically all the characteristics of mercenary forces. The use of armed contractors, including foreign nationals, by the U.S. is much closer to a violation of the Geneva Convention, and is illustrative of many semantic games played during war time.

The U.S. used thousands of foreign civilian contractors in Afghanistan and Iraq for non-combat support roles, such as cleaning crews, cooks, and other support roles where they did not carry weapons. The end of the draft and the creation of an all-volunteer military brought about significant changes in what members of the services do. In the old days, they peeled potatoes, cooked, washed dishes, cleaned toilets, washed their uniforms, and cut hair. For all practical purposes, the military has ended most of those menial but necessary tasks. An army of third country nationals from such low-wage countries as the Philippines, Bangladesh, Sri Lanka, Myanmar, and their Asian neighbors were hired through private contractors to carry out those tasks. While the local workforce in Afghanistan and Iraq suffered from high unemployment, instead of hiring them, the U.S. imported foreign workers. Why? In part, because *the locals could not be trusted!* They could have had links to the insurgency and present a serious internal security problem. When the people one is trying to assist cannot be trusted to perform menial support tasks, something is very wrong. If we cannot trust the locals, how in the world can we expect to be successful in *nation-building*?

Thousands of foreign contractors were hired to provide security services as guards. While deployed to Iraq in 2008-2009 with the U.S. Army Human Terrain program, the base where I worked (Phoenix) in the Green Zone of Baghdad was protected by Ugandan "mercenaries" in uniform carrying AK-47 rifles, and at night I slept at another nearby base (Blackhawk) protected in my sleep by Peruvian "mercenaries," also in uniform and carrying AK-47 rifles. That was – to say the least – very strange. The American Embassy was also protected by mostly Peruvian "mercenaries," working for a company contracted by the Department of State to provide security. Something was very wrong with that picture.[199]

I heard that there were former Chilean military commandos working for Blackwater, one of the American security guard companies, but I never ran into them. I did run into some former Chilean military sergeants employed by the company that provided guards to the American Embassy in Iraq, although most of them were Peruvian. Apparently the use of these contractors did not violate the UN Convention against the use of mercenaries adopted in December 1989 (UN Resolution 44/34, which was in force on 20 October 2001). The U.S. and many other countries have not signed the Convention.

Several of the leading companies providing security protection, including Blackwater and DynCorp, did a lot of stupid stuff that resulted in civilian casualties. Other companies, including Triple Canopy and Global Strategies, who provide similar security services to the Department of State (DOS), are somewhat better, but are close to the dictionary definition of *mercenary forces*. Incidents resulting in non-combatant casualties were caused by trigger-happy "cowboys" in their twenties with prior military experience hired to work as security guards with limited training in some of the difficult tasks normally associated with police rather than military functions. Without a doubt these contractors had to perform difficult and dangerous tasks, but inadequate recruitment and training added to the challenges they faced. The UN commissioned controversial studies that called these contractors a new form of mercenary activity.[200]

What was behind the use of private security PMC's to protect American diplomats and an army of civilian contractors working for the Department of State, the Agency for International Development (AID) and the DOD contractors? The policymakers did not want to send more troops to reduce costs, avoid political controversy, manage the challenge with an all-volunteer military, and possibly to reward some friends. A lot of money was made by contractors! Young men, a lot of them former military, made a lot of money as civilian contractors, but company executives laughed all the way to the bank. Wages of between $200,000 and $300,000 were common for young cowboys who would not have any chance of making that kind of money back home. Their selection and training was not the best, leading to multiple incidents in which innocent civilians were killed as collateral damage.

Moral and ethical contradictions

Historically, some combatants from all nationalities at some point commit atrocities in war, despite international conventions that outline what is and is not acceptable. Enhanced Interrogation techniques (EIT) used by the CIA were justified and approved by the Justice Department and senior policymakers, including the President. Members of Congress in the Intelligence Committee of the House and Senate were informed of these very limited practices. In hindsight, they may seem improper, but in the heat of the moment right after 9/11/2001 when everyone was concerned about additional attacks on the homeland, they were accepted by policymakers. In the traditional ways of Washington, everyone claims "*virginity*," and "*lack of knowledge*," while others play political games. Other things happened that were significantly more important because they took place outside of the approval channels.

In April 2004, the first accounts of mistreatment of enemy prisoners, including physical, sexual, and psychological abuse, at the Abu Ghraib prison in Iraq were made public.[201] Although the news media linked the abuse of prisoners by *rogue soldiers* to a policy of subjecting them to EITs, the perpetrators were *acting on their own*, for their own personal entertainment. Members of the 372nd Military Police Company, 320th Military Police Battalion, and the 800th Military Police Brigade were involved. Their actions were inconsistent with the high standards of conduct and ethics that military personnel are expected to observe.[202]

One of the leading abusers, an Army reservist and mastermind of the maltreatment, was a "*corrections officer*" at the State Correctional Institution in Greene County, Pennsylvania, and previously at the Fayette County Prison. At both locations he was known to have abused prisoners, and had multiple formal accusations for racial remarks and beatings.[203] The behavior exhibited in Iraq was a mirror image of widespread abuse in American prisons, as supported by contemporaneous studies made on the subject.[204] The real scandal is that prison guards in the U.S. engage in the type of behavior that surfaced in Iraq, but similar widespread activity in the U.S. does not lead to a public outcry for reform.

In September 2010, the news media carried details of how 12 soldiers attached to the 2nd Infantry Division near Kandahar in southern Afghanistan had murdered Afghan civilian non-combatants and mutilated their corpses to take "war souvenirs," in addition to using hashish. They intimidated other soldiers so that they would not denounce their actions and lied to investigators.[205] In March 2011, trophy pictures of soldiers posing with dead Afghan civilians were made public.[206] In January 2012, video was posted on *YouTube* showing several US Marines attached to the 3rd Battalion, 2nd Marine Regiment, urinating on dead enemy combatants, apparently made between March and September 2011.[207] All of these controversial violations of the *Uniform Code of Military Justice* are not historically unique, as there have always been rogue elements and are not representative of the Department of Defense.

During WWII, soldiers of the 180th Infantry Regiment killed about 71 Italian and German prisoners of war in July, 1943, in Sicily (See *Biscan Massacre*).[208] Soldiers from the M Company, 3rd Battalion, 157th Infantry Regiment, 45th Division of the U.S. Seventh Army shot and killed German soldiers guarding the Dachau concentration camp after they surrendered, as documented by U.S. Seventh Army IG investigation. The German prisoners had not been directly involved with what had gone on at the camp, and had only been assigned temporarily as the SS perpetrators of the abuses had abandoned the area.[209]

In the Pacific theater, surrendering Japanese soldiers were frequently killed, according to some reliable published accounts.[210] (Japanese soldiers routinely killed many allied prisoners of war and some American soldiers wanted to pay them back. See massacre at Palawan in the Philippines.) There are numerous reports of American troops collecting body parts as souvenirs from fallen Japanese soldiers, triggering an order to the troops threatening disciplinary action for such deeds, issued in September 1942.[211] During the Korean War American troops massacred civilian non-combatants at No Gun Ri. During the Vietnam War both sides committed atrocities. Captured American soldiers were tortured and killed by the Communists. Several American soldiers were prosecuted for killing civilian noncombatants, and at least 36 cases of war crimes were prosecuted by court-martial, resulting in at least 77 convictions. The most known cases took place on 16 March 1968 at My Lai, when somewhere between 400 and 500 civilians were massacred.[212]

Despite historical incidents in which the high standards of conduct and ethics expected of the military were violated, the U.S. has a long tradition of respecting fallen enemy combatants, and providing ethical treatment, as witnessed by the fascinating story of *Project Jennifer*, to recover the Soviet Golf class diesel electric ballistic submarine SSB k-129, which sank off Hawaii in April 1968.[213] The cause of the sinking was probably due to the malfunction of a missile. The sub carried between three and five SS-N-5 SLBMs. The crew of 97 sailors perished. It sank about 17,000 feet down hitting the bottom of the ocean floor. That's about one and a half miles down. The Soviets were not able to find it. The U.S. Navy on the other hand did, using specially equipped research submarines. The CIA joined in the search and dared to start a recovery effort based on cutting edge R&D. The result was the construction of the *Hughes Glomar Explorer*, a 63,000-ton deep-sea salvage ship especially built for this project.[214]

According to published reports, about half of the submarine was salvaged, including two nuclear-tipped torpedoes and cipher/code equipment. The remains of several Soviet sailors were recovered. After the collapse of the Soviet Union, the U.S. revealed to the Russian Government that the remains of six Soviet sailors had been recovered from the Soviet submarine in 1974. They were given a formal burial at sea, according to the standard Soviet protocol. A videotape of the formal ceremony was given to President Boris Yeltsin. It showed the ceremony, the playing of the Soviet anthem, the American and Soviet flags, and the burial at sea. It was all done in a very tasteful way, showing respect for sailors who were doing their duty and died as heroes for their country. That is an example of one of the things that separates *us* from the Communists. We beat them with our decorum, our humanity, and our respect for basic human rights.

When the IC finally traced Osama bin Laden to his hideaway at Abbottabad in Pakistan, and was taken down on 2 May 2011 by a team of Navy Seals, his body was handled with respect and buried at sea within 24 hours of his death, according to Islamic traditions. His corpse was not desecrated, despite the fact that he was the mastermind of the 9/11 terrorist acts that resulted in, at least, 2,977 victims, including at least 372 foreign nationals, all of them civilians, except 55 military personnel killed at the Pentagon. The body was taken from Abbottabad to the Bagram base in Afghanistan, and on to the aircraft carrier Carl Vinson for burial at sea, after the body was washed, wrapped in a white sheet and placed in a weighted plastic bag, Islamic rituals in English and Arabic were carried out before the body was released into the sea from a flat board.

It only takes a few unethical soldiers to destroy the reputation of all the men and women in uniform. Honorable, patriotic, and ethical rank and file members of the armed forces represent the majority of Americans in uniform. War places soldiers in dramatic and dangerous situations that affect them psychologically, particularly when faced with enemies that do not respect international conventions, purportedly target civilian non-combatants, fire on medical personnel and helicopters clearly marked with a Red Cross sign, and systematically torture and execute prisoners. Without adult supervision, young soldiers can go rogue and trigger the types of incidents that took place in Iraq and Afghanistan.[215]

Mistreatment of enemy combatants is bad enough. Mistreatment and sexual assault on your own is beyond incredible. According to a DOD report, there were over 26,000 cases on sexual assaults in the military during 2012, which is equivalent to an average of more than 70 sexual assaults daily involving military personnel. To compound the problem even more, guilty verdicts were overturn by general officers.[216] And, based on an internal Pentagon investigation, more military men than women – roughly 14,000 of the victims - were victims of sexual abuse by other men during 2012.[217] It was estimated that about 26 percent of the assaults took place in combat zones. Historically, throughout the ages these problems have existed in all military organizations, and the US is not exempted from the problem. However, the notable increase in cases of sexual assault in the U.S. military is indicative of a *serious deterioration of the culture.* As in so many areas, the trend shows that there is a serious need to *redirect the direction that the country is taking.*

The Real Cost of War

There are numerous estimates of the real cost of military operations in Afghanistan and Iraq since 9/11/2001. The Congressional Research Service as of December 2014 estimated that both wars had so cost $1.6 trillion up to that point:

- Operation Enduring Freedom (OEF) for Afghanistan and other counterterror operations: $686 billion
- Operation Iraqi Freedom (OIF)/Operation New Dawn (OND): $815 billion
- Operation Noble Eagle (ONE), enhanced security for military bases: $27 billion
- War designated funding not directly related to Iraq and Afghanistan wars: $81 billion

These numbers do not cover the future cost of care for wounded veterans, many left with handicaps that will not allow them to return to the workforce for a long time, if ever, in addition to medical costs.

These unfunded liabilities will have to be paid by future generations of taxpayers for the next 50 to 60 years. As the conflict in Iraq was rekindled in 2014, nobody knows what the final cost will be.[218] Fighting Jihad will be a "long war" which has no clear end, and no clear objectives, other than to protect the American people from nefarious actors.

Policymakers have been discussing overhauling the management of the national defense establishment for a very long time. As far back as 1986, a *Blue Ribbon Commission on Defense Management* issued a report with suggestions for improvements, which were partially implemented afterwards. However, with the end of the *Cold War* in 1991, many of the suggestions of the *Commission* became obsolete. Despite the change in objective conditions, the defense establishment was resistant to meaningful change, and so were policymakers. They came to the Epiphany after the collapse of the Soviet Union that there would be a "peace dividend," and started to cut back programs across the board, as they opined that there was justification to reduce defense expenditures.

The tragic reality that emerged during the conflicts in Afghanistan and Iraq is that the defense establishment was not ready to deal with the new problem set. The military did not have sufficient trained and experienced experts in COIN; lessons learned in the past could not be easily retrieved; it did not have the proper equipment to deal with IEDs, despite the experiences of the Vietnam War, when crude IEDs caused a high percentage of American casualties; and as witnessed by the need to rotate troops through both conflicts over and over again, showed that the size of the force was not adequate. Policymakers and military leaders bamboozled themselves into thinking that the defense establishment was ready in 2001 to deal with the challenges that emerged after 9/11. They thought that they could operate "on the cheap," without affecting the outcome. The results of poor decisions in the procurement system, planning and budgeting, training, and government-industry accountability became evident through numerous unanticipated problems. The right equipment was not available, from vehicles for troop transport to effective body armor. The problems are particularly unsettling because the country cannot afford to mismanage national defense.

So-what?

War is disorderly and chaotic drama, sprinkle with lots of stupid things. As James Madison stated, the discretionary power of the Executive to declare war can be seductive, and no nation can preserve its' freedom in the midst of continual warfare.[219] Realistic ways for paying for national defense should be incorporated into current accounts, balancing tax revenue with current expenses, instead of passing a burden to future generations of taxpayers. President Dwight Eisenhower warned in his farewell address on 17 January 1961 about the dangers posed by corporations that supply goods and services to the military and their formal and informal links to military and civilian bureaucracies and elected officials. Without a doubt national security depends on the ability of private sector R&D and ingenuity to provide the military advanced weapons systems second to none. However, these same private companies exercise unwarranted influence and frequently engage in immoral, unethical, and illegal practices, which undermine civil liberties and the democratic process. The extensive use of contractors led to considerable waste, fraud, and mismanagement.

Did we learn anything? Proposed budget cutbacks will reduce the size of the Army to about 420,000 by 2016, which will put it at its smallest size since 1939. Thousands of reservists and active duty airmen will be eliminated. The personnel of the Navy and the Air Force will be reduced. New weapon systems will be reduced. At a time when the country is facing the growth of Islamic insurgent networks these reductions are not wise. Traditional threats from Russia, North Korea, China, Iran, are growing. It will be impossible for American defense institutions to deal with multiple war fronts at the same time.

Warfighting has morphed over the years, particularly since Vietnam in the 1960s, past 4th generation warfare into the current 5th generation warfare, where there are no definable front lines, and a lot of the "fighting" takes place in unconventional and hybrid fronts through the Internet, unmanned aircrafts, and by networks of sleeper agents, "lone wolves," deranged would-be-terrorists, drug-trafficking organizations, and all kinds of criminal networks. Unconventional tactics target civilians, as well as people in uniform. The new normal has no rules. The new reality creates the need for multiple alternative capabilities, but more reliant than ever before in intelligence.

VI – DYSFUNCTIONAL ECONOMIC MANAGEMENT

Economic System: *All the elements and activities associated with production, distribution, and consumption of all goods and services; There are four types of economic systems: Primitive, Free Market or Capitalist, Planned or Socialist/Command Economic Systems, and Mixed Economic Systems.*

Impoverished America

Americans tried to fix the world while neglecting the home front, and it shows. The American economy still reigns supreme, but the future is uncertain. An estimated 46.5 million people live in poverty, and median family income continues a ten year fall.[220] Just as it was in 1965, about 15 percent of the population continues to live in poverty, despite the so-called *War on Poverty* and all the social legislation enacted since the late 1960s. Wages are flat, or retreating. In 1999-2000, the median income was $54,473. By 2011 the median income had dropped to $49,434, increasing slightly towards the end of the year to around $51,413.[221]

Panhandler on the corner of Lee Hwy and Washington Blvd in Arlington, Va. on 29 June 2013. Two years later, he is still there as of October 2015. The picture was taken by the author, No known restrictions on publication.

As of December 2013, Americans had endured 59 months of above 7.3 percent unemployment.[222] One of the consequences of high unemployment is that the unemployed and their families have lost access to employer-provided benefits, including medical, dental, vision and other types of insurance, as well as access to 401-K retirement savings plans.

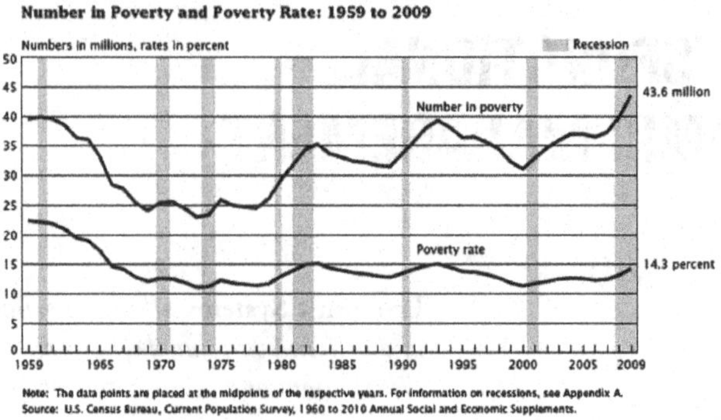

Official data from the US Bureau of the Census clearly show that the poverty rate has not changed much since 1965, despite dipping about three percentage points during the period between 1969 and 1978, and again around 1998-99 to return to around 15 percent in 2009. After the creation of numerous programs to help the poor and billions of dollars in investments in anti-poverty programs, the situation has not changed much in about 45 years.

- One in three U.S. adults have debt in collection (about 77 million people)[223]
- More companies are closing than opening[224]
- U.S. wages are down 23% since 2008 – jobs lost paid ~$61,637, and new jobs pay an average of ~$47,171[225]
- Approximately 1.3 million students in public elementary, middle, and HS, were homeless during the 2012-13 school year – an 8% increase over the previous year[226]

In Arlington, Virginia, one of the wealthiest counties in the country, located less than 5 miles from the U.S. Capitol, there are multiple panhandlers at key intersections every day of the week. For example, they are present at every corner around the East Falls Church Metro Station. Some claim to be homeless disabled veterans. Others claim to be sick and homeless. Others carry signs that say that they are homeless, unemployed, and have small children. Throughout the downtown area of the District of Columbia, there are numerous homeless living on the streets in plain view of policymakers.[227] While billions of dollars are sent overseas to places like Afghanistan, Egypt, Haiti, and Iraq for "nation building," there are Americans living in extreme poverty, about 10 percent of the bridges are in dire need of rebuilding, and the nation's infrastructure is not being maintained and expanded at the rate needed to maintain economic leadership in the world and American workers employed.[228]

It has become harder for people to enter and remain in the middle class. The gap between the wealthy and the poor has grown since 2007. The liberated spirit of the people is undermined by a dysfunctional economic system. The nation needs to reinvent itself to truly be *exceptional* and to revive the American dream that has roots that go back to 1776. Despite social programs to assist the poor, 17.2 million household or about one in seven, were food insecure in 2011, based on data from the U.S. Bureau of the Census. It is immoral to allow poverty to exist and do nothing about it, but it is more immoral to create expectations and then mismanage programs to help the poor. Perhaps James Madison, Benjamin Franklin, and Thomas Jefferson were correct in their observations about the proper role of government in helping the poor. As they observed government programs to help the poor have a way of undermining people's ability to improve their economic situation. The solution may be to make it easier for entrepreneurs to start and expand businesses and create viable jobs.

Youth idealism and hope is being torpedoed every day with potentially dangerous consequences. The cost of education and the debt that many students will carry for the first 10-20 years of employment has soared. However, educational institutions are not programmed to teach and train students for the jobs of the future.[229] There is not enough collaboration with industry to see what skill sets will be needed in the future. In the past, many Americans stayed with one employer until retirement age. This is seldom possible anymore. In order to see significant pay increases, people most change jobs and even careers several times in their lifetime and may be forced to move to another part of the country. The days of growing up in one town, working and retiring there is becoming more and more rare. There is no sense of loyalty to an organization because retirement benefits are now a thing of the past. Even the American military has new restrictive policies which do not allow soldiers to reach retirement eligibility.

To address the challenge of massive poverty government imposes taxes on the earnings of the most successful to pay for so-called anti-poverty programs, including food stamps, housing and income subsidies, health care programs like MEDICAID. Confiscation and redistribution do not accomplish anything more than providing a temporary palliative rather than attacking the root causes. This is something that several of the Founding Fathers correctly addressed 239 years ago. There is nothing wrong with assistance programs as a *temporary* measure in times of crisis, or to help the elderly, the handicapped, the sick, but not as a *permanent* way of life for people who if given the opportunity to work could take care of their own needs.

Numerous *counterculture* components introduced since the 1960s have undermined the economic system. Who wants to hire a dude speaking in gangster rap, with long hair, nose rings, tattoos, and pants without a belt and showing their underwear or the crack of their butt?[230] Traditional moral order has turned into obscene moral disorder and destructiveness. In theory, the private sector is free to function as the dynamic force in the economy, but increasingly the public sector acts like a parasite. Competition, technological innovation, lower prices, and superior management allows for the survival of the best companies. In practice the public sector exercises increasing controls over economic activity, including unnecessary bureaucratic procedures, regulations, and upsetting the concept of survival of the fittest companies.

This homeless person was on the grounds of the US Capitol, across from the US Supreme Court on 10/12/2013. As policymakers engaged in gridlock and the government the author, No known restrictions on publication.

This is a picture of a homeless person at the corner of 19th and M Streets NW, Washington, D.C. on 10/12/2013. This is another example of the hundreds of homeless

The national debt

> **The budget should be balanced, the treasury should be replenished, public debt should be reduced, the arrogance of officialdom should be tempered and controlled, and the assistance to foreign lands should be curtailed, lest our Nation become bankrupt. People must again learn to work, instead of living on public assistance.**
>
> **Marcus Tullius Cicero**
> **Circa 55 BC**[231]

On 5 August 2011 Standard and Poor's (S&P)[232] downgraded the U.S. Government's debt. Fiscal deficits and the growing national debt were obviously to blame, and the rating agency's opinion of the *Budget Control Act of 2011* fell short of what is needed to address these problems. Although the dysfunctions of the economic system have deep roots, the elements that pushed the economy to the edge of the cliff are relatively recent. Republican and Democratic administrations made serious errors of judgment and mismanaged the economy year after year, but excelled in making unintelligent moves since 2001. Many unintended consequences of programs created with good intentions have boomerang because of consistent failures to look ahead to prevent catastrophic outcomes. As of 8 November 2015, the outstanding public debt was approximately $18.6 trillion dollars. Deficit financing simply will push the economy over the cliff. As of May 2015, at least 32 of the 50 states are facing budget deficits, and numerous cities are on the edge of bankruptcy.

With the end of the *Cold War* as the Soviet Union collapsed in 1991 there was a shared hope that defense spending could be reduced. Both, President George H. W. Bush and UK Prime Minister Margaret Thatcher, discussed what they called the "peace dividend," as they hoped that spending on national defense would at least remain flat and allow for redirecting funds to social programs and infrastructure development. At the time, the U.S. faced record budget deficits.[233] In 1994, a newly elected Republican Congress forced the Clinton Administration to negotiate a bipartisan agreement to eliminate the budget deficit and start paying down the debt. What actually happened is that defense spending was reduced, but entitlement programs continued to grow, and little was done to improve public sector management.

A plan to address the national debt and balance the budget resulted from considerable bi-partisan heated discussions starting on or about 1994. Finally the *Balance Budget Act of 1997* was enacted with bipartisan support. The economy at the time was booming, unemployment was at a bare 4 percent, and in some parts of the country practically full employment was reached.[234] Federal spending as a percentage of the gross domestic product (GDP) was reduced to about 18 percent. In 1999, for the first time in a quarter of a century, Congress and the Clinton Administration produced a debt reduction plan based on projected budget surpluses, which would have eliminated the outstanding sovereign national debt, at the time amounting to about $3.8 trillion, within ten years. Some Republicans wanted to cut taxes, while some Democrats wanted to expand social welfare programs. Alan Greenspan, the Chairman of the Federal Reserve, argued in favor of retiring the debt with the surpluses, which would have further reduced the cost of government operations.[235] Instead of eliminating the debt, it has been tripled since then.

By FY 2000, a surplus of $236.2 billion was reached, although this figure was not entirely accurate due to some of the gamesmanship associated with government accounting, but it was an excellent accomplishment. Spending cuts to the defense and intelligence budgets were, without a doubt, too deep in hindsight.[236] The economy suffered a blow in March 2000 due to an irrational growth in the Internet sector and related technology fields, and the discovery of illegal accounting practices, which led to the collapse of WorldCom, Global Crossing, NorthPoint Communications, and other companies, which in turn dragged down other high technology players, and produced numerous business failures. The market value of companies traded in the stock markets fell by over $5 trillion.

President George W. Bush was elected in November 2000, with a plan to reduce taxes instead of continuing to pursue the goal of reducing the national debt. President Bush signed into law the *Economic Growth and Tax Reconciliation Act of 2001*, enacted on 7 June 2001, which lowered tax rates. As the implementation of these tax cuts were being discussed, came the attacks on the homeland of 9/11/2001. Instead of placing the tax cuts on hold, the Bush Administration and Congress went ahead and cut taxes, in part to address the economic downturn that came about after the terrorist attacks, although the economy had already started to cool down due to the bursting of the Internet bubble. Financing two wars in Afghanistan and Iraq without tax collections to support them was not wise. There were terrible miscalculations made by DOD, the intelligence community (IC), and policymakers.[237] They decided to ignore what multiple experts were saying about the escalating costs and the warnings provided before the invasion of Iraq. The basic truism that nothing can be had for free was ignored.

The economy suffered additional severe losses after the 9/11/2001 terrorist attack, which destroyed considerable infrastructure associated with the New York Stock Exchange. The relatively mild economic recession resulting from the burst of the *dot.com bubble* the previous year became a lot more complicated, with a resulting drop in previously projected government revenue. Unwisely, the *Jobs and Growth Tax Relief Reconciliation Act of 2003* accelerated tax cuts, under the premise by ultra-conservative elements that erroneously claimed that the cuts would increase government revenue and eliminate the national debt by 2010.[238]

The tax cuts produced a decline in tax collections of about 12 percent in 2002 and 2003, but the economy recovered and unemployment went down to 4.2 percent, close to the level of the late 1990s. As the economy recovered, tax collections rebounded from 2004 to 2007, increasing tax revenues by about 44 percent, until the housing bubble collapsed in late 2007. Government spending skyrocketed well beyond the increased tax collections. The gains made after the enactment of the *Balance Budget Act of 1997* in the reduction of the debt-to-GDP ratio were lost, together with the budget surplus reached in 2000.

The so-called Global *War on Terror (GWAT)*, and military operations in Afghanistan and Iraq increased government expenditures, without enacting taxes to cover defense spending, which would have received considerable support right after 9/11/2001, when the country was united behind the need to punish the perpetrators and prevent future attacks. By Fiscal Year 2005, the government was bleeding a record $364 billion in deficit spending. Supplemental budget appropriations for defense simply destroyed the hopes that existed back in 1999 of paying down the national debt. Irrational deficit spending stimulated the economy and triggered higher inflation, which in turn further increased government expenditures. By late 2008, the debt-to-GDP ratio reached almost 68 percent. The national debt doubled.

Increased defense spending was not the only action leading to larger deficits. President Bush signed into law in 2003 an expansion of MEDICARE, to include prescription drug benefits, which although well-intended and welcomed by the elderly with limited income, it was not supported with new sources of income, i.e. taxes. When the legislation went into effect in 2006, it was supported by a co-pay of $35 monthly and a $250 deductible, for a plan that paid up to $2,250 annually in prescription medicines. In general, government expenditures increased by over 52 percent during the two presidential terms of President George W. Bush, with *discretionary spending* growing by over 95 percent.

Any semblance of "Conservative" fiscal responsibility was abandoned, with the creation of over 1800 subsidy programs that were not supported by new revenue streams, which caused the deficit and the national debt to balloon. All the economic theories presented to the public were seriously flawed, in part because they did not really adhere to so-called *free market economics*. Policymakers kicked down the road the predicted economic problems, including the unfunded liabilities associated with the Social Security and Medicare programs and other entitlements resulting from the *New Deal* and the Great Society programs. Behind the scenes another serious financial crisis was building and it finally exploded around 2007: the sub-prime mortgage crisis, or "*housing bubble*."

Budgetary showdowns and brinkmanship over honoring the government's obligations are far removed from the views of the

Founding Fathers. George Washington in a 1793 message to the House of Representatives said:

> *No pecuniary consideration is more urgent than the regular redemption and discharge of the public debt; on none can delay be more injurious, or an economy of the time more valuable.*[239]

At the time of this Presidential Message in 1793, the national debt was equivalent to an estimated 32.27% of GDP and had a value of about $75 million. By 1835, the debt had been totally eliminated. During the Civil War the national debt increased to $2.7 billion. By the end of WWI, the debt had increased to $25.5 billion. As a result of WWII the national debt reached an all-time peak of 121.96% of GDP in 1946, but it rapidly declined after the war. In 1974, the national debt was again down to about 32.27% of GDP. From that point on, it increased to 69.87% of GDP in 2008 and 83% of GDP in 2010.[240] According to the Congressional Budget Office (CBO), as of mid-September 2013, the national debt was about 73% of GDP.[241]

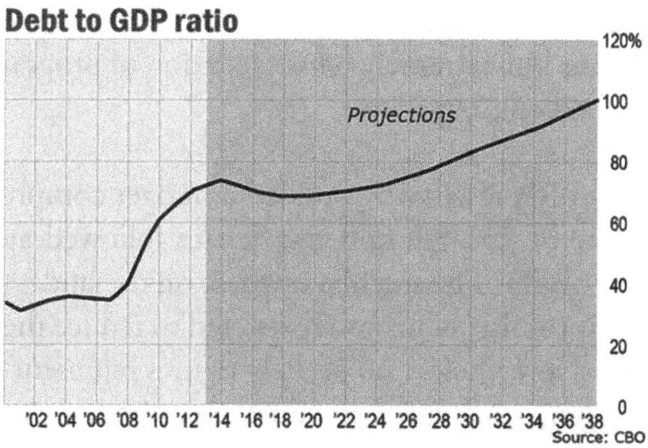

The CBO long-term national debt to GDP ratio projections and budget outlook is grim, unless action is taken to reduce government deficits. Without automatic budget cuts under the "sequester" mandated by the *Budget Control Act of 2011* the debt could potentially reach the unsustainable equivalent of 190% of GDP by 2038.

Further increases in the debt are unsustainable in the long run. The full faith and credit of the country is at stake. Policymakers have to come to terms with unsustainable entitlement programs, including Social Security, MEDICARE and MEDICAID, as well as increasing interest rate on the national debt. Pigheaded refusals to negotiate solutions put in jeopardy the future of the country. The Founding Fathers took steps to address the national debt from the Revolutionary War, including combining all the debt from the states and national government and it became a matter of national honor to pay it and establish national credit. They did not engage in rhetorical mind-games over the national debt or balanced budgets.

Despite all the gloom and doom over budget deficits, tax revenues increased in 2013, and the budget deficit was reduced in FY 2013 due to increased tax revenue, sequestration, and other reductions in government expenditures. Austerity measures started to work, although entitlement programs continue to grow. Some government programs of wealth redistribution through the tax system are unsustainable and need to be either redesigned or eliminated. Higher and higher taxes are depressing the labor market, and undermining the safety-net programs that leftist pied pipers support and causing serious dysfunctions to the economic system. The future of the country's financial system, as well as the health of the entire world-wide financial system is being wrecked by good intentions but extremely poor execution of programs with very serious unintended consequences.

The House of Representatives passed a budget compromise for FY 2014 with a vote of 332-94, and the Senate followed approving the deal by a vote of 67-33. The suicidal impasse on the budget was averted through the compromise, which was expected to reduce the deficit by at least $20 billion. Nevertheless, all of these figures represent a huge farce. They hide the large unfunded liabilities acquired through multiple government programs, as for example, pension funds, including Social Security. We continue to ignore reality and to live a dream, but sooner or later the dream will become a nightmare. According to the Congressional Budget Office (CBO), the budget deficit for FY 2014 was expected to decline to $514 billion, which will be equivalent to 3% of GDP.[242] This estimate assumes that there will be no legislation that changes the approved budget. Current baseline projections for the next ten years estimate that in FY 2015 the deficit will fall again to $478 billion, or 2.6% of GDP. However, deficits are expected to start rising again in FY 2016 and beyond, and spending goes up more rapidly than the GDP.

THE FINANCIAL REPORT OF THE US GOVERNMENT

Total Assets	$2.75 trillion
Liabilities	$18.85 trillion
Net worth	Negative $16.10 trillion (18% of GDP)
Unfunded additional liabilities	Negative $38.55 trillion (~422% of GDP)

Source: US General Accounting Office, *The Financial Report of the US Government*, 2012.

Housing crisis: 2007

The American economy has suffered from poorly evaluated decisions based on good intentions. The "housing bubble" in 2008 has its' roots in good intentions starting as far back as 1992, when President Bill Clinton announced during the presidential campaign his plan to push for more affordable housing. President George H. W. Bush had already signed into law the *Housing and Community Development Act* of 1992, which amended the charters of Fannie Mae and Freddie Mac, pushing both organizations to issue more mortgage loans to low-income families, with specific goals set annually by the Department of Housing and Urban Development (HUD). By 2007, the authors expected an increase of 55 percent in the issuance of risky loans. Thus, the ideas that eventually led to the crisis of 2008, have deep roots that go back to a bipartisan series of not-well-thought-out tinkering with what was not broken, without regard to unintended consequences, and in violation of a basic concept taught to children in a traditional nursery rhyme as far back as 1797…

Humpty Dumpty sat on a wall,
Humpty Dumpty had a great fall.
All the king's horses and all the king's men
Couldn't put Humpty together again[243]

One of the components of the plan espoused by the Clinton Administration was to entice private pension plans, which were already having their own problems, to invest in mortgage financing to lower income families. Investments by pension plans in an affordable public housing program were conceived as a safe investment that would result in great benefits for everyone. That initial idea failed, as labor unions and pension plans refused to go along, as they were already concerned about the mounting pension crisis. Nevertheless, the Clinton Administration continued its' efforts by pushing Fannie Mae and Freddie Mac, as well as banks, to provide more financing to lower income families to purchase homes.[244]

By July 2008, the predicted crisis arrived. The Treasury Department and the Federal Reserve took heroic steps in an attempt to avoid a total collapse, including considering a government takeover of Fannie Mae and Freddie Mac, but the damage had already been done. Toxic debt was widely held by many institutions who could not meet their financial obligations. Fannie Mae and Freddie Mac had to be placed into a conservatorship by the Federal Housing Finance Agency (FHFA), to be followed by lawsuits, investigations, the finding of fraud, kickbacks, conflicts of interest, mismanagement, business failures, and lots of taking heads and news media pundits discussing a crisis that they failed to address when they should have. Over 22.5 million families lost their homes to foreclosures since several government actions created the conditions that led to the collapse of the real estate market in 2008, leading to a world-wide economic crisis. Although not all of these foreclosures were linked to the *Housing and Community Development Act* of 1992, well over half of these foreclosures were beyond the average normal rate of foreclosures in the preceding 20 years.

As a result of the economic meltdown ensuing from the mortgage mess, global economic growth was affected, precipitating a sovereign debt crisis in Europe, high unemployment, a drop of in stock market prices by approximately 57 percent from the peak level of 2007, a huge loss in the net worth of American families, a dramatic increase in the number of poor people, the failure of many business enterprises, including financial institutions like Lehman Brothers and Merrill Lynch, and emergency government intervention to save other financial institutions from collapse, including AIG, Bear Sterns, several large banks, and the automotive sector.[245] Very few countries escaped the negative ripple effect of the American economic crisis.

NUMBER OF FORECLOSURES 2000-2012

Year	Number of Foreclosures	Number of home repossessions
2012	2,300,000	700,000 Estimate
2011	3,920,418	1,147,000
2010	3,843,548	1,125,000
2009	3,457,643	945,000
2008	3,019,482	679,000
2007	2,203,295	489,000
2006	1,215,304	268.532
2005	801,563	268,532
2006	640,000	
2003	660,000	
2000	470,000	
Total	21,089,690	

Sources: Source: RealtyTrac, Federal Reserve, Equifax, StatisticBrain

Heroic efforts to save the economy

Heroic efforts were made to address the sub-prime mortgage crisis, including the enactment of the *Emergency Economic Stabilization Act of 2008*, to bail out the financial system and restore confidence. Although President George W. Bush signed the bill into law, most of the action took place under the Obama Administration. The Federal Reserve committed close to $8 billion to rescue the financial system, in addition to the $700 billion committed through the *Emergency Stabilization Act* and the creation of the *Troubled Asset Relief Program (TARP).* At least 936 entities received a total of over $608 billion in government assistance, of which at least $367 billion have been paid back as of mid-September 2013.[246] The government may eventually recover most of the money and could even stand to earn a profit, but the concept goes against a basic tenant of the Capitalist system, and creates a questionable precedent which may encourage well-intentioned dumb programs in the future that will again end up in failure.

A basic tenant of the Capitalist system – a key element of traditional Conservative philosophy - is that *the right to succeed comes with the right to fail*, and perhaps, painful as it may have been, some of the entities that were bailed out should have been allowed to fail. However, if action had not been taken the economy would have plummeted even further and it is impossible to tell what the picture would have looked like.

Enter the Obama Administration in January 2009, and to deal with the economic downturn, deficit spending was increased to unprecedented levels. Everyone claimed lack of knowledge of what was going on. *Virginity!* They were all innocent. Nobody would take responsibility for the housing mess, unwise tax cuts, runaway deficits and resulting economic crisis. Policy decisions that were adopted, allegedly, to expand home ownership among the lower economic class and ethnic minorities had the opposite effect of wiping out their savings and dreams. The Obama Administration, counting with majorities in Congress enacted an economic recovery plan to be financed by additional and massive government deficit spending.

Budget deficits and the national debt ballooned again during the first administration of President Barrack Obama, approaching the size of the Gross Domestic Product (GDP), which was estimated at about $14 trillion in 2009/2010. A messy situation became messier, despite the fact that as a US Senator President Obama had rationally pointed out on a floor speech in the Senate on 16 March 2006 the problems associated with budget deficits and an increasing sovereign debt:

> *The fact that we are here today to debate raising America's debt limit is a sign of leadership failure. It is a sign that the U.S. government can't pay its' own bills. ... I therefore intend to oppose the effort to increase America's debt limit.*

Somehow the debt problem curiously looks very different depending on the peculiar angle from where it is viewed. Commonsense is the least common of the senses inside the Washington Beltway.

Under President Obama taxes were increased to the top tax earners making more than $400,000 per year, but the results were similar to what was done under the previous administration. Huge government operating deficits were covered by borrowing and printing money, which eventually could produce hyperinflation, which will hurt people with limited income and retired people who do not have their pensions indexed for the true cost of inflation. The tax increases, bleeding of the Federal budget, and unparalleled increases in the national debt led to the creation of the *Tea Party* movement in 2010, and the election of a new wave of Conservative Republicans to office.

The next crisis could be generated by the Federal Reserve's policy of purchasing mortgage-backed securities (MNSs) and U.S. Treasury securities monthly since the crisis of 2008 to stabilize the financial system. By September 2013, the Federal Reserve Board had acquired over $2 trillion in U.S. Treasury securities and over $1l3 trillion in MBSs, for a combined total of over $3.4 trillion. Printing money to cover these huge amounts of debt could trigger hyperinflation and weaken the economy further.

Guns and Butter: Not for free

Reagan proved deficits don't matter...[247]

Vice President Richard Cheney

The *"good life"* cannot be had for free. Policymakers consistently mismanage government programs and do not link current expenditures and projected expenditures to projected tax revenues. They act as if they are expecting that funding miraculously will appear to cover the costs of their mismanagement. Without a doubt, national security is a priority because the very existence of the country depends on deterrence that can only exist with a military that is second to none, and able to defeat enemies in conventional and unconventional warfare, including asymmetric conflicts, cyber-attacks, and terrorism. The attacks of 9/11/2001 were in part the result of unwise budget cuts affecting the intelligence community. Nevertheless, defense spending could be cut by eliminating duplication, mismanagement, corruption, and abuse.

As the nation ages, demographics have to be taken into account to protect the elderly with viable retirement programs and affordable health care. Without support to education and R&D, the future health of the economy is at risk. It is unrealistic to continue to add more and more government programs that deviate from the basic role of government starting with what is constitutionally mandated, and what is reasonably added because the world has changed in the past two hundred years.

Numerous entitlement programs have to be rationalized, eliminating the ones that do not work or are duplicative of other programs. Social Security needs to be placed on sound footing based on facts not fiction. Health care is perhaps the most critical area after Social Security, in part because it covers about 21 percent of GDP, and because it is in many ways a fallacy to think that society will let millions of people go without treatment. Society as a whole ends up paying for the uninsured in one way or another, so it makes sense to come up with a viable program.

Health Care

Rather than dissecting the health care challenge into manageable components in which there is bipartisan agreement, as for example, outlawing denying insurance coverage to people with so-called pre-existing conditions, the Obama Administration counting on majorities in the Senate and House of Representatives enacted a complete overhaul of the system, the *Patient Protection and Affordable Care Act* (PPACA – known as *Obamacare*), on 23 March 2010. Many of the provisions were not carefully studied, and the law was enacted without due analysis of potential unintended consequences. On 28 June 2012, the Supreme Court upheld the constitutionality of PPACA/Obamacare, but the implementation is complicated by numerous unintended effects, including the loss of employment or reduction in work hours of workers by employers to avoid certain provisions of the legislation that would render their businesses unprofitable. Precisely due to the multiple complications associated with healthcare reform previous attempts failed. Instead of separating specific areas of reform for which there was bipartisan support and clear solutions, the enactment of a comprehensive plan complicated the subject.

As the baby boom generation reached retirement age in 2012, around 10,000 people began to retire every day. As they aged, baby boomers will require medical care at an increasing pace. As demand increases, the number of physicians is declining, and as many older physicians retire, there are few new ones to take their place. At the same time, the population is expanding, making the shortage of medical professionals even more acute in the coming years.

For example, there is a shortage of nurses. Community colleges and colleges should be actively involved in training an adequate number nursing professionals with government support to address the shortage, yet hardly anything is being done about it. With so many people unemployed, there should not be any need to import foreigners to clear bed pans, clean hospitals, clinics, and nursing homes. Visit a few nursing homes and take a look around and see if you find any native-born Americans working at these facilities other than in administration. Even the physicians and nursing staff are foreigners. (More on this subject will be covered on Chapter IX – *The Immigration Debate.*)

Redistribution of wealth

The 18th century American Revolution predates the development of Socialist ideologies. The Founding Fathers shared egalitarian ideas emanating from Judeo-Christian ethics, moral traditions and values, and secular ethics and concepts of right and wrong. They wanted to reduce human suffering and promote well-being. Regardless of the root of their ideology, religious or secular, they wanted to redress the human condition, but in ways that differ from 20th and 21st century agendas for redistribution of wealth. For the Founding Fathers the society they were creating would be fairer, more humane, and less cruel. However, as James Madison put it, *"charity is no part of the legislative duty of the government."*[248] But that was then, and this is now. We are in the 21st Century, not the 18th century.[249]

Socialist ideas surfaced in the 19th century, and some have been adopted. The challenge now is to find a middle ground between the views of the Founding Fathers and all the legislation enacted since the 1930s to help the needy, with a four key variable in mind: Is it necessary and is it affordable? Does it work? Can it be amended to make it work better? If it does not work, fails a cost/benefit analysis, and cannot be fixed, then get rid of it. The dysfunctional economy cannot be blamed solely on Socialist ideas, but on lack of planning, poor execution of programs, and serious unintended consequences of implementing altruistic ideas without fully analyzing the potential outcomes. The *screw up fairy* has to be kicked out of Washington! It is impossible to avoid her visits once in a while, but she should be encouraged to take up residence somewhere else.

Political gridlock

Political gridlock led to the creation of the concept of "*sequestration*," or automatic spending cuts which were mandated under the *Budget Control Act of 2011*, which were set to start on 1 January 2013, if an austerity plan was not worked out prior to that time.[250] Across the board cuts of about $85 billion from Fiscal Year 2013 through 2021 mandated under sequestration are not realistic.[251] Taxes are a necessary evil, but they should be levied in such a way that they do not kill the goose that lays the golden egg. Taxes should not strangle the entrepreneurial spirit that is a basic component of the free enterprise system and the economy.

At the state, county and municipal level, government debt and unfunded liabilities are a serious problem, but the situation is not the same across the country. Thirty seven (37) state constitutions have provisions requiring balanced budgets, but each state has its' own peculiar definition of what constitutes a "balanced budget" and how debt financing can be structured for capital expenditures and multi-year major projects. Unlike the Federal Government, states cannot print currency or issue debt obligations without a revenue stream to repay the debt. All the states except Vermont have some form of requirement to operate with balanced budgets. Nevertheless, state governments have a cumulative debt that surpasses $4 trillion, including many unfunded pension liabilities for state employees. California has a debt of over $700 billion; New York is second, with a debt of over $350 billion. Texas has a debt estimated at over $283 billion, New Jersey's debt is estimated at over $182 billion, and Illinois has a debt of at least $150 billion. Policymakers do not have any idea of how they will meet these obligations, but continue to pile up more liabilities.

At the municipal level, there is an estimated debt of at least $2 trillion, most of it resulting from fiscal mismanagement, unfunded liabilities associated with pension and health plans for city workers and retirees, bonds associated with costly Pharaonic projects, and reductions in the tax base due to social disorganization and crime, leading to resident flight. At least twenty seven (27) municipalities have filed for bankruptcy between January 2010 and June 2014, including San Bernardino, CA, Stockton, CA, Harrisburg, PA, Jefferson County, AL and Detroit, MI. Among the cities facing budget shortfalls are Cincinnati, OH, Camden, NJ, New York, NY, Chicago, IL, Baltimore, MD, San Francisco, Los Angeles, San Jose and San Diego, CA. The strategy to deal with the problem is similar. They are shutting down recreation and community centers, libraries, schools, fire department and police stations, cutting employees and reducing services. They are increasing property taxes, installing speed sensors and red-light cameras to raise money, which in turn irritate people and push them out to suburbia, which in turn further reduces the tax base in a vicious cycle. People feel that they are being ripped off in multiple ways to generate revenue.

What is eminently clear is that politicians of both parties are unable to explain convincingly their views on budget deficits and the national debt, or how they would deal with both challenges. The U.S. Government collects annually more taxes than any other country in history, but spends over $1.1 trillion more than it takes in. The top 5 percent income earners pay 59% of all income taxes, the bottom 50 percent of people (earning less than $33,000) pay less than 3 percent of all taxes collected, but left-wing agitators accuse the top income earners of not paying their fair share. If a majority of people are living off the tit of the state, they will vote for candidates for public office that promise to continue them on the *Gravy Train*, completely undermining the democratic process.

Unfunded liabilities

The earlier discussion of fiscal deficits and the size of the sovereign debt does not include all the unfunded liabilities of the government at all levels, particularly liabilities linked to pension funds. The estimate of unfunded liabilities could be at least $60 trillion, but the actual amount could be much higher. Government retirement programs resemble a series of Ponzi schemes. A classical Ponzi scheme is a pyramid investment swindle in which supposed profits are paid to early investors from money invested by later participants. Hypothetically, when the Social Security and associated programs were created, a population pyramid would exist forever into the future, with few older people at the top, supported by a wide younger and growing population at the base of the pyramid.

Life expectancy at birth in 1935 (both sexes, all races) was 61.7 years. By 1950, it had increased to 68.2 years. By 1980, life expectancy had increased to 73.7, and by 2010, it had increased again to 78.7 years. With people living longer, the number of people collecting a pension has increased well beyond the original calculations. At the same time, American families became smaller, as they elected to have fewer children. The program began to resemble a Ponzi scheme, in which the original investors collected their retirement, but future generations of retirees may not be able to collect their full pensions.

Since 1990 alone, reproduction rates declined overall to below replacement level. The fertility rate was estimated at 2.01 per woman, when to replace the population a rate of at least of 2.1 is needed. After WWII, there was a baby boom starting in 1946. In 2011, the babies that were born in 1946 reached age 65. From 2012 on, every year another wave of members of the post-war baby boom will be reaching retirement age, and since the population has not been growing, there will be fewer and fewer young working people paying into the Social Security fund. As a result, the looks of the population pyramid began to change. As time passes, there are more and more people at the top, and fewer young people at the bottom. to support the older retired population.

There are solutions, but policymakers don't seem willing to take steps to deal with the challenge. They continue to increase Social Security payroll taxes by moving the cap slowly. The cap in 2008, 2009, and 2010 was left at 6.2 percent of income up to a maximum limit, which is moved up every year. In 2009 and 2010, the cap was on gross wages was $106,800 (Social Security Wage Base), resulting in a maximum tax of $6,621.60. The wage base went up to $110,000 in 2011, $113,700 in 2013, and $117,000 in 2014. (The maximum payroll tax in 2014 is $7,254.) It is projected to go to $119,100 in 2015. This is one way to address the shortfall of funds in the Social Security program, but more changes are needed.

Median income for a family in 2007 was $49,777, according to the Bureau of the Census, often with more than one family member working. What is median income? *Median income is the amount which divides the income distribution into two equal groups, half having income above that amount, and half having income below that amount."* Often, more than one family member works, and each one pays the Social Security payroll taxes. People who earn more than the wage base, are not taxed the 6.2 percent on income earned beyond the cap. Maximum benefit payments are also capped. People who earn large incomes maintain their right to a retirement, but that retirement is capped for everyone based on the amount workers and their employers paid into the system. A person who earns $200,000 in income in 2014 will pay Social Security taxes up to the cap of $117,000. If that high-income person retires in 2014, the pension would be based on the amount paid, or $2,642. (The average gross monthly benefit in 2014 for a single person is $1,294.)

President Richard Nixon, a Republican, proposed to increase benefits under Social Security. In a special message to Congress on Social Security dated 25 September 1969, Nixon requested a ten percent increase, in addition to attaching a schedule to the cost of living to provide "peace of mind to those concerned with their retirement years, and to their dependents." At the time, there were about 25 million people receiving cash payments from the program, and about 92 million workers were contributing to the program. To pay for the increase in payments, Nixon proposed an annual gradual increase in worker contributions starting in 1972, to strengthen the system and keep future benefits related to the growth of worker wages, and to meet part of the cost of increased coverage, and from then on the base would automatically be adjusted to account for inflation.[252]

Congress increased Nixon's proposal to a 20 percent increase in monthly payments. On 22 May 1970, Nixon issued a statement praising the House of Representatives for passing the bill expanding coverage, and issued another statement praising Congress again on 18 May 1971 for further increases to the scope of the original Social Security plan, including a plan to create 200,000 new public sector jobs for people on welfare, and issued another statement on 22 June 1971 praising the House approval of the Welfare Reform and Social Security bill. Then, on 28 December 1971, he signed into law H.R. 10604, amending the Social Security Act, including an extension of Medicaid benefits to assist the medically indigent. On 3 January 1974, Nixon signed H.R. 11333, with additional benefit increases, including supplemental security income benefits for the aged, blind, and disabled.[253]

As in so many other areas, there is a *united state of amnesia* about important historical events. If President Roosevelt was responsible for the enactment of Social Security back in the late 1930s, President Nixon expanded the original program substantially between 1969 and 1974. Neither party can claim a monopoly in the enactment of social legislation to help the poor, the elderly, and the disabled. Both parties are responsible for actions that built in *system failure*, by not paying attention to the fiscal responsibility for sustaining the programs based on actuarial information and basic common sense. Thirty years later, as the first wave of "baby boomers" born in 1946 reached retirement age the sins of the past are knocking on the door.

What happened to the contributions to the Social Security fund? Well… the funds were not put in a "locked box" or invested so they would grow. Instead, like in a Ponzi scheme they were used to pay grandparents and the parents of the baby boom generation their pensions, just as in a classical pyramid fraud. The early investors took back their original investment and more, and the later investors are in trouble. To compound the problem, the Federal Government began to borrow from Social Security funds to pay for current expenses and issued bonds (IOUs) to the Social Security Administration.

The population has increased by about one million immigrants annually since 2000. The idea behind has been that young immigrant workers would help to make up for the low birth rate of American women. The problem is that the immigrants bring along their elderly parents, who often end up collecting Social Security (SSI), without ever having contributed to the program. If they entered the country legally, they are covered. The way it works is that the younger legal immigrants get a job, establish economic *bona fides*, and request visas for their parents signing a document by which they promise to take care of their needs. However, after the parents have been in country legally for five years, they can apply for SSI, even if they never worked and contributed to Social Security. Even if they do not become citizens, as long as they are in the country legally, they can receive about $700 monthly from the SSI program. Their children do not have to honor the document they signed pledging to take care of their parents after five years. If they become incapacitated and destitute in their old age, the government picks up the tab for placing them in nursing care or hospices. At to the fact that many immigrants work in construction and are paid in cash, they underreport their earnings and pay much less in Social Security taxes that they should.

There are other serious problems associated with government pension plans for employees at all levels of government. At the Federal level, each government agency receives an operating budget, which is used to pay for all expenses, including the wages of the employees of each agency. Upon the retirement of the employees, the administration of the pensions is passed to the Office of Personnel Management (OPM). Each agency is not required to put away a portion of their "current operating budget" to fund the liability associated with the retirement of the employees of the agency. That burden is passed on – unfunded- to the OPM.

In a normal 20-25 year career, government employees pay between $100,000 and $130,000 through payroll deductions to their retirement plan. Once they retire, in two or three years they will have been paid back all the money they put in. From then on, the government has to pay the retirements from current operations for 10 to 30 years, plus survival benefits for the spouses. Because the government agencies were not required to set aside money to fund the pension liability, nobody cared about the problem, since OPM will have to deal with the subject eventually. *Don't worry, be happy… deal with today… who cares about tomorrow!*The old pension system was reformed in 1987, forcing Federal employees to contribute to Social Security in addition to their government retirement plan, but as we already explained, that does not solve the problem with both systems in jeopardy.

At the state and local level, if workers are covered by a government-sponsored pension plan, each worker pays into that plan, but is exempted from paying for Social Security. If the government pension plan fails, the workers are damaged not only due to the failure of their retirement plan, but also because they are not covered by Social Security because they never contributed to the program. At the Federal level, this issue was resolved in 1987, when new employees were required to participate in both, the government retirement, as well as Social Security.

At the county, municipal and state levels, the situation is critical in many jurisdictions, depending on the management of the pension programs. With the advent of government employee unions and collective bargaining, pension plans have been instituted that often go beyond the government's ability to pay. In difficult economic years, often money is not put into the retirement plans. In other cases, the management of the funds has been unusually bad. In other cases, the fund managers did not understand the investments they were making and ended up losing lots of money. For example, before the housing bubble, they invested in schemes that used mortgages that were illogical and basically unsecured as collateral. When the bubble burst in 2008, huge amounts of money were lost, leaving the pension plans in many counties, municipal, and state governments with a huge mess and unfunded liabilities.

Some states operate their pension plans with sounder management and have avoided these problems, but the vast majority is in trouble, including large states like New York and California. The much-criticized decision of both, the Bush and Obama administrations to intervene to save the financial system, was in part necessary in order to save many pension plans that would have gone under otherwise. They may go down the drain anyway, but for other reasons.

According to a study by Boston College Center for Retirement Research, based on a survey of 126 state and municipal pension programs found that as of 2011, they were similarly unfunded by approximately $1 trillion.[254] Add to this amount the unfunded pensions for the military and for federal employees, as well as Social Security. Add to the number the unfunded liability to take care of wounded veterans who will need health care and income support forever. Add to the number the unfunded liability to support their families. The figure is much larger than the approximately $17 billion in sovereign date of the national government. The potential train wreck gets closer and closer as each day passes and nothing is done to study the problem and come up with solutions.

$9.6 TRILLION UNFUNDED LIABILITY

As of June 2013, the Social Security Board of Trustees estimated that the program faced $9.6 trillion in unfunded liabilities covering the next 75 years (2087). In other words, the program has promised benefits to people now alive, despite a shortage of revenues to cover the benefits.[255]

There are viable alternatives to the way Social Security functions. For example, the so-called Chilean model, which takes the 10 percent taken from payrolls, just as the it is currently done in the US, but instead of the government making use of the money, it is invested in the stock market. Each worker has his/her own personal account, and can track how the investments are doing. During the 30+ since 1981, years that this program has been in place, the system has produced enough profits to provide workers when they retired about 87 percent of the money they were earning while working. About 73 percent of the money has been earned from profits earned by the investments, and the rest from returning the original contributions. This model replaced a previous similar to the U.S. Social Security system and shared some of the same problems. Since its' inception in 1981, around thirty other countries have copied the Chilean model. Despite normal stock market ups and downs, the privatized system has steadily produced excellent returns on investments through cost-averaging.

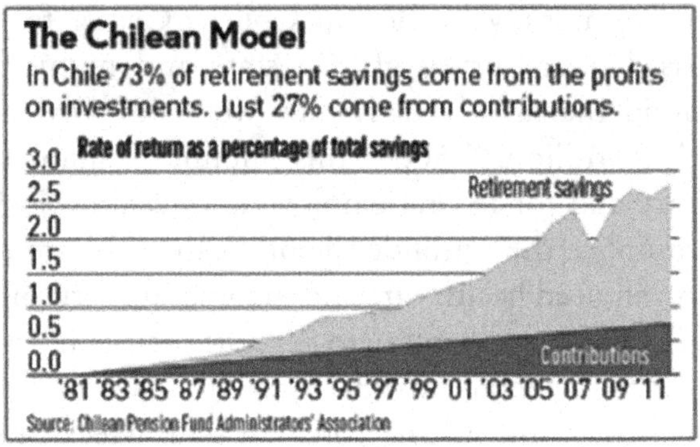

Sources: Chilean Pension Fund Administrator's Association, and Investor's Business Daily, "Yes, Chile's Private Pension Model Works, Big Time," 26 September 2013.

The public must be weaned away from the entitlement mentality. Ignoring the problem or overblowing the problem to make it sound like total gloom and doom, is not a solution. This situation will become very "flammable" in a few more years when it becomes clear that the funds are not there to meet the commitments that have been made to the aging population.

Fraud, waste and corruption

The incidence of fraud, waste and corruption in government is stunning. What is even more impressive is that a lot of it is hidden behind a *façade* of patriotism and national defense needs. The kleptocracy resembles the multi-headed serpent-like *Lernaean Hydra* of Greek mythology, but the political system has failed to produce a Hercules to confront and slay the beast. Corruption undermines American's faith in government and demoralizes and destabilizes the culture. The Government Accountability Office (GAO) came to the conclusion in 2006 that overhauling *Federal Financial Management* was crucial to reduce the long-term fiscal imbalance.[256] The first step in the overhaul process is to fund an expand auditors and Inspector General

Operations throughout the government. Despite recent successes in dismantling MEDICARE fraud, for example, many more fraudulent operations ripping off this program alone would save taxpayers a lot of money. And then… there is DOD.

Three days before leaving office President Dwight D. Eisenhower in a famous speech warned about what could be conceived as the Hydra's one "immortal head" that requires special treatment, the so-called *Military-Industrial Complex*. President Eisenhower described it this way: *In the councils of government, we must guard against the acquisition of unwarranted influence, whether sought or unsought, by the military-industrial complex. The potential for the disastrous rise of misplaced power exists and will persist.*[257] Like the mythical beast, when Inspector General and other counter-corruption prosecutors cut off one of the heads of the Hydra, for each head cut off, it grows two more even more virulent heads. In the DOD procurement world, subcontractors and multiple agents mask considerable corruption, including payoffs and kickbacks, and multiply like the head of a Hydra. The rackets never get truly smashed as they should be, in part because the perpetrators are too big to fail. They act as if they are exempt from all laws and regulations that apply to everybody else in the country.

According to a DOD report dated 20 October 2011, and reproduced in the website of U.S. Senator Bernie Sanders (I-VT) practically all the large defense contractors have engaged in "*systematic fraudulent behavior*." According to the report, DOD paid $573.7 billion in the past ten years to more than 300 contractors involved in civil fraud cases that resulted in judgments of over $1 million, $398 billion of which was awarded after settlement or judgments of fraud. When awards to parent companies are counted, "DOD paid over $1.1 trillion in the past ten years just to the 37 top companies engaged in fraud." The report went on to point out that another $255 million went to 54 contractors convicted of hard-core criminal fraud.[258] Somehow they get away with it!

Lockheed Martin, for example, is not only the top DOD contractor; it is also at the top of the list of companies that have been caught in fraudulent activity, with at least 59 cases of documented corruption since 1995, resulting in fines, penalties and settlements worth over $606 million dollars.[259] In 2000, the Department of State fined the company $13 million for a violation of the *Arms Control Export Act* linked to the illegal transfer of sensitive information to China related to space launches.[260] The number of bribery scandals involving Lockheed goes way back to the 1950s, and not only involves domestic wrongdoing, but expands to its' international operations, which has resulted in scandals in Germany, Italy, the Netherlands and Japan involving the sale of military and civilian aircraft, which resulted in multiple violations of the *Foreign Corrupt Practices Act.* At the state and county level, the company has also built a reputation for questionable practices to avoid paying taxes.[261] Lockheed Martin has been found guilty in multiple investigations of violations of racial and age discrimination by the Equal Employment Opportunity Commission (EEOC). In 2008, Lockheed Martin was paid $10.5 million "to settle charges that it defrauded the government by submitting false invoices on a multi-billion dollar contract connected to the Titan IV space launch vehicle program.[262]

After 9/11/2001 DOD contracting doubled to about $400 billion annually by 2008, as compared to defense spending during the 1990s. Nevertheless, there was a drop of 76 percent in the number of fraud cases referred to the Department of Justice for criminal prosecution during the George W. Bush Administration. According to an FBI report, the number of DOD procurement fraud cases dropped from 213 in 2001 to only 86 in 2008. Nevertheless, criminal activity continued and increased, including numerous cases involving contracting in support of the wars in Afghanistan and Iraq.[263] As the DOD *Report to Congress on Contracting Fraud* prepared for Senator Sanders, criminal activity was considerable, but investigators and prosecutors did not seem to be properly staffed and pushed to protect the interests of taxpayers.

After 9/11/2001, to the end of 2011, the U.S. Government had spent over, over $770 billion dollars on private contractors to support military operations and construction projects in Afghanistan and Iraq. Corruption has been widespread. To address the problem the *International Contract Corruption Task Force* (ICCTF) was set up in 2006 to investigate and prosecute American companies and individuals suspected of corruption.[264] In addition, the *Special Inspector General for*

Afghanistan Reconstruction (SIGAR) and the *Special Inspector General for Iraq Reconstruction* (SIGIR) were created to provide additional resources to investigate and prosecute contract law violators. Based on estimates made public by these investigative units, more than $30 billion in taxpayer funds were lost to waste and fraud. Numerous investigations came to similar conclusions about inadequate planning, unsustainable projects, waste, fraud, bribery, and corruption in the construction of hospitals, clinics, schools, roads, and support services for American troops, civil servants, and civilian contractors. Numerous military officers have been convicted for bribery associated with the awarding of contracts to American and foreign suppliers.[265]

Afghan and Iraqi corruption is endemic, but it was enhanced by American corrupt contractors. According to the *Commission on Wartime Contracting in Iraq and Afghanistan*, as much as $60 billion were lost to contract fraud and abuse since the 2001 incursion into Afghanistan and the invasion of Iraq in 2003.[266] The political will for implementing anti-corruption reform has been lacking, and as a result, the credibility of the entire system is undermined. An ethical compass is needed to truly put the system in the right direction and address citizen complaints about misconduct throughout government, and decreasing incentives for engaging in illegal activity.

The suicidal regulatory environment

The business community has been tied in regulatory knots for years. The huge number of irrational regulations has become an obstacle to progress. There are at least 31 government agencies that enforce the regulatory framework. The more regulations, the more that government has to grow to enforce them. A regulatory framework that stifles private investment and economic growth is suicidal. Although environmental regulations are increasing exponentially, the problem affects many other areas of the economy, with and without justification. Every regulation on the books should be re-evaluated to identify those that are truly justified to protect the public and eliminate those that do not produce any discernable benefit.

THE REGULATORY MESS

There are at least 32 government agencies that have some kind of regulatory authority. Some regulations are mandated through legislation, while other regulations are drafted and enforced by the agencies without involvement by elected officials. There is nothing intrinsically wrong with regulations. They exist to protect society, the echo system, facilitate commerce and other important areas. However, excessive regulations generated by political extremists are a hindrance to progress and undermine the entire regulatory system.

1. Agency for Toxic Substances and Disease Registry
2. Bureau of Ocean Energy Management, Regulation and Enforcement
3. Center for Food Safety and Applied Nutrition
4. Centers for Disease Control and Prevention
5. Commodity Futures Trading Commission
6. Consumer Product Safety Commission
7. Drug Enforcement Administration
8. Endangered Species Program
9. Environmental Protection Agency
10. Fair Housing and Equal Opportunity
11. Federal Aviation Administration
12. Federal Communications Commission
13. Federal Maritime Commission
14. Federal Mine Safety and Health Review Commission
15. Federal Motor Carrier Safety Administration
16. Federal Transit Administration
17. Fish and Wildlife Service
18. Food and Drug Administration
19. Grain Inspection, Packers and Stockyards Administration
20. International Trade Commission
21. Interstate Commerce Commission
22. Marine Mammal Commission
23. Migratory Bird Conservation Commission
24. Nuclear Regulatory Commission
25. Occupational Safety and Health Administration
26. Office of National Drug Control Policy
27. Office of the Comptroller of the Currency
28. Pension Benefit Guaranty Corporation
29. Pipeline and Hazardous Materials Safety Administration
30. Postal Regulatory Commission
31. Securities and Exchange Commission
32. Surface Mining, Reclamation and Enforcement

Economic and Political "System Integrity"

The most important aspect of a country's economic system is its' unimpaired integrity, soundness, and freedom to function without absurd and excessive government regulations. This includes the relative ease of obtaining permits to start a new business, the burden placed on business by the regulatory environment, transparency, clear rules, and accountability. The perceived and real level of corruption or wholesomeness of a system is key determinants of the viability of an economy. An economy should be judged not only in terms of production and consumption of goods and services, but also on the wealth represented by the labor force and its' culture, values, education, political structure and its' legal system.

Unpleasant as it may be for ultranationalists, *the U.S. is not the top-ranked country in basic economic freedom*. Promoting the myth of "*exceptionalism*" in this area is not accurate. The U.S. is ranked #17, has lost ground in the past few years, and is scored behind Hong Kong,[267] Singapure, New Zealand, Switzerland, United Arab Emirates, Mauritius, Finland, Bahrain, Canada, Australia, and the UK. According to the *Index of Economic Freedom* produced by The Heritage Foundation and *The Wall Street Journal* ranks the U.S. as #10 in the world.[268] Historically, the U.S. has scored better, between #5 and #7. Countries with top ranking in economic freedom generally enjoy the top per-capita GDP in the world, in addition to more investments, lower unemployment and top life satisfaction.[269] They generally have lower top marginal income and payroll tax rates, less government regulations, a better legal system of property rights, and make it easier for entrepreneus to start a new business. Limitations in freedom are irreconcilable with a well-functioning economic system.

Corruption and cronyism undermine the integrity of political institutions. From political party bosses and patronage to financial contributions in exchange for championing business interests, and corruption in politics has been has been central to American politics for a very long time.[270] Corruption distorts government operations and reduces efficiency, as regulations and piled on top of more regulations, in part to cater to one or another interest group. Naturally the U.S.

ranking in the *Index of Economic Freedom* suffers. Members of both political parties have been found guilty of curruption going all the way back to the 1870s. The problem just got worse after the 1960s.

Since the organizations behind the *Index of Economic Freedom* are generally regarded to be right-of-center politically, their findings should be compared with the findings of more impartial European "thinktanks," as for example, the *Democracy Index*, compiled by *The Economist Intelligence Unit*, which measures the state of democracy in 166 countries based on 60 variables. The U.S. was ranked #21 on the list, in part due to poor political participation, because the American electorate has a low voter turnout for elections.

Transparency International's *Corruption Perceptions Index for 2012* ranked the U.S. as #19, behind Denmark, Finland, New Zeland, Sweden, Singapore, Switzerland, Australia, Norway, Canada, Netherlands, Iceland, Luxenboug, Germany, Hong Kong, Barbados, Belgium, Japan, and the UK.[271] The Index was published by the European Commission. In the variable of *e-Government Readiness*, which evaluates "*transparency*" as a function of openness, communication, and accountability in delivering government information and services to citizen, the U.S. does not score very well. The lack of direction, including the dysfunctions of the economic system are linked to the low voter participation in U.S. elections.

One potential problem with majority rule and democracy is that if everyone did show up on election day, the lower income earners could potentially create even more dysfunctions in the economic system. When over 40 percent of the population is receiving some form of government assistance, it would be easy for pied pipers to make promises of additional government largess, and promote class warfare. Mob rule is not a fictional impossibility when just about every American is affected by the dysfunctions of the economic system, the number of poor people expands, unemployment remains high, and and the median income retreats year after year.

ECONOMIC FREEDOM DWINDLING

According to the 2014 *Index of Economic Freedom,* the U.S. dropped out of the top ten most *economically free countries*. Countries with the higher ratings outperform others in economic growth and long-term prosperity. Countries with the lowest rating normally are affected by high unemployment, deteriorating social conditions and economic stagnation. The U.S. has been steadily losing standing as one of the top economically free countries. The size of the U.S. sovereign debt and government deficits influences the country's standing, as these are signs of economic problems, including a reduction in economic freedom.[272]

The *Organization for Economic Cooperation* (OECD) and the *New America Foundation* made an assessment of higher education in the U.S. for the purpose of providing an outsider's view on the challenges to American competitiviness.[273] According to the report made public in July 2013, the U.S. needs to pay more attention to quality, coherence, and transparency if the country is to continue to be a leader in postsecondary education. According to the study, one in three American jobs will require Career and Technical Education (CTE), but increasing costs, widely varying quality standards, and other issues present risks for future competitiveness.[274] According to the report, the previous generation of Americans had one of the highest levels of both high school and post-secondary attainment in the world, but the situation has deteriorated and the current generation is challenged by higher skills in competing countries.

According to the OECD report, despite many outstanding features, the U.S. needs to improve post-secondary CTE, career-focused associate degrees, post-secondary certificates, and industry certifications. High school graduates are relatively weak when compared with other OECD countries. Post-secondary education needs more quality assurance. Quality standards for certification and accreditations of schools should to be revised. Students are marketed by schools to participate in programs that do not really qualify them to join the workforce. The OECD recommended better workplace training and partnerships between CTE institutions and employers to help graduates transition into employment. As compared to OECD countries, American students invest in post-secondary education but the return on investment is dubious due to many programs of questionable value.

Despite a high per pupil investment, the average American adult has lower basic skills in math and literacy than other countries. The U.S. ranks 16th out of 23 countries in literacy and 14th in problem-solving in technology-rich environments. Adults in Australia, Canada, Finland, Japan and other countries have significantly higher basic skills than Americans in everyday tasks. Without a doubt the integrity of the economic system is affected when the U.S. ranks fairly low as compared to other countries in basic skills of the workforce, despite a huge per capita investment in education.

Mounting Trade Deficits

After about 75 years of steady trade surpluses, the U.S. has suffered 40 years of unsustainable trade deficits since 1975. The bleeding of wealth out of the U.S. has to be stopped somehow, as a critical component of any plan to reenergize the economy. There has been considerable philosophical debate over the significance of trade deficits, with a tendency to believe that the problem would take care of itself. However, "free markets" are a fiction of the imagination. There is a common sense principle that indicates that every institution and individual should live within its' means. Just as the public sector has to balance the budget, the nation has to at least reach trade equilibrium or balance.

Around six hundred years ago European rulers established colonies all over the world to obtain raw materials and reduce their dependence on foreign suppliers. The colonies served as markets for finished goods. European rulers understood the basic principle that it was essential to export more than was imported. This basic principle for the prosperity and security of a state was the basic component of what was denominated *Mercantilism.*[275] The concept was challenged by Adam Smith (1723-1790), who proposed free trade and competition as a way to reduce costs and promote economic development. Smith believed that the lowest cost producer should prevail, and government should not intervene in the economy.

Smith promoted the principles of *laissez-faire*, but within reason. His views were part of the basic rationale for Americans to seek independence. Together with John Locke (1632-1794), Voltaire (1694-1778), and Rousseau (1712-1778), Smith's ideas were picked up by Américan revolutionaries who incorporated them to the basic economic plan for an independent country. Locke theories about the "laws of supply and demand" that cause prices to rise and fall proved accurate. Locke advocated that a country should seek favorable trade balances. Voltaire supported policies directed at achieving positive trade balances. Adam Smith supported duties on imports as a component of national defense. Smith did not reject the basic principle that a country should at least aim for a balanced external trade, even though he disliked Mercantilism.

Some 19th century economists, as for example, Frederic Bastiat (1801-1850), argued that trade deficits were a sign of a successful economy, but there were caveats. He argued against protectionism and all forms of government interference with free trade, while advocating that the full economic picture should be taking into account for making decisions, including the long-term potential consequences. During the 19th century American trade deficits were linked to the need to import machine tools so that factories could be built, including factories to build more efficient American machine tools. When the American economy was being built from scratch, capital goods had to be imported. The expansion of the railroad system required a huge amount of iron and steel, as well as machinery and tools. Trade deficits were the result of *investments for growth*, not the result of imports of consumer goods and luxury goods. By 1900, the United States had industrialized, and started to pile trade surpluses steadily until 1975.

The situation that has emerged since 1975 has nothing to do with building up the productive capacity of American industry. When the mounting problem became eminently clear, policymakers dismissed the deficits as something temporary. The concepts that Adam Smith wrote about in the 19th century were not allowed to function. The principal competitors of the U.S. do not practice free trade, and tinker with their currencies in ways that do not allow market forces to truly function. There is a big gap between theory and practice.

Nobody is perfect. In 1988, President Reagan in a speech delivered in Cleveland said that the U.S. trade deficit was a "*sign of strength.*" This line of thinking may have been paraphrasing the free market views of Milton Friedman (1912-2006), who opposed import quotas and tariffs, and government regulations. Although generally praised for his intellectual abilities, Friedman was not always correct. Friedman believed that trade deficits would be corrected by "free markets." Countries that have trade deficits would see their currencies fall, and that would make their own products cheaper and imported products more expensive. As imports became more expensive, people would be discouraged to purchase imported products. As a country's products become cheaper, they would become more competitive in international markets, and exports would increase. Thus, free markets would eventually balance a country's international trade. In the real world these market forces *do not* function as Friedman predicted. The so-called "free markets" are anything but free.

Another argument made to justify trade deficits is that there are other factors that influence the flow of money in and out of the country. For example, the American economy is a powerhouse in the services sector, including such things are license fees, royalties for patents and other intellectual property, insurance, financial services, passenger fares, and the like. In the export of services, the U.S. continued to enjoy a trade surplus and as late as 1999, the export of services amounted to about $272 billion, producing a surplus of about $81 billion. When taken into account, the international trade in services helped to offset the trade deficit in goods, however, it only reduced the deficit by about 25 percent. Since 1999, the amount offset by export of services has been reduced further. The average monthly surplus in the export of services as of 2011 has been reduced to about $14 to $16 billion, whereas the deficit in the export of goods continues to climb. The basic flow of money has been going in the wrong direction since 1975, through seven administrations of both parties.

President Reagan played lip service to the concept of allowing free markets to solve the trade deficit problem, but in practice, he took action to control some aspects of the problem. For example, when international agreements to reduce steel imports did not work, he took action to protect domestic producers. He imposed tariffs and import quotas on specialty steel imports. By the time action was taken, already thousands of American jobs in the steel industry had been lost as factories shut down because they could not compete with imports from Brazil, Canada, Japan, Mexico, South Korea, Spain, South Africa, Sweden, Taiwan and other countries.

The electorate may not have a clear perception of all the problems and challenges faced by the national economy, but people are not stupid. They know that the process of dismantling the industrial might of the country has to be reversed. Economic policy should have as a key goal to make it profitable to produce most of what we consume in American farms and factories. Achieving self-sufficiency and improving competitiveness for American products is not incompatible with respecting fair and open international markets. The effect of such a program would be increased employment, a more vibrant economy, and increased revenue for government at all levels, which in turn would help defray the cost of programs to help the truly needy. The U.S. has suffered serious economic damage through a process of deconstruction of the nation's industrial base. Other competing economies have grown at the expense of American workers. All the idealism associated with globalization led to failure. It turned out to be a temporarily uplifting Utopian disaster.

Energy Production

For over thirty years imports of crude oil and petroleum products constituted the largest share of the U.S. trade deficit. The U.S. has been the largest importer of crude oil in the world, accounting for about 25 percent of all the oil that moves in world markets, even though other countries are more energy dependent than the U.S. (For example, Germany and Japan need to import over 90 percent of the energy they consume.) The U.S. is energy rich, but incompetently managed. Despite the gross mismanagement by policymakers, domestic energy production has been increasing helping to moderate imports at a slow but steady pace. Natural gas exploration and production, has been expanding due to the discovery of vast resources that can be exploited with advanced drilling technology. Vast Coal deposits continue to be used to generate electricity, but due to government regulations from the EPA, new plants have not been built with "clean coal" technologies, because the requirements are too stringent.

Despite all the disincentives that policymakers have created for the development of domestic energy resources, the U.S. is decreasing energy imports, but it is a slow process, which will not produce energy independence for a few more years. As of 2009, about 24 percent of U.S. energy consumption was imported, and with the introduction of more efficient vehicles, better insulation, increased gas production, more renewable energy technology, and additional oil production, it is expected that by 2025 the percentage of imported energy will decline to around 18 percent. That process could and should be accelerated. It is now predicted by some experts that the U.S. will achieve self-sufficiency in crude oil and gas much sooner, despite government interference.

U.S. DOMESTIC CRUDE OIL PRODUCTION 2007-2012
Energy Information Administration, U.S.DOE

YEAR	MILLION BARRELS PER DAY
2008	5.000
2009	5.353
2010	5.479
2011	5.652
2012	6.498
2013	7.5
2014	**8.46 Estimate**
2015	**9.26 Estimate (other estimates are higher: EIA estimates 9.65)**

The may be able to cover all its energy needs by 2016.

The U.S. consumes about 18,000 barrels per day in liquid fuels.
(Motor gasoline, distillate fuel oil, and jet fuel.)

Despite the enactment of the *Energy Policy Act of 2005*, and the *Energy Independence and Security Act of 2007*, the U.S. continues without a comprehensive energy policy. The 2005 Act was partially amended by the *American Recovery and Reinvestment Act of 2009*, which was driven by environmentalists seeking funding for alternative biofuels, and loan guarantees for innovative technologies, as for example, in solar, wind, and geothermal energy. All of these laws place more restrictions on oil and gas drilling and on the use of coal than the number of incentives provided to unproven and uneconomic alternative energy sources based on existent technologies. About the only area that received attention that had been lacking for several decades was nuclear power, including support for building several new nuclear power plants. These laws did not provide much if any support and instead complicated the development of the technologies that are moving the country to energy independence, namely, oil shale, tar sands, and hydraulic fracturing for natural gas production.[276]

Despite all the environmental roadblocks, North America (Canada, United States, and Mexico) is expected to become energy independent from the rest of the world by 2020.[277] Increased production of shale natural gas, gas liquids, and increased domestic production of crude oil in the U.S. is expected to overcome the need to import fuels from world markets. The U.S. is expected to increase gas and coal exports to energy dependent countries, such as China. In some parts of the country it may still be necessary to import some fuels, but that will more than be made up by exporting from other parts of the country.

Coal mining is a key component of any energy plan to achieve energy independence. Coal is mined in 25 of the 50 states, and an important export category. In 2011, the U.S. produced 1,004 metric tons of coal, and exported 85 metric tons. Over 90 percent of the domestic coal production is used to generate electricity, but the percentage has dropped from about 50 percent to 37 percent, due to increasing regulations, as well as the increasing availability of domestic natural gas. The battle over carbon dioxide and other greenhouse gasses produced by burning coal could be the subject of many books. The basic problem with coal is that there is no viable comprehensive energy plan, and like in other areas, there is action without direction other than a concerted effort by environmentalists to shut down coal production. Coal miners and their families are suffering due to all the stupidity produced by wealthy environmentalists that may mean well, but don't know what they are talking about most of the time. And the poor coal miner families suffer!

Downspiral of Basic Industry

One significant cause of the overall economic mess is the demise of capital-intensive heavy industry which is the key component of the industrial base. It includes mining, iron, steel, shipping, coal, oil refining, industrial machinery, chemicals and plastics. While the industrial base of Japan, Germany, the UK, France, Italy and most of Central and Eastern Europe, the Soviet Union and China had been damaged during WWII, the American industrial base had been untouched. All the major powers had to invest in rebuilding, and by 1960 the principal world economies had new and more competitive industrial base that had incorporated new technology to factories built since 1946. Some of that reconstruction was paid by American taxpayers through such programs as the European Recovery Plan, known as the Marshall Plan.

The U.S. did not invest in rebuilding and updating its' industrial base, with the exception of technology to support the race for supremacy in space, and military technology to compete with the Soviet Union in the *Cold War*. The steel industry, for example, had outdated factories by the 1970s. Like other heavy industries, steel factories are part of the supply chain for other products, selling primarily to other industrial customers, not end products directly to the public. For example, the automotive industry relays on the steel industry to build vehicles.

All the elements needed to be a world leader in the iron and steel sector are present in the U.S., including abundant and exceedingly rich iron ore, abundant coal, and the rail transportation infrastructure to bring it all together. The Carnegie Steel Company by the mid-1890s had exceeded production in the UK and other European producers. U.S. Steel by 1901 had become the largest and lowest cost steel company in the world. Bethlehem Steel, the second-largest American steel company not only operated steel plants, but also operated shipyards and produced specialty steel for building skyscrapers and bridges and armor for the military. During WWII it built over 1100 ships for the war effort. American basic industry out-produced all other countries and made the U.S. the leading military power in the world.

Failure to invest in innovation after WWII led to eventual filing of bankruptcy by Bethlehem Steel in 2001. U.S. Steel was a much smaller company by 2002 than what it had been a century earlier, but remains the largest producer in the U.S. and #12 in the world. In 1986 it changed its' name to USX Corporation, reflecting a more diversified company away from the original core business of steel production, but in 2001 it reorganized again and recreated U.S. Steel with what was left of the original steel-related businesses, and acquiring assets from other smaller producers that had gone bankrupt. Republic Steel, the third largest American steel producer, like the two larger competitors, went into a downward spiral and became uncompetitive by the 1970s. It declared bankruptcy in 2001, after having merged in 1984 with Jones and Laughlin Steel. China is the top steel producer (~684 Mt), Japan is second (~108 Mt), the U.S. is third (~86 Mt), India is forth (~71 Mt), and Russia is fifth (~68 MT).

The U.S. economy continues to be the largest national economy in the world, with an estimated GDP of over $16.6 trillion in 2012, more or less equivalent to a quarter of the market value of all goods and services produced world-wide. The U.S. is the largest manufacturing country, and is the leading agricultural producer. Despite increasingly serious problems with the infrastructure, the U.S. is the world-leader in transportation systems, including highways, rail, waterways, and air links. It continues to be a magnet for foreign investment, which totals over $2.4 trillion, more than any other country. Despite an increasing regulatory environment and a judicial system that progressively meddles in economic activity, the economy continues to be driven by the private sector. Nevertheless, manufacturing of durables comprises 6% and non-durable manufacturing another 6% of GDP. Construction accounts for 4%, mining for 2% and agriculture 1% of GDP. The combined retail and wholesale trade account for 12% of GDP. State and local government accounts for 9% and the Federal Government for another

5% of GDP. The combined government sector (9+5=12% of GDP) is 2% higher than manufacturing!

Catastrophic errors in judgment by business executives, organized labor, elected officials, and government regulators steadily undermined basic industry. Compounding the problem of heavy industry is that weakness in this sector can disrupt other subsectors that depend on heavy industry for raw materials. Stricter environmental legislation enacted since the 1970s pounded another nail into the coffin of heavy industry, as higher costs made it less competitive with producers in other countries with less restrictive legislation, and with newer plants that could be more easily adapted to environmental protection technologies.

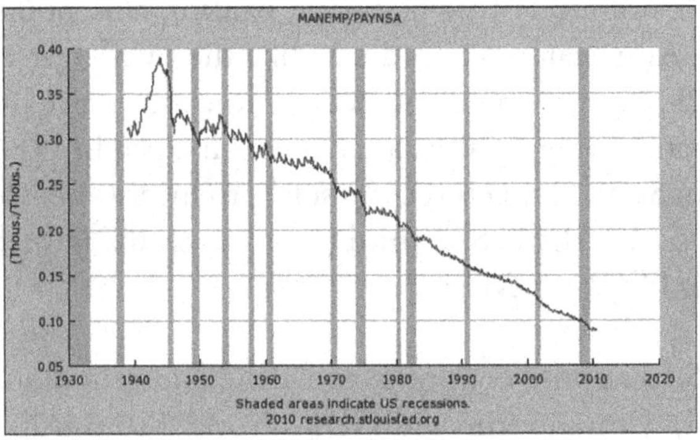

EMPLOYMENT IN MANUFACTURING IN THE US[278]

In 1955, about 35% of American workers were employed in industry, but by 1980 the percentage had dropped to between 25 and 30%.[279] Between 1997 and 2006, the number of American workers employed in manufacturing dropped from about 17 million to about 14 million, and the trend continues to point to additional job losses in the future, based on official U.S. Department of Labor (BLS) statistics. Manufacturing jobs have declined by an estimated 40% since the late 1970s, particularly in the manufacture of labor-intensive production, such as shoes, textiles, apparel, leather products, wood products, paper products, furniture, computers and electronics.

Increasing government regulations contribute to the problems affecting the industrial sector. For example, on 20 September 2013, the Environmental Protection Agency (EPA) announced a ban on new coal plants without expensive and unproven emissions controls. In the meantime, solar storms during 2013 were less than in the previous 100 years, and the earth's average temperature in the current cycle was reached in 1998. Sea surface temperatures along the Equator have cooled, and the earth may be about to start a new period of cooling instead of warming up. Forecasting the heating or cooling of the earth is a tricky business because scientific research on the subject is in its' infancy. Controlling pollution and protecting the environment makes sense, but *voodoo science* is not a proper way to study climate change.

Agriculture and Agro-Industry

The agricultural sector is an exception to the decline experienced by other areas of the economy. During the 19th century American agricultural productivity underwent a steady growth through the introduction of new mechanical planters, sickles, reapers, harvesters, irrigation, chemical fertilizers, barbed wire, tractors and many other inventions. Inventors like John Deere (1804-1886) introduced new machinery, and scientists like George Washington Carver (1864-1943), pioneered research to find new uses for agricultural products. People of all races, ethnic backgrounds and widely different educational backgrounds contributed to the steady advancement of the agricultural sector. This steady improvement continued into the 20th century. In 1930 one American farmer could feed 9.8 people domestically or overseas. By 1950 the same farmer could feed 15.5 people, and by 1970 one American farmer could feed 75.8 people.

Exports of agricultural products increased, even in the face of competition from other countries. The number of small farmers in the U.S. declined, as well as the number of farm workers, in part due to productivity gains and the growth of large agricultural companies that achieve economies of scale with large land holdings. Due to world population increase and economic development in China and India, countries with large populations, the demand for American agricultural products is predicted to continue increasing. Agro-industry adds value to raw agricultural products, further contributing to exports and job creation. As productivity increases and less agricultural workers are needed, the population has to move to other sectors where they can find employment, even if it affects a traditional way of life in rural areas.

American companies that produce agricultural machinery were faced with increasing international competition and protectionism after WWII. Italy, for example, enacted legislation in 1952 to support their domestic agricultural equipment industry, blocking access by American suppliers. South Korea followed suit with similar protectionism coupled with government supported export driven policies. The U.S. became a major importer of Korean tractors. China and India became important competitors for agricultural machinery. Although the United States continues to hold a leading position with top manufacturer like Deere & Company there is increasing competition from multinational companies, including CNH Global of Italy and the Netherlands, AGCO of Germany, Kubota and Iseki of Japan, Mahindra & Mahindra of India, and other producers from all over the world.

The U.S., China, Germany, Italy, India, France, Brazil, Canada, Korea and the UK are the top producers and exporters. While American equipment companies experienced significant roadblocks to enter foreign markets as other countries created their own domestic producers, the U.S. opened up the door to foreign competition. Through the process of globalization, multinational companies have taken over the agricultural machinery sector, and it has become practically impossible to place a national tag on the leading global suppliers of agricultural machinery. The U.S. market share has diluted since WWII, but some U.S. producers like John Deere & Company continue to hold a leading position, despite trade rules and government regulations that hinder American companies.

American companies continue R&D to increase agricultural productivity, but now they find roadblocks from people who want to stop all progress. For example, through genetic engineering, genetically modified (GM) seeds produce more abundant crops without the need for agricultural chemicals. Biotechnology could be the key to feed an expanding world population. Corn, cotton, potatoes, rice and soybean seeds that produce faster growth and resistance to pathogens have been invented, but despite wide scientific consensus that they do not pose risk to humans, ecologists have blocked their use in many countries and the importation of American GM products, particularly in the EU. In the U.S. at least 25 GM crops have received government regulatory approval to be grown commercially as of 2013.

Agriculture and agro-industry continue to be key sectors of the American economy which continue to present excellent expansion possibilities. However, the future depends on the support and incentives provided by government for companies to invest without excessive regulations heavily affected by politics rather than true science. The current battleground involves GM crops. It is too early to tell which way the wind is blowing as politics are blocking scientific advances. Like the ancient cosmologists that held that the Earth was flat, modern day ecologists are ready to use Holy Scriptures to contradict modern day scientists, as Copernicus and Galileo were persecuted by the Inquisition in the past.

Textiles and Apparel

The domestic textile and apparel industry predates the arrival of European settlers, as many indigenous tribes weaved cloths for about 1200 years before their arrival.[280] European settlers imported most textiles manufacturing equipment until around 1790, when British spinning wheels and the spinning *jenny* started to be replaced by water-powered equipment manufactured in New England, New Jersey, New York, and Pennsylvania. Throughout the 19th century American inventors introduced new power looms and weaving machinery that steadily increased worker productivity. Electrical equipment was introduced by the beginning of the 20th century, further increasing productivity.

From New England and New York, textile industries expanded to the South, particularly North Carolina, where thousands of new jobs were created. But despite the productivity achieved with new technology, workers in the mills were among the worse treated anywhere. Long hours in cramped conditions and child laborers were common in the late 19th and early 20th centuries. These conditions have been a constant for centuries in all cultures around the world to the present. These problems have been addressed earlier and better in the U.S. than in any other competing country. Changes did not take place without the growth of organized labor and a long history of strikes to produce collective bargaining contracts that steadily increased safety and created generally better working environments.[281]

Like the agricultural sector, the American textile and apparel sector has the highest worker productivity and is considered to have the most advanced industrial equipment in the world. However, over 900 factories have closed since 1996. Over 80,000 jobs have been lost in North Carolina alone. Numerous communities throughout the southern states have lost textile factories. The former workers of the textile mills have not found alternative employment anywhere close to the income they earned before, and many have become permanently unemployed. The promised restructuring of the industrial base has not materialized. Older workers have been unable to find alternative employment.

In 1965, about 95 percent of the apparel worn by Americans was domestic-made, but by 2012, about 98 percent was imported, mostly from China. And the apparel enters for the most part duty-free. The decline of the American garment industry is an important component of the country's economic regression. Why should thousands of American workers remain unemployed, while foreign workers produce textiles and apparel for American consumers? Can a country depend exclusively on imports of apparel? Somehow, that does not make sense. How did this industrial sector that leads the world in labor productivity and technology come unglued? The enactment of strict environmental rules, government regulations, and excesses by employers and unions are each partially responsible.

Most countries enacted protectionist legislation that made it illegal to import textiles and apparel, or priced imports out of the market through high tariffs and import quotas. Some of this protectionist legislation has been slowly disappearing, but they continue to exist. American policymakers tried to protect the domestic textile and apparel sector through a combination of high import duties and import quotas, but at the same time they came up with contradictory foreign policy decisions that accelerated the steady decline of the apparel sector.

Explaining *freakonomics* is not easy, because many features do not make any sense at all.

The U.S. Congress repeatedly tried to expand protectionist legislation and a system of import quotas, but consistently ran into presidential vetoes. The Reagan Administration, while repeatedly supporting the free flow of trade, in practice maintained a mixed set of actions to address trade issues. To stop an inflow of Japanese electronic products, President Reagan ordered a 100 percent tariff on selected Japanese electronic products, particularly semiconductors. He ordered a 45 percent duty on Japanese motorcycle imports essentially to protect American icon Harley Davidson. However, when Congress passed a bill in 1988 to imposed additional limits on imported textiles, apparel, and shoes, President Reagan vetoed the legislation, and Congress failed to override the veto in a vote of 272 to 152, short by 11 votes from the required two-thirds majority for the bill to become law over the president's veto.

Again in 1990, Congress passed another similar bill, like the one vetoed by President Reagan in 1988, but President George H. W. Bush, like his predecessor, vetoed it. In January 2005 all the global quotas were lifted, and this action was followed by a new flood of imports particularly from China. Policymakers in Washington apparently gave up on saving textile worker's jobs. Even the U.S. Army procured barrettes made in China for American soldiers! No other country would put up with politicians that act repeatedly against their own people's best interests.

During the Reagan Administration, in 1984, a foreign policy decision was made to create the so-called *Caribbean Basin Initiative* (CBI) for the purpose of providing tariff and trade benefits to Central American and Caribbean countries to create employment, counteract leftist movements, and create incentives for people to stay home instead of illegally migrating to the U.S. One of the ways the administration defended the program was by making the case for American companies to continue producing components in the U.S. to be assembled in the CBI region, instead of closing down altogether and reestablishing new production plans in Asia. The apparel industry in particular was targeted by U.S. Department of Commerce employees (U.S. Department of

Commerce, International Trade Administration) with a promotional campaign to invest in the CBI area and create offshore assembly lines for pre-cut apparel for final assembly in one of the beneficiary countries. Somehow, despite the bills that Congress tried to enact to protect domestic textile and apparel manufacturers, they enacted the CBI, going along with President Reagan's foreign policy decision, even though it was contradictory to what they had been trying to do through protectionist legislation.

The CBI program did not achieve the level of success that had been hoped for, but American jobs were lost. With the enactment of the *North American Free Trade Agreement* (NAFTA) under the Clinton Administration in 1994, Mexico provided superior advantages than what the CBI countries could offer, and the textile and apparel production drifted there. Thousands of American jobs in the textile and apparel sector were lured away attracted by lower wages, and a U.S. Government program that endorsed the export of American jobs. Government employees, whose wages were paid by American workers through taxes, undermined American workers by contributing to the export of their jobs.

Protectionism can only artificially help to maintain an industrial sector alive temporarily. If a sector is free from competition through artificial means, there are no incentives to invest in productivity gains and R&D to develop better products. Every country that has enacted import substitution legislation and imposed protective tariffs on imported goods has failed to achieve their intended goals. However, there is a role for government in assisting private companies to remain competitive. For example, tax incentives to make it more cost effective for entrepreneurs to introduce new technology to remain competitive. It is an effective way to address foreign competition from countries with cheaper labor rates. Allowing companies to write off capital goods over a shorter period of time provides an additional incentive for the business community to introduce new technology to maintain leadership and remain competitive. Instead, the business community has been faced with high taxes that render many sectors unable to meet foreign competition.

In the case of the textile sector there have been numerous errors on the part of the business sector. Running illegal cottage industries, sweat shops, paying low wages, and abusing immigrants willing to work in hidden production facilities is not the way to compete in the textile and apparel sector. Organized labor demands beyond the employer's ability to pay also leads to the eventual failure. Government is not the only culprit for the failure of the textile and apparel sector. It is the combination of multiple factors that has resulted in massive unemployment in this sector that once employed tens of thousands of American workers. Is there a way back? No.[282] There is practically no way to recover the textile and apparel sector. The world has moved on. Just because a sector is in trouble, it is not an excuse for implementing a policy of industrial euthanasia, which is essentially what has been applied to the textile and apparel sector. Policymakers seemed to have come to the conclusion that it was the patriotic duty for the sector to commit suicide for the sake of implementing bizarre foreign policy ideas.

Automotive Sector: The Gloomy Story

The American automotive industry grew during the 1920s through innovative techniques, such as the assembly line introduced by Henry Ford, which dropped the per unit price. There were multiple auto manufacturers, but General Motors, Ford and Chrysler each held between 20 and 25 percent market share. Smaller and less competitive companies slowly began to disappear. With the enactment of the National Labor Relations Act in 1935, and the Creation of the United Auto Workers Union (UAW), the collective bargaining process brought about better wages and better working conditions, but the only way industry could afford to cover the additional costs was to continue growing and kicking the liabilities of the pension plans forward.

During WWII the assembly lines were redirected to support the war effort. However, as soon as the war ended in 1945, manufacturers went back to producing cars. Over 21 million cars were built and sold in 1945. The U.S. auto industry was not only building for the domestic market, but was also exporting all over the world. The top three auto makers, GM, Ford, and Chrysler, set up factories in Europe and Latin

America to meet local demand, thus reducing the export of cars made in the U.S. Foreign competitors in Europe and Japan rebuilt their factories and began to produce for their markets and for export. They built smaller and more fuel efficient cars, and introduced innovations as they build new factories. U.S. manufacturers continued to operate the old factories, with more limited introduction of new technology.

By 1970, several factors merged to torpedo the auto industry. Consumers demanded safer cars, after successful litigation by Ralph Nader forced the industry to rethink car designs with safety in mind.[283] New government regulations forced the industry to invest in environmental technology, while the UAW aggressively approached collective bargaining with higher demands for wages and benefits, leading to strikes that undermined competitiveness in the early 1970s. The Nixon Administration's decision in 1971 to go off the gold standard brought about inflation, and the introduction of wage and price controls, which restricted the industry's ability to set prices based on production costs. An embargo of oil exports to the U.S. imposed by the Organization of Arab Petroleum Exporting Countries (OAPEC) in response to U.S. backing of Israel during the Yom Kippur War in October 1973 precipitated a new crisis. The devaluation of the dollar, plus the new found power of OPEC, led to much higher fuel prices, which triggered a demand for fuel efficient vehicles. The price of fuel in the U.S. went from about $0.38 per gallon in May 1973 to around $0.55 in June 1974. American companies were behind other producers in fuel efficiency, pushing buyers to purchase imported cars.

A stock market crash in 1973-1974, plus the political and economic uncertainty emanating from the Watergate Scandal, further destabilized the automotive sector. Reengineering vehicles to comply with new government efficiency regulations added costs, which could not be passed on as a result of wage and price controls. Shortages of fuel, fuel rationing programs, and the state of the economy reduced the demand for vehicles. The automotive industry in the middle of the economic mess, denominated "*stagflation*" had to phase out front engine/rear wheel drive to more efficient front engine/front wheel drive designs. Japanese fuel efficient cars took advantage of the consumer rejection of gas guzzlers contributing to a drop in American car sales that lasted until the 1980s when fuel prices dropped. By 1985, the average car made in the U.S. improved its mileage performance from an average of 13.5 miles a decade earlier to an average of 17.4 miles per gallon of fuel. But to achieve greater efficiency huge investments were needed to retool.

The shakeup of the American automotive industry during the 1970s resulted in the closing of several assembly lines and a reduction of about 10 percent of production from the 1969 level. The slump in demand led to a reduction in production, leading to huge layoffs and the start of endemic unemployment in the rust belt. Suppliers to the larger companies went bankrupt. Production of parts and components was shifted overseas. The American Motors Corporation (AMC) brand disappeared, and its' assets were bought by Renault. Chrysler came close to bankruptcy by the middle of 1979, and was only saved by a government-guaranteed loan.[284] Ford was kept afloat by profits from foreign operations, as it bled from domestic operations. General Motors lost market share to foreign competitors, slowly losing its role as the largest auto manufacturer in the world to Toyota.

When fuel prices went down in the 1980s, the American automotive industry went back to producing larger vehicles and successfully introduced minivans, SUVs, and more pick-up trucks, with Chrysler leading the way after recovering from near death. Foreign manufacturers followed their lead, as the American public forgot the experience of the 1970s and bought the larger vehicles. Minivans, SUVs, and pick-up trucks became popular through the 1980s and 1990s. When fuel prices went back up around 2008, the gas-guzzling SUV and pick-up truck culture went into crisis. The price of these used vehicles dropped by about 24% overnight. Sale of new ones dropped as demand for fuel efficient vehicles went back up. Once again, factories making the large fuel guzzlers were shut down, bringing about another crisis. By 2008, Japan was producing over 5.5 million cars, China 9.3 million, and U.S. production had decreased to 8.75 million, while Germany produced 6.0 million.

President George W. Bush's Administration provided Chrysler and General Motors $17.4 billion in loans in December 2008 to keep them from going into bankruptcy. In exchange, they had to implement a plan to regain competitiveness. The UAW and the companies had to work out a new realistic collective bargaining agreement that included a cut in benefits and wages. The Canadian Government joined the effort to save both companies with parallel bailout funds. Over one million direct and indirect jobs were at stake. President Obama's Administration provided $43 billion in additional funds in exchange for more concessions. With this assistance, both companies started a recovery, leading to profitability and recovery of the funds provided by the government five years ahead of time, as the companies emerged from bankruptcy. Taxpayers did not lose money and many jobs were saved, but many of the problems could have been avoided with better corporate and union leadership. One of the results of all the upheaval in the automotive sector was the destruction of multiple pension plans, leaving thousands of workers without coverage or reduced pensions.

Automotive Sector: Alternative Analysis

There is another side to the story of the American automotive sector. Since the energy crisis of 1973, the leading German, Japanese, and Korean manufacturers have invested in vehicle factories in the U.S., for the most part in the south, where there are labor laws that do not give the edge to the UAW. The most interesting aspect of these factories is that several of them produce the top ten cars with the highest percentage of American content. For example, Toyota turned out to be the leader in the 2010 lineup of vehicles with the highest percentage of American components, not one of the three American companies (GM, Ford, and Chrysler). The American companies – however that is defined - have a high percentage of parts made in Canada, Mexico, Japan, and other countries.

As a reaction to concern for the future of the domestic vehicle industry, Congress enacted the "The American Automobile Labeling Act (AALA) in 1992, with the hope that if American consumers were aware of the domestic content of cars sold in the U.S., they may prefer to purchase the ones with the highest American content. The AALA covers cars, vans, pickup trucks, and SUVs. The Act went into effect in 1994, requiring a label on all vehicles covered stating the country of origin and the percentage value of the American and Canadian parts content, and place of final assembly. Contrary to expectations, repeated surveys of consumers has indicated that buyers do not seem to be aware of the labeling, are not very concerned about the information, and do not seem to factor in the source of the components as a key decision for purchasing a vehicle. In addition, it turned out that Japanese vehicle manufacturers Toyota and Honda compared very well with vehicles made by GM, Ford, and Chrysler.

Just because the three American vehicle manufacturers lost market share since 1973 to foreign companies, it does not necessarily mean that autoworkers have lost their jobs to foreign workers. While the rustbelt lost jobs, Alabama, Georgia, Indiana, Kansas, Kentucky, Illinois, Mississippi, South Carolina, Ohio, Texas and West Virginia benefitted from foreign investment to produce cars in the U.S. BMW, Honda, Hyundai, Kia, Mercedes-Benz; Nissan, Toyota and Volkswagen have manufacturing plants in the U.S. In the meantime, Detroit lost about 25 percent of its population in the past 30 years, and so have other key population centers in the old rust belt. Where did they go? It is not very clear if they moved to the states where the foreign auto makers set up their new factories.

The health of the automotive manufacturing sector in the U.S. is not necessarily as bad as it is portrayed to be. Just because the three American giants are not anywhere close to what they once were, does not mean that all is lost. For example, foreign companies manufacturing in the U.S. repatriate their profits, but so do GM and Ford from their own business operations overseas.

Foreign Investment Contradictions

Misdirected nationalism and ignorance has affected the flow of foreign investment and job creation. Few people really know anything about statutory restrictions on foreign investment, and many of the restrictions on the books no longer apply because the world has changed and technological advancement have made old regulations *de facto* irrelevant.[285] Many states modified their tax structure during the 1980s to attract foreign investment. Just about every state has economic development offices that try to attract foreign investment. For example, since 1968 the Illinois Department of Commerce & Economic Opportunity has a West European Office in Brussels. The Office of Trade and Investment (OTI) tries to attract foreign investment, in addition to helping Illinois companies to export to Europe. The Virginia Economic Development office not only maintains an office in Brussels, but also maintains offices in London, Shanghai, and Tokyo. Tennessee has investment development offices in Canada, China, Germany, and Japan. Nevertheless, not everyone supports foreign direct investment in the U.S.

When I was stationed in the Netherlands in one of my business trips back home in 1994, I visited Asheville, NC and Knoxville, in eastern Tennessee. I was surprised to see numerous store fronts and shops with signs that read "*AMERICAN OWNED.*" While both states were trying to attract foreign investment, the people of that region of Appalachia (Blue Ridge, Black Mountains, and Smoky Mountains) were clearly showing bigoted and ultranationalist tendencies that went against economic development of the region.[286] I was curious to learn more about the regional attitude when at the western end of Tennessee they were enjoying hundreds of new jobs due to the then recent opening of a Japanese-owned car manufacturing plant. Nissan's factory in Western Tennessee had opened in 1983, and already around 1,736 people were employed at the factory. I talked with shopkeepers, auto repair garage owners, and owners of small restaurants exhibiting the billboards that read "*AMERICAN OWNED*" in an attempt to understand what that was all about. They questioned the motivations of foreigners to invest in the US, were concerned about foreigners taking control of American businesses, expressed national security concerns, but could not explain what they meant. They told me that foreign investors were "subverting" the "American culture," however that is defined.

I thought that the views about foreign investors "*subverting the culture*" was indicative of the ignorance that drove the regional concerns. Despite the diversification in foreign investment flows into America, the fact is that British investors continue to be the principal foreign investors, followed closely by the Japanese, Dutch, German, and French. These countries – except Japan - are intimately linked to the *Mayflower* and the initial waves of immigrants to the original 13 colonies, which makes linking investments with dilution of the culture questionable. It was obvious to me that my interlocutors could not have defined specifically what they meant by "*subverting the culture*."[287]

The Nissan factory in Western Tennessee had opened in 1983, and already employed around 1,736 workers. I visited Memphis in 1994, as part of the opening ceremonies for a new direct flight by Dutch airline KLM from Schiphol International Airport in Amsterdam. Once again, I went out and talked to people, including businessmen who were invited to a trade event organized in connection with the start of direct flights to the Netherlands. I presented market opportunities for American exports to the Netherlands, a country with which traditionally the U.S. enjoys substantial trade surpluses, as Dutch companies import American products and redistribute them to other countries throughout Europe.[288] The difference in popular attitudes towards foreign trade and foreign investment in the east and west ends of Tennessee were remarkable.

After about thirty years of direct foreign investment in vehicle manufacturing, Tennessee is ranked No. 1 as the top auto manufacturing state with over 150,000 direct jobs in the automotive sector. Volkswagen had hired over 2,000 workers for their new plant in Chattanooga, and more jobs were expected as the plant starts to build the specially designed Passat for the North American market. Nissan was hiring more workers in Smyrna to manufacture lithium-ion batteries for all-electric cars. Altogether, as of 2011, there were over 860 suppliers for the growing vehicle industry. The Knoxville area was ranked as one of the top high technology hubs in the U.S. in part due to foreign investment. Hopefully some of the chauvinistic mentality against foreign investment is a thing of the past. As of 2007, foreign direct investment in the U.S. employed over 5.5 million workers or about 4.7% of the employed work force. More recently, it is estimated that the number of American workers employed in manufacturing plants owned by foreign investors has increased to about 12%.

The silliness about foreign investment in Appalachia was not unique. In 1975 President Gerald Ford issued Executive Order 11858, which created the Inter-Agency *Committee on Foreign Investment in the U.S.* (CFIUS), to review potential national security implications of foreign investment. Despite concerns, CFIUS hardly ever meets or takes any action other than for window-dressing. In 2006 the potential purchase by Dubai Ports World of a couple of British companies would have given them control of six American ports brought the issue of foreign investment and national security once again to the front pages of newspapers. The Dubai company cancelled their plans and the issue went away, but not without creating considerable discussion on the subject of national security and unrestricted foreign investment. Both political extremes, from the far right to the far left have shared some of the same absurdity about foreign investment.

In most countries there are restrictions to foreign investment and generally the more restrictions the lower the level of economic development. Nationalism tends to be irrational, and reactionary, confusing basic patriotism with anti-foreigner frenzy. Liberals and left-wing politicians in the U.S. have even mistakenly provoked racist and anti-foreign extremists' views that are remarkably similar to the views of right-wing extremists at the other end of the political spectrum. Lunatics at the far ends of the political spectrum share many dumb views.

The lack of clear direction and ignorance about the benefits of foreign investment produce a very dysfunctional environment. Political leaders frequently show their ignorance and contribute to misdirecting public opinion. This absence of a clear policy contribute to slowing down job creation. There is evidence that the states that have gone all out to attract foreign investment have dramatically increased employment and triggered domestic investment to complement foreign investment. Companies that supply services flock to an area receiving foreign investment, increasing the labor base, and the purchasing power of the population.

1988 PRESIDENTIAL CANDIDATE DUKAKIS ON THE EVILS OF FOREIGN INVESTMENT

While most state governments were aggressively seeking foreign investment, during his failed presidential campaign in 1988, Massachusetts Gov. Michael Dukakis tried to capitalize on public apprehension, despite mounting evidence that they were creating thousands of new jobs for American workers.[289] By that time in 1988, there were already around 3 million American workers employed by foreign companies. Some argued that many of the jobs existed already and that all that foreign investors had done was to purchase a pre-existing company and continued pre-existing jobs. Dukakis warned that the level of foreign investment and ownership had become a threat to national security. To complete the anti-foreign investment stand, one of the Dukakis television campaign ads featured an insensitive and racist message about the dangers of foreign investment with a Japanese flag.[290]

Deregulation: Unintended Consequences

Just about every time policymakers decide to tinker with the economy they produce serious unintended consequences. Usually, they introduce more regulations into the economic system. However, in the mid-1970s policymakers decided to *deregulate* key sectors without proper analysis of the potential unintended consequences. The *Screw-up Fairy* made another visit to Washington. At the time, the American economy had been shaken by the failure of companies that had become uncompetitive for one reason or another. Some of the companies that failed had thousands of workers participating in company pension programs, which collapsed when the companies went bankrupt.[291]

The decision to deregulate was made with a heartbreaking background. The tragedy of thousands of elderly workers and retirees losing their pensions had led Congress to enact the *Employee Retirement Income Security Act* (ERISA), leading to the creation of the *Pension Benefit Guarantee Corporation* (PBGC), as an independent agency of the U.S. Government.[292] PBGC was created to protect and encourage the continuation of private pension plans, and avoid their catastrophic failure as companies filed for bankruptcy. PBGC is funded from premiums paid by workers participating in retirement plans, assets (investments) made by these plans, and the recovery of assets from the estates of companies that declare bankruptcy and fail to meet their obligations to retirement plans. Bankruptcy courts generally have favored unsecured creditors over pension plans for redistribution of assets of failed companies, placing considerable stress on the ability of PBGC to take over the pension plans of failed companies.

All pension plans seek to moderate risk by investing in entities that produce a steady revenue stream and are sheltered to some extent from the normal ups and downs of the stock market. At about the same time that PBGC was created, policymakers decided to consider deregulation of economic sectors that had been allowed to function as monopolies under government supervision: *telephony* and the *airline sector*. Deregulation introduced a new factor of distress to sectors that had previously enjoyed prosperity. The deregulated companies failed, carrying with them pension plans that had been previously stable. Their stability had attracted investment from other public and private pension plans, which became indirectly affected by the failing deregulated companies. These failures made the work of PBGC even more complicated.

The decision to deregulate led to additional company failures, which carried with them their pension plans, which had previously enjoyed considerable stability. The failure of previously regulated companies produced a serious economic impact well beyond damaging direct employees, because many private and public pension plans traditionally invested heavily in telecommunications and airline companies, because they were "stable" and annually produced profits as regulated companies. Through deregulation, previously viable pension plans covering millions of workers had the rug pulled from under them. Not enough thought was given to the possible consequences of creating a deregulated environment in light of what was already taking place.

Breakup of the Bell System

At the tail end of the Nixon Administration in 1974, the DOJ filled an antitrust lawsuit to dismantle the AT&T conglomerate, which for about 100 years was the principal provider of telephony throughout the U.S. The so-called "Bell System" or "Ma Bell," provided Americans and Canadians with the best telephone system in the world.[293] Bell Labs and Western Electric, subsidiaries of AT&T had a top research and development (R&D) program, and produced domestically all the telephones and associated equipment needed. The Federal Communications Commission (FCC) regulated the operations of the conglomerate, which was a government sanctioned monopoly under the *Communications Act of 1934*. Some elected officials pushed the DOJ to break up the system based on the expectation that competition would bring about benefits for the public.

Deregulators did not take into account the potential ugly side of what they were doing. The "free market" was difficult experience for AT&T. Attempts to expand into the new computer age which came about at the same time in the early 1980s, convert the system from analog to digital, and other innovations after the dismantling of the conglomerate prove to be a bridge too far, and what was left of the original Ma Bell failed. The name brand was bought out by SBC Communications for about $16 billion in 1995. The current AT&T is not the same as the pre-antitrust company. It stems from one of the seven "baby bells" or regional operating companies created in 1983 from the old AT&T, namely Southwestern Bell Corporation, which changed its name to SBC Communications in 1995, and purchased what was left of the original Ma Bell at a fraction of its original value before the conglomerate was broken up. Later on, the new AT&T acquired Bell South, another one of the seven Baby Bells. The reconstituted company bought back about half of the original components of the old company. (Possibly in an attempt to put parts of *Humpty Dumpty* back together again.)

Although the new AT&T is now one of the largest companies in the country and the world, in 2000, the company was in trouble and forced to restructure again, as it came close to bankruptcy. Who got hurt?

The employees of AT&T and subsidiaries, who before deregulation were paid excellent wages, and were covered by an outstanding benefits package that included a retirement plan, were hurt. Since then, just about everything has grown backward to the detriment of workers. According to PBGC, as of 31 December 2011, the unaudited fair market value of the Plan's assets was $45,888,552,000, and the estimated liabilities were $57,065,843,000.[294]

Competition allowed new companies to enter the telephony business, and with the advent of the Internet, cellular phones, VOIP (Voice over Internet), satellite telecommunications, and related technologies, the sector continued to expand and introduce new ways for people to communicate. Over one million people are employed in the sector. Communications have dramatically improved through the invention of new technologies which would have been introduced anyway with or without deregulation. Americans have more choices than ever before and the telecommunications revolution has been a key driver of the economy. That is undeniable. But there is the *ugly side* of deregulation. Basic telephony costs, namely the cost of a basic landline (fixed telephony) has more than double, which affects low-income consumers who do not need and cannot afford all the new gadgets. As many as 200,000 jobs have been lost since 2000, particularly in wired communications. The telecommunications sector continues to provide better than average wages, but the benefits do not compare well to pre-1978 days.[295] Cell phones and practically all the associated technology is imported from China, Korea, and Europe. Bell Labs and Western Atlantic no longer provide the equipment, which means that not only have jobs been lost, but national security is affected when we are dependent on imports of a critical technology. Both companies went the way of the dinosaurs.

DOW JONES MARKET INDEX

Rank	1960	1980	2000	2010
1	General Motors	Exxon Mobil	General Motors	**Wal-Mart**
2	Exxon Mobil	General Motors	Wal-Mart	Exxon Mobil
3	Ford	Mobil	Exxon Mobil	**Chevron**
4	General Electric	Ford Motor	Ford Motor	General Electric
5	US Steel	Texaco	General Electric	**Bank of America**
6	Mobil	Chevron Texaco	IBM	ConocoPhillips
7	Gulf Oil	Gulf Oil	Citigroup	**AT&T***
8	Texaco	IBM	AT&T*	Ford Motor
9	Chrysler	General Electric	Altria Group	**JP Morgan Chase**
10	Esmark	Amoco	Boeing	**Hewlett-Packard**

Turnover among the largest companies in the U.S. has taken place for the past 200 years due to multiple macroeconomic changes, including innovation. Eight of the top 25 companies did not exist or were very small in 1960. In the ten years between 1999 and 2009, there was a turnover of 50 percent of the 500 top companies. Of the original Fortune 500 list compiled in 1955, only 71 were still on the list 50 years later. * Note: The AT&T listed above is not the same AT&T conglomerate broken up by government anti-trust action in 1983.

Airline Deregulation

In 1978, Congress deregulated the airline sector through the enactment of the *Airline Deregulation Act*. The goal was to create competition between carriers, improve service, and reduce price. The system, as it was constituted before deregulation, was efficiently regulated, and provided service to many communities that would not have received service from air carriers otherwise. The Civil Aeronautics Board regulated routes, fares, schedules, and every subsector of the civil aviation sector. Pan American Airways had a monopoly of international routes, and five companies, namely American, Eastern, Transcontinental, United, and TWA, operated domestic flights. All the airline companies had excellent benefits packages for their employees, including pension plans, and they were profitable. They operated for the most part with American manufactured aircraft, which were produced by American workers who also enjoyed excellent benefits and pension plans. After deregulation, American workers suffered a considerable reduction in their benefits, including pensions, and thousands lost their jobs.

Commercial aviation has weathered many problems since deregulation and passenger traffic has grown about 5 percent annually. Low-cost carriers have come about, but by offering their employees lower wages. Initial pricing advantages through competition have produced an unstable set of companies and pushed large traditional companies to bankruptcy. The quality of service has declined. The traveling public is faced with numerous new fees for things that were always covered by the price of the tickets. Many communities have lost access to air transport, as the carriers concentrate in larger urban areas from where they can generate more business. Due to the fear of terrorism after 9/11/2001, security costs have skyrocketed, placing an additional burden on the carriers, as well as the traveling public.

Regulations have come back, covering an increasing number of areas, from denied boarding compensation, to the time that passengers can be left inside planes that experience departure or arrival delays due to weather conditions or other factors. After thirty years, deregulation has led not only to bankruptcies but to a series of mergers and acquisitions, leading to the creation once again of large dominant carriers, often at the expense of the employees, who have suffered reductions in wages and benefits. The public is not happy with the results. Since 2001, over 100,000 airline jobs have been lost, and the number of flights serving an increasing number of communities have been lost or reduced, despite the cited annual increase in passenger traffic.

Braniff Airways ceased operations in 1982. Frontier Airlines failed in 1984 and the assets were bought to start People Express Airlines in 1985, but finally shut down in 1986. Eastern Air Lines filed for bankruptcy in 1989, unable to compete with low cost new carriers, and faced with considerable labor unrest. Pan American World Airways failed in 1991. PanAm had been a profitable airline, with considerable cash reserves, operating around 160 airplanes covering just about every point in the world before deregulation, although the company was already handicapped by other government policies which put it at a competitive disadvantage with other carriers. The purchase of National airlines in 1980 to obtain domestic routes proved to be a costly mistake. The bombing of Pan Am Flight 103 over Lockerbie, Scotland in 1988, contributed to the demise of the company, which was already in trouble.

TWA filed for bankruptcy in 1992, and seemed to emerge as a more competitive company, but financial problems resurfaced and went out of business. American Airlines bought some of the assets in bankruptcy court in 2001. After initially benefiting from deregulation, which provided the company an opportunity to expand, Continental Airlines was forced to reorganize under bankruptcy protection in 1983. The old labor agreements were set aside to sharply reduce costs, and new more favorable contracts for the employers came about. Continental emerged from bankruptcy in 1986 as the third largest airline in the country. However, Continental was forced into bankruptcy again in 1990, and once again managed to emerge successfully. Continental Airlines merged with United Airlines in 2010. The combined companies became the second largest carrier after Delta Air Lines. AMR, parent company of American Airlines filed for reorganization under bankruptcy in November 2011. A proposed merger with US Airways was announced in February 2013, but regulators initially did not approve the merger, which was finally approved after the new company agreed to give up some gates; the merger created the world's largest airline.

After about 30 years, deregulation has led to the creation of four dominant carriers who control about 80 percent of the traffic, less choices for the traveling public, much higher fees and fares, and less competition. It is not wise to fix what is not broken, and it is a good idea to explore possible unintended consequences, because putting *Humpty Dumpty back together again* is not possible. The medicine for alleged maladies has turned out to be worse than the alleged problems triggering decisions to tinker with basic components of the economic system. We are back to about the same number of dominant carriers and a much worse situation for the workers and the public. That is how *freakonomics* works.

So What?

The American economic system needs an overhaul. It would make sense to revive the moral courage of 1776. First and foremost the Founding Fathers were *patriots*. For them, *corruption was the greatest threat to liberty*. They thought that the true value of a man lies in his moral behavior, and took pride in sacrificing private passions for superior public interests. Behind many aspects of the dysfunctional economic system is selfishness and criminal behavior. Improper plans, failure to analyze intended and potential unintended effects of policy decisions and mismanagement result in the conditions that allowed criminals and idiots to come close to sinking the entire financial system. The economic and political systems are designed precisely to encourage and inspire smart solutions taking into account all possible angles before decisions are made after distilling from political debate the best ideas from all sides. The people's representatives are supposed to embody and stand for the views of the electorate, but with the idea of reconciling differences, finding the middle ground, and enacting legislation that makes sense. The *spirit of compromise* is missing. Political gridlock was far from the intentions of the Founding Fathers.

The Constitution was based on the notion that government rests on the *consent of the governed*. Enacting legislation without proper evaluation of every aspect of transcendental changes, such as the *Patient Protection and Affordable Care Act of 2010*. This legislation is an example of how dysfunctional the system has become. Enacting legislation without reading all the details and ironing out every aspect of implementation is contrary to the way the system was design to work. The Founding Fathers were split ideologically on economic principles, but shared basic notions of *laissez-faire*, a doctrine which upholds an economic system with limited government intervention, and allows citizens freedom of action.

The United States has plentiful and diversified natural resources, including crude oil, natural gas, and coal. Basic industry, primarily energy-intensive metal-working industry has the advantage of plentiful supplies of domestic raw materials.[296] The key to economic development is industrial revival through fair and competitive taxes comparable to other countries, shortened depreciation schedules, support for R&D, and streamlining the regulatory process.

VII – CULTURAL DECADENCE

"Every kingdom divided against itself is headed for destruction."

Matt. 12:25

Social System and Civil Society

The American *"social system"* is comprised of the norms, values, and ethics that govern interrelationships between all individuals, races, ethnic groupings, formal and informal organizations, family groups, economic classes, religious affiliations, and institutions that form the structure of the nation. The *"system"* comprises multiple *"subsystems"* of people and groups that have affinities that bring them together. The *"social system"* embodies multiple complex components that interact with each other based on traditions, shared thinking, passions, and collective wisdom, which transmitted from one generation to another constitute the *culture* of the nation.

What is *civil society*? It is a concept with multiple components and variables. It involves shared values and interests, as well as *un-coerced* collectively negotiated actions of a community of people. It includes the private and the public sectors, non-governmental organizations, religious and professional organizations, labor unions, advocacy groups and numerous other institutions and organizations that voluntarily bring together people with similar affinities, interests, purposes or values, whatever they may be. There are many definitions, but what they all have in common is *respect for the rights of other members of society*, as well as classical liberal values, and respect for democracy.[297]

One of the most interesting political science studies of the United States was written by British jurist, historian, and statesman, Viscount James Bryce (1838-1922) in the mid-1880s, with the title *The American Commonwealth*. Bryce was concerned about British ignorance and misunderstanding of the former colonies.[298] At the time, there were about 60 million people in the U.S. and the Union consisted of 38 states and territories that were later to become states. Bryce's transcendental study described the American political system and American society. Americans were optimistic about their future, and the economy was expanding, even if there were periods of recession. America was *respected* and was progressively increasing its' influence in world affairs. A new preeminent world leader was being forged, opined Bryce.

If Bryce conducted a similar analysis in 2015, he would be more concerned about the American ignorance of their own country's history and the widespread misunderstanding of the Constitution in which the country's political and economic systems rest. Back in the 1880s, British elites assumed that the U.S. was a vulgar, uncultured, and rustic country barely starting to industrialize. In 2015 Americans seem to be deconstructing the country, with an increasingly vulgar culture, with schools that are barely educating young people. The economy is suffering from a process of de-industrialization. In world affairs, the U.S. has been losing influence as the economy deteriorates and military conflicts overseas end inconclusively. American civil society is challenged internally and externally in ways that could not have been predicted back in the 1880s.

Tolerance, Pluralism, and the Counterculture

American society has been increasingly willing to allow people the freedom to live their lives however they want, even if it involves self-destructive behavior. *Live and let live!* The spirit and letter of the American Constitution supports the notion of personal liberty, with the rational assumption of reciprocity and respect for other people's rights. Predators, cheaters and sociopaths are not necessarily willing to provide *reciprocal tolerance* under an umbrella of pluralism and respect so that everyone benefits. Loudmouths and bullies have been allowed to have their way. American culture has been overtaken since the 1960s by a *counterculture* that is in opposition to traditional mainstream civil society, and do not really accept the concept of tolerance and pluralism. Particularly serious is the growing intolerance of those who preach tolerance. They only remember the First Amendment to the Constitution when it suits them. For all practical purposes, we are witnessing the results of evil social engineering.

At times it is not clear if American society is suffering from cultural decadence, or advancing towards a progressive "Utopian" multicultural, tolerant, pluralistic society, where there is no difference between right and wrong. Some writers have obsessed with comparing the American experience since the 1960s as a predictor of a fate similar to that of the Roman Empire.[299] Some aspects of the recent American experience are dreadful, but it is far from reaching the level of disruption suffered by the Roman Empire.

Many of the changes since the 1960s have corrected weaknesses and strengthened *the system*. Greater diversity, tolerance and pluralism are positive changes that reinforce and bolster the nation. However, when there is a failure to learn from the past, and illogical nonsense is poured into the mix, the result is not pretty. Over 5000 years of collective wisdom reflected in the Old and New Testaments and Judeo-Christian traditions cannot be ignored or cast aside as irrelevant. There are thousands of years of wisdom (good judgment and accumulated knowledge) in the *Bible*. The most dangerous sign of what is taking place is the slow death of free speech.

American cultural values have been deliberately torpedoed by snake-oil salesmen promoting morals, lifestyles, and behavior contrary to those of established in mainstream society. These include the *hippie* movement that emerged in the mid-1960, the associated drug culture, and the general nihilistic mayhem that followed. In other words, the masses were indoctrinated with the idea that *morality does not inherently exist*, and all moral values are abstractly contrived. Sadly, the *turn on, tune in, and drop out* culture started in the 1960s has taken hold and is a big contributor to economic problems affecting the country, particularly high youth unemployment. Traditional moral order has turned into *obscene moral disorder and destructiveness* that has nothing to do with creating a more tolerant and pluralistic society.

Breakdown of the American family

American society is suffering from challenges that set it apart from other countries. In 2013, an estimated 48 percent of all first born children, and about 40 percent of all children, were born to unwed mothers. Single mothers make up the majority of households. (Out of an estimated 12.2 million single parent families in 2012, more than 80 percent were headed by single mothers.) About two thirds are White, one third is Black, and about one quarter is Hispanic.[300] We are faced with moral catastrophe, resulting from secular and "*progressive*" ideologies associated with the counterculture of the 1960s. The tsunami of change since the 1960s has resulted in failure, not in a more harmonious society. The huge prison population is to a great extent the result of the breakdown of the American family. It is predictable that in the future the prison population will continue to grow unless something is done to recover old values.

Marauding "Flash Mobs"

One of the most significant additions to outrageous behavior in 2011 was the introduction of a new twist to American culture: the *flash mob*. Intimidation through the threat of violence just because people look different or are perceived to be a member of another social or economic class is a form of terrorism. What causes this type of outrageous behavior? Is it inspired by class warfare rhetoric or political pied pipers who blame the "establishment elites" and the business community for the economic problems affecting the country? Does it result from the Hollywood culture transmitted through movies packed with violence and wrong role models that glorify gangs and criminal behavior? Is it inspired by *Gangsta rap* music? Do the roots go as far back as the violence promoted by the Black Panthers in the late 1960s? The answer to these questions is that they all converge into wild mob action. These are some examples of *flash mob* activity:

- (2011-02-24) A mob of about 50 teenagers swarmed and carried out a massive shoplifting exercise at a Holiday convenience store in St. Paul, Minnesota.
- (2011-05-04) A mob of Black teenagers "swarmed" a convenience store on Sunset Road in Las Vegas. The mob darted into the store and snatched items from the shelves and ran out. Surveillance video cameras recorded the scene.
- (2011-04-28) Five Black men were arrested and charged with assault and battery in an unprovoked brutal attack on a white gay teenager

outside a store in Rock Hill, South Carolina. Surveillance video helped to identify the suspects.

- (2011-05-22) A flash mob of about two dozen male and female Black teenagers swarmed a Dunkin' Donuts store in Greenwich Village, New York, terrorized employees, and made off with drinks and sweets from the store, and left after damaging some of the equipment.
- (2011-06-27) A mob of about 50 Black teenagers attacked a white family in South Akron, Ohio, as they walked out of an event at the Firestone Stadium. The teenagers in the mob were shouting "this is a Black world" and other similar slogans.
- (2011-06-28) A flash mob of Black teenagers beat, trampled and robbed people on North Broad Street in Philadelphia after attending the Susquehanna Community Festival in North Philadelphia.
- (2011-07-29) A mob of younger teenagers attacked and robbed pedestrians in downtown Philadelphia. A judge acting on the case characterized the actions as "hunting humans for sport."

BROTHERS AND SISTERS DEAL WITH THE WHITE STORE OWNER THAT ROBS BLACK PEOPLE.

- (2011-08-17) A flash mob of teens ransacked a Germantown, Montgomery County, Maryland 7-Eleven store.
- (2011-08-18) A flash mob of female teenagers ransacked a convenience store in North East Washington, D.C.
- (2011-08-26) A mob of teenagers after a high school football game at the Independent School District Johm Kincaide Stadium entered an Exxon Tiger Mart on Interstate 20 and South Polk Street in Dallas, attacked a store clerk, and robbed the store. Other people were attacked in the vicinity of the store.

These are only a sample of incidents between February and October 2011. Where are the signs of the so-called *"post-racial society"* that supposedly emerged after the election of President Obama in 2008? Numerous arrests were made, but because many of the perpetrators were minors, they got away with light sentences. Many were never caught, in part because there was no interest in catching them, despite video evidence about what they did. *Tolerance should not be extended to criminal activity!*

Promoting Racial Violence since the 1960s

The following two drawings were taken out of the *Black Panther Coloring Book for Children.* They promoted the idea of Black people assaulting white store owners, who were classified as thieves that stole money from Black. These ideas over time influenced generations of young people who do not see anything wrong with such things as the flash mobs that attacked multiple stores all over the country in 2011. The second picture promotes the assassination of policemen. These are factual reproductions of the efforts to promote revolution and civil strife. These people were not peaceful protesters or true defenders of the interests of Afro-American people. They are criminals that belong in jail. The flash mobs that surfaced in 2011 are a reflection of years of indoctrination of youth by groups like the Black Panthers.

I personally took the pictures that follow by the Reflecting Pool, located between the Lincoln Memorial and the Washington Monument during one of the anti-war demonstrations between 1968 and 1970. Hundreds of naked demonstrators waving Viet Cong flags, smoking marijuana, and high on other drugs had sex in the open. This is an example of trash promoted by the New Left that contributed to the "*counterculture*" that developed in the United States over time. When Islamic extremists point to the America as a sick society, these are the types of images they have in mind. The *Occupy Movement* born in 2011 was nothing but a continuation of the same trash with roots back in the 1960s. And… thus Muslim extremists hold that our entire society is corrupt, has moved away from God, and needs to be obliterated. Increasing racial tensions in the country are in part the result of years of indoctrination of youth in support of revolution and racial warfare. The events of Ferguson and Baltimore in 2015 have deep roots that go back to the 1960s.

Note: The Black Panther Coloring Book for Children was first printed in 1968, allegedly created by James Anthony Teemer, a 23-year-old Sacramento, CA, college student who was a member of the BPP. The Central Committee of the BPP debated if it should be published, and a run of about 1000 copies was printed by the LA chapter of the organization. According to an article in the *San Francisco Examiner* (Teaching Grade Schoolers Revolution, 6/20/1969), the publication was distributed at the Sacred Heart Catholic School and other schools in the Bay Area, Oakland, and Sacramento. It was also distributed at the St. Augustine's Episcopal Church in Oakland. It was 23 pages long, and did not contain a copyright notice. The BPP and other leftist groups have alleged that the FBI under the COINTEL program was behind the coloring book because some people linked to the publication may have become FBI informers. The *Senate Permanent Subcommittee on Investigations* under Senator John McClellan carried out an extensive investigation on the BPP. No prove has ever surfaced that supports the allegation that the FBI was behind the publication to smear the BPP. The BPP was an organization of thugs who wanted to be part of a revolution to overthrow the US Government. Only two original copies of the publication are known to exist. One is at the Law Library of the University of California at Berkeley, and the other at the University of Virginia library. The Library of Congress has photo copies of the original publication. (Accession No: OCLC: 81619820, class descriptor: LC: E185.165) It is not clear if the publication was first printed in LA or Oakland, CA.

THE ONLY GOOD PIG, IS A DEAD PIG

BROTHERS AND SISTERS DEAL WITH THE WHITE STORE

Picture of a crowd of naked and semi-naked anti-war demonstrators bathing in the *Reflecting Pool* in Washington, D. C. This fountain is located between the Washington Monument and the Lincoln Memorial., circa 1969. Notice the Viet Cong flag. The picture taken by the author, No known restrictions on publication.

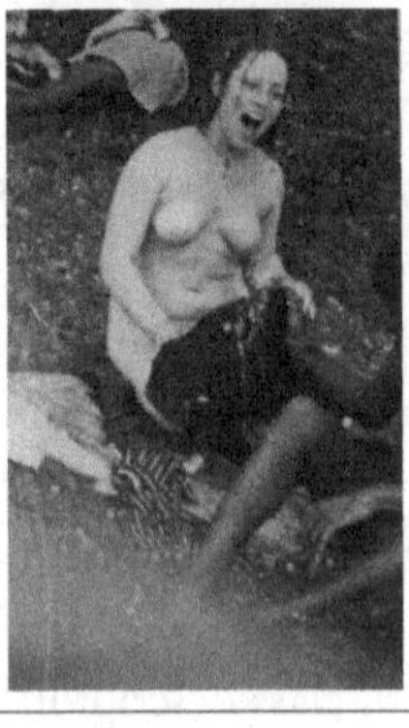

Age of Aquarius

When the moon is in the Seventh House
And Jupiter aligns with Mars
Then peace will guide the planets
And love will steer the stars

This is the dawning of the Age of Aquarius
The Age of Aquarius
Aquarius! Aquarius!

Harmony and understanding
Sympathy and trust abounding
No more falsehoods or derisions
Golden living dreams of visions
Mystic crystal revelation
And the mind's true liberation
Aquarius! Aquarius!..

The 5th Dimension (1967) From the musical "Hair"
By James Rado & Gerome Ragni

Leftist poster in the late 1960s calling for armed revolution and the killing of policemen.
(Author's collection)

Note: The image on the left is that of Dr. Ernesto "Che" Guevara, an Argentine adventurer and Communist who found his way to Mexico and joined Fidel Castro and a group of about 80 men as they prepared to travel by sea to Cuba to start guerrilla warfare in 1956 to overthrow the government of Fulgencio Batista. The Cuban Armed Forces discovered the landing and decimated the group. Guevara was one of about a dozen men who managed to reach the mountains. Instead of acting as a physician for the guerrillas, Guevara turned into a commander, but in practice his image was well above his actual military knowledge. He was an assassin who delighted in executing people opposed to the Communist revolution after 1959. His more radical views caused friction with the Castro brothers, leading to his departure to Africa (Congo) and eventually to Bolivia, where he was killed as he tried to start a Communist revolution, but the Indian farmers did not want any part of it. The picture taken by the author, No known restrictions on publication.

Breakdown of the Educational System

According to the U.S. Bureau of the Census, there are ~83,000 public schools in the country, of which ~49,200 are primary schools, ~15,300 are Middle Schools, and ~11,900 are High Schools. Approximately 11,900 combine several levels of education. Roughly 14,300 schools (17.2 percent) experienced serious violent incidents during the school year 2007-2008. There were at least 58,300 serious violent incidents reported to school authorities. According to the most recent data available, during 2009 a total of 7.7 percent high school students reported being threatened or injured with a weapon on school ground.[301]

The ethnic breakdown of the students threatened or injured is noteworthy: 9.4 percent of Black students, 9.1 percent of Hispanic students, 6.4 percent of white students, and 5.5 percent of Asian students were victims of school violence. The worst situation affected American Indian and Alaskan natives with 16.5 percent being subjected to assault on school grounds.[302] Information is not readily available on the breakdown of incidents by urban, suburban, and rural schools. Although school violence may not be the prime reason for increasing ignorance, it certainly is not conducive to a proper learning environment.

The "culture" of hooliganism is anchored in the homes and in the school system. When school administrators, teachers, parents, and law enforcement authorities fail to control bullying, assaults, and other forms of violence, society as a whole suffers. Parents are primarily responsible for the misbehavior of their children, not teachers and school administrators, who have to work with the students as they arrive with all their baggage. Violence against teachers is a growing problem, with over 250,000 teachers annually (about 7 percent) threatened or attacked by students, particularly in city schools, according to a study by the American Psychological Association.[303] The problem is not new. As far back as 1969, *Time Magazine* published an article about the then new growing violence against teachers, more or less about the same time as the drug culture was spreading among young people, together with "revolutionary" leftist politics. According to the article, some teachers were starting to pack concealed guns to work![304]

The assumption that we have arrived at a "*post racial*" society is a myth. Racial tensions continue to exist and they are part of the problem. The primary victims of Afro-American crime are usually other Afro-Americans. Gang crime in large urban areas, like Chicago, generally entails Black-on-Black and Hispanic-on-Hispanic violence. The level of social disorganization can best be described as having reached *a critical state*. American society is increasingly characterized by violence, and untreated people with serious psychological issues.

Violent Videogames

Videogames involve the interaction between an individual "player," and a visual video device, either a computer or stand-alone game device, which provides feedback to the player. Videogames are a big money-maker, producing an estimated $18 billion in annual sales, under the protection of the First Amendment to the Constitution. The principal providers of violent videogames are Activision Blizzard, Electronic Arts, Take-Two Interactive Software, and GameStop. They compete by trying to outdo each other with visions of carnage, dismemberment, disembowelments, decapitations, impalements, manslaughter, massacres, police killings, ultra-violent kills, and victims wailing in pain. This was the sequence of market introduction of the most violently-rated games: Postal (1997), Soldier of Fortune (2000), Grand Theft Auto III (2001), Manhunt (2003), DeadSpace (2008), MadWorld (2009), Call of Duty: Modern Warfare 2 (2010), Splatterhouse (2010), God of War III (2010), and Mortal Kombat (2011). What is wrong with these videogames? They apparently have psyche-desensitized young people to violence.

Linking violent videogames with an increase in violence is impossible due to contradictions in crime statistics. Empirical evidence seems to show that violent crimes have steadily decreased in the U.S. since 1997, when violent videogames were progressively introduced into the market. Despite the decrease in the crime rate, the number of incidents of mass murder by mentally-challenged people has increased, as witnessed by such incidents as Columbine (1999), Virginia Tech (2002), Northern Illinois University (2008), Tucson (2011), the Denver theater massacre, the attack on the Sikh Temple, and the slaughter at Sandy Hook

Elementary in 2012. Perhaps mentally challenged individuals are more susceptible to violence inspired by videogames.

While some of the perpetrators of these crimes are known to have played videogames, they were exposed to violent movies, violent song lyrics, as well as the overall gun culture, which is fed from many different angles. Videogames are marketed in Canada and Western Europe as much as in the U.S. and there are no comparable lists of incidents of mass murder carried out by mentally-challenged individuals. To be fair, even though many of these games are repugnant, there is insufficient evidence to establish a direct link between videogame violence and mentally unstable people who carry out mass murders.

Dark Music Subculture

In the 1960s rock bands contributed to the creation of a drug subculture. More recently, an equally dangerous *heavy metal* violent subculture developed in Europe, particularly in Germany and the UK. This type of music pushed violent lyrics and more extensive debauchery on young people. For example, the German band KMFDM, which surfaced around 1984, threw animal entrails at audiences during life performances. Eventually, the recordings entered the U.S., with such wonderful lyrics as *"Kill Motherfucking Depeche Mode."* By 1991, the band and the new trend that had started in Germany had found a niche in Chicago. KMFDM in association with a new band called Excessive Force released new albums with such titles as *Conquer Your House* and *Conquer Your World*, Blitzkrieg, *Megalomaniac, Ride the Bomb, We Like War,* and *Finger on the Trigger*.

The key perpetrator of the Columbine High School massacre in 1999 had posted on an Internet website the lyrics of the KMFDM songs *Son of a Gun* and *Stray Bullet*. The day of the school shootings, April 20, 1999, coincided with the birthday of Adolph Hitler. Among the followers of the new music wave are white supremacist groups and neo-Nazis. Nevertheless, the original date for the massacre may have been 19 April, which coincided with the Oklahoma City bombing of the Federal building, and the Waco Siege, covered on Chapter I. It is impossible to know what the real intended day for the shooting was.

Musicians involved with these bands, including the composers of the songs, denied that they were a bad influence on young people or that they promoted violence. These are partial lyrics of one of the songs, released in 1997, that had attracted the attention of the perpetrators of the Columbine massacre:

"Stray Bullet"[305]

I am your holy totem
I am your sick taboo
Radical and radiant
I'm your nightmare coming true
I am your worst enemy
I am your dearest friend
Malignantly Malevolent
I am of divine descent

I have come to rock your world
I have come to shake your faith
Anathematic Anarchist
I have come to take my place

I am your unconsciousness
I am unrestrained excess
Metamorphic restlessness
I'm your *unexpectedness*

I am your apocalypse
I am your belief unwrought
Monolithic juggernaut
I'm the illegitimate son of god

Gangsta Rap

Another aspect of music and violence is *Rap music* and *Gangsta rap*, which came out of Afro-American society, particularly among the very poor living in urban ghettos and failed housing projects. The Bronx section of New York City is regarded as the birthplace. The initial beat moved from profanity to more and more violent tunes and lyrics since the early 1980s. The lyrics promoted sex, drugs, and graphic violence, demeaning Black women and stereotyping them as prostitutes. The more profanity and violence in the lyrics, the closer the genre moved to mainstream. Among the key performers were Dr. Dre, Vanilla Ice, M C Hammer, Scarface, N.W.A., Ice-T, Eminem, and KRS-One. They competed in glamorizing violence through lyrics that promoted shootings, robbery, violence against women and promiscuity. According to the literature on the subject, among the most violent rap songs are: *Kim*, *The Day the N***az Took Over*, *X is Coming For You*, *No Tears*, and *97'Bonnie & Clyde.*

It is questionable to what extent the wave of mass-murders since the late 1990s is linked to rap and gangsta music. With one exception, the perpetrators were young and mentally-challenged white males.[306] On the other hand, the so-called *flash mobs* are generally composed of young Black male and female participants. This *genre* may be more of an inspiration for flash mobs than mass murder incidents. The perpetrators of the worse incidents of mass murders have been white and Asian; only two Afro-Americans were the perpetrators of a series of shootings in the District of Columbia Metro area.

American parents and even Conservative talk show hosts who once in a while attack gangsta rap don't know much if anything about the filth of the lyrics, and that is part of the problem. Americans do not seem to listen anymore to what is going on around them. Do Afro-American church leaders ever listen to the filth that is being used to brainwash young people? First Amendment Rights or not – this is trash. The Founding Fathers without a doubt did not have protecting trash like this when they wrote the Bill of Rights.

Vulgar America (with a British twist)

> **We're more popular than Jesus now; I don't know which will go first, rock n' roll or Christianity.**
>
> **John Lennon**[307]

Vulgarity is something indecent, rude, or offensive to good taste or propriety, but historically, societies have evolved and changed the definition of what is and is not acceptable behavior, and what is and is not conceived as tasteless. However, trash is always trash, regardless of how popular some aspects of vulgarity may become acceptable in American culture. From jazz at the beginning of the 20th century to the introduction of Rock-and-Roll in the 1950s, perceptions of vulgarity in music changed. Society slowly accepted what originally was disapproved, and so we progressed to *Psychedelic Rock* and protest songs in the 1960s, and *Punk Rock* in the 1970s, and *Rap* starting in the 1980s. What originally was viewed as primal and uncouth rhythms accompanied by vulgar lyrics became acceptable and regarded as harmless, not as examples of moral decay.

Vulgar lyrics increased during the 1960s, and continued to expand through the 1970s. This is not an effort to make music a *Bogeyman*. I am simply pointing out that music has a tremendous impact in society, as a way of persuading, manipulating, and influencing people to accept or not accept subliminal messages in the lyrics of popular music. Thus, twisted values and morals that were unacceptable in the 1950s became acceptable by 2000. Popular music perverted the minds of young people by endorsing irresponsible sex, smoking, drinking, and drug use, as well as the use of violence as an acceptable way to solve any problem. Psychedelic music contributed to the use of LSD and other drugs on college campuses. Thank *The Grateful Dead*, *Country Joe and the Fish*, the *Jefferson Airplane*, and *The Yardbirds* for their contribution to the drug culture.

Under the cover of *artistic expression* vulgarity has been oozing through society and corrupting the minds of young people to the point that nobody understands the parameters of current "indecency standards." Cursing and obscenities are the norm from television sitcoms to standup comedy to song lyrics. Motion pictures are a venue for promotion of irresponsible behavior, and pimps, prostitutes, and drug dealers are presented as ubiquitous in society, and are even assigned some redeeming social values to make them *"acceptable"* even during "family-hour" in television programming. I do not believe in *"conspiracy theories"* and I am convinced these performers are too stupid to plan and carry out any conspiracy. However the damage they cause is real. They generally make fortunes peddling their garbage, while maintaining an image as "*Progressives*" who are concerned about the poor and discriminated minorities, when in fact they exploit the poor and minorities and grab their money and run to the bank laughing at their victims. It happens because *"we the people"* allow it to happen.

Criminal Violence and Mental Illness

On average 34 people are murdered every day with guns in the United States. In 2009, there were 16,799 homicides across the country, of which 11,493 were carried out with firearms. The murder rate, as well as the rate of violent crime has fallen since then, despite a considerable increase in the number of people that own firearms. There are many factors that come into play, from changes in demographics to more strict prosecution of people who commit violent crimes. There are over 320 million firearms in private hands, according to estimates made by the Bureau of Alcohol, Tobacco, and Firearms, independent research institutions, and the National Rifle Association (NRA). Regulation on firearm brokers and on private gun ownership are generally respected by law abiding citizens, but the problem arises when other people, including minors, and mentally challenged, and criminals get hold of weapons.

The challenges associated with dealing with mental illness are not unique to the U.S. Every country is affected by behavioral and emotional disorders and how to address them. To start with, diagnosing a mental illness and the degree of impairment is complicated. Based on published statistics, somewhere between 4 and 5 percent of Americans are affected by some form of mental illness, with the highest concentration in the 18-to-25- year-old bracket. As of November 2015, there were about

320 million people living in the U.S. of which between 12 and 16 million suffer some form of mental illness. According to the *Diagnostic and Statistical Manual of Mental Disorders*, there could be around 11.4 million adults with serious mental illness.[308] Most of these people are not institutionalized, and many have not even been diagnosed as suffering from a mental illness. The "system" to take care of the mentally ill is broken, which compounds the problem of establishing and enforcing gun control legislation, because there is no complete database of people who should not have access to guns.

The issue of criminal insanity is highly controversial, as the legal profession uses "cognitive" insanity as a means to defend lawbreakers. Without a doubt, many people who commit crimes are not able to discern right and wrong, are mentally impaired, and are incompetent to stand trial. The issue is further complicated by mentally retarded criminals, who clearly are not mentally competent. Instead of ending in institutions that can provide needed care, they end up in jail instead. Based on a study carried out in 2010, using 2004-2005 data, it was determined that there were three times more seriously mentally ill persons in jail and prisons than in hospitals. It was further determined that at least 16 percent of inmates in jails and prisons (about 319,918 individuals) have a serious mental illness. In 1955 there was one psychiatric bed for every 300 Americans. In 2005 there was one psychiatric bed for every 3,000 Americans, of which the majority was filled with court-ordered "forensic cases," and not really available.[309] What happens when the large population of criminally insane individuals completes their sentences? They are released without any kind of follow up or treatment, which leads to a high rate of recidivism.

Americans are stunned every time a new incident of gun violence takes place, but not enough to make changes. According to existing legislation, only law abiding people of sound mind can obtain a firearm. The argument goes that criminals, by definition, do not abide by legislation, and *guns do not kill people, people kill people.* Despite the obvious, energy is directed at gun control, instead of directing energy towards finding solutions to the mental health crisis.

The gunmen who opened fire on a movie theater in Denver, CO in July 2012, the Sikh Temple in Oak Creek, WI in August 2012, and the Sandy Hook Elementary School in Newtown, CN in December 2012, all used a combination of military-style assault rifles and handguns.[310] The deranged gunman who ambushed and killed two volunteer firemen and wounded two others in Webster, New York when they responded to a house fire on 24 December 2012 used a similar .223-caliber Bushmaster AR-15 style assault rifle as the one used in the Newtown massacre ten days earlier. Police found that he also had other types of guns, which had been acquired from a woman who bought them for him several days before. As a convicted felon it was illegal for him to purchase or own firearms.[311] Based on published reports, all three perpetrators were mentally-challenged.

The perpetrator of the Denver theater massacre was under the care of a mental professional. The perpetrator of the Newtown massacre was mentally challenged and apparently his mother was about to confine him to a mental institution for treatment. The shooter of the firemen in Webster had served 17 years for killing his 92-year-old grandmother in 1981. The perpetrators of the Newtown massacre and the shooting of firemen in Webster, NY killed their own mothers before they acted against other victims.

Where is the problem? The proliferation of gun-ownership, the apparently large number of people with mental problems that are not receiving treatment, or a society that fails to seriously address these issues? The source of the problem may go back to the 1960s when left-wing psychiatrists had an epiphany: *confinement of the mentally ill constituted a violation of their constitutional rights.* They could be released and given a pill daily to control their mental problems. Not only are thousands of schizophrenics roaming the streets, but the entire society is suffering from schizophrenia derived from the interminable debate over taxes and the size of entitlement programs.

Although mass shootings like the massacre of children in Newtown, Connecticut in December 2012 grab national attention, there is an even more serious side to the availability of firearms. The domestic front is not peaceful. There are many nefarious actors, from criminal elements to home-grown extremists, in addition to a large number of mentally ill people that periodically make the U.S. resemble a war zone. For example, in June 2014 two Las Vegas police officers were having lunch when they were shot and killed by a white supremacist anti-government extremist couple who wanted to start a revolution.[312] Despite the mounting need to address the challenge of mental illness, the growth of extremist ideology, and the availability of guns to people who should not have access to them, nothing is seriously done. Too many interest groups get into the debate and nothing is done. The country continues to move ahead without a bearing, led by politicians who have no idea of where "true north" or the "magnetic north" are or the difference between the two.

There are groups that openly promote violence. Take a look at the Black Panther's coloring book reproduced in the previous pages. There was *a clear effort to promote class warfare and racial conflict*, and now we are harvesting what was planted years ago by radicals. Somehow, society is going after children in school that make a "paper gun," or draw a gun, or even make a gun with their hands and fingers and point to another child in play, and suspend them from school. On the other hand, there is nothing done against would-be "revolutionaries" like the Black Panthers, when they display weapons and use inflammatory language. Perhaps it is a lot easier to go after a 7-year-old girl who innocently brings a plastic knife to school to cut a birthday cake, than to have the gonads to confront a violent 200 pound 18-year-old male with an attitude.

Criminal Justice System in Crisis

Once upon a time – before the arrival of civilization - humans lived according to the *law of the jungle*, in a totally hostile environment where survival was a struggle between pray and predators. Slowly, humans developed a *social contract* for practical reasons, and became willing to live under *rules of behavior* that granted power to a central government in exchange for *clear rules* and protection from predators. The concept of "*civil society*" developed over time, with multiple variables, but a key component is *un-coerced, voluntary, collectively negotiated actions* of a community of people who share similar values and interests. People come together with other people with similar affinities, interests, purposes or values, and sharing *respect for the rights of other members of society.* That is how the American Revolution came about after rejecting British colonialism. It is also how the American system of government came about.

A key component of *civil society's* compact is the *Criminal-Justice System*, which is:

> *...supposed to focus on defining, investigating, and punishing wrongdoing that is considered damaging to society, not just to individuals. The goal is to protect society by deterring such conduct through the threat of capture, conviction, and sentencing.*[313]

Americans expect their government to enforce *the rule of law* and protect them from law violators and predators, but that delivery has been increasingly short of the expectations of most citizens. According to English philosopher Thomas Hobbes (1588-1679), humans of free will surrendered certain rights driven by self-interest. They consented to submit to authority, to live under certain rules, and to be governed by a "*legitimate*" political power, in exchange for protection. Hobbes held the view that humans would revert to the *law of the jungle* if government would no longer protect them from violence and uncertainty.

Other philosophers, as for example, John Locke (1632-1704) claimed that mankind knows what is right and wrong, lawful and unlawful, and that the most important role of the state is to ensure that the rule of law and justice is enforced.[314] For Locke, resorting to violence is not acceptable, unless mankind's freedom is in danger of being relinquished. Locke proposed that government exists with the consent and approval of the governed. German philosopher Immanuel Kant (1724-1804) believed that all human experience is the basis for the concept of cause and effect, and that reason would prevail over passion. Despite different views, they seem to agree that when authorities fail to protect the governed, and the structure of government (social contract) fails, the people will revert back to taking the law into their hands.

We seem to be going back to *the law of the jungle*. Americans – particularly *Liberals* – have developed the mythology that white police officers spend their day hunting down Afro-Americans. *Conservatives* on the other hand, create their own mythology that police officers spend their days protecting Afro-Americans from their own kind. When the rules of civil society turn into Anarchy, insecurity becomes universal, the *Criminal-Justice System* falls apart, and the door is opened for a return to a world where only the strong and the fittest survive. Some Americans are taking the law into their own hands because they feel that the system is failing them.

Highest Incarceration Rate in the World[315]

The convict population in federal prisons increased from 25,000 to ~219,000 between 1983 and 2013. The unprecedented increase puts the U.S. in first place among all countries in the world. The U.S. is a leader in the rate of homicides as a percentage of the population, and the number of fatal police shootings in the first half of 2015 set a new record.[316] These figures are indicative of the deterioration since the 1960s, particularly due to the *turn on, tune in, and drop out* drug culture, which has hurt youth in general, but particularly Afro-American and Hispanic/Latino youth. The left-wing new-left culture, closely tied to the *drug culture* is nothing but a *new and virulent form of racism*. When youth copies the jargon, the dress code, the drug culture, and all other associated worthless non-sense promoted by Hollywood movies, rap music, and the subgenre gangsta rap, they clash with the prevailing culture and end up unemployed, in poverty, behind bars, maimed, or dead.

The growth in drug related criminal activity led to the enactment of legislation in 1968 to stiffen penalties during the Johnson Administration. Under the Nixon Administration additional legislation to stiffen sentences was enacted in 1970, and once again in 1986, penalties were increased during the Reagan Administration. Although currently regarded as "excessive," there were ample reasons to stiffen penalties. In hindsight, the legislation led to a huge increase in incarceration, and an accompanying increase in the number of people who have a criminal background, particularly young African American males.[317] Despite stiffened sentences, in 1992, there were more serious crimes committed than in the previous twenty years. During the Clinton Administration, additional legislation was enacted to impose even stiffer penalties, and in addition, the Federal Government funded the hiring of over 100,000 more police officers throughout the country.

Finally, the crime rate began to drop steadily, and by 1999 the homicide rate had dropped to its lowest point since 1966, and the demand for narcotics was down to levels not seeing in twenty years. The Clinton Administration claimed to have played a pivotal role leading the FBI, DEA, Customs, Border Patrol and other Federal agencies to step up effective law enforcement. In 2000, there were 15,362 murders. The cumulative effect of the harsher sentences helped to reduce violent crimes, but produced the disproportionate rise of racial minorities among the prison population. It was an indication of the negative impact of the 1960s *counterculture*, the failure of many anti-poverty programs, and the increase in social conflicts. By 2010, there were 12,996 murders, of which the victims were 47% were White, and 50.4% were Black. The perpetrators were 53.1% Black, 44.6% White, and other minorities 2.3%. By 2011, the number of murders declined to 4.8 per 100,000 people in the country, the lowest murder rate since 1963, in part because a lot of potential murderers were in prison.

Between 2003 and 2013 the prisoner population at the federal level increased by 27 percent, according to the Federal Bureau of Prisons (BOP). The *Anti-Drug Abuse Act of 1986* set in place mandatory minimum sentences, which contributed to a rapid increase in the prison population. The approximate number of Federal prisoners as of December 2013 was estimated at around 219,000, dispersed over 119 prisons. The largest percentage of the prison population was sentenced for drug offences. Violent crime, on the other hand, has been steadily declining since 1997. Taking discretion away from the courts is nonsense, but sadly many judges act irresponsibly, and legislation had to be enacted to exercise some control over their actions.

When the number of Federal prisoners is added to prisoners at the state and county level, there are at least 2,266,800 adults incarcerated. Another 4.8 million adults are on parole or probation. Taking all of these numbers into account, about 3 percent of the population is under some form of "correctional" supervision, although clearly based on the numbers, few if anybody is getting "corrected." The rate of recidivism is high. It is estimated that about 68 percent of prisoners released are rearrested within 3 years and at least 50 percent go back to prison. About 40 percent of the prison population is composed of Afro-Americans, compared to a presence in the over-all population of about 13.6 percent (including Blacks who have Spanish surnames or "Hispanic-Blacks.") Minorities in prison represent a disproportionate number to their presence in society. These figures do not even take into account over 70,000 juveniles under detention.

Police Misconduct

> **It's only when you see a mosquito landing on your testicles that you realize there is always a way to solve problems without using violence.**[318]

In addition to the increasing prisoner population, there has been *an epidemic of police misconduct cases*, including aggravated rape, sexual battery, possession of child pornography, pimping, drug trafficking, racial profiling, searches without warrants, theft of public funds, brutality, and trigger-happy police officers involved in unnecessary shootings. Numerous cases of obstruction of justice, tampering with and suppressing evidence, torturing suspects to obtain confessions, and conspiracy with prosecutors to suppress evidence frequently come to light in the news media. These are some examples of the dysfunctions in the law enforcement system.

- On 3 October 2013, a mentally-challenged Afro-American woman with a one-year-old baby in the car led police in a high-speed chase in downtown Washington from the White House vicinity, where the driver struck a barrier, to the Capitol, until finally she crashed her vehicle into a police barrier. She never exhibited a weapon, although her vehicle could be classified as a weapon. Police opened fire in two locations and killed her with multiple shots, despite knowing that there was a baby in the car. If they had to shoot, why did they have to fire multiple times? Why so many bullets flying with a baby in the car? The fear of terrorism in the District of Columbia is so high that excessive force was used unnecessarily by over-zealous police to kill an emotionally disturbed person with six bullets.[319]

- On 18 November 2013, Police in New Mexico stopped an Afro-American woman doing 71 MPH in a 55 MPH zone. She was driving a mini-van with five of her children. After an altercation with police, she started to drive away and stopped again. Police tried to get her to come out of the car forcibly. At that point, her 14-year-old son came out of the car to defend her mother, who was being dragged out of the car by police. As additional police cars responded to the scene, the family got back in the car and drove away with the kids scared and screaming. Police opened fire on the van packed with children. Miraculously they were not hit by the bullets.[320] The driver was charged with five counts, including child endangerment, and the 14-year-old with battery on a police officer. Nevertheless, police improperly fired at least three times on a car packed with children. Apparently the incident started when police demanded payment of a fine immediately because the vehicle had out-of-state license plates and the driver did not have the money.
- An Afro-American man was gunned down in Charlotte, SC, on 15 September 2013, after he had a serious accident with his car and walked to a nearby house to ask for help. Police arrived and as he ran to the police car for help, he was shot ten times. The policeman was charged with voluntary manslaughter. There were three police officers present, more than enough to handle an unruly unarmed person, but in this case, the victim was not unruly and was only asking for help. The victim was a college graduate, working two jobs.[321]
- A white 23-year-old senior at the University of the Incarnate Word, in San Antonio, Texas, was shot multiple times and killed by a campus policeman on 6 December 2013. After a short altercation, the policeman pulled out his gun and shot the student about six times.[322] The student was allegedly driving erratically and above the speed limit and was stopped by police while walking to an apartment complex where he lived. The police officer called for assistance, but the call was routed to the wrong police department, but instead of waiting, he went ahead and tried to make an arrest before help arrived. The student apparently resisted, and the officer

drew his gun and shot the student. The student had been on the Dean's List, was a campus television news anchor and did not have a police record.

- An 84-year old Chinese man was pulled aside by police in the Upper West Side of New York City on 19 January 2014 for jaywalking on Broadway and 96th Street in the early evening. The old man did not speak English well, and did not understand what was happening. As police were writing him a ticket, the old man started to walk away as he did not understand what was going on. At that point, several police officers jumped the old man, threw him the ground and left him beaten and bloodied, requiring a trip to St. Luke's Hospital to have his head wound stitched. He was charged with jaywalking, resisting arrest, disorderly conduct, and obstructing governmental administration. What was the justification for beating up a senior citizen who did not understand what was going? Did police bother to reason that perhaps the old man could have been hard-of-hearing, not fluent in English, or affected by Alzheimer's?[323]
- On 30 May 2014 the CBS affiliate in Atlanta reported that a 19-month-old toddler had been critically injured by an exploding "police flash bang" in front of his face after it was tossed into his playpen during a raid in a home in Habersham County, Georgia. The toddler had a 50-50 chance of survival, and if he survives, he will be scared for life. The Chief of Police noted that they had not seen toys or any other indication that there was a child present. The Georgia Bureau of Intelligence (GBI) reportedly claimed that there was no need for further investigation.
- On 12 February 2015, an elderly grandfather from India was visiting his on in Madison, Alabama. Sureshbhai Patel went out for a walk in front of his son's home, when a neighbor called 911 to express concern about *"a skinny black guy…"* who had not been seen around before… and was walking around the neighborhood. Police arrived and Officer Eric Parker approached the man and attempted to question Patel, who does not speak English. Without any justifiable reason, the old man was slammed to the ground, suffering serious injuries. The incident was captured on video. Officer Parker was fired, arrested, and charged with assault in the third degree. A law suit was filed in Federal Court for excessive force and for stopping the old man without cause.

Prosecutorial Misconduct

Numerous cases of prosecutorial or judicial misconduct surfaced during 2013, resulting in innocent people going to jail for crimes they did not commit, including capital murder convictions. The variety of misconduct includes bribes to fix cases, coercing witnesses, perjury, intentionally withholding exculpatory evidence, deliberate mistakes, mishandled DNA evidence, paid snitches coached to lie under oath, witnesses paid to lie, and convictions based on speculation and innuendo. Some of the cases uncovered in 2013 had roots in the past. About the only positive thing that can be said is that *the system is not totally broken*, as eventually the truth has been discovered and corrections have been made in many cases. In other countries misconduct exists and few corrections are made to release the innocent. However, it is practically impossible to discover and rectify all the cases resulting from misconduct. These are some the examples:

- In Wilkes-Barre, PA, two judges pled guilty of taking millions of dollars in *kickbacks from two privately run jails* to send juvenile suspects to prison for minor offenses. The young detainees were sentenced without receiving legal assistance from a lawyer, in hearings that lasted a few short minutes. The investigation revealed that kickbacks amounted to at least $2.6 million.[324]
- A fifteen year old boy was convicted in 2001 of capital murder for allegedly killing a 74-year-old woman in 1996 in Culpepper County, VA. The conviction was tossed out for prosecutorial misconduct. A federal court ruled that *prosecutors improperly concealed evidence that could have helped the defense*. As a result of the work of the University of Virginia Innocence Project Clinic the case was resolved.[325]
- A 19-year-old Black youth was convicted of capital murder in Texas in 1995, and served 15 years in jail before being exonerated through DNA evidence and *evidence suppressed at time of trial.* Centurion Ministries, a prisoner-advocacy group investigated the background of the case and uncovered that a prosecutor withheld information that pointed to another man as the perpetrator of the crime.[326]
- A former Williamson County, Texas, District Attorney only served four days in jail of a ten day sentence for *criminal contempt of court in the wrongful conviction of a man who served close to 25 years* for

> killing his wife. The former prosecutor was also sentenced to 500 hours of community service and disbarred. When the misconduct was identified, the former prosecutor was serving as District Judge. In his previous capacity he failed to disclose that he had tampered with evidence in 1987. The erroneously convicted man was released from prison after DNA testing linked the crime to another man, who was found guilty of the crime earlier in 2013. The Houston law firm Raley & Bowick and Barry Scheck of the New York-based Innocence Project was instrumental in solving this case. As a result of this case the Texas Legislature enacted the *Michael Morton* Act of 2013, requiring prosecutors to open their files to defense attorneys before any trial begins.[327]

It is obscene that members of the judicial system involved in cases like these get away with relatively light punishment. Readers' reaction to news media articles on these cases has been strong, calling the outcome *a travesty of justice.*

Exonerations in the United States, 1989 – 2012
Report by the National Registry of Exonerations
Total Exonerations Recorded = 873

Table 13: Exonerations by Crime and Contributing Factors

	Mistaken Witness Identification	Perjury or False Accusation	False Confession	False or Misleading Forensic Evidence	Official Misconduct
Homicide (416)	27%	64%	25%	23%	56%
Sexual Assault (203)	80%	23%	8%	37%	18%
Child Sex Abuse (102)	26%	74%	7%	21%	35%
Robbery (47)	81%	17%	2%	6%	26%
Other Violent Crimes (47)	51%	43%	15%	17%	40%
Non-Violent Crimes (58)	19%	52%	3%	3%	55%
ALL CASES (873)	43%	51%	15%	24%	42%

Source: Exonerations in the United States, 1989 – 2012
Report by the National Registry of Exonerations

There are cases where the courts went in the opposite direction and failed to impose reasonable and appropriate sentences for law violations. For example, a judge in Montana sentenced a rapist to 15 years in prison, but with a suspended sentence for all but 31 days in jail. The victim was a 14-year-old student who the judge opined that she "*seemed older than her chronological age.*" The victim committed suicide. The perpetrator of the statutory rape was a 49-year-old high school teacher who claimed that he engaged in consensual sex with the victim.[328] Prosecutors had asked for 20 years in prison with 10 years suspended. After considerable public reaction, the judge issued a statement that he would reconsider the sentence. State law requires a two-year mandatory minimum prison term for such a case, and apologized after public demands that he resign. However, the sentence could not be recalled without going through a lengthy appeal process by the prosecutor.[329]

One of the basic problems with the judicial system is the unusual situation which allows for elections of judges. This is a rare situation worldwide. Voter participation in these elections is generally low.[330] Instead of a "merit system," electing judges places politicians in charge of deciding on judicial proceedings. Business organizations and individual business executives who contribute financially to these campaigns to elect judges expect and receive favorable treatment. Judges naturally and unconsciously side with the interests that help them get elected. The impartiality of the courts is questionable when the judicial system depends on elected judges instead of experienced lawyers selected for appointment by a process involving the state bar, nomination committees, governors and state legislatures based on merit.[331] Twenty-two of the 50 states use elections to fill State Supreme Court seats. A merit-based system could be a more adequate way to administer justice.

WHO IS IN CHARGE OF PUBLIC SAFETY?

There are approximately 683,000 police officers working in state, county (boroughs and parishes), and municipalities, including several thousand employed at colleges and universities, and U.S. territories and Puerto Rico. There are another 120,000 law enforcement personnel working for the federal government, at the Federal Bureau of Intelligence (FBI), Drug Enforcement Administration (DEA), Bureau of Alcohol, Tobacco, Firearms and Explosives (ATF), the U.S. Marshals Service, U.S. Customs and Border Protection CBP), U.S. Immigration and Customs Enforcement (ICE), the U.S. Secret Service, U.S. Coast Guard (USCG), the Transportation Security Administration (TSA), the U.S. Federal Protective Service (FPS), and the U.S. Bureau of Prisons (BOP). Altogether there are over 800,000 law enforcement personnel in the country. There are about 18,000 law enforcement agencies employing over 1.1 million people, including over 100,000 part time law enforcement officers, including deputy sheriffs. According to the National Police Misconduct Statistics and Reporting Project (NPMSRP) capturing statistics in 2010, there were ***4,861 cases of misconduct involving 6,613 law enforcement officers and 6,613 victims, including 247 fatalities.*** The largest percentage of these cases (23.8%) involved excessive force, 9.3% involved sexual misconduct, fraud and theft 6.8%. and false arrests 6.8%. The states with the largest incidence of misconduct were LA, MT, MS, WV, OK, AK, NM, TN, IN, OR, CT, and CO.

As previously pointed out, it is estimated that between 4 and 5 percent of the general population suffers from some kind of mental challenge. Despite background checks, apparently law enforcement across the board are representative of the general population, as witnessed by between 4 and 5 percent committing some type of violation of their rules of engagement or engage in some form of misconduct.

Ferguson, MO. - Vignette

On 9 August 2014, Michael Brown, an 18-year-old African-American, 6'4" with a weight of around 292 pounds, entered a *Quik Trip* convenience store, at around 11:52 A.M. accompanied by Dorian Johnson.[332] Brown carried out a strong-arm robbery of a box of *Swisher Sweet* cigars (value $48.99) and manhandled a frail older man much smaller than him.[333] The scene was captured by video cameras and is *undeniable*.[334] The victim in the incident was an Arab immigrant from Kuwait. St. Louis, MO attracts investments by Indian, Korean, Arab, Latin American, and other immigrant entrepreneurs who are willing to invest their family savings and long hours of work to scrape a meager existence. For that, they are frequently victimized by young hoodlums who shoplift, carry out armed robbery, and flash mobs that flood into convenience stores and walk away with everything they can carry.

Michael Brown captured by video camera during the robbery of convenience store about 15 minutes before he was shot. He clearly manhandles the store owner in this picture. Picture was released by the Ferguson Police Department. No known restrictions on publication.

Immigrant business formation rates are higher than for non-immigrants, and they hire more employees, normally from the poor neighborhood around their shops. They contribute to the economy, but are frequently victimized by criminals. Racial friction between Black youths and immigrant-owned neighborhood gas stations and convenience stores is widespread.[335] These victims cannot be blamed for slavery or generations of racial discrimination. They are targeted in part due to years of violent propaganda from such groups as the Black Panther Party telling children in such publications as the *Coloring Book* that it is justified to attack businessmen who are ripping them off. At one end of the idiocy pole they are faced with white *racist nativists* with limited education and income, and, at the other end, by idiots who complain all the time about racism, yet they practice it against a vulnerable population. *Both ends of the spectrum are out of control!*

Within a few short minutes of the violent robbery, Darren Wilson, a 28-year-old white policeman stopped Michael Brown and Dorian Johnson for jaywalking. A police dispatcher had put out an alert explaining that a Black male with a white T-shirt had just robbed the *Quik Trip* convenience store.[336] An argument followed and Brown became verbally abusive and violent, punching the police officer in the face, and there was a struggle to take the officer's hand handgun.[337] The gun went off inside the police vehicle during the struggle. Brown and his friend tried to run away but he turned, and according to published reports, charged back towards the police officer. The officer fired multiple times and shot him dead. The details of the incident had to be investigated, as there were multiple conflicting stories.[338] Darren Wilson was taken to the hospital after the incident with injuries to his face resulting from the altercation with Michael Brown. An autopsy revealed that Brown had smoked marijuana, based on toxicology tests. Before an investigation could be completed, all hell broke loose.

Was Brown an innocent teenager, or a criminal that had just carried out a strong-arm robbery? The evidence is overwhelming that *he was not a candidate for sainthood.* Does it matter that Michael Brown had been smoking marijuana prior to these incidents? Yes, it is indicative of the general drift that started in the 1960s to widespread use of controlled substances, including marijuana, which contributes to irrational situations like this. Could some other alternative have been used other than firing a gun multiple times? Probably, but one thing is to pontificate about it and another thing is to be placed in the situation faced by the police officer. That is why we have a Criminal-Justice System to pass judgment after all the facts are properly analyzed. There are numerous cases of unjustified police shootings, but *not every case is unjustified!*

Within hours, demonstrators gathered to protest the police shooting, well before information was released about Michael Brown's participation in a strong-arm robbery before the altercation with police. The demonstrations turned into violent riots over the next few days, as agitators portrayed the shooting as *an execution of an unarmed teenager.*

Poor education, poor housing, high unemployment, widespread poverty, despair, and self-destructive behavior are part of the mix of factors that contribute to root causes of this type of violence. Nevertheless, *nothing justifies irrational behavior and disrupting the rule of law, or hurting innocent people!*

All the investment in federal anti-poverty programs since the 1960s apparently failed. Black unemployed youth continue to target the stereotyped "*gouging merchants*," particularly immigrants, who set up shops in poor neighborhoods. They are tempting targets for mobs that lack any solidarity with people who are struggling just like they are to earn a living. When all is said and done, it will be the Black community who will have lost jobs and places to purchase what they need, and the town will lose tax revenues, which will further affect the delivery of services to the community. Several of the stores looted were owned by Black-American entrepreneurs. Property values in a town with over 60% African-Americans plummeted right after this incident. Guess who got hurt?

Add to the equation the participation by self-appointed charlatans– such as Jesse Jackson and Al Sharpton, who flock to every incident to exploit it for whatever benefit they can get. Jesse Jackson showed up in Ferguson and started passing the hat to collect donations, stir up the masses and contribute to hostilities.[339] Al Sharpton called the police shooting a "*defining moment*," and called for Congress to stop providing hand-me-downs of military weapons to police departments, and called the release of the video showing the strong-arm robbery by Michael Brown an attempt by police to "smear" the slain teenager, who was clearly a bully and a thief who belonged in jail.[340] The news media provided microphones to numerous cons to blame what happened on "racism" and "structural inequality." Outside agitators and *would-be revolutionaries* flocked to Ferguson to take advantage of the situation to promote anti-establishment violence. *What happened was precisely what the coloring book told Black children to do!* Have Jackson and Sharpton ever commented on the *Black Panther Coloring Book*?

The shooting of Michael Brown was described as an execution, and incendiary language to promote violence was used by the numerous troublemakers who flocked to Ferguson, and the news media put many of them on the air, acting like vultures trying to outdo each other finding the most extremist troublemakers. The *Quik Trip* store robbed by Michael Brown was one of the first to be looted and burned. The owner's son during a television interview said that they had lost thousands of dollars and would be unable to rebuild. Nobody seemed to give a rat's derriere about the people whose businesses were looted and burned down.

Police allowed the mob to destroy private property without confronting the hooligans with an appropriate level of force. About 30 businesses were destroyed. The news media failed to point out how hard-working small business owners were not provided protection. Some went home and returned with their own guns because law enforcement officials would not protect them or their property. When the system fails, people take the law into their own hands. Is that the new direction Americans want for the country? The *law of the jungle*?

The rush to judgment and the justification for violence are part of the *counterculture* that has emerged with the assistance of the "*grievance industry*." Black agitators think that they are justified in torching and looting businesses and attacking police with bricks, bottles, and Molotov cocktails. Policymakers, elected officials, at all levels, failed to protect the public. Police officers were instructed to allow violent mobs to rampage and carry out numerous acts of vandalism and arson without any fear of arrest.

THE NATION OF ISLAM AND THE FERGUSON VIGNETTE

The Black Panther Party is not alone in promoting violence against police and members of the business community, particularly foreigners. The leader of "Nation of Islam," Louis Farrakhan used the vignette in Ferguson as an excuse to attack Koreans, Chinese, Indian, and white store owners for not giving a damn about the Black people in the communities where they operate. In a rant referred to as "a sermon," on 24 August 2014 he called Ferguson *a microcosm of what is going on around the country...* And the rant produced thunderous applause by his audience at the mosque. By an extension of his remarks then, Black people apparently have the right to rob Arabs and Asian people...[341] The Constitution provides Farrakhan the right to free speech, but does society have to be tolerant of his racist remarks and his calls to violence? By accident, he left out Jews, who are frequently attacked similarly.[242] He frequently demonizes of the LGBT community and gets away with it... in part because leftists are willing to accept "theological errors" from anti-American troublemakers like Farrakhan.[343]

A pattern of elected officials abdicating their responsibility to preserve law and order was established long ago. The situation in Ferguson was part of a pattern. On the evening of 18 August, with National Guard troops deployed to Ferguson, police came under fire and about 75 people were arrested during violent protests, at least two of the arrestees had Molotov cocktails and guns. Most of the people arrested were outsiders. The lynch mob would love to get their hands on the policeman who shot Michael Brown without examining all the facts in a truly honest judicial process. The news media stood around waiting for something to happen, and by their very presence created an incentive for political *vedettes* to pontificate while doing nothing to reestablish order.

Once again, on 25 September, rioting and looting started after the Ferguson Police Chief apologized for having allowed the body of Michael Brown to remain where he was shot for over 4 hours.[344] A memorial that had been built slowly at the site of the shooting was set on fire the previous day. These developments, as well as non-related incidents elsewhere angered a large segment of the Black community again.[345] The violence in Ferguson was led by multiple outside agitators, including neo-Communist and Anarchist groups that want to overthrow the US Government and start and world-wide Communist revolution to bring down Capitalism. A good number of the troublemakers arrested on 18 August, for example, arrived from as far away as California and New York to take part in the rioting.

President Obama and his Attorney General Eric Holder failed to enforce the rule of law. Instead of appearing to side with the mob out to lynch the police officer, who may have acted properly and without any intention to violate anyone's civil rights, they should have maintained neutrality. Instead of focusing on agitators from all over the country, they ignored the true victims, essentially the local business community and the population they serve.[346] The one clear evidence of bullying, racism, and criminal behavior was perpetrated by Michael Brown when he robbed the convenience store and manhandled the attendant.

At rallies in preparation for new violent demonstrations if Officer Wilson was not indicted there was talk of "revolution" and of dying on the streets... "*People have a right to go out and express their rage in a manner that is equal to what we have suffered.*"[347] Society has the duty to enforce the rule of law and defend innocent business owners whose property is attacked by hoodlums or would-be-revolutionaries. People under a democratic system of government have the right to express their views in peaceful demonstrations, but when they violate the rights of other people they may have to be granted their right to die in the streets in fulfilment of their desire to stage a violent revolution. Revolutions are not dinner parties. And many of the revolutionaries end up as victims of their own rhetoric. Remember what happened to Robespierre in the French Revolution?

Finally, on 24 November, over three months after the shooting, the Grand Jury's decision was announced. Officer Darren Wilson was not charged with any criminal offense, which by default means that *he acted properly*. The Grand Jury was presented by Prosecuting Attorney Robert McCullock with all the evidence available, and the members reached the decision not to indict. Within seconds after the announcement the looting and vandalism started again, leaving at least 25 stores set on fire, police cars and other vehicles were torched, and hundreds of thousands of dollars in property damage. There were at least 80 arrests, but police and National Guard troops let the situation get out of control. At least two dozen people were injured needing life-saving immediate medical emergency care. Protests took place in at least 37 states and in about 130 locations throughout the country.[348] Many of the businesses looted and destroyed were minority-owned! Once again, the *law of the jungle* returned, as authorities did not enforce the rule of law. Missouri Governor Jay Nixon (D) failed to protect civil society from criminal elements and would-be revolutionaries. Small business owners had their dreams destroyed, and their families and the families of all the workers who lost their jobs as their places of employment went up in flames end up suffering as a result of the lack of gonads of elected officials to protect innocent people.

Michael Brown's step father, Louis Head, an ex-con with a long list of prior convictions, married to Brown's mother, used a microphone to incite the rioters: *Burn this bitch down!*[349] Facts do not matter anymore. Numerous witnesses testified in support of Officer Wilson, including African-Americans who provided the facts about what happened. Michael Brown was a wanted criminal who had committed a strong-arm robbery minutes before his altercation with Officer Wilson. He was not an "*innocent*" unarmed 18-year-old, and the facts examined by the Grand Jury showed that he had attacked the police officer. The people who contributed to the creation of *a beast* include Michael Brown's step father who clearly was not a good role model.

President Obama went on national television right after the decision not to indict Officer Wilson to ask for calm, as using split screens the news media was showing the looting, vandalism, and stores set on fire. Instead of backing up the findings based on facts, he reminded citizens that he still had an investigation ongoing by the Department of Justice in a clear political witch hunt that looks and smells like *a case of reverse racism*. The so-called *post-racial age* has become a farce precisely because for leftist would-be revolutionaries keeping the fires going is good business. It took months, but a Justice Department investigation cleared Officer Wilson.

Bottom line: The *Counterculture* is Responsible

Michael Brown was a victim of the *counterculture*. He was a child of divorced parents, his mother remarried and the step-father turns out to be a criminal who has served multiple stretches in jail for dealing in narcotics, and a long list of other criminal activity. The destruction of Afro-American families due to ill-conceived welfare legislation which required the absence of fathers to qualify for benefits, the large number of children born to single mothers, the inconceivable percentage of abortions, the images promoted by Hollywood of what is "cool," – remember *Super Fly*?[350] – Drug abuse, free love, exploitation of women, and criminal behavior was presented as "cool." In real life, the promoted stereotypes end up producing tragedies like what happened in Ferguson. The *webcomic stories* are not very comic in real life. Michael Brown was heading for a serious prison sentence for felony assault and robbery after trial as an adult if he had not been killed. The responsibility for the Ferguson tragedy is shared by all the entities that profit from feeding multiple *counterculture* elements to young people.

It Takes Chutzpa!

In early November 2014 Michael Brown's parents traveled to Geneva, Switzerland, to request international assistance, accusing the U.S. of violating their son's human rights. They did not mention that their son was video-recorded as he carried out a strong-arm robbery and manhandled a frail older man much smaller than him a few minutes before he was shot by a police officer, whom he also physically attacked. What kind of jurisdiction does the *United Nations Committee on Torture and Other Cruel, Inhuman or Degrading Treatment or Punishment* have over a criminal incident that took place in the United States?[351] Who paid all the expenses for this trip to make a statement against police brutality in the U.S.?

"Heifer Dust" Happens

Following a pattern that has played out several times prior to the Ferguson incident, a Glendale, MO police sergeant with 35 years of service posted a rant with severely developmentally challenged racist comments on Facebook on 21 August 2014. He stated that the protesters should be "*put down like rabid dogs*" and ranted against President Obama. He called himself a "*killer*" who would shoot without regard to race… "*I personally believe in Jesus Christ as my lord savior, but I am also a killer… I've killed a lot…If you do not want to get killed, don't show up in front of me… I'm into diversity. I kill everybody, I don't care…*" He added that he retired from the Army because he refused to take orders from "*an undocumented President…*" Extremist idiots like this provide ammunition to the idiots at the other extreme… and irresponsibly provide the excuse for troublemakers to take advantage of the situation. The sergeant was rightfully suspended from his job.

In March 2015, the Justice Department made public the report of their investigation of the criminal justice system and police operations in Ferguson. The report pointed out a pattern of corruption and racism. Essentially, the criminal justice system was turned into a "profit center" by the municipal government, by imposing huge fines for traffic violations, targeting more-often-than not poor people and minorities. The Chief of Police, the Ferguson City Manager, and a judge that was a principal participant in these improper schemes to exploit the population through an improper use of law enforcement resigned. The situation found in Ferguson is not unlike other towns and cities throughout the country, including Washington, D.C. Racism, selective law enforcement, unnecessary roughness, and the morphing of law enforcement into a system to collect revenue through unfair practices is endemic.

Beavercreek, OH - Vignette
The NYPD Chokehold Vignette

About a month before the Ferguson incident, on 17 July 2014, several officers of the NY City Police Department in Staten Island attempted to place Eric Garner, a 6'5", 350-pound Black male for selling untaxed cigarettes, a misdemeanor. Garner verbally objected, complaining that police was picking on him. He had at least 30 prior arrests for similar petty offenses.[352] Technically, *he was resisting arrest* – even if he did not resist physically.[353] By not cooperating, he forced police to escalate the situation to the next level. One police officer, Daniel Pantaleo, moved in from behind and placed Garner on a chokehold, as three other police officers moved in to wrestle him to the ground and rolling him onto his stomach. Garner repeatedly complained *"I can't breathe!"* but police continued with the very physical arrest using what appeared like excessive force. Within a few short minutes 43-year-old Garner, who suffered from asthma and had heart problems was dead of a heart attack. The medical examiner after performing an autopsy came to the conclusion that Garner died from the chokehold and chest compression when he was restrained by police, and ruled the incident *a homicide*. However, Officer Pantaleo was not indicted by a 23-member Grand Jury.

Should police officers have used other non-violent tactics to defuse the situation in an attempt to get cooperation from Eric Garner? The quote from Mahatma Gandhi placed at the beginning of the section on police misconduct logically applies here: *"It's only when you see a mosquito landing on your testicles that you realize there is always a way to solve problems without using violence."* In hindsight, perhaps a non-violent means of dealing with the situation should have been applied, as the officers *did not* intent to kill Eric Garner.

The term *homicide* is frequently misunderstood. It does not necessarily imply that a criminal violation took place. It means that a human being was killed. It does not imply that *a murder* has been committed. A homicide can be justified or unjustified, depending on the particular circumstances. In this case, *police brutally*, resulted in the unintentional killing Eric Garner. On 4 December 2014, a week and a couple of days after the Ferguson grand jury announced its decision not to indict Officer Wilson for the shooting of Michael Brown, a NY grand jury of 14 White and 9 non-White people decided not to indict NYPD officer Pantaleo for using excessive force.

In this case, the entire incident was videotaped and just about everyone, including Conservative news media commentators expected an indictment due to the *brutality* and apparent *lack of good judgment* shown. Immediately a mixed crowd of protesters took the streets of New York City. Attorney General Eric Holder within minutes of the grand jury announcement went on national television to tell the public that DOJ was conducting an independent investigation to determine if there had been civil rights violations in this case. Once again the nation was witnessed another tragedy in which different people expected different outcomes.

Garner was married and had six children, as well as a long list of arrests for non-violent criminal offenses, for the most part for acting as a *street hustler* to scratch a living. Officer Pantaleo also had a history of lawsuits – two such cases after about 300 arrests - in which plaintiffs alleged false arrest, civil rights violations, and other allegations of police misconduct. Chokeholds have been banned by the NYPD for over twenty years, but they continue to be used.

Why did the police target Garner for arrest? First, the business community in the area where the incident took place complained to police about his loitering in the area, disrupting the normal flow of customers, and engaging in arguments with other people. Second, Garner had a history of loitering and approaching people transiting the area to sell them single untaxed cigarettes, a misdemeanor. Third, Garner had at least 31 similar arrests. The NYPD was reacting to citizen complaints, not just because Gardner was a known recidivist who apparently did not understand that he was not allowed to do what he was doing. The highest ranking police officer and in command when the arrest was made was a female Afro-American sergeant, which means that racism was probably not the driving force behind the decision to make an arrest.

The news media covered just about every angle to the story, exploiting the existence of the video recording of the arrest, which for the average viewer clearly showed unnecessary roughness, particularly after Garner was heard saying at least eleven times that he could not breath. Police should have released the chokehold at that point, considering that he was for all practical purposes on the ground on his chest and could easily have been handcuffed. Very few people did not take issue with the use of excessive force in this incident. There was considerable agreement that what happened was outrageous.

The news media failed to analyze some important common elements to both, the Michael Brown and the Eric Garner tragedies, as well as many other similar cases. In the fifty years between 1964 and 2014 in which numerous civil rights and anti-poverty legislation have been enacted, the system has failed to make much progress. The poverty rate is about the same. Most welfare programs have failed, particularly the Afro-American community. The crime rate among Black Americans has increased dramatically, to the point that one-in-three young Black males is either in jail, has been in jail, is out on probation, or awaiting trial. Something is very wrong with this picture. The common element is *the catastrophic influence of the counterculture* that appeared in America at about the same time in 1964.

The *counterculture* has encouraged young people to *drop out* from mainstream culture, adopt a different lifestyle including making a living by hustling in the streets, including selling "*loosies*" (un-taxed cigarettes), as Eric Garner had been doing for a long time to survive precariously. His buyers were other poor people who do not have the money to purchase a highly taxed pack of cigarettes. Once upon a time, Garner worked as a horticulturist for NY City, but somehow became unemployed and apparently could not find alternative employment.[354] He suffered from cardiovascular disease, a heart condition, diabetes, asthma, sleep apnea, seriously overweight, and without a doubt was not receiving adequate healthcare.[355] Finding employment for a person with his health handicaps certainly could not be easy. Young people, particularly minorities have been encouraged to challenge authority, without taking into account that the lyrics of *Gangsta Rap* that promote risky behavior leave out the consequences or anti-social behavior.

A significant related case was the indictment of the 22-year-old Hispanic man who filmed the arrest of Eric Garner with his cell telephone on 2 August 2014 on two third-degree felony counts for gun possession, after he was seeing by NYPD counter narcotics unit placing a .25 caliber Horton handgun into the waistband of 17-year-old Alba Lekaj, who was found to be in possession of a small amount of marijuana. Orta had other pending charges for a variety of criminal offenses, including third-degree assault, robbery, and possession of controlled substances. Both, Orta and his wife claimed the police was acting in retaliation for filming the arrest of Eric Garner about three weeks earlier. The NY City Patrolmen's Benevolent Association countered by pointing out that criminals like Ramsey Orta try to benefit by demonizing the good work of police officers.[356]

The *counterculture* promotes tolerance of illegality, and a mindset that encouraged inflammatory racialist rhetoric. There is a criminal underworld that operates in line with Timothy Leary's *Turn on, tune in, drop out.* Nobody bothered to tell young people that pranksters and law violators have a very high probability of ending up in jail or killed in confrontations with police. Life is not a rock festival, but the lyrics of Country Joe and the Fish – *I–feel-like-I'm fixin'-to-die-rag*… may be how things end for people who live outside the law, as witnessed by the Ferguson and Staten Island tragedies.

A Pattern of Failure

The following contemporary incidents are indicative of the failure of the criminal-justice system.

Beheading in Oklahoma. On 26 September 2014 a 30-year-old Afro-American with a police record converted to Islam and began to proselytize co-workers to become Muslims in Oklahoma. After an altercation at Vaughan Foods, Alton Alexander Nolan, AKA Jah'Keem Yisrael, went home and returned with a large knife and, apparently, at random grabbed 54-year-old grandmother Collen Hufford and ritually beheaded her while chanting Islamic expressions in Arabic. Nolan attacked and wounded another female employee, and was only stopped when company executive Mark Vaughan, who is also a reserve sheriff deputy, shot him. As in so many other cases, the perpetrator had *previous arrests for marijuana and cocaine with intent to distribute*, assault and battery, and traffic violations going back to 2006. In March 2013 Nolan was arrested for possession of a controlled substance and resisting arrest. He *had served time in jail for assaulting a policeman* and had a long rap sheet! He had posted pictures of himself on Facebook in Islamic dress and made jihadist comments. Other Muslims attending services at the Mosque in Oklahoma that he frequented said that he had converted to Islam while incarcerated and was known to be more radical than members of the Nation of Islam. *Why was he out on the streets?*

A convicted assassin is made into a role-model. On 1 October 2014, it was reported that a convicted assassin had been selected to be a commencement speaker at a college in Vermont. In December 1991, 25-year-old Police Officer Daniel Faulkner was shot in the back, and as he lied wounded on the ground in Philadelphia, he was again shot between the eyes by Wesley Cook, a former member of the Black Panther Party. From espousing Black Nationalism under a revolutionary Marxist ideology, somehow old members drifted to Islamic extremist views and became influenced by revolutionary extremist Islam. Wesley Cook changed his name to Mumia Abu-Jamal and became a Muslim after he was arrested, tried, convicted, and sentenced to death by a jury of 10 Whites and two Afro-Americans. The case was appealed all the way to the US Supreme Court, where the conviction was upheld. Nevertheless, the death sentenced was vacated and converted to life in prison without the possibility of parole due to a technicality.[357] Incredibly, Goddard College invited this assassin to be the commencement speaker.[358] The excuse was that he had become a winning journalist from prison, from where he chronicles the so-called "human condition." Among the assassins claim to fame is that he was allowed to take college classes from prison, and earned a BA from the same college in 1996. Among his long-term supporters are the Hollywood celebrities, NAACP, Human Rights Watch, Amnesty International, and Communist organizations from all over the world. All kinds of distortion of the facts have been used to justify the unjustifiable. They claim that he is *a victim of racist justice.* Goddard College is a small school located in Plainfield, VT, where apparently students are taught to glorify police killers. *What a way to grab national headlines!*[359] Despite the protestations of elected officials and relatives of the victim, this criminal who *should have been executed long ago*, has been turned into some kind of role model for young people. *American society tolerates the intolerable and then wonders why the country is heading in the wrong direction towards Anarchy.* But for how long will Americans allow situations like this to continue?

Survivalist/Extremist shoots a policeman. On the night of 16 September 2014, a survivalist, and declared enemy of the US Government named Eric Mathew Frein shot and killed a police officer and wounded a second outside the Blooming Grove police barracks in Pennsylvania using a .308-caliber rifle, and fled into the Poconos Mountains. Frein was charged with criminal homicide of a law enforcement officer, unlawful flight to avoid prosecution, and several related charges. *Frein is representative of violent extremists* who surfaced in the past thirty years, including Eric Rudolph, an anti-abortion activist who committed several murders and exploded an IED at Centennial Olympic Park during the 1996 Summer Olympics in Atlanta in 1996, killing one person and wounding over 100 other people.[360] More recent examples include Jerad and Amanda Miller, who shot and killed two policemen during their lunch break at a dinner, and Frazier Cross, a neo-Nazi, former KKK member, and White supremacist and activist arrested on 13 April 2014 for shooting three people at a Jewish community center in Overland Park, Kansas. Cross had a history of arrests linked to hate group activity, including for illegal tinkering with explosives.[361] Frein had a criminal record starting as far back as 2004, when he was charged with burglary and grand larceny and failed to show up for trial. Over 1000 law enforcement officers were involved in tracking Frein through the Poconos using sophisticated tracking gear and dogs. U.S. Marshalls finally captured Frein after seven weeks searching at a cost of about $10 million. Frein, a right-wing extremist, claimed that he acted in an effort to reclaim "*the liberties we once had*."[362]

Extremist elements from both ends of the political spectrum have existed for a long time. The picture above was taken circa 1968/69 by the author of members of the American Nazi Party demonstrating in front of the White House. The FBI tracked these groups to protect society from potential violent lawbreakers. The author has many years of experience dealing with all sorts of extremists. As the case of Eric Mathew Frein clearly shows, it is not only Black extremists who target law enforcement officers who are working to protect civil society against evil.

No known restrictions on publication

Off the Pig!
Black Panther Party Coloring Book

On Saturday 20 December 2014, two NYPD officers were murdered by a would-be revolutionary Afro-American Muslim assassin, in part as a result of years of brainwashing of Black youth with insurrectionist rhetoric

Two NYPD officers were assassinated in an ambush in Brooklyn as they sat in their police car. Both officers, Rafael Ramos and Wenjian Liu, were members of minority groups (Hispanic and Chinese). The gunman, Ismaaiyl Abdullah Brinsley, posted on Instagram that he was going to kill policemen as retribution for the killing of Michael Brown and Eric Garner. This incident was the product of years of incitement of this type of violence by extremist groups. The assassin posted the message *"I'm putting Wings on Pigs today..."* and in Facebook he added: *"I Always Wanted to Be Known for Doing Something Right... But My Past Is Stalking Me and My Present Is Haunting Me."* As other criminals, he was a converted Black Muslim. How long will American society put up with incendiary rhetoric by extremist elements calling for violent revolution? Will Americans ever link the violent rhetoric of such groups as the Black Panther Party and assorted lunatics like the Nation of Islam to racial conflict? How about the incendiary comments of charlatans like Al Sharpton? The growth of the *counterculture* since the 1960s has contributed to the growing climate of crime and violence in the country. When the system fails to bring under control the slow drift towards the *law of the jungle* the result will naturally be complete Anarchy. *Undiagnosed Mental illness?* As in other similar cases, mental illness may have contributed to the tragedy.

Brinsley
Picture released by the NYPD.
No known restrictions on publication

***The* Law of Probability *and* Hamartia[1]**

With a population of 321 million people, it is a numbers game... An infinitesimal percentage of people are touched by tragedies, but tragedies occur daily, and any of them can become a catalyst for conflict. Perpetual recidivists, including criminals with some form of mental illness, are allowed to roam free to continue victimizing innocent people. Law enforcement officers are part of the population and reflect the same characteristics. Even if thorough background investigations are carried out before hiring law enforcement officers, certain applicants suffering some form of mental illness are not weeded out. It only takes a relatively small number of mentally unfit people to produce episodic tragedies. Anybody can make the wrong judgement, misinterpret or misapprehend facts, act based on inadequate knowledge, or simply make a mistake. There is a chain of cause-and-effect tragedies that unfortunately are part of the compass of daily life for over 321 million people.

[1] Tragic flaw and ironic consequences...leading to catharsis (cleansing).

The pattern of *undeniable* police misconduct and tensions between Americans of different races continues unabated. Sometimes the culprit is obvious, unmistakable, and undeniable, but other times it is unclear, obscure, and practically impossible to easily identify who did what to whom, or why. Regardless of the facts, there are demoniacal people who take delight in upsetting the peaceful course of life. Apocalyptic predictions are not justified, but without a doubt something has to be done to stop the tragic never-ending chain of events that are leading to catastrophe. The situation is not just the product of *happenstance* or *happenchance*, or part of a complex plot. It is a large country, and the possibility of something going wrong somewhere is high.

In early April 2015 a white policeman in N. Charleston, SC, was filmed shooting a Black man eight times in the back, as he ran away after a traffic stop for a malfunctioning tail light. The driver had outstanding arrest warrants for not paying court-ordered child support, and was possibly concerned about being arrested after the police officer checked his credentials. Other officers who arrived at the scene of the shooting failed to render medical assistance expeditiously to 50-year-old Walter Scott. After the senseless incident, Police Officer Michael Slager was fired and charged with murder. The incident was captured on video. Few people would argue in defense of a clearly improper act.

Police misconduct victims, contrary to numerous news media accounts, *are not limited to Blacks!* On 9 April, San Bernardino County, CA, sheriff's deputies were filmed brutally beating 30-year-old Francis Pusok, a white man, after he was arrested as he attempted to flee detention on horseback. The county settled the case out-of-court within days with a payment of $650,000. There was no denying the facts after a KNBC news helicopter videotaped and broadcasted the entire incident as it was happening. Pusok is no saint, as witnessed by several prior run-ins with the law, including charges of resisting arrest. Days after he was compensated by the county he was detained again under suspicion of wrongdoing. Nevertheless, there was no justification for the brutal beating he received from a racially and ethnically mixed group of law enforcement personnel.

On 14 April, a 73-year-old Robert Charles "Bob" Bates, a wealthy businessman working as a Reserve Deputy Sheriff, shot and killed an unarmed Black male in Oklahoma, who had been attempting to flee from police after he was caught illegally selling weapons. The unpaid Deputy Sheriff claimed that he "*confused*" his handgun with his Taser and accidentally shot Eric Courtney Harris.[2] He was charged with 2nd degree manslaughter for culpable negligence. The incident was captured in a dramatic video, when the Reserve Deputy said *"Oh, I'm sorry. I shot him!"* The wounded man was begging for help, as he explained that he was losing his breath, but instead of helping, another deputy sheriff told him *"Fuck your breath,"* as he kneeled on the neck of the mortally wounded man… and continued making comments, like *"Shut the fuck up…"* A follow-up investigation found that Robert Charles "Bob" Bates had very deficient training to be working in the Sheriff's Office. Clearly, there was no denying the facts on this case.

Two days before, on 12 April, another 25-year-old Black man with at least 18 previous arrests, was detained by several policemen in Baltimore and put in a paddy wagon used to haul prisoners to central booking. Freddie Gray had a long history of run-ins with police, mostly on drug violations, and just a month earlier he had been charged with second-degree assault and destruction of property. The reason for the arrest was not clear, but apparently he ran from police, and when they tackled and searched him, he was found in possession of a switchblade knife in one of his pockets. Possession of a switchblade knife is punishable by up to one year in prison and a fine of $500, but in this case, the switchblade may have been within the legal limits, was closed, and inside one of Mr. Gray's pants pocket. He was a recidivist, but that was no excuse to arrest him in the absence of evidence of a law violation.

Gray's spinal cord was mysteriously severed, and he suffered other injuries while on police custody on his way to central booking, but not necessarily consistent with a whipping. Upon his arrival, police requested paramedics and Gray was taken to a hospital emergency room, but by then, he had lapsed into a coma. On 19 April Gray died.

---

2 Eric Courtney Harris had a criminal record. For example, on 31 August 2014 he was arrested and released on an $8,044 bond pending trail. On 15 February 2013, he was arrested again for possession of marijuana.

The case had to be investigated to find what actually happened. Without a doubt several instructions for police officers were not followed. For example, he was not secured by a seatbelt when he was placed inside the van. No evidence of a police beating was captured by cameras and made public. The biracial police team carried out the arrest, which makes it very difficult to tag what happened as an "*incident of racism.*"

As had taken place in Ferguson a few months before, all hell broke loose on 27 April after Freddie Gray's funeral. Contrary to undeniable evidence captured on video, as in the prior two cases in South Carolina and Oklahoma, there was no "smoking gun." Six police officers were suspended pending the result of several investigations at the state, local, and Federal level. The usual group of self-elected "community leaders" and national agitators engaged in "*Blackexploitation*" attended the funeral, all calling for restrain, but hoping for the opposite, because that is how they function. Always jumping to conclusions, before investigations are carried out, and findings lead investigators to deductions, assumptions, and a valid set of conclusions. And the national news media dropped just about everything else to focus on the tragedy. Instead of a chorus, as in ancient Greek plays, they parade a series of improvised pundits and broadcast their soliloquies. More often-than-not, the so-called "authoritative experts" provide braggadocio opinions that are far from reality.

Contrary to the background in previous incidents, such as the case of Ferguson, Baltimore has a Black female Mayor, Stephanie Rawlings-Blake, a Black Police Commissioner, and a racially mixed police force that is about 50 percent Black. The Congressman for the District is a reputable Black leader who has worked for his people during a long career in politics. Yet, something went very wrong. Was there a failure of leadership, or are conditions so extreme in the country that that violence is inevitable?

Shortly after the funeral, rioting started, leading to the arrest of over 250 *hooligans,* at least 144 vehicle fires, including police cars, and the destruction of numerous buildings by looting and arson. About thirty police officers were hurt needing attention at a hospital ER, with at least two needing hospitalization. Although President Obama and Mayor

Rawlings-Blake used the term "*thugs,*" talk'ing heads in the news media claimed that the term "*thugs*" has become "*racialized*" and considered a "*racist*" description of the perpetrators. *It takes the cake!* Some news media extremists and "*Blackexploiters*" accused the Mayor and President Obama, both Black, of using racist terminology. To be clear, the rioters were lawbreakers, hoodlums, and street gang members. If they cannot be called "*thugs*" something is very wrong.

The rioting was planned through "social media" by high school students and teenage gang members calling for a so-called "*purge.*" Even in a poor area, school kids have smart phones with access to "social media," which have become tools for criminals. There is high unemployment, poverty, numerous unmet needs, but expensive high tech phones are widely available. It would be hard to explain that to masses of poor people in just about any other country. How do they get the smart phones? How do they afford the monthly charges? Drug dealing is a lucrative part time activity for some teenagers… and the proceeds go to indulging in expensive toys and expensive snickers.

Black teenagers started throwing bottles, bricks, and rocks at police shortly after 3:00 p.m. Looting and arson began within one hour of the end of the school day. Despite the growing conflict, police response was very limited, and the disturbances were allowed to grow without quick police response. Firefighters and police trying to extinguish fires were attacked and prevented from saving property. The same pattern of appeasement that took place in Ferguson, Missouri, a few months earlier was used again. Damn the business community, nobody seem to give a rat's ass about what happen to store owners and their employees. Police was instructed to "*stand down*" because the poor little darlings were just letting off steam.

Dozens of shops, restaurants, bars, gas stations, and other businesses were ransacked. The neighborhoods affected and the entire Baltimore Metro area may be affected for years, as businessmen will be reluctant to rebuild and new investors will stay away. As a result, community frustrations are bound to increase, as the availability of jobs will decline, and people will have to travel far to meet their needs. Property prices will decline, more buildings will be boarded up, and everyone will argue about who or what is responsible for the outcome. Fifty years after the 1968 riots the scars are still visible, so it may take another fifty years before the damage can be repaired.

The Mayor of Baltimore announced a nightly curfew around 8:00 p.m. *but starting the following day instead of immediately!* It took another hour before she announced that schools would be shut down the following day. In the meantime, as reinforcements from the State Police arrived, the rioters continued to control the situation. Law enforcement and political leaders claimed that because the rioters, at least initially, were between 13 and 16 years old, they did not want to use force. Before the disturbances came to an end over 450 arrests were made, and they turned out to be over 18 years of age except in rare exceptions.

Even a church-sponsored housing program for elderly Black poor people was torched. At least eighty elderly people will have to wait to rebuild a project with a price tag of over $80 million. Will they live long enough to ever receive the benefits of such a facility? Many of the small business destroyed were owned by Black entrepreneurs and poor hard working immigrants. Some businessmen stood guard with baseball bats, guns, and guard dogs to protect their property. Another step was taken back to the *law of the jungle.* When people lose trust in government that is what happens.

What happened in Baltimore is typical of what many Black communities experience all over the country. They feel that they are under siege by criminal elements at one end, and by law enforcement officers prone to misconduct at the other end. Street gangs control many neighborhoods, challenging law enforcement officers and society. Traditional Black families have been destroyed, and an estimated 72 percent of all Black children are being born out of wedlock. Yes, there is social injustice, but why? After trillions of dollars spent since the 1960s in social programs have failed miserably. The *counterculture elements* and horrible management of programs to help the poor are to a great extent responsible for the failure of the education system. Misguided and misdirected young people are guided by the wrong models. As could have been predicted, in the month that followed the riots the murder rate in Baltimore escalated. At least 31 people were victims of the climate of violence, and the majority were Black-on-Black killings. During the Memorial Day weekend 28 people were shot, including children, and 9 of the victims died.

On Wednesday 29 April, copycats in several cities including Boston, Detroit, Ferguson, Minneapolis, New York, San Diego, and Seattle, staged demonstrations in solidarity with the protests in Baltimore. In New York City at least one police officer was hurt when struck by a bottle as violent demonstrations after rallies in Lower Manhattan, around the Holland Tunnel, Union Square, and around Times Square. Over 100 arrests were made, many of them white leftist extremists – for engaging in their own version of *Blackexploitation.* They were trying to turn the situation into a violent confrontation with police in support of the so-called "*Black struggle*" and revolution. At least eleven protestors were arrested in Denver for obstructing traffic and resisting police orders. In Ferguson, three people were shot and several were arrested in separate incidents, as protesters blocked streets, looted some stores again, and threw rocks and bottles at police.

The first week of May brought about a continuation of the domestic war between police and criminal elements, most of whom happen to be Black. On 2 May 2015, plainclothes New York City 25-year-old police officer Brian Moore was shot in the head by a Black criminal with a long rap sheet. Moore passed away on 4 May, becoming the fifth officer killed on the line of duty in the city in 2015. The killer was arrested for first-degree murder and other charges. The ambush was similar to the fatal ambush of two other police officers who were murdered in Brooklyn in December 2014.

As police officers die trying to protect citizens from criminals in The Big Apple, press reports indicated that visitors to Central Park were being mugged by gangs of at least a dozen Black teenagers. Despite numerous muggings over the second weekend of May, no arrests were made. The city's Police Commissioner called the rash of muggings and aberration… insisting that *the park remains one of the safest places in America*, which says a lot about the pathology of crime and punishment in New York City and the entire country.

A week after Officer Moore was killed in New York, two police officers in Hattiesburg. Miss. were shot and killed after a routine traffic stop. White Police Officer Benjamin Deen made the traffic stop, and Black Police Officer Liquori Tate, answered a request for backup. The killers were brothers Curtis and Marvin Banks, both well-known felons with multiple prior arrests. According to their mother, Marvin is a drug user and alcoholic, and may be mentally ill. His brother Curtis, a girlfriend is charged as accessories to murder, and a third friend was charged with obstruction of justice. All four are Black. As frequently happens, a Black policeman was killed by four Blacks, so the case falls within the category of Black-on-Black crime.

Without engaging in apocalyptic predictions of gloom & doom, it is evident that the system is blinking red, and anything could happen if nothing is done about it. There are multiple examples between April 2014 and May 2015 of a *pattern of system failure,* as society is left unprotected from predators. Victims of crime are denied their right to justice. Criminal elements are going in and out of prison to commit more crimes, and so-called "*correctional institutions,*" are allowed to function as "*crime universities.*" When the system fails to properly enforce the law, police authorities are enticed to impart justice as judge, jury, and executioner, as they get tired of dealing with the same violators over and over again. Sadly, sometimes they get away with it, as the *climate of impunity* extends to both, criminals and rogue law enforcement officers.

Freddy Gray's Arrest Record

20 March 2015: Possession of a Controlled Dangerous Substance

13 March 2015: Malicious destruction of property, second-degree assault

20 January 2015: Fourth-degree burglary, trespassing

14 January 2015: Possession of a controlled dangerous substance, possession of a controlled dangerous substance with intent to distribute

31 December 2014: Possession of narcotics with intent to distribute

14 December 2014: Possession of a controlled dangerous substance

31 August 2014: Illegal gambling, trespassing

25 January 2014: Possession of marijuana

28 September 2013: Distribution of narcotics, unlawful possession of a controlled dangerous substance, second-degree assault, second-degree escape

13 April 2012: Possession of a controlled dangerous substance with intent to distribute, unlawful possession of a controlled dangerous substance, violation of probation

16 July 2008: Possession of a controlled dangerous substance, possession with intent to distribute

28 March 2008: Unlawful possession of a controlled dangerous substance

14 March 2008: Possession of a controlled dangerous substance with intent to manufacture and distribute

11 February 2008: Unlawful possession of a controlled dangerous substance, possession of a controlled dangerous substance

29 August 2007: Possession of a controlled dangerous substance with intent to distribute, violation of probation
28 August 2007: Possession of marijuana
23 August 2007: False statement to a peace officer, unlawful possession of a controlled dangerous substance
16 July 2007: Possession of a controlled dangerous substance with intent to distribute, unlawful possession of a controlled dangerous substance (2 counts)

NOTE: This record of arrests are limited to violations recorded in Baltimore, Maryland, and does not take into account possible arrests in other jurisdictions. Why was Freddy Gray out of jail? Without a doubt, Freddy Gray's future victims were bound to be other Afro-Americans.

COUNTRY	HOMICIDE COUNT	RATE PERCENTAGE of INHABITANTS
Argentina	1,868	4.6
Canada	492	1.4
China -PRC	13,410	1
Chile	541	2.9
France	675	1.1
Germany	690	0.8
Italy	529	0.9
Russia	**14,574**	**10.1**
Spain	390	0.8
Sweden	91	1
UK	753	1.2
US	**14,722**	**4.7**

The United States suffers from one of the highest rates of homicide in the world, second only to the Russian Federation, and considerably more than Western European countries and Canada.

TRAGEDY AT THE MOTHER EMANUEL AME CHURCH

A deranged white 21 year-old-male entered a Bible study meeting at the Emanuel African Methodist Episcopal Church in Charleston, SC, and shot nine innocent worshippers on 17 June 2015. His profile was typical of perpetrators of these types of crimes. A high school dropout, with a history of drug and alcohol abuse, a history of mental illness, and arrests, was proselytized by racist extremists and brainwashed. One arrest was linked to the manufacture of *Subozone* (buprenorphine and nalozone) a habit-forming controlled substance used to treat opiate addiction. In a Facebook profile the attacker had posted the historical flags of Rhodesia and South Africa when they were ruled by a White minority, as well as a Confederate flag and advocated for white supremacy. He justified his hate crime with racist comments. How was a person with this profile able to get a gun?

Is the US turning into a Police State?

A "*police state*" is defined as *a political unit where there is repressive control of the population by the arbitrary use of power by police and other arms of the state.* Repressive control can take many forms, from constant monitoring through technical means, or through informers and spies. Historically, there have been many different styles of repressive dictatorships that used creative ways to force obedience through brutal means and psychological manipulation. If America became a police state it would be a disastrous conclusion, or the *Götterdämmerung* to American Constitutional Democracy. It would be the ultimate destruction of the spirit of the Founding Fathers. There are dangerous signs that "*the system*" is in crisis, as a battle between good and evil plays out.

Extremists play up flaws in "the system" to describe the U.S. as resembling the dehumanized totalitarian government portrayed by George Orwell in his 1949 novel *Nineteen Eighty-Four*, with omnipresent government surveillance. Extremists take advantage of every opportunity to play up some incidents, when, in fact, generally the country continues to be the ultimate representative Constitutional

Democracy and shining light for freedom, although in desperate need of a correction in direction. In recent years, convoluted means of law enforcement have emerged that are undermining key aspects of the *Bill of Rights*, because a terrific amount of heifer dust in the air is making it very difficult to ascertain why things are happening, and there are numerous contradictions playing out.

Big Brother is Watching

There has been a steady increase in the use of traffic control cameras allegedly to reduce accidents and casualties. Nevertheless, many jurisdictions are increasingly relying on traffic fines as a *revenue source*. The cameras have produced the unintended effect of turning law enforcement into a form of *regressive taxation* which hurts the poor. To complicate matters, private companies have become providers of equipment, as well as "*partners in business*" for government authorities. Suppliers offer to provide all the technology at no cost in exchange for permission to install cameras, and in turn, they split the "profit" with the government. Thus, instead of a means to reduce accidents and casualties, traffic cameras become a money making operation – *a cash cow* - far removed from the original intent of improving traffic patterns and reducing accidents and casualties.[363] *Not even George Orwell could come up with this angle back in 1949!* The prognosis points to even more video surveillance, including policemen wearing cameras as part of their uniform, together with weapons and handcuffs.

Police Industrial Complex

As if we did not have enough with the so-called *Military Industrial Complex* made famous by President Eisenhower in his farewell address, now we have an emerging *Police Industrial Complex*. Another relatively recent development are privately owned and operated detention centers or privately owned jails. Thus, private investors have a financial incentive to advocate for stricter sentences and longer prison terms.[364] There are documented cases of corrupt judges in collusion with companies that own and operate jails to apply harsher sentences to increase the prison population and associated profits. (See the previous section on

Prosecutorial Misconduct.) Prisons have become a cash cow for some people.

Is there something very strange going on behind the scenes? The statistics are incredible. In 1989 only 3% of American adults had a felony conviction, but by 2000, the number had increased to 6.5%, and as of 2014, it has increased further to 8.4%.[365] Is an approximate increase of 700% in the prisoner population between 1974 and 2014 the result of increased criminal activity alone, or are there other reasons, such as the advent of privately owned and operated prisons and associated corruption? It would be reasonable to suspect racism, due to the high percentage of people in prison who belong to racial and ethnic minorities. It would also be unreasonable to deny that there are very violent Black criminals, who generally target their own kind.

Abusive Practices

Abusive police practices have always existed, particularly if officers were convinced that they could get away with *imparting justice* as they saw fit.[366] When confronted with a revolving door in the judicial system, with the same people being arrested and released over and over again, some police officers feel justified in acting as judge, jury, and executioner. They want to exercise their power to get rid of whomever they want, silently.[367] Has there been an increase in abusive practices since the 1980s, or is the advent of new technologies exposing abusers, who can no longer hide in the shadows by intimidating witnesses? Since the proliferation of cellular telephony in the 1980s there has been a steady increase in the number of witnesses to police abuse who can document, with video recordings, how law enforcers become law violators. Abusive police officers all over the country have lost their jobs and been prosecuted for violating basic human rights.

Videotaping has become a very effective way to protect citizens against abuse by police officers.[368] Perhaps the most famous case is that of Rodney King, which took place 3 March 1991, when police pulled him out of his car after a high speed chase in Los Angeles, and five officers proceeded to beat him up mercilessly.[369] A witness videotaped the incident using a camcorder from his apartment and released it to the news media. Four of the arresting officers were charged with assault and using excessive force. Three were acquitted of assault and the jury failed to reach a verdict on the use of excessive force by the fourth officer, despite the video recording of the incident.[370]

Since the Rodney King incident video recordings have played a significant role in law enforcement. In the Ferguson, Dayton, and Staten Island cases discussed in the previous section, video recordings played a key role in the investigations. However, there are many more instances where recordings have become the detonator for follow-up incidents. For example, a man who appeared to be mentally challenged was handcuffed by police officers from the Antioch Police Department near San Francisco, CA. The detainee was tasered, hit with a baton, and then subjected to an attack by a police dog to the point that the man was left bleeding and in severe pain. Several witnesses began recording the incident with their cell phones. Police officers forced witnesses, to erase their recordings, and confiscated several cell phones. They even pulled a lady out of her car to force her to give up her phone.[371] Technically, police need to get a search warrant before they can view recordings from confiscated equipment. Incidents of overkill or brutality have resulted in firings and convictions of police officers, and for that reason, police officers do not want witnesses, particularly recordings that can be entered as evidence in court against them. Have the cameras reduced police brutality? The issue has not been studied seriously, because it would be necessary to have data or evidence of cases of brutality before the advent of camcorders to answer the question, and such data is not available.

Different states have different legislation about such recordings, and there are inconsistent interpretations of the Constitution. For example, in New York and Massachusetts, it is legal to record police officers while performing their duties. Nevertheless, numerous witnesses have been arrested for videotaping police in the performance of their duties in both states.[372] Federal courts have sided with the rights of citizen to record police incidents. The lack of a consistent way of handling these incidents across the country add to the increasing disunity in a country that is called The *United* States of America.

Civil Libertarians, the ACLU, left-wing and right-wing groups have objected to law enforcement use surveillance for a very long time. Video surveillance is supposed to be governed by the Fourth Amendment to the Constitution, and, technically, intelligence and law enforcement agencies must show a court that they have probable cause that there is evidence of criminal activity that can be secured through video surveillance to obtain a search (recording) warrant. The hypocrisy of these groups is that the very technology that they object to has been instrumental in clarifying right and wrong in cases of police brutality. Subversives are always going to protest any means of identifying them before they have an opportunity to carry out their fantasies as revolutionaries through terrorism.

Fourth Amendment rights could be violated by increasing government surveillance, but not using these technologies could result in a repeat of the *big surprise* received on 11 September 2001. Is warrantless surveillance justified or a clear violation of the concept of unreasonable search and seizure? As long as terrorists are unable to carry out a successful attack the public debate will continue, but if they happen to "score big" the opposite public outcry will materialize overnight.

A legislative attempt to place limits on data collection was narrowly defeated in the House of Representatives by 217 to 205 on 23 July 2013.[373] In January, 2014, several Federal judges, members of the Foreign Intelligence Surveillance Court (FISA) unanimously objected to and rejected the notion of an "*independent advocate*" to the FISA court to increase transparency and oversight in reaction to allegations of excesses in domestic and foreign intelligence surveillance programs.[374] After the Ferguson incident and the decision of the grand jury not to indict the police officer who shot Michael Brown, President Obama announced a plan to use Federal funds to provide personal video cameras to police officers all over the country as a way of reducing police misconduct. This is typical of left-of-center American politics... *they want to have their cake and eat it too...*

Mismanagement of the Prison System

If cell phones with cameras were allowed in prison, the pictures that could be produced of abuse by guards would make the Abu Ghraib scandal child's play.[375] In September 2014 the Department of Corrections of the State of Florida fired 32 "correction officers" for abusing and murdering prisoners. The decision was made just before *The Miami Herald* was about to publish an article about the long list of complaints and evidence of prisoner abuse.[376] The Abu Ghraib scandal continues to hurt America's reputation ten years after prisoner abuse images were released. If more details were released about what goes on in American prisons, the odyssey would certainly damage any claims of moral superiority.[377] Charles Graner, the convicted perpetrator of the most serious abuses and ring leader was a corrections officer in Pennsylvania, where he had already gained a reputation for abusing prisoners. He worked at SCI-Greene, where he took part in at least one "savage beating" of a prisoner in 2004. But this monster had been involved in numerous cases of sadistic treatment of prisoners going back to the late 1990s.[378]

Sadistic violence, including rape and sexual abuse against prisoners is endemic, in some states more prevalent than others, but present throughout the country. A study carried out by the Justice Department revealed in January 2014 that sexual abuse in prisons across the country was on the rise, and that around 49% of the cases involved guards.[379] (The Justice Department report noted that about a quarter of all incidents of staff sexual harassment were committed by females, an obvious reference to Lesbian attacks on female prisoners. This could be another derivative of the *counterculture* of the 1960s, although Lesbians have been around since the ancient times.)[380] An ACLU report issued in 2014 reported that abuse of immigrants in privately-run prisons.[381] Despite these findings, few guards are removed from their jobs, and few are ever prosecuted. This situation in the prison systems adds fuel to the growing *culture of impunity*.[382]

Abuse by Privatized Probation System

In a number of states the management of the probation system was privatized or contracted out to private companies for the purpose of reducing government expenses. Although the intensions may have been good, in practice, a very abusive and corrupt system was created. For example, if a driver is stopped by police for speeding and is unable to pay the fine and court costs, a private company is granted the authority to collect payment in monthly installments, plus a handling fee. Poor people who are unable to pay are hit with additional fees and fines and even hauled into jail. An initial fine of perhaps $200 may increase exponentially turning the law violator into practically a slave of the predatory practices of the service provider. The poor, and particularly minority poor, are the primary victims of the compounding abusive practices. The private-probation companies rake millions of dollars from the people who can least afford to deal with this situation. Offenders end up becoming virtual slaves of the companies that have been granted these contracts. The service providers want to see higher fines and more clients, and have a natural interest in enticing or corrupting judges to generate more income. The concept, as applied in practice, lacks proper oversight and transparency, and suffers from similar weaknesses as privatized jails, or privatized traffic control cameras. In a functioning democracy, the state should not delegated or outsourced to private companies functions that logically should be in control of elected officials, who are in turn controlled by voters.

Militarization of Law Enforcement

Citizens are questioning the program to pass down military-style weapons from the DOD to police forces around the country, and the proliferation of special operations squad teams that resemble military Special Forces. As the homeland is increasingly exposed to terrorism, there is a reasonable justification to create special teams to deal with the problem. However, how much is enough? There have been numerous cases where law enforcement authorities dressed in paramilitary uniforms mistakenly entered a home and roughed-up innocent people, and even killed young children, while conducting raids based on warrants with the wrong address or carried out no knock warrants without proper surveillance to detect the presence of innocent bystanders. These mistakes have taken place all over the country, from Atlanta, to New York City, to Peoria.[383] Innocent people who thought that criminals had entered their homes to rob them and used their weapons for self-defense ended up shot and killed by SWAT teams.

Local governments have paid millions of dollars to victims of these poorly-planned and executed raids. Is the problem tied to military-style weapons, or a growing reckless and aggressive *cowboy mentality*? Racism is a frequent component of incidents of police brutality. However, that is a simplistic analysis of a greater problem. Behind ethnic conflict, there is poverty, shortage of opportunities for upward mobility, and competition for power and resources. Ultimately, the outcome of the growing number of conflicts between police and different population groups could lead to class warfare. The growth of right-wing and anti-government militia groups is part of the same phenomenon. These groups target law enforcement just as much, if not more, than extremists at the left-wing of the political spectrum.

Department of Homeland Security (DHS)

The creation of the Department of Homeland Security (DHS) in November 1992, as a result of the 9/11/2001 terrorist attacks, was an attempt to combine the previous areas of jurisdiction of 22 Federal agencies into one unified agency. It *did not* create a repressive organization, and DHS may not even be very effective. The same or similar functions already existed before DHS was created. The creation of DHS was a classical American idiom: *to close the barn door after the horse has bolted.* The problem is that after the imaginary horse escaped, a very real mountain lion was still in the barn with us! The threat of Islamic extremist terrorism was then, and continues to be very real, despite a DHS budget of over $61 billion annually, and 240,000 employees.[384]

DHS has worked for a dozen years to improve its' performance and implement more effective plans to protect the homeland, but it would only take another case like the events of 9/11/2001 to discredit the agency. Terrorists only have to pull off a successful attack once to send DHS into a spin. A GAO report published on 26 April 2013 found multiple areas of fragmentation, overlap, duplication, and potential cost savings.[385] The assessments made of DHS by multiple organizations *do not* point out any activities that resemble what occurs in true police states. There is a growing body of literature on the subject of policing and the key aspects of the Criminal-Justice System analyzing the subject from different angles, which shows that the system continues to provide freedom of expression, which would not be found in true repressive police states.[386]

Seizing Assets Without Justification

On Sunday 12 October 2014, *The Washington Post* published the paper with a large headline: *Seized Assets Fuel Police Spending.*[387] The article highlights how millions of dollars in assets improperly seized by police organizations and Federal agencies, including ICE and DEA, have been used to purchased military-style equipment, as well as to cover local budgets for police departments. In 1993, *The Orlando Sentinel* won a Pulitzer Prize for exposing in a series of articles how the Volusia County Sherriff's Office had improperly seized several million dollars from mostly minority drivers who were never charged with a crime. Instead of declaring illegal these practices, the situation was made worse after 9/11/2001. Without indictments or search warrants, law enforcement has been violating individual rights protected by the Constitution. The Criminal-Justice System is being pulled apart in numerous ways, and this just happens to be one of the most egregious and appalling ways in which *the system* is being undermined. It is all part of the so-called asset forfeiture programs at the U.S. Department of Justice, and at odds with basic civil liberties and the Constitution.

This program should be analyzed in historical terms, as the issue was one of the triggers to the American Declaration of Independence and the Revolutionary War that followed. The so-called *writs of assistance* permitted British customs officials to search homes, warehouses, ships or any other location without a need to show cause on a whim, and seize assets. The driver for the *writs of assistance* was the British effort to stop trade between Americal colonials and the French West Indies and to stop smuggling of highly-taxed molasses, sugar, and other items. The British justified ransacking of property with their need to increase their revenue to pay for their costly wars by cracking done on people suspected of participating in illegal trade and not paying duties.

Boston lawyer James Otis (1725-1783) went to court in 1761 to argue about the legality of the powers assigned to British customs officials as a violation of basic rights the American colonists, but was defeated. This legal challenge, known as the *Petition of Lechmere*, argued that writs were a violation of fundamental principles of law. Americans have a long-standing negative view of government entering and seizing property simply based on suspicion without probable cause and a valid warrant issue by a court. Americans do not like government to violate what they conceive as one of their *basic inalienable rights*, to the point that they started a revolution.[388]

One of the unintended effects of the creation of DHS was the introduction of more aggressive rules for searches, authorizing law enforcement organizations across the country to stop anyone that could be suspected of contraband or drug dealing. As a result, police departments have seized millions of dollars from people who have never been charged with a crime. Thousands of innocent people have spent fortunes in legal fees to recover their assets, and many more have either not been able to get the money back, or lost a substantial portion as a result to what eventually will be taken all the way up to the Supreme Court, and will be found to be a clear violation of the Constitution. It is inevitable that Americans will demand that legislation that authorizes these actions be rescinded.

Police officers have even seized Sunday church collections on their way to be deposited in a bank![389] If there is something that can lead to rousing passions among Americans is to witness something of this nature, even if the alleged justification is to fight crime. This form of illegally seizing assets has become a *cash cow* for jurisdictions all over the country. As in other aspects of law enforcement, private companies have surface to provide law enforcement tools to engage in questionable and without a doubt unconstitutional activity.[390] Instead of providing law enforcement a tool to fight drug trafficking organizations (DTO's), the legislation has been misused to hurt the innocent. *Washington Post* investigators analyzed a database of hundreds of thousands of seizures, and exercised great diligence to smoke out the truth by interweaving scores of police officers victims.[391] In at least 41% of the cases the government agreed to return the confiscated property when the rightful owners challenged the government in court, in exchange for the victims agreeing not to file a law suit to recover damages.

Contrary to the concept that everyone is presumed to be innocent until proven guilty, in the case of seized property, the owners have to prove that their assets were acquired legally to get them back. It should be the burden of the state to prove that any asset was obtained illegally before it can be seized. One of the incentives for misuse of the DHS regulations that allowed for this miscarriage of justice to take place is that it authorized local law enforcement agencies to keep a percentage of the assets they take from their rightful owners, thus creating an improper way to cover law enforcement budgets. *The Washington Post* investigators found that of 298 police departments and task forces, they have been able to cover about 20% of their annual budgets with the assets seized since 2008. At least two states, Iowa and Kansas have refused to participate in the program, suspecting that the legal authority could be found to be a violation of civil liberties protected under the Constitution.

The Washington Post found numerous cases where the victims were members of minority groups, including Blacks, Hispanic, and Chinese. A large number of these victims got their money back, but after months of legal battles, business loses, and the loss of confidence in *the system*. Without a doubt the aggressive seizure of assets has caused serious damage to drug trafficking organizations and organized crime. But at what price? Indicators of potential criminal activity have been misused against innocent people. Fighting crime is important, but protecting basic individual freedom is even more important if the system is to function in a rational way.

Irrationality Thrives

In 1999 a 6-year-old kid took a camping utensil that had a knife, fork and spoon to school, after joining the Cub Scouts. He wanted to use it to eat at school and show it off. In the process, he violated the *zero-tolerance* school policy and was suspended from school. Additionally, he faced a 45 day sentence in the school district's reform school. The Christina School District in Delaware apparently did not have a choice.[392] Common sense is a thing of the past. A 7-year-old was suspended from school for three months for pointing a pencil and saying POW-POW! Another 8-year-old boy was suspended from school for using his finger as an imaginary gun. A 7-year-old was suspended from school for eating his strawberry pop tart into the shape of a gun. A third-grade girl was expelled from school because grandma sent her to school with a birthday cake for her classmates along with a knife to cut it. The knife was used by the teacher to cut the cake, which was happily eaten by the kids, but afterwards, she alerted the school principal, who proceeded to expel the child due to the *zero-tolerance rules*. The incident made the headlines of the *ABC* newspaper in Spain on 28 March 2014. Americans were accordingly displayed as total idiots, without the paper having to spell it out.[393]

Insanity can be defined as *a case of extreme foolishness, legal incompetence or irresponsibility*. These types of irrational incidents are taking place across the country as idiocy has prevailed among elected officials and policymakers. In the meantime flash mob violence goes unpunished. It is utterly unreasonable to enforce stupid rules without exercising common sense, while serious criminal activity goes unpunished. Totalitarian monstrosities can easily result from insane decisions that result from not using common sense. It is irrational to go after small children for incidents in which there was no malice, while really bad actors escape punishment.

Children aiming sticks as guns, lined up against a brick building. Washington, D.C. (?), circa 1941. Prints and Photographs Division, Library of Congress. In 2015 the child would be accused of harboring evil thoughts, possibly suspended from school, and placed in a foster home or reform school. On 23 November 2014 police in Cleveland fatally shot a 12-year-old child at a playground because they mistook a toy gun for a real one. No known restrictions on publication

So What?

The criminal-justice system is in crisis, as evidenced by the large number of people incarcerated, and the number of cases of police and prosecutorial misconduct. The crisis is the byproduct of the cultural decadence affecting American society since the 1960s. In the tragedies covered in the previous pages, there is a psychopathology present on all sides to the point that it is difficult to identify who is really at fault. Law enforcement officers are suffering from low morale, and it is increasingly difficult to recruit good personnel with the correct attitude. Police officers are constantly bombarded by verbal and physical attacks and accusations of wrongdoing.

A toxic mix of disenfranchisement of Black youths, poverty, unemployment, poor education, racial profiling, hyper-active targeting of minorities with such practices as *stop and frisk*, lead to confrontations in which police forget that they are supposed to be protecting everyone. Some law enforcement officers use confrontational, rigid, gun and nightstick tactics instead of a more flexible and subtle approach and street psychology to deal with people and gain their cooperation. Some officers act as judge, jury, and executioner, and engage in brutality because *they have lost faith in the system*. Some law violators act in ways that could signal that they are seeking *"suicide by cop,"* by adopting a confrontational approach instead of following orders. People engage in racially-motivated rioting, because they feel that *the system* fails them, and they have the right to revert back to *eat or be eaten* or *might makes right*. There are simply too many behavioral dysfunctions occurring across the board. Americans seem to be reverting to the *law of the jungle* because they no longer trust government to protect them.

There are many marginalized groups including undereducated whites who blame their problems on African-Americans or immigrants, or both. Some Afro-American political activists blame whites, immigrants and everybody else for their problems. There are segments of the population that blame other people for their inability to find well-paying jobs, for their own poverty, and these frustrated people can come out from both extremes of the political spectrum. *American society is suffering from collective schizophrenia.*

All the misfortunes faced by civil society become more acute due to an absence of enlightened leadership able to pull the country back from heading to a primitive stage without law or morality, in which people take pleasure in the pain and weakness of others. Extremists at both ends of the political spectrum share similar traits. Pathologically insecure and marginalized crackpots cluster in paramilitary and right-wing militias at one end, and left-wing unruly mobs at the other end of the spectrum demonize each other. Irrationally, they see the world in absolute and uncompromising terms with no grays or middle ground. Fanaticism is leading to the creation of a complex phenomenon that is resulting in *virtual ungoverned spaces* throughout the country where antisocial extremists rule.

VIII – POPULISM AND SOCIAL ENGINEERING

> **When even one American – who has done nothing wrong – is forced by fear to shut his mind and close his mouth, then all Americans are in peril.**
>
> **Harry Truman**

Charismatic Messianic Leaders

The rise of left-wing charismatic messianic leaders with a folksy appeal is scary.[394] They claim to be mobilizing the working-class and pushing for redistributive policies as a way to deal with social and economic problems. The mobs they attract are far from representing a grass-roots Democracy or the so-called "*working class.*" They attract mobs of frustrated people who can easily be proselytized and manipulated with calls for an expansion of entitlement programs and redistribution of wealth. They use anti-establishment rhetoric, as they ignore that *wealth first has to be created* and that by attacking Capitalism, all they do is *destroy wealth,* and do not help anybody but themselves.

However, this is not new. As far back as the 1890s there were similar populists railing against banks and railroads and what they called "*nonproductive speculators*" and the "*overbearing greedy and corrupted rich people*" who controlled the economic and political systems of the United States. In those days, left-wing populism was associated with racist and anti-immigrant rants, just as current day right-wing populists suffer from the same malady. Socialists and Anarchists have deep roots in American History, just as right-wing anti-establishment extremists have deep roots. The two extremes are closer to each other in many respects than what their leaders reveal.

Right-wing elements have developed their own version of populism and doomsday scenarios. They cannot wait for a total meltdown to be able to say "*We told you so...*" They are hoping for the masses to throw up their hands and rush to Washington to clean house. Along the way to the Capital they hope to meet Liberal politicians running out being chased by a mob of former followers screaming... "*You lied to us... Instead of deliverance you brought us Armageddon...*" All right-wing prophesies fulfilled... Social Security programs bankrupted, total collapse of the healthcare delivery system, the *Barbarians* breaching the walls along the nation's borders led by Beelzebub in person. And of all these scenarios would be playing out in record cold temperatures, as a result of climate change, as the end of America as you know it comes to pass. These conflicting visions of the future, show that the country drifts without direction. Americans are confused by convoluted rhetoric that fuels an unthinking herd into unguided mob rule.

Traditional Western theology, morality, and philosophy have been turned upside down by new-style theologians, philosophers, psychologists, poets, novelists, playwrights, teachers, politicians and Hollywood. The U.S. has become a prime exporter of radical cultural decadence to the world. Liberty has been slowly transformed to *"libertinism,"* a form of freethinker philosophy that rejects many of society's established mores. It involves more than freethinking, promiscuity, pornography, and infidelity. It includes the "*dumbing*" down of American culture. Our enemies take advantage of the situation to paint the U.S. as the "incarnation of evil," while they camouflage their own dastardly actions behind a façade of high moral standards. There is a dogmatic denial by Liberals and Conservatives that anything is wrong with their views, while both extremes point fingers at each other blaming the other side for contributing to decadence, corruption, immorality, lack of interest in solving the economic problems of the masses, and just about every conceivable evil.

These are just a sample of the political figures involved in scandals in the recent past resulting in forced resignation or criminal convictions: Marion Barry, Sandy Berger, Henry Cisneros, Duke Cunningham, Edwin Edwards, Walter Fauntroy, Mark Foley, Jim McGreevey, J. Dennis Hastert, Guy Hunt, Bob McDonnell, Evan Mecham, Robert Ney, Dan Rostenkowski, Robert Torricelli, and Jim Traficant. They are White, Black, and Brown, and represent all ethnicities present in the American population, Democrats and Republicans, and come from all parts of the country. Most people do not have any idea of who the people in this list are. The issue is a true example of bipartisan cooperation, like taxidermists and veterinarians working together... *either way they give you your dog back.*

Politicians do not have a monopoly on decadence and impropriety. Several prominent tele-evangelists have ended up in jail or discredited for fraud, cavorting with male or female prostitutes, pedophilia, stealing from church collections, tax evasion, mail fraud, money laundering: James O. Bakker, Jimmy Swaggart, Jim Whittington, Ted Haggard, and numerous Catholic priests and members of the hierarchy of the Church. There are demented tele-evangelists who claim that Islamic terrorism is the result of sinful behavior in the U.S. and a form of punishment from God. Elements of the so-called *"religious right,"* push a political agenda that seeks to criminalize homosexual relationships and deny basic rights to homosexuals in a range of critical areas: employment, housing, and families.[395] They resemble Iranian Shi'a Muslim extremists who persecute, arrest, torture and hang homosexuals in that country. On the other side, there are leftist preachers who endorse the Communist dictatorship in Cuba and every other leftist cause, regardless of how they restrain or persecute religious people (and homosexuals in the past). And, the homosexual activists who demand that everybody else accept and endorse their views regardless of their own moral and ethical convictions take the cake!

PASTOR WITH AIDS HAD MULTIPLE AFFAIRS WITH HIS PARISHIONERS

America without a compass......

The pastor of the Shiloh Missionary Baptist Church in Montgomery, Alabama disclosed to his parishioners in October 2014 that he had AIDS, and that he had multiple affairs with women inside the church, but had not disclosed to them that he was infected. He also disclosed to church attendants in another sermon that he was a drug user. When the deacons voted to fire him, the pastor refused to leave and instead changed the locks and the parish's bank accounts. The deacons filed a law suit accusing the pastor of "*debauchery, sinfulness, hedonism, sexual misconduct... violations of the Ten Commandments... and knowingly spreading a sexually transmitted disease.*[396]

Scandals in the sports world abound. Everyone seemed surprised when a child sex abuse scandal broke out at Penn State in November 2011, but it was only the latest in a series of events that triggered public outrage. The list of schools involved in numerous shenanigans involving varsity sports has been growing for years, including Boise State, CCNY, Connecticut, LSU, Michigan, North Carolina, Southern California, Southern Methodist, Tennessee, and West Virginia, to mention only a few. Gambling associated with baseball took down Pete Rose in 2004, and the use of steroids took down Alex Rodriguez in 2009, after affecting José Canseco and other players. Doping allegations were levied against Lance Armstrong, multiple time winner of the Tour de France. (He finally confessed to doping in January 2013.) Tiger Woods made the headlines with another juicy sex scandal. Quarterback Michael Vicks was convicted and served time for illegal dog fighting. The ultimate award for depravity without a doubt can be awarded to NFL Hall of Famer O.J. Simpson, currently serving a long prison sentence in Nevada. The image of the superstar athlete as role models for children has been seriously damaged by fake injuries, doping, sex, drugs, gambling, point-fixing, and other criminal schemes.

One of the things that glue together Islamic Jihadists and other violent extremists is their perception of the U.S. as *a decadent imperialist power that is bound for destruction and only needs a push to make it fall.* Subversive elements always masquerade their evil intentions behind some vision of a better future, and they also need to demonize something or someone. The U.S. is a favorite easy target, because *Americans make it an easy target.* Enemies of the U.S. do not have to invent, all they have to do is quote from American newspapers the details of the scandal *du jour.* In the quest for increased freedom, the discourse in the U.S. has polarized public opinion, fueling extremists at both ends of the spectrum. Perfectly good concepts like *"diversity"* get tainted with the introduction of extreme points of view to force people to accept things that may insult their personal moral or religious convictions. There is an internal clash of civilizations within the country which in some ways resembles the global clash of civilizations between Western Culture and Islamic extremists. Political radicals and fanatics at both end of the spectrum hate the *sonsofbitches* at the other extreme, and both hate the moderates in the middle. And the talking heads stimulate the rancor.

Moral Cataclysm: Historical Roots

If someone is gay and he searches for the Lord and has good will, who am I to judge? We shouldn't marginalize people for this. They must be integrated into society.

Pope Francis I

In the *Book of Genesis* of the *Old Testament*, there is a story about the prosperous kingdoms of Sodom and Gomorrah, and three other nearby cities named Admah, Zeboim, and Bela, along the River Jordan, near the Dead Sea. According to the story, the people of these kingdoms deviated from moral traditions and engaged in all forms of sexual deviations and crimes against nature, and were destroyed by war, plus a natural or supernatural (divine) cataclysm; Possibly, in the form of a major earthquake, a meteor, and resulting fires. The Christian *Bible* (*New Testament*) and the Islamic *Quran*, cover the ancient story derived from the *Book of Genesis*. Why would God punish the people of these cities? Allegedly they were destroyed due to their inhospitality, humiliation of strangers, economic crimes, lack of compassion for the poor and the needy, arrogance, sadism, aberrant behavior, perverse sexual depravities, and impenitence.[397]

People with strong religious convictions, point to the story of Sodom and Gomorrah as a predictor of where the U.S. is heading. They predict a moral catastrophe and a major tragedy in the making. At the other end of the spectrum, of the secular "*Progressive*" variety, they say: *Take off the rearview mirrors and drive on... That was then and this is now... We need to know the past, but we need to deal with the present and the future... and not be influenced by traditions that block the creation of a pluralistic new world with greater tolerance and diversity.* American society and culture is facing a tsunami of change, but nobody knows if the nation is pre-destined for complete failure or blessed to come out with a more harmonious society. Nobody knows where we are going!

Government in the Bedroom

Among the most absurd, controversial, and vicious issues of our day, is the national sexual-freak show. On 26 June 2015, the U.S. Supreme Court ruled in a 5/4 decision that the Constitution guarantees a right to same-sex marriage. Contemporaneous to this transcendental decision, ISIS celebrated "Gay Love" by tossing four more Syria, as a large crowd gathered to watch the execution.[398] After years of debate, it is obvious that not everyone around the world shares the concept of "*equal dignity*" in the eyes of the law on this subject. Since 2003, American's views on the subject took a radical turn, and by 2015 the polls reflected that the majority of the population favored doing away with traditional legislation regulating sexual relations and kicking the government off the bedroom.

Should government regulate what goes on in the bedroom? If homosexual and transgender people have a basic constitutionally-protected right to same-sex marriage... What about polygamy? If consenting adults do not have any conflicts with polygamy, or if their religion allows for polygamy, on what basis can government prohibit polygamy? Will Muslims and orthodox Mormons file lawsuits claiming that their rights are being violated if same sex marriage is legal, but polygamy is not? What about bigamy? What about pedophilia? What about incest? What about people who have a sexual attraction to animals (zoophilia and bestiality)? And, let's not forget about necrophilia! Where is the reference in the Constitution to any of these issues one way or the other? The decision by the Supreme Court opens the door to multiple other transcendental cultural and legal changes. Now that the country started down this road putting *Humpty Dumpty* back together again will not be easy, as the drift to the edge of the abyss accelerates, as we enter unchartered territory.

Morality comes from free people who influence the culture of the country under the Constitution, except that the Constitution is being turned into a pretzel. Only monogamy and marriage between men and women had been allowed by law since the Constitution was enacted in 1791, until recently.

HOMOSEXUAL RELATIONS: THE INTERNATIONAL REALITY

In at least 76 countries homosexual relations are illegal, and considered to be a deviation from traditional sexual relations. According to the United Nations High Commissioner for Human Rights, there has been an increase in violence against lesbians, homosexuals, bisexual, and transgender people, including at least 1,612 documented murders between 2008 and 2014. In many countries consensual homosexual relations are punished by death. In Muslim countries in particular, homophobia and transphobia are widespread.

A Latter-day Saint with his six wives c.1885
Library of Congress Collection
LC-USZ62-83877 Call # LOT 11888 No known restrictions on publication

Same-sex Marriage

> ***Marriage has got historic, religious and moral content that goes back to the beginning of time, and I think a marriage is as a marriage has always been, between a man and a woman...***
>
> **Hillary R. Clinton**[399]
> After this statement was made in January 2000, she backed civil unions in October of the same year.

On 26 June 2013 a divided Supreme Court ruled "unconstitutional" a ban on same-sex marriage in California, which had resulted from a referendum. The Court ruled against the *Defense of Marriage Act* (DOMA), because it denied liberties protected under the due process clause of the Fifth Amendment. That decision was a preamble to the decision of 26 June 2015, legalizing same-sex marriage. As a Historian, I do not remember any other case in which a civilization repudiated its religious faith and morality and survived.

For the "historically illiterate," multiple Supreme Court decisions were later superseded by Constitutional Amendments. For example, in 1857 the Court declared that Blacks were not and could never become American citizens, had no rights which the white man was supposed to respect, and could justly and lawfully be reduced to slavery. In 1895, in another landmark ruling the Court found income taxes, particularly taxes on interest, dividends and rents, unconstitutional, because they unfairly taxed the people with the highest incomes. Both decisions were later superseded by the Thirtieth and Sixteenth Amendments to the Constitution in 1865 and 1913. Just because the Supreme Court decides to interpret the Constitution in a given way, it is not necessarily the end of the story.

Under DOMA, key federal benefits, including Social Security, pensions and bankruptcy protection did not apply to homosexual couples legally married in states that recognize same-sex unions. DOMA (Public Law 104-199, 110 Statute 2419), enacted on 21 September 1996, allowed states to refuse to recognize same-sex marriages performed legally under the laws of other states, and did not recognize them as spouses for the purposes of federal laws for federal benefits. DOMA had been legally enacted in 1996, with large majorities in both houses of Congress, and signed into law by President Bill Clinton. In both landmark rulings, the Supreme Court acted against legislation that had been enacted democratically, with the support of the majority of the voters in California, and by duly elected Members of Congress, and signed into law by the President. In the absence of a complicated process to amend the Constitution, Supreme Court decisions hold.

The Supreme Court's decision of 26 June 2015, will have a considerable economic impact, as it expands benefits and government liabilities that had not been factored into the equation. The decision reflected significant changes in the way of thinking of the American population. The drift towards a secular state, contrary to shared religious doctrine, is self-evident. After 50 years of indoctrination, young people reflect what they have been taught by people who are products of the 1960s *counterculture*. These decisions are a natural outcome.

The U.S. Conference of Catholic Bishops called for a constitutional amendment to "protect the unique social and legal status of marriage." The Vatican has taken a similar position against same-sex marriage, and the Catholic Church is not an institution that changes basic doctrine on the basis of which way the wind is blowing. Pope John Paul II denounced legislation in the Netherlands in 2000, which made same-sex marriage legal. Pope Benedict XVI expressed his opposition to same-sex marriage in December 2012 in his annual Christmas address. Pope Francis I has described same-sex marriage as *the work of the devil*, and opposed legislation in his native Argentina to legalize it in 2010. In his first encyclical published on 5 July 2013, Pope Francis reiterated that "*marriage is a union of one man and one woman.*"[400]

The Southern Baptist Convention disagreed with the Court. Frank S. Page, President and CEO, Executive Committee of the Southern Baptist Convention, called the decision "mind-boggling." Galen Carey, Vice President of the National Association of Evangelicals disagreed with the Court. Richard Land, President of the Southern Evangelical Seminary commented that it was a "*devastating day for traditional marriage and religious freedom... God created marriage and He has defined its' parameters, regardless of what the majority of Supreme Court justices might think.*" Ralph Reed, chairman of the Faith & Freedom Coalition commented that the decision was "*stunning and an indefensible display of judicial activism.*" The national Orthodox Jewish organization Agudath Israel called the decision a grievous insult to the sanctity of marriage.

On the other side of the argument, "*Progressive*" religious leaders and organizations agreed with the decision of the Supreme Court, as part of a process to ensure that all human rights of people are recognized, and all citizens are provided true equality under the law. Several Liberal Jewish organizations, including the American Jewish World Service, the American Jewish Committee, the National Council of Jewish Women, and the Union for Reform Judaism, the Central Conference of American Rabbis, Women of Reform Judaism, and the Religious Action Center of Reform Judaism, agreed with the finding of the Supreme Court. Bishop Mariann Edgar Budde, of the Episcopal Diocese of Washington, as well as other Episcopal organizations issued statements in support of the Supreme Court. Other Christian congregations, including the United Church of Christ, the Methodist, and the Unitarian Universalist churches, support same-sex marriage.

With such divergent opinions, it is important to understand Greek, Roman, and Judeo-Christian traditions, established practices, conventions, and ethics. The current trend is irritating for people who respect "basic traditions." For them, issues like same-sex marriage are more than an annoyance. They represent an unacceptable violation of basic moral principles and Judeo-Christian traditions. However, there is considerable mythology about so-called *Western Cultural Roots.*

There are plenty of examples of sexual *aberrations* in Greek and Roman cultures. Alexander the Great (356 BC - 323 BC) had a male lover named Hephaestion, who was approximately of his same age, and led military units and managed military logistics for him. Alexander's father, Macedonian King Philip II, was bisexual, and was assassinated in 336 BC by a former homosexual lover. The beginning of the Roman Empire, which succeeded the Roman Republic, is normally placed during the rule of Gaius Julius Caesar Octavianus (27 BC to 14 AD), generally referred to as *"Augustus."* Although morally corrupt, he is regarded as the first and greatest Roman emperor. He was a practicing homosexual and pedophile who enjoyed the company of young boys. Homosexuality is nothing new, as these examples reveal.

Greek and Roman cultures shared multiple examples of what could be described as *sexual aberrations*, including bisexual and homosexual practices and pedophilia. Homosexuality and sexual abuse of young boys is discussed frequently in Greek texts (See: *pederasty*). Greek mythology, including the *Iliad*, discusses the relationship of the demigod *Achilles* and *Patroclus.* This relationship is said to have inspired Alexander the Great in his relationship with Hephaestion.[401] Public debaucheries, and every form of lewdness, were the rule during the Roman Empire, building on Greek traditions. Thus it could be said that *what historically has been considered extreme forms of immorality, depravity, pornography, smut, and related matters, are well ingrained in Western civilization all the way back to its' origins in ancient Greece and Rome.* In other words, to attack current or modern immorality as an affront to Western civilization is *not necessarily accurate.* On the other hand, Christian civilization provides a different set of guiding principles together with Jewish culture. Muslims are even less inclined to accept homosexuality. In Saudi Arabia they go to the extreme of sacrificing animals who are witnessed engaging in same-sex acts!

Judeo-Christian Traditions

According to the Hebrew Bible, polygamy was frequently practiced in ancient Jewish society, although it was *discouraged* by Mosaic Law. The Torah, or the first five books of the Hebrew Bible, regulates the practice of polygamy with complicated rules for such things as inheritance. Men were allowed to have more than one wife, but women were only allowed to have one husband. There is sufficient historical precedent for constitutional lawyers to claim that since the Hebrew Bible discussed polygamy, even if discouraged, it should not be illegal.

Christians - even in the early days – rejected the notion of polygamy. At the start of the Reformation around 1525, Martin Luther (1483-1546), one of the most influential Reformers, did not see any reason in Scripture to prohibit a man from having multiple wives. Fundamentalist members of the Church of Jesus Christ and Latter Day Saints (Mormons-LDS) practiced polygamy until around 1890, when it was declared improper and subject to excommunication, although some Mormons continue to practice polygamy, even though it is not only illegal, but a practice rejected by the Mormon Church under considerable legal pressure.

On 8 July 1862, President Abraham Lincoln signed into law the *Morrill Anti-Bigamy A*ct, which specifically targeted the Mormon practice of plural marriage, although he instructed government authorities not to enforce the new law. The *Edmunds Anti-Polygamy Act* was enacted in 1882, and signed into law by President Chester A. Arthur, which expanded the previous anti-bigamy law to include cohabitation. Under this law, being a member of the Mormon Church was made illegal, simply because the Mormon doctrine of plural marriage was illegal, even if a member did not engage in plural marriage! Over one thousand Mormon men were arrested and prosecuted under this law for unlawful cohabitation. In 1887, the *Edmunds-Tucker Act* went further by disincorporation of the Mormon Church, because it fostered Polygamy, and church property was confiscated. Mormons had no choice but to change their doctrine, in violation of the basic premise of freedom of religion. In 1890, the US Supreme Court upheld the seizure of Mormon Church property in *Late Corporation of the Church of Jesus Christ and Latter-Day Saints v. United States.*

If same sex marriage is legal, under what legal or moral justification can polygamy be kept illegal when practiced by consenting adults? In many Muslim countries polygamy is allowed based on interpretations of the Quran and Sharia Law, which allows a man to have up to four wives. Even when modern laws in Muslim countries declare polygamy illegal, the practice is tolerated.[402] Why should legislation in the U.S. prevent Muslims from practicing polygamy? The First Amendment to the Constitution, which states that *"Congress shall make no law respecting an establishment of religion, or prohibiting the free exercise thereof..."* Constitutional lawyers could argue that Muslims are being denied the free exercise of their religion, in light of legalization of same-sex marriage.

Significant Aberrations

And then... there is *zoophilia* and *bestiality*, namely, the practice of having sex with animals. The Hebrew Bible specifically condemns the practice with the death penalty as a *crime against nature*. Nevertheless, in classical Egyptian, Greek and Roman mythology there are multiple examples of Gods having sex with humans (Zeus, for example). Christian theologians condemned bestiality right from the beginning. This is not a *hypothetical issue*... On 16 June 2011, a man was arrested in Richland County, Ohio, for having sex with multiple animals, including a 3-year-old shepherd mix.[403] In 2012 a man was arrested in Clearwater, Pinellas County, Florida for having sex with a pit-bull mix dog.[404] A thirty-one year-old man was arrested in Marion County, Florida in September 2012, for having sex with a miniature donkey.[405] Again, what is the legal difference between same sex marriage and bestiality? Under Hebrew and Christian traditional practices, both, the person and the animal involved were put to death. Lawyers could have a ball with this one! Is the Constitution being interpreted in such a way as to comply with a particular religion that has a problem with zoophilia and bestiality?

And then for the *pièce de résistance*, there is *necrophilia*, or having sex with a dead person, or an erotic attraction to corpses.[406] Abominable as it may be, it is not as exceptional as it may seem, as several cases are documented in the U.S. since 2007. For example, a 24-year-old man was convicted in 2007 for having sex with a 92-year-old woman's corpse at the morgue of the Holy Name Hospital in Teaneck, NJ.[407] A funeral home director in Houston, TX was arrested in October 2009, and charged with a misdemeanor for abusing a corpse.[408] Another man was charged in Geneva, Ohio, with necrophilia in January 2011.[409] In March 2012 an employee of a funeral home in Toledo, Ohio, was arrested for abuse of a woman's body at the funeral home.[410] In January 2013, a 61-year-old male nurse was arrested and charged with necrophilia in Los Angeles, CA, for having sex with a corpse at Sherman Oaks Hospital.[411] This aberration is not limited to men. According to an article in *Psychology Today*, "*One female apprentice embalmer claimed that during the first four months of her employment, she'd had sex with an average of ten corpses a month.*"[412]

Despite these arrests, *there is no national legal standard on necrophilia.* In several states, necrophilia is considered a felony: Alabama, Arizona, Florida, Iowa, Oregon, Washington, and Wisconsin. However, in other states it is considered a misdemeanor, including Connecticut, Colorado, New York, Texas, Ohio, and Hawaii. As of February 2012, in 22 states it was illegal to have sex with corpses, and at the time, In other words, *in 28 states necrophilia is not illegal,* and bizarre as it may be, there was *no Federal law against it either!* In fact, in many countries there are no laws against having sex with a corpse.[413] If it is not illegal under Federal law to have sex with a corpse, why should same sex marriage be illegal? If same-sex marriage is legal, and if in most states necrophilia is not illegal, and if there has not been Federal legislation against necrophilia, why should it be prohibited? If *necrophilia* is not illegal under Federal law, why should same-sex marriage be illegal?

The Great Moral Struggle of Our Age

Once the floodgates are opened to legalize what has been regarded as "*sexual aberrations,*" all legislation dealing with what traditionally has been regarded as "*sexual misconduct*" has to be put on the table. Otherwise, it could be alleged that the state is discriminating illegally against what some people believe are their God-given right to engage in whatever form of sexual relationship they want. And, the Constitution does not deal with sex, which means that *it is not a point of reference on the subject.* Sex is not mentioned once in the Constitution. And thus we get closer and closer to the abyss. Generally, society has been moving toward increased tolerance, but where are the parameters of what is and is not reasonable, moral or legal? America lacks a moral compass...

While the issue of same-sex marriage has been widely debated, laws that prohibited exogamy, or the ban on mixing of people from different racial groups, including sexual relations, cohabitation and marriage, were ignored for decades. These laws existed in many states of the Union until a Supreme Court decision in 1967 declared them unconstitutional. However, as already mentioned, in some of the same states that prohibited exogamy, necrophilia was legal, and in some, having sex with a corpse continues to be legal. Something is very wrong with this arbitrary and convoluted situation.

In some countries, particularly in Muslim countries in the Middle East, Central and South West Asia, there is legislation that bars marriage outside one's tribe, even if there are no racial differences. Historically, racial mixing has taken place going back to the origins of mankind, in part due to military conquests and the institution of slavery. Genome Research has found considerable evidence in genetic material of mating between human migrations from Africa, Europe, and Asia, going back to prehistoric times more than 11,000 years ago. Subspecies of Homo sapiens also mixed tens of thousands of years ago.[414] Hybridization has a long history![415] What are the consequences of tinkering with cultural and historical traditions that go back hundreds of years? There is no way to realistically keep people of different races from mating. As already pointed out, there are people who like to fornicate with animals and corpses! Lawyers could argue that American society should have learned long ago that *government should stay out of the bedroom*, as exogamy laws clearly showed. Americans don't know where they are going with all of this...

Misreading of Scripture to support just about any cause is a favorite past time of extremists of all kinds. On the question of racial intermarriage, there are sections of the Hebrew Bible that seem to oppose it, in part due to concerns about mixing with people that followed different religions, as for example, Greeks.[416] The Christian Bible, on the other hand, proclaimed that *people are one in Christ Jesus*, regardless of where they came from.[417] Although originally Christians preached only to Jews, and were mainly Jewish converts, Christianity was opened to everyone. There were no prohibitions for Christians to marry people of other tribes or races.[418]

After the arrival of Islam, considerable forced interracial breeding took place as Jewish and Christian women were taken into slavery and as concubines. When Europeans arrived in the Western Hemisphere after 1492, they interbred with Native Americans from Tierra del Fuego in South America to the northern tip of North America. When African slaves were imported, they interbred with Europeans and Native Americans. When large numbers of Chinese were imported to the Americas, particularly after the end of the slave trade around 1850, most of the Chinese were indentured servants, composed of only males, with only a few Chinese women, leading to interbreeding with Black women, Native Americans, whites (however defined), as well as with mixed peoples from earlier inter-racial breeding. The same happened elsewhere, as European colonial powers expanded throughout Africa, the Middle East, and all corners of Asia. No legislation, religious edict, or punishment could stop it then, and it does not make any sense to try to stop it now.

The Supreme Court decision in 1967 made legal what was already de facto a widespread practice throughout the America, in some areas above board, and in other areas, particularly in the southern states, hidden in plain sight. The so-called "abomination," was widely practiced. As modern ethics and morality had long incorporated the practice of interracial mating, the Supreme Court only legalized what was already de facto. Homosexuality has been around for a very long time, as depicted in numerous historical documents going back to Greek and Roman times. The existence of important homosexual military figures in the past puts into question the theory that more homosexuality, translates into a more peaceful species.[419] Did the Supreme Court act once again on what was already *de facto* a widespread practice throughout the U.S. on 26 June 2013 and 26 June 2015?

Memorial for Prussian General *Friedrich Wilhelm von Steuben* at Lafayette Park in Washington, D. C. General von Steuben, a well-known homosexual, served with George Washington in the American Revolutionary War and is credited with teaching critical improved essential military drill discipline at Valley Forge. He participated in the decisive Battle of Yorktown as a Major General in the American Army.

Picture taken by Rafael Fermoselle on 9/19/2015.

Once policymakers start moving down the road to make legislative changes regarding sexual preferences, it will be impossible to put *Humpty*

Dumpty back together again. The complicated issues associated with same-sex marriage will open the floodgates to even more controversy and numerous unintended consequences. Decisions by the U.S. Supreme Court are not necessarily free of serious miscarriages of justice. As previously mentioned, in a seven-to-two decision on *Dred v. Sandford* in 1857, the Court ruled that African-Americans were not citizens, and regardless of their status as free or slave, had no standing to sue in Federal Court.

The Supreme Court ruled that the Federal Government could not regulate slavery, and did not have any jurisdiction outside of the original states that formed the Union. Slaves were declared personal property, and their owners could not be deprived of their property under the Fifth Amendment, which prohibited the taking of personal property without due process of law. The 14th Amendment to the Constitution, adopted on 9 July 1868, clearly defined citizenship and overruled *Dred Scott v. Sandford.* It took another 100+ years to dismantle racial segregation and discrimination and enforce equal protection under the 14th Amendment. What may seem rational and legal at one point in history may become irrational and illegal years later, because societal standards change. However, as in other areas, the U.S. is navigating dangerous waters without a compass, and there is no way to put the toothpaste back in the tube…

Where are the opinions of unbiased legal scholars?

Deconstructing the line of reasoning of these legal decisions is challenging. Humpty Dumpty told Alice in Wonderland – "*When I choose a word, it means just what I choose it to mean – nothing more nor less.*" So, what is *a natural condition in humankind*? What is covered by Constitutional rights, assuming something is *a natural condition in humankind*? Should courts interfere with natural conditions? Should the news media be devoting so much space to sexual preferences? Should anybody give a … about the first openly homosexual basketball, football, or baseball player?

We are Who We Are!

Defining the meaning of "equal rights" continues to be a challenge for Americans, despite the Bill of Rights, which was approved in December 1789, when the states ratified the first set of amendments to the Constitution. At the time, slavery was still legal, and many of the people who voted for the Bill of Rights were slave owners. So much for the concept of equality and equal rights! The majority, or at least, the majority of the people who qualified to be part of the electorate at the time, we can speculate, supported slavery. Otherwise, they would have done something about it.

American society has for all practical purposes accepted that discrimination and harassment of homosexuals constitutes a grave abuse of basic human rights. It is possible that "gay marriage" will eventually become a non-issue and the traditional interpretation of marriage solely as a union between a man and a woman will go with the dinosaurs and slavery. Enter volatility of the masses, and the ability of opportunists to influence the populace to take and retain power. The majority of the population in 1970, 1980, and even in 1990, would have rejected the notion that the demand for homosexual rights had any similarity with the Afro-American Civil Rights Movement. Afro-American leaders, would not have accepted any parallels or similarities.[420] But the world of 2015 is very different. A new moral sense is in the making. Either national leaders have been swayed by public opinion, or national leaders have swayed the populace to accept that homosexuals are entitled to have their views and rights respected.

"Majoritarianism"

Tocqueville, in his famous book *Democracy in America* (1835) expressed the view that democracy has a tendency to degenerate into *soft despotism*, and *a tyranny of the majority*. He described "*soft despotism*" as the illusion of the masses that they are in control, when in fact they have limited influence over the government, and are "*manipulated*" by charismatic leaders. Tocqueville expressed concern about the risk of developing a tyranny of the majority. Democracy and majority rule can easily turn into *Ochlocracy*, or *mob rule*.

In the past, the majority actively oppressed homosexuals and made them second class citizens. Now the masses are moving in the other direction. Homosexuals have the right not to be persecuted or denied their basic human rights, but should they have the right to persecute or deny freedom of thought to people who object to the *homosexual agenda* as immoral?

Not everyone is jumping into the "*next social revolution*" with a new sense of morality. The right of a minority to express its view that same sex marriage is immoral should be protected, and people who for religious or other moral convictions object to the new trend in American culture should be shielded because *they are exercising a basic Constitutional right to present their objections,* poses an important issue. That is what the First Amendment is all about. We may be collectively living a fictional story *in extremis* with the wrong interpretation of morality, possibly leading to the erosion of American values and self-destruction. *But Americans have been doing that since the 1960s!*

What is the point of "*making an issue*" because someone "comes out" and announces that they are homosexual? Homosexuals have been around as far back as Greek and Roman times... Why do they have to insist in marching on the New York City or Boston Saint Patrick's Day Parade with a banner? What does it have to do with the festivities? Homosexuals may have been marching in these parades for generations! Who cares about a homosexual basketball or football player "coming out" – does it affect the game in any way? The issue is simply – *Can the individual play well?* Who cares about their sexual orientation? They should not be victims of discrimination, but *they do not have the right to demand to rub it in, on everyone else!*

On 21 January 2013, members of the St. Louis, MO, Lesbian and Gay Band Association were granted the honor of being selected to participate in the Second Inaugural Parade for President Barack H. Obama. Although for some people, there was nothing wrong with that, there are many people who object on moral grounds, and dislike the demagoguery of those who place passion over reason, and could not care less about who gets offended. A lesbian and gay marching band does not play very well in Moscow, Beijing, Teheran, Kabul,

Baghdad, and Pyongyang, and in most African capitals. It does not lead to much respect for Americans in countries like Afghanistan, Algeria, Egypt, Ethiopia, Iraq, Jordan, Kazakhstan, Kuwait, Lebanon, Morocco, Nigeria, Uganda, Oman, Pakistan, Saudi Arabia, United Arab Emirates, and Uzbekistan, to mention only a few countries with large Muslim populations. In 27 or 54 African countries recent legislation has been enacted criminalizing homosexual activity. In the Russian Federation, likewise, the trend is going in the opposite direction, criminalizing all forms of proselytism in favor of the homosexual agenda. *The American image suffers internationally!*

There is bi-partisan support for same sex marriage, including a *Republican Unity Coalition* that supports a gay-straight alliance. For example, on 25 September 2013, former President George H. W. Bush and his wife Barbara Bush, attended the same-sex wedding of a couple of longtime friends in Maine.[421] The former President was an official witness and signed the marriage license. Same-sex marriage became legal in Maine in December 2012. His son, President George W. Bush opposed same-sex marriage and supported a constitutional amendment to outlaw it in 2004. However, First Lady Laura Bush, as well as their daughter Barbara Bush, differed with his views and supported same-sex marriage.[422]

In July 2013, former President George W. Bush used a Bible to make a comment that people should not judge same-sex marriage, which may indicate that he changed his mind from the views he expressed in 2004, and again during his re-election campaign in 2006. In a video interview he said: *I shouldn't be taking a speck out of somebody else's eye when I have a log in my own.*[423] Supposedly ultra-Conservative former Vice President Richard Cheney has a daughter, Mary Claire Cheney, who is openly homosexual. Mary C. Cheney filed an amicus *curiae* brief with the Supreme Court in 2013 in support of same-sex marriage in the *Hollingsworth v. Perry* case. She is the mother of two children and has been married to Heather Poe since June 2012. Considering these evolving views among prominent Republican leaders, it is understandable that there was no objection to a gay marching band participating in President Obama's inaugural parade in January 2013. Note that as of May 2015, 19 countries had legalized same-sex marriage, the last being Ireland, where in a referendum voters accepted the change by a margin of 62 to 38 percent, despite opposition by the Catholic Church.

Is majority rule always right? Was Tocqueville correct? The key to the answer resides in the First Amendment to the Constitution. The rights of people to express their views have to be protected, or the country can drift to a dangerous form of dictatorship. The masses are not always right.

Is that all there is?
Alternative analysis

The St. Louis, MO, Lesbian and Gay Band Association marched in the parade in Washington, D.C. on 21 January 2013 honoring President Barrack H. Obama, and the next day the sun came out like any other day. The earth was not hit by a meteorite, an earthquake did not open a sinkhole on the ground to swallow the White House, and people went about their business like any other day.

Remember listening to a stanza of a pop song by Jerry Leiber and Mike Stoller that Peggy Lee sang around 1969 that said… *And when I was 12 years old, my daddy took me to the circus, the greatest show on earth, there were clowns and elephants and dancing bears, and a beautiful lady in pink tights flew high above our ears… And as I sat there watching, I had the feeling that something was missing, I don't know what, but when it was all over, I said to myself, "Is that all there is to the circus?"* And the lyrics ended with: *Is that all there is, is that all there is? If that's all there is my friends, then let's keep dancing, let's break out the booze and have a ball, if that's all there is.* Peggy Lee won the Grammy Award for Best Female Pop Vocal Performance with the song.

Should the American people be cynical, disenchanted, or the starry-eyed? Who wants to go back several centuries to the time when the entire marching band would have been burned alive at the stake? Surprisingly, a thorough search on the Internet DID NOT show any negative articles on the subject. Perhaps American society is truly willing to accept a more inclusive society, or people are cowed to accept transcendental cultural changes and the "*new morality.*" How other people around the world see what is going on in America is another story. Who is gaining the high ground? We may have very difficult years ahead…

Decriminalizing Narcotics

> **As has been well documented, I smoked pot as a kid, and I view it as a bad habit and a vice, not very different from the cigarettes that I smoked as a young person up through a big chunk of my adult life. I don't think it is more dangerous than alcohol..."[424]**
>
> **Barrack Obama**

Since the 1960s there have been many suggestions about the potential benefits derived from the decriminalization of narcotics. The *Select Committee on Narcotics Abuse and Control of the 101st Congress* studied the issue in 1989. The catalyst for the study was a speech by Kurt L. Schmoke, then Mayor of Baltimore, to the U.S. Conference of Mayors in which he claimed that the existing drug policies had failed, and suggested legalization and decriminalization as a way of solving all the problems associated with narcotics addiction. Chairman Charles B. Rangel and the Committee produced a list of findings resulting from the many hours of testimony. Chairman Rangel decried the notion as stemming from frustration and exasperation with the Nation's mushrooming drug crisis, and opined that such a move would be *a tactical error that could result in a nation full of drug addicts.*

A Gallup poll survey conducted at the time found that about 75 percent of those surveyed were opposed and nearly 70 percent felt that legalization would aggravate an already serious situation. The Committee found that there was no commonly agreed upon approach to the issue of legalizing narcotics, and the public remained opposed to the idea. No data was available to support the theory that legalization would result in less crime or a decrease in experimentation with drugs, or a decline in the number of addicts. As a result, the Committee concluded that *legalization should not be considered.*[425]

Since 1989 a lot has changed. Marijuana has been decriminalized in several states and the District of Columbia. Narcotics continue to be a scourge, young people in particular have their lives destroyed, and around two million people are in jail, for the most part as a result of crimes linked to narcotics. Racial minorities continue to be the overwhelming percentage of victims, but do not own a monopoly of the problem, as over time the problem has moved to suburbia and to small towns from large urban centers. The so-called *War on Drugs* continues to be *a failure*, because elected officials have failed to use political, military, economic, diplomatic, and informational tools to truly destroy drug trafficking organizations (DTOs), the street gangs that control the retail end of the business, and the middlemen and corrupt officials who benefit from the trade.

The entire society forgets how the problem got started in the first place in the 1960s in association with the rise of the New Left and the *turn on, tune in, and drop out* culture. When there was a need for effective leadership to deal with the nascent challenge it just simply did not exist. *America continues without direction and without leadership with brass gonads to really address a problem that is affecting the entire society!* We could shoot down the planes, sink the speed boats -- and now using submarines, and kill the traffickers... but that takes what our political leaders do not have. *America continues in the wrong direction!*

To illustrate the trend, in September 2014, the Berkeley City Council in California approved unanimously an order to stores selling "medical marijuana" to donate two per cent (2%) of their volume of sales to patients that claim they need the weed for medical use but make less than $32,000 annually in income. The program was mandated to start in August 2015. In other words, elected officials in the City Council are going to be providing for free marijuana to poor people. Obviously, *the country is going to pot!*

On 10 March 2014, Attorney General Eric Holder noted that there is an "*urgent public health crisis*" in the country as a result of a huge increase in heroin-related deaths. He even went as far as to suggest that "first responders" should carry *naloxone* in a kit to reverse a heroin overdose after a 45 percent increase in deaths caused by heroin addiction between 2006 and 2010. This was a surprising statement, considering the trend to decriminalize marijuana and question the so-called *War on Drugs*. This problem was predictable and is partially related to the War in Afghanistan 2001-2014.[426] What has happened is that the arrival of cheap heroin, mainly from Afghanistan, has become readily available and a new drug of choice. Islamic insurgents financed their war by trafficking in heroin, and international organized crime moved the drugs to Russia and Western Europe, and eventually the heroin reached North America. Predictably, with the relaxed law enforcement, in a few years the situation will be considerably worse, unless some degree of *sanity* is reintroduced into the culture. *And... yes... gonads... to stop it!*

According to a Gallup poll taken in 2013, it was estimated that about 58 percent of the American people support the legalization of marijuana. The Federal Government banned marijuana in 1937, and it continues to be illegal according to federal law. However, legislation was enacted in 1996 in California that made "medical" marijuana legal. Another 19 states and the District of Columbia followed with similar legislation. Colorado expanded the concept by making recreational use of marijuana legal as of 1 January 2014. Other states, including Washington, will follow later in 2014. Among the excuses for a change in legislation at the state level were that money will be saved by not arresting and locking up marijuana peddlers and users, and by taxing production and sale of pot. Colorado expects to make around $600 million annually in taxes on pot. Former Congressman Patrick Kennedy is fighting back despite his Liberal politics. After years of indulging in drugs, he has taken an aggressive position totally opposed to liberalizing and decriminalizing pot. He favors mandatory screening for marijuana addiction and supervised education to prevent further drug use.[427] Finally someone shows some degree of sanity!

Intimidation and the First Amendment

INTIMIDATION means to make people fearful. Generally, proof of actual fear is not required in order to establish that a coercive environment exists. Intimidation may be inferred from conduct, words, or circumstances reasonably calculated to produce fear. Americans are intimidated to accept changes that contradict their own moral values and convictions as never before. For example, making any comment against same-sex marriage or legalization of marijuana can result in losing government jobs at all levels of the public sector. Practically the same situation exists in private sector employment. For all practical purposes the First Amendment of the American Constitution is useless as the climate of intimidation grows in the country.

Leftist extremists and pro-dope liberalization activists do not want to remember that Michael Brown had been smoking pot before the incidents that led to him being shot and killed by a police officer! Michael Brown could be a poster child for victims of the counterculture. Dylann Storm Roof, the 21-year-old perpetrator of the murder of nine people at the Emanuel African Methodist Episcopal Church in Charleston, SC, was a known drug addict, and had been arrested for manufacturing, possession, and distribution of controlled substances, including cocaine, methamphetamine, LSD, and other drugs. Was drug use linked to his extreme racist views? Why is it that outcasts of different races and persuasions have drug use as a common aspect of their profile?

Religion and Secular Ethics

> **To one who has faith, no explanation is necessary.**
> **To one without faith, no explanation is possible".**
>
> **Thomas Aquinas**[428]
> **(1225-1274)**

The Founding Fathers shared egalitarian ideas emanating from Judeo-Christian ethics, moral traditions and values, as well as secular ethics. Even those who were not religious shared similar ethical views based on logic and reason, a sense of moral responsibility, and secular principles of justice and universal morality. They were influenced by the philosophers of the *Enlightenment* and wanted to reduce human suffering, and promote well-being, regardless of their religious or secular ideology. Jefferson was instrumental in advocating that the government should be NEUTRAL - not secular - on the question of religion views, and not promote, endorse, or fund any particular religion or religious institutions.

Even those people who were moved by secular ideology were respectful of Christianity and believed that religion could play a beneficial role in American society. However, since the 1960s society influenced by a *secular counterculture* has gained ground attacking anything spiritual, particularly anything associated with Judeo-Christian culture, from displaying the Ten Commandments in government buildings, to nativity scenes, or crosses in government offices.[429] Multiculturalism has become a tool to promote and protect just about any culture, spiritual, or nonspiritual views, except Judeo-Christian traditions. Faith, reason, and traditions are being challenged by 21st century secularism and new forms of intolerance like never before.

Traditional Western theology, morality, and philosophy have been turned upside down by new-style theologians, philosophers, psychologists, poets, novelists, playwrights, teachers, politicians and the Hollywood crowd. America has become a prime exporter of radical cultural decadence to the world. Liberty has been slowly transformed to *"libertinism,"* a form of freethinker philosophy that rejected many of society's established mores. It involves more than freethinking, promiscuity, pornography, and infidelity. It includes the rejection of many of society's established mores, and the "*dumbing*" down of American culture. It includes numerous ways for self-destruction, from the use of narcotics and hallucinogens, to body-piercings, tattoos, and mutilations to freak out other people or for self-punishment.

Counterculture elements have attempted to replace the traditional *Merry Christmas* greetings with *Happy Holidays,* so as not to "offend" anybody, except Christians. Instead of tolerance for atheists and agnostics, a climate of intolerance has been created against Christians. Numerous previously alien religious festivals, be they Islamic or Buddhist, or anything else, are highlighted and promoted as part of an effort to create *a more tolerant society*, but the whole idea of tolerance is absent in relation to respecting Christian traditions like Christmas or the Jewish holiday of Hanukkah. Americans generally want to maintain their own unique culture and identity, while being respectful of other culture, *but that implies a two way street.*

The growth of what is starting to resemble *mob rule* is pushing the culture into intolerance for anybody who dares to exercise their right to free speech and freedom of conscience, which are protected under the First Amendment. For example, people who for religious convictions do not support homosexuality and same sex marriage are immediately attacked as homophobic, when in reality they may be tolerant of others and may only be asking for *tolerance for their own views*. Peace depends on the respect of other people's rights to freedom of conscience and freedom of speech. *What is good for the goose is good for the gander.*

Historically, there were periods in which some religious groups, such as the Quakers, Mormons, Jehovah's Witnesses, and Church of Christ, Scientist, were perceived as out of "*mainstream Christianity*," resulting in persecution, confiscation of their property, and mob attacks. The rights of free speech and freedom of religion granted by the Constitution were violated. Catholics were discriminated in some parts of the country. There were victims of anti-Catholic riots in Boston, Philadelphia and elsewhere in the 19th century. Atheists have been discriminated for their views, which are equally protected by the Constitution. However, what the *counterculture* is promoting in the Second Millennium is different from previous periods of intolerance, because the basic Judeo-Christian traditions and culture are under attack by promoters of a secular counterculture. They do not want a neutral government; *they want government to prohibit the free exercise of religion!*

Americans are more religious and have a higher church attendance than most countries around the world. Nevertheless, regular church attendance is down, in part because people are having problems with their image as church-goers. On the one hand, they over-report church attendance, because they want to be perceived as *good Christians*, however defined, but at the same time they are constantly indoctrinated by secularists that *religiosity* is somehow equivalent to *intolerant behavior* and *right-wing chauvinism*. The image of a resilient religiosity in the U.S. may not reflect the new reality.

ESTIMATED CHURCH ATTENDANCE STATISTICS

COUNTRY	ATTENDANCE	COUNTRY	ATTENDANCE	COUNTRY	ATTENDANCE
Malta	75%	US	43%	**Greece**	27%
Poland	63%	**Italy**	31%	**Spain**	21%
Ireland	46%	**Portugal**	29%	**Canada**	20%

These estimates of church attendance are based on a Gallup polls taken since 2004. Generally people are torn between being perceived as good Christians, and over-report, and not being identified as troglodytes by secularist who are constantly blaming religion for societal problems. Weekly church attendance may be closer to between 17 and 20%, based on an average of several research polls.[430] However, a Gallup poll taken in December 2013 revealed that 40% of Americans reported that they had attended religious services in the previous week.[431]

The U.S. has a history of generating messianic leaders who are expert recruiters of followers with their facial expressions, their mannerisms, their long diatribes, and simplistic explanations for just about every evil affecting society, while promising redemption. Usually, they have a scapegoat to blame. Since the 1960s there has been a notable increase in messianic leaders who blame Capitalism and "*the system*" for all the problems affecting society, as for example, Jim Jones, founder of the *Peoples Temple*, who led 909 people, mostly racial minorities, to *"revolutionary suicide"* by drinking cyanide in 1978. Despite a checkered past, and a history of arrests, Jones was able to recruit a large cast of followers for his brand of "*Apostolic Socialism*."[432] Among his infamous lines was: *"If you're born in Capitalist America, racist America, Fascist America, then you're born in sin. But if you're born in Socialism, you're not born in sin."*[433] Despite his deranged views, Jones was able to obtain high-level political contacts with Democratic Party figures, including San Francisco Mayor George Moscone, California Governor Jerry Brown, First Lady Rosalynn Carter, and Vice Presidential candidate Walter Mondale. After the Jamestown massacre they ran for the hills…

Another example of leftist preachers is Jeremiah A. Wright, Jr. former Pastor of the Trinity United Church of Christ in Chicago. Despite once serving in the U.S. Navy and Marine Corps, he became a promoter of *Black liberation Theology*, blaming racism and poverty for affecting Afro-American families and mal-distribution of wealth on Zionist Jews, Capitalism in general and America:

> *Not God Bless America – God Damn America… — that's in the Bible — for killing innocent people. God damn America, for treating our citizens as less than human. God damn America, as long as she tries to act like she is God, and she is supreme. The United States government has failed the vast majority of her citizens of African descent…"*[434]

Somehow these convoluted mixes of Judeo-Christian and Marxist rhetoric confuse the masses. Why? People desperately seek spiritual answers, miracles and solutions for their problems.

Right-wing pied pipers use similar histrionics. They have a list of grievances which they use to recruit followers. A good number of them have been proven to be charlatans who have landed behind bars in the past twenty years.[435] They have an intoxicating and seductive pull for nymphets, out-of-control youth, idealistic and impressionable people with confused spirituality, society castaways, xenophobic people, criminal elements, aggressive misfits, and drug addicts.

Apocalyptic visionaries, regardless of political linings, target and recruit essentially the same type of gullible people. How did Jim Jones manage to get 914 people to accept *revolutionary suicide* to protest racism and Fascism in 1978? How did David Koresh manage to convince at least 75 followers to accept communal living, a highly regulated and disciplined life, and to gather a huge arsenal of weapons to fight off government agents trying to execute an arrest warrant? How did he manage to convince them to stage some kind of a murder-suicide pact in 1993? How did Luc Jouret, a *New Ageist* homeopathic doctor manage to recruit people for the *Order of the Solar Temple* and convince them to engage in a murder-suicide pact between 1995 and 1997? How did people get convinced to join the *Heaven's Gate* cult and commit suicide in 1997, expecting to be picked up by some kind of a spaceship linked to the tail of the Hale-Bopp comet? How can civil society *legally* counteract the ability of these *apocalyptic visionaries* to recruit people? Islamic extremists do not have a monopoly on recruiting suicidal people.

Protection of the freedom of conscience, religion, and freedom of speech is selective, as long as it does not conflict with the emerging *counterculture*. Intimidation of people with convictions that go contrary to the emerging *counterculture* is rampant. The masses are rejecting the spirit of tolerance by refusing to acknowledge the validity of other views. Americans are increasingly diverting from the egalitarian ideas emanating from Judeo-Christian ethics, moral traditions and values, and secular ethics shared by the Founding Fathers. Polarization is evident, but like in other areas, *the direction of the country in terms of religious convictions is ill-defined and contradictory.*

Since his election in March 2013, Pope Francis I has moved to place the Catholic Church alongside the people by reducing formalities, grandeur and the traditional script, and establish a clear direction to assist the needy. Pope Francis is an example of leadership to address social issues and economic justice. Within the constitutional parameters concerning the relationship of church and state, a compassionate commitment is necessary to address the needs of the marginalized. Trust in *the system* has to be restored, just as much as Pope Francis wants to restore and expand religious faith and devotion to God through a *compassionate ministry* to the needy. Nevertheless, as a strong anti-Communist, I am concerned about his participation in efforts to bring about rapprochement between the Castro regime in Cuba and the United States. I do not forget the thousands of victims of that Communist dictatorship for one second.

Helping the poor should not involve stealing from others. The *Ten Commandments* clearly *prohibits taking private property*. There are very negative consequences when the commandment is misinterpreted as "*redistribution of wealth*." The ancient Hebrews understood and honored private property rights, and that understanding was inherited by Christians and Muslims. In Leviticus the concept of stealing includes fraud in trade, and not paying workers their due wages as a form of oppression and robbery. It warns about not desiring another person's possessions. The *New Testament* suggests hard work to have something to share with people in need. In other words, wealth has to be created, it should not be stolen. The wealthy, on the other hand, are prompted to be *voluntarily compassionate.*

Islamic faith directs the faithful to help the needy. Reformer Martin Luther ascribed the commandment not to steal to God's desire to protect private property rights. John Calvin preached that the commandment against stealing extended beyond money, or merchandise, or lands, to every kind of right, including tormenting workers by not paying them their due as a form of theft. Calvin asserted that Christians should help to relieve people in need, assisting their want out of one's own abundance. The commandment should not be confused with preaching Socialism or an attack on Capitalism. *It is critical not to be confused and establish the proper direction for America.*

So What?

America is on trial. Americans are facing a war of principles and philosophy. Islamic extremists are assisted in their efforts to proselytize by the Hollywood trash producers who not only damage American youth by promoting irrational and outrageous behavior, but convey to international audiences a picture of the U.S. as a den of snakes, run by rogue CIA operatives in cahoots with corrupt politicians, who exploit the masses. Americans are portrayed as eccentric and weird people covered with tattoos, body piercings, strung out on drugs and alcohol, dressed with low-cut pants with half their butts sticking out. American women are depicted as whores before they have their first menstruation. Hollywood has produced and exported an image of the U.S. as *a country riddled with a culture of evil.* Add violence to the mix through movies, music, videogames, and social networks and *Americans are portrayed as Satanic.*

In the quest for increased freedom and tolerance, the discourse has polarized public opinion, fueling extremists at both ends of the spectrum. Perfectly good concepts like *"diversity"* get tainted with the introduction of extreme points of view, and a concerted effort to force people to accept things that may insult their personal, moral or religious convictions. There is an internal clash of civilizations within the country, which in some ways resembles the global clash of civilizations between Western Culture and Islamic extremists. We are prisoners of extremist ideologies, which turns the right of free speech to an instrument of self-destruction. There is no moral balance between church and state. Government regulations are forced on religious institutions in violation of their convictions.[436] People are increasingly afraid to express their views, as new forms of censorship pick up momentum, as the country moves to mob rule.

Americans are no longer optimistic about their future as they were towards the end of the 19th century, when James Bryce published *The American Commonwealth.* Society seems to be increasingly hostage to disparate groups, from drug lords to firearm dealers, and from street gangs to pompous *talking heads* and political pundits. We are deconstructing the country, with an increasingly vulgar culture, and multiple efforts to coerce civil society into accepting immorality disguised as secularization, emancipation from religion in general and Christianity in particular. Progressives cast traditional morality as irrational and try to coerce society to accept the correctness of their ideology. Common sense and traditions are supposed to make way for their new *correctness* and *modernity*, in which nothing is good or bad anymore.

Public opinion makers try to coerce and manipulate the public; there has always been a counterbalancing act by other public opinion makers with different points of view. In today's environment, the national news media, including right-wing radio and television talk show hosts broadcast daily diatribes to influence the opinion, emotions, attitudes, and behavior of the populace, in part by intimidating people with their vision of a catastrophe ahead. On the other side, there are left-wing elements that intimidate the public to the point that people are afraid to make any comments that could be classified as *not-politically-correct.* The end result is that people are generally intimidated, to the point that the First Amendment rights are rendered useless. Anyone who refuses to accept social disorder, immorality, irresponsible fiscal management, demonizing of the wealthy, or class warfare, is turned into an outcast. What we are facing is internal disorder and *a society with a broken inner moral compass.*

IX – THE IMMIGRATION DEBATE

Gobbledygook (Nonsense)

Nothing is more representative of the breakdown of the rule of law in America than the subject of immigration, which is entangled in nonsense, making it challenging to frame the discussion. The roots of the problem go back to 1942, in the middle of WWII, when there was a shortage of agricultural workers, and the so-called "*bracero program*," was started. By 1954, the program to allow for temporary workers, mainly from Mexico, to enter the country during planting and harvest time and return home had deteriorated into an uncontrolled flow of immigrants. Immigrants continued to cross the border for seasonal employment and returned home, with a relatively limited number staying permanently without visas. During the 1980s the flow of workers from Mexico was increased by Central Americans fleeing the wars between Communist insurgents and military governments receiving American assistance to win the regional proxy wars that were part of the *Cold War*. Five administrations accepted the flow of refugees, Reagan, Bush 41, Clinton, Bush 43, and Obama. They did little to nothing about it. Obama went further by violating the spirit, if not the letter of the Constitution.

Despite a resurgence of *Nativists* and other anti-immigration agitators, most Americans were not into scapegoating immigrants for every imaginable problem. Unemployment was low during the 1990s, until the dot-com bubble recession that started in 2000. After the 9/11/2001 terrorist attacks unemployment climbed further, reaching two digit numbers after the housing crisis in 2008. In 2013, based on polling, only a small percentage of the population really cared about immigration reform. People were more concern about their steady erosion of purchasing power and unemployment. The solutions proposed did not take into account the unintended consequences of acting without properly analyzing the problem.

The immigration picture took a dramatic turn in June 2014, when a massive invasion of children began arriving at the border with Mexico, and erroneous projections were made that as many as 240,000 children mainly from Honduras, El Salvador, and Guatemala would try to enter illegally. According to a Gallup poll, the percentage of Americans citing immigration as the top problem affecting the country spiked to 17%. Americans focused on the problem as never before, but the issue only lasted in the front pages for about two months, until President Obama announced that he would issue an Executive Order on 20 November 2014 to address illegal immigration. The result of the mid-term elections in November 2014 did not dissuade President Obama from going ahead with his own plan, usurping Congressional responsibilities.

From about 1925 to 1965, when immigration rules were revised, an average of about 175,000 immigrants entered the U.S. annually.[437] Over the next 20 years over 500,000 new immigrants arrived annually, with a greater diversity of cultures. Between 2000 and 2010 another 14 million people arrived.[438] Thousands of people from countries and cultures not previously represented in the U.S. in large numbers entered legally and illegally. Supporters of the legislation that allowed for a more diverse immigrant population denied that American culture would be negatively affected. Everyone was expected to live happily and enjoy a greater diversity. That has not happened, and the old systems in place to help immigrants assimilate into American culture were dismantled. The concept of *multiculturalism* was introduced during the 1960s as a new *counterculture* began to expand.

Americanization Abandoned

Within a few days of my arrival in the U.S. in 1962, my uncle registered me to attend the so-called *Americanization School*, which was operated by the D.C. Public School system. It was not free, despite being part of the public school system. The school was located at the John Quincy Adam's School on 19th Street NW, about a block away from the intersection of Connecticut and Florida Avenues, right behind where the Washington Hilton Hotel was under construction. I had studied English in Cuba starting in first grade, and my mother provided additional language training practically every evening during the school year. However, I needed a crash course so that I could start my junior year at St. John's College, a Catholic military school in September. The goal was to *mainstream* me, not to keep me in some bilingual program.

The Americanization School was attended mostly by the sons and daughters of foreign diplomats and international employees of the World Bank, International Monetary Fund (IMF), Inter-American Development Bank (IDB), Pan American Health Organization (PAHO), Organization of American States (OAS), and other organizations headquartered in the city. Most students *were not* immigrants and were planning to return to their countries when their parents' tours of duty ended or retired from the institutions were they worked. The teachers not only taught English, but even more importantly, educated the students on acceptable American cultural mores. Awareness of multiple body gestures and language differences was essential to blend in successfully. I was aware of many of these important subtleties. For Cubans 90 miles away from the U.S. mainland and exposed to American television and movies, these subtleties were generally understood, but for students from far away countries with different cultures, this was a critical part of the program.

American society had some interesting peculiarities, some of which I found perfectly justified and some that I found unacceptable. Washington was at the forefront of the Civil Rights Movement, but in 1962 there were still discriminatory practices that I thought were obscene. I did not like how Afro-Americans were treated, but I found myself incorporating into my daily routines some precautionary practices. I walked about 15 blocks to and from the Americanization school from my home in Georgetown from a wealthy upscale area, past a section of Embassy Row, and ending up in an area in transition, near public schools that were *de facto* segregated. The immediate area around and east of the school was predominantly Black.

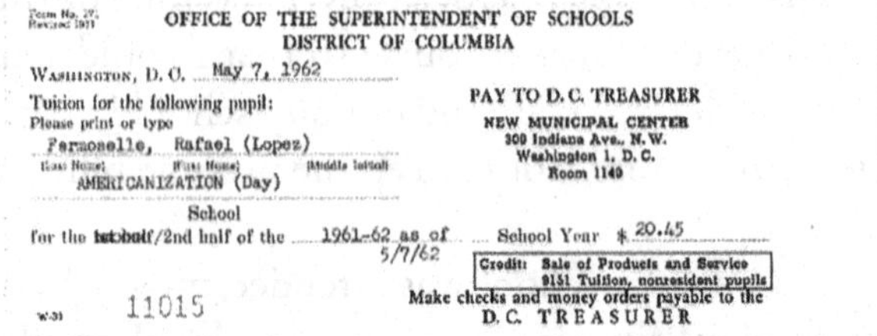

OFFICE OF THE SUPERINTENDENT OF SCHOOLS
DISTRICT OF COLUMBIA

WASHINGTON, D. C. May 7, 1962

Tuition for the following pupil:
Please print or type
Fermoselle, Rafael (Lopez)
(Last Name) (First Name) (Middle Initial)
AMERICANIZATION (Day)
School
for the 1st half/2nd half of the 1961-62 as of 5/7/62 School Year $ 20.45

PAY TO D. C. TREASURER
NEW MUNICIPAL CENTER
300 Indiana Ave., N. W.
Washington 1, D. C.
Room 1140

Credit: Sale of Products and Service
9151 Tuition, nonresident pupils

Make checks and money orders payable to the
D. C. TREASURER

W-31 11015

School registration for the Americanization School was not free, even though it was part of the public school system of the city. To put it in context, $20.45 for about two months of schooling when the minimum wages were at $1.05 per hour was not cheap. No known restrictions on publication

At the time, I do not remember friction between Latin American and Afro-American kids, or any instances of discrimination because I was not Anglo. There were very few Spanish-speaking immigrants at the time other than Cuban exiles, and they did not concentrate in the Capital, with the exception of professional elites educated in the U.S. before the 1959 revolution. However, I could sense that there were important signals in the air that I had to understand to avoid problems. Almost fifty years later, the same public schools are *de facto* segregated, as the student body is almost 100 percent Black. About 50 years later, now the adjacent Columbia Road and Kalorama neighborhood is packed with Spanish-speaking immigrants.

Things were not perfect then, and are not perfect as I write these pages, but there has been progress. The idea of an Afro-American of mixed race elected to the presidency, and Herman Cain, another Black man running against him and leading in many polls during a portion of the primary campaign in 2012 was totally out of the picture back in 1962. But in some other important areas there has been significant deterioration in the political, economic, and social systems. One area where there has been a serious deterioration is the elimination of programs design to incorporate immigrants to American culture. A serious effort should be made to bring back the Americanization programs, if we are serious in maintaining unity of purpose in the country. Perhaps Americans – not just immigrants – need to be put through an Americanization school to bring back "*core values*."

I don't know when, but the old Americanization School that was operated by the Public School system in Washington, D.C. disappeared. It had been established in 1919. Similar schools around the country designed to incorporate immigrants to American culture, went the way of the dinosaurs. The concept of *multiculturalism* had replaced the old concept of the America as a *melting pot* of cultures. The 1960s *counterculture* was already exercising considerable influence on the direction of the country: rebellion against traditional authority, experimentation with narcotics, psychedelic drugs and marijuana, Bohemian lifestyles, the sexual revolution, and alternative lifestyles based on fun and lots of theatrics, civil disobedience, and leftist politics.

Theory and Practice

Readers should not be confused. This entire discussion is *academic*, because the "*problem*" is illegal immigration – not legal immigration. Illegal immigrants come to make a living and send money back to their families. These concepts of Americanization, multiculturalism, and related *are not applicable* because they are far removed from the daily reality of their lives. These philosophical concepts are "irrelevant," when a person is standing outside a Home Depot hoping to be hired as a day worker so that they can buy food and pay for some hole where they can spend the night. If they have a family with them in the U.S., they hardly have any time to relax or attend school. At best, they have a link with a church or a religious organization that offer a mix of basic services and hope through faith. The forces of good and evil are at play all the time. Those that survive for a few years and develop some kind of stability, manage to learn some English, and through osmosis become *Americanized.* There are real success stories that emerge from very difficult and brutal circumstances.

Multiculturalism vs Melting Pot

Since the 1960s, the old concept of "*Americanization*" of immigrants, as well as the metaphor of the nation as a "*melting pot*" of cultures were put aside *in favor of "multiculturalism."* The alternative concept was based on the desirability of building a new "*Utopian metaphor*" of America as a *mosaic of distinct cultures* in a multiracial society. Public schools that had programs to ease the assimilation of immigrants into American culture were shut down. New *"bilingual"* programs were introduced in schools throughout the country. Instead of teaching English intensively to assimilate and educate immigrants, an investment was made to educate children of immigrants in their own language, as well as in English.

Contemporaneous with the introduction of *bilingualism*, the concept of *multiculturalism* was introduced, as the greatest discovery since sliced bread. Since the early immigrant arrivals in the 17th and 18th centuries, immigrant groups tended to cluster together for reasons of language, culture, and religion. A similar unplanned phenomenon happened during the 19th and the early 20th centuries. Germans, Polish, Irish, Italian, Chinese, Cuban, and Jewish immigrants from different nationalities clustered together in their own neighborhoods in Philadelphia, Boston, New York, Chicago, Baltimore, Miami, and other large metropolitan areas. They had their own butcher shops, ethnic grocery stores, cultural centers, newspapers, churches, and other institutions tied to their countries of origin. The older people continued to speak their native languages as their children learned English in their schools. Over time, they assimilated into American culture without necessarily dropping their native cultures. New York, Philadelphia, Boston, and Chicago, for example, were *multicultural* cities 100 years before the left-wing *multiculturalists* "invented" the term. There really was nothing new with *multiculturalism*, other than an attempt to downplay American culture.

Should the US move away from the concept of *multiculturalism* and return to the metaphor of the American *melting pot*? It is impossible to answer the question without examining how the concept played out in Western Europe. Without a doubt, *multiculturalism* and *religious pluralism* has been a failure in Western Europe. Whereas in the United States the traditional idea was to build a new American culture resulting from a "*melting pot*," for Europeans with their own native cultures with deep historical roots the concept resulted from the application of "*Progressive*" ideas, and to be more welcoming and "*open-minded*" to immigrants.

Since the 1950s, Europe has received wave after wave of Muslim immigrants who stand apart, refuse to integrate, and are threatening the very existence of European cultures. Instead of accepting English, French, Dutch, Danish, Swedish, Italian, and Spanish cultures, they try to recreate the very cultures that resulted in their need to flee to Europe. Right-wing populist parties are growing throughout Europe as a result of a strong backlash against the intellectual vision of *multiculturalism* and *diversity*. After years working on the creation of a supranational European Union, there is a revival of national identity, including the things that bind people together, as for example, the cultural and religious background and solidarity of the citizens of one nation. Basically, people are starting to question who can be a *legitimate* fellow citizen.

In The Netherlands (Holland), the clash of cultures has been particularly significant. The Dutch were open-minded and supportive of many components of the secular *counterculture* introduced since the 1960s. They liberalized drug laws, decriminalized pot, legalized prostitution, and introduced tolerance for lesbian, gay, and transgendered people. Every leftist idea associated with the 1960s *counterculture* became the norm. Then as the Muslim immigrants, mostly from their former Dutch colonies of Indonesia and Surinam, as well as Moroccan, Algerian, Turkish, Bosnian, and Iranian people began to arrive in large numbers, conflicts began to develop. Dutch "*tolerance*" turned out to be incompatible with Muslim culture. By 2014, about 6 per cent (6%) of the population of The Netherlands is composed of Muslim immigrants and their Dutch-born children. Due to numerous incidents, Dutch "*tolerance*" is going the way of the dinosaurs.[439]

Wilhelmus Simon Perus Fortuijn (Pim Fortuyn), a prominent far-right Dutch nationalist, who was an openly homosexual Catholic politician called Islam a backward culture, and clashed with them because of their opposition to gay rights. On 6 May 2002, he was assassinated by Volkert van der Graaf using the excuse that Fortuyn was scapegoating and targeting Muslim immigrants because of their general opposition to gay rights. Fortuyn wanted to put an end to Muslim immigration because he thought that it was incompatible with the Dutch culture of tolerance and respect for human rights. Fortuyn held that Muslims were trying to implement sharia law, and import Islamic refusal to accept democracy, women and LGTB rights.

On 2 November 2004, Dutch film director, author, and actor Theodoor "Theo" van Gogh was assassinated by Mohammed Bouyeri, a second generation Moroccan Muslim, who was well-known to police for promoting Islamic extremist ideology, and armed jihad in the Netherlands. Theo van Gogh was riding his bicycle to work – a typical Dutch way of getting around – when he was stabbed eight times by Bouyeri. The assassin was captured within minutes after a gunfight with police. The assassin and his followers had among their targets for assassination Ayaan Hirsi Ali, a Somali-born Dutch woman who was campaigning against female genital mutilation as part of Muslim rituals.[440] At the time, she was a member of the Dutch House of Representatives. She had authored a screenplay for Theo van Gogh for a movie entitled *Submission*, in which abused Muslim women were featured. These incidents triggered firebombing of Muslim schools and mosques, which in turn triggered Muslim attacks against Christian churches. Tolerance is giving way to *Islamophobia.*

A country with a solid reputation for tolerance and open-mildness is dropping multiculturalism as a national policy after experiencing numerous problems with the Muslim immigrant community because they *refuse to integrate* or to respect Dutch culture. Multiculturalism fails when immigrants refuse to accept the culture and values of their host country and the Dutch are getting anxious (uneasy). The clash of Muslim and European civilization is not unique to The Netherlands. In France legislation was adopted to ban the burga in public places, as an affront to women's rights and safety. All the ideas of liberty, fraternity, and equality, engrained in French culture are incompatible with Muslim immigrant culture.[441]

Muslim riots broke out throughout France in 2005, in part due to racial discrimination, and a stream of legislation to forbid key aspects of Muslim culture, from wearing of a hijab to the operation of food stores in violation of local sanitary laws.[442] High unemployment, poverty, and xenophobia have produced a high incidence of crime perpetrated by Muslim youths, and French jails are packed with them.[443] Radical

Islamic organizations surfaced all over France, and attacks against Jews proliferated all over the country. The riots of 2005 led to the deportation of a large number of troublemakers, and calls by far-right politicians to deport all illegal immigrants and even the revocation of French citizenship of naturalized rioters.

In March 2012, a radicalized 24-year-old French-Algerian Muslim, Mohammed Merah, and a former insurgent in Afghanistan, opened fire on a Jewish Day School in Toulouse, killing a rabbi and three young children.[444] The perpetrator also shot and killed three unarmed French soldiers in uniform at Montauban to protest French involvement in the Afghanistan conflict. The three assassinated French soldiers were Muslim, who obviously did not share the same extremist politics. Merah was killed in a shootout with police on 22 March 2012. Thousands of people marched in Paris and other French cities in tribute to the victims. Naturally, *Islamophobia* grew as a result of these incidents. Within days France arrested and deported at least 20 radical Islamic imams back to their home countries. The terrorist attacks in Paris in January 2015, particularly the assassination of graphic artists and cartoonist at the satirical French newspaper *Charlie Hebdo* brought together a broad coalition of people opposed to Islamic terrorism. The French – and other Europeans - are clearly agitated and worried. And then came the terrorist attacks in November 2015 in Paris, which added close to two hundred more victims of Islamic extremists.

The British experience with Muslim immigrants has been extraordinary. On 7 July 2005, in a coordinated suicide attack the public transportation system was targeted by terrorists. Four bombs exploded on board underground trains and a double-decker bus in London causing 52 civilian deaths and injuring over 700 other civilians during the morning rush hour. Three of the terrorists were British-born sons of Pakistani immigrants, and one was a Jamaican convert to Islam. On 23 March 2013, two Nigerian-born British citizens shouting *Allahu Akbar* and "*you will never be safe*" attacked an off-duty British soldier with meat cleavers, and attempted to behead him near London's Royal Artillery Woolwich army barracks. Both attackers were shot and captured by police. As usual, British politicians, including Prime Minister David Cameron, made comments to the effect that "*there is nothing in Islam that justifies this truly dreadful act…*" The British public does not buy all the *heifer dust* any more than Americans when similar comments were made after 9/11/2001 and other Islamic terror attacks in the U.S.[445] All of a sudden the Brits are realizing that it is important for nations to take control of their borders.[446]

In the U.S. "*multiculturalism*" becomes a problem when immigrants refuse to accept American culture and values. There is an interesting and significant contradiction that emerges when the *Progressives* and *secularists* that gave birth to the *counterculture* and the concept of *multiculturalism* are confronted by immigrants that are radical opponents to their views. When the principal proponents of the *counterculture* promote a secular society, and try to drive religion from public life, they run head-on into Muslims that hold the opposite point of view, as they believe that religion should drive all phases of life. For Muslims, particularly extremists, the American *counterculture* is unacceptable and sinful. They are appalled by feminism, freedom for LGBT, same-sex marriage, and related. Funny thing… "*Progressives*" do not see it, or refuse to recognize that they would be among the first to have their heads chopped off by radical Islamists for their views.

Immigration Reform Failure

The *Immigration and Nationality Act of 1965* (PL 236, as well as the *Immigration Reform and Control Act of 1986* (PL 99-603) failed to accomplish their intended purpose. The idea was to increase border security to stop the flow of illegal immigrants and provide a legal process for those already in country to stay and obtain residency papers. What happened was that more people entered the country illegally. A simplistic analysis of why that happened concludes that more people entered illegally because they thought that they would eventually have their status legalized. Other geopolitical factors came into play, particularly the wars in Central America as Communists tried to seize the area, and the U.S. fought back. This regional subset of the Cold War triggered the displacement of refugees that were allowed to enter and stay in the U.S.

The wars in Afghanistan and Iraq, as well as conflicts throughout the Muslim world are directly responsible for the huge influx of

Muslims immigrants from countries that historically never played a major role in immigration to the U.S. Many of them worked for the U.S. Government in their home countries and were either promised visas, or were forced into exile, as they became classified as *collaborators*, and targeted by extremists for helping American military forces or diplomats. Due to these threats they were granted visas for their safety. This is part of a tradition in American foreign policy. After the collapse of South Vietnam in 1975 and the Communist takeover, thousands of Vietnamese who worked for the U.S. took off like bats out of hell – and with reason. Slowly, the so-called "*boat people*" made it to the U.S. as refugees. More recently this process has been repeated with immigrants from Iraq and Afghanistan.

Gridlock on Immigration Policy

Despite an effort by a bi-partisan group of legislators in 2014, the so-called *"Gang of 8,"* it was impossible to enact new immigration policy.[447] The House of Representatives would not go along with the Senate plan. The "*Gang of 8*" proposed a path for illegal aliens to legalize their status and eventually qualify to apply for citizenship, but only after people waiting for permission to enter legally with a permanent residency. The senators' plan included a system to reduce visa application backlogs with fast tracking residency permits for people with U.S. university degrees in science, technology, engineering or math. Their plan would improve the E-Verify program to confirm that new hires have work permits. Finally, they proposed a plan for work visa options for low-skill and agricultural workers. They did not address the key point of creating a national ID card. President Barrack Obama announced on 20 November 2014 his own plan to overcome the immigration gridlock through a controversial Executive order. Regardless of the legality of "legislating" through Executive Order, the measure is only temporary and the country continues to *navigate without a compass.*

Immigration in a Historical Context

People conveniently forget that "native-born Americans" have had problems with new immigrants, starting with the "real" Native Americans who experienced the loss of their lands to European settlers starting in the 16th century. Few if any immigrant group has been spared ethnic bigotry, as evidenced by the long list of disparaging ways of referring to them: *Abbie, Asian nigger, bohunk, chink, ching chong, dagos, fritz, ginzo, gook, greaseball, hymies, hunkies, micks," "kikes, Pollacks, sheeny, wop,* and *raghead.* As the number of Latin American immigrants increased, new derogatory terms came about, including *beaner, spic, spigotty*, and *wetback*, to mention only a few. Some immigrants, as for example the Chinese, were specifically discriminated against by such legislation as the *Anti-Miscegenation Act of 1889* and the *Cable Act of 1922*, which prohibited Chinese men from marrying white women, and terminated American citizenship for white women who dared to marry an Asian man.

Criminal activity and particularly ruthless criminal gangs are not a new phenomenon associated only with Hispanic/Latino gangs that have surfaced since the 1980s. The descendants from such 19th century Irish gangs as the *Dead Rabbits*, the *Daybreak Boys*, the *Patsy Conroys* and the *Roach Guards* have clearly been assimilated into American society. Back in the 19th century Irish immigrants were regarded as subhuman apes and genetically inferior. The same applies to the descendants of Jewish gangs, such as the *Eastmans*, which surfaced in lower Manhattan and Brooklyn in New York City in the 1890s.

During Prohibition Irish, Jewish, Italian and other ethnic criminal immigrant gangs raged in Boston, Chicago, Cleveland, Minneapolis-Saint Paul, New York City, Philadelphia and other American cities. Although some crime families of the Sicilian Mafia (*Cosa Nostra*) are still functioning, Italian immigrants were assimilated into American society and contributed to strengthening the country across the board. The same thing is happening with Latin American immigrants.

Illogical Non-Sense

The shenanigans and transgressions of the rule of law linked to illegal immigration result from a climate of corruption and illogical nonsense that are part of the bizarre "new normal." The way immigration legislation was drafted and implemented does not work. All the problems are periodically compounded by rules that cause more problems than they solve. We can't come up with an effective program to deal with the issue of illegal immigration, but instead a bad situation is made worse by acting without considering unintended consequences, and the population ends up in more danger than ever before.

For example, in the past, anybody could easily get a driver's license, regardless of immigration status. Licensed drivers who own a vehicle are required to purchase accident insurance. There are an estimated 12 to 15 million illegal immigrants. For many of them the operation of a vehicle is necessary to earn a living. With or without licenses they will drive. Drivers without licenses are bound not to have accident insurance either. Thus, by trying to deal with a set of potential problems, a much greater danger to the community at large has been created. A lot of people are driving without a license and without insurance because the system prevents them from getting both. Is there anything more stupid? Yes. There are no national standards. Each state has its own policy on the subject.

Every year millions of drivers unlawfully drive without insurance, causing serious problems for accident victims resulting from unpaid health and car repair bills. This causes insurance premiums to increase to cover victims if they are hit by uninsured drivers. In Virginia alone, about 9 percent (9%) of the drivers involved in accidents are uninsured, with the worse cases in 2007 in New Mexico (29%), Mississippi (28%), Alabama (26%), Oklahoma (24%), and Florida (23%). According to the Auto Insurance Association, and the Institute for Highway Safety, they have no evidence that illegal immigrants cause increases in the cost of auto insurance or the number of highway accidents, but I have serious doubts about how these statistics are analyzed so as not to violate *political correctness.*

About 29 percent of all prisoners are immigrants, representing about 27 different nationalities, but most of them are from Mexico. The problem with criminal activity among Spanish-surnamed legal and illegal immigrants is serious, but it needs to be put in perspective.[448] About 59 percent of the people incarcerated in the U.S. are white-Americans (Whatever that means); and about 37 percent are African-Americans, who only make up about 12 percent of the population of the country. Spanish-surnamed people in the U.S. account for about 16 percent of the population, however, they represent about 35 percent of the people incarcerated. It is impossible to carry out a proper analysis of the meaning of these statistics from the typical mindset using simplistic descriptions of the immigration mess.[449]

Statistics of prison populations are not accurate.[450] Many illegal immigrants use fake identification. Once arrested illegals are fingerprinted, photographed, and an effort is made to figure out who they are and where they came from. If they are deported and come back they can assume new identities, but they are easier to identify because we have them on file, but do not necessarily know their true identity. A substantial number of illegal immigrants incarcerated did not commit a violent crime that would normally land a perpetrator in jail, but because of their immigration status, they are arrested as local authorities try to get DHS to deport them. There are about three times more African-American males incarcerated than Spanish-surnamed prisoners regardless of immigration status or nationality, as a result of mandatory sentencing laws, and stiff penalties for drug violations and the destruction of Afro-American families by the *counterculture*. But how does the system classify a person of African ancestry when they happen to have a Spanish surname? How does the system track a Dominican, Puerto Rican, Colombian, Panamanian or Cuban if they happen to be Black? What is more relevant, the name or the race of the individual?

Historical antecedents, high unemployment, poverty, sub-standard education, the legacy of growing up in crime-infested housing projects, and dependency on welfare generate lifestyles that lead people to think that there is no need to work for a living, and that it is easier to live off the tit of the state, and that it is easier to engage in criminal activity than to take low-paying jobs. These are the factors that have contributed to a large number of African-Americans in the prison population. Likewise, they will contribute to a continued rise in criminal activity among Spanish-surname people, regardless of their immigration status. A growing sense of entitlement to government handouts is creating conditions that are bound to make criminal activity harder to handle in the future. The *U.S.* has become a cradle of social problems, weather we want to admit it or not.

There were at least another 50,000 illegal immigrants in federal prisons as of 2005. About 19,000 illegal immigrants were in state prisons. Criminal violations resulting in their incarceration included arson, assault, auto theft, burglary, drug smuggling, extortion, homicide, human trafficking, intimidation, kidnapping, rape, robbery, weapons violations, as well as violations of American immigration laws. There is a high rate of recidivism, particularly for Mexican-American drug offenders. There are numerous violent Mexican prison gangs, but nothing is done about it.[451] This is part of an overall senseless practice of tolerating all kinds of gangs within prison walls, when they should be smashed to take members out of the mindset that they have any power to control anything or even to think that they will eventually be let out to continue their illegal activity.

According to DEA, criminal activity related to narcotics is regionally dominated by different ethnic groups.[452] For example, Meth in New York and New Jersey is peddled principally by Filipino, Mexican, and white-American networks. Heroin distribution is controlled by African-American, Asian, Colombian, Dominican, Mexican, Pakistani, and Nigerian, West African, and Puerto Rican networks. Cocaine distribution is controlled by African-American, Colombian, Dominican, Jamaican, Mexican, Puerto Rican, and white-American networks. Marijuana is distributed by African-American, Cuban, Dominican, Colombian, Jamaican, Mexican, and White-American networks. Along the Pacific Coast control of the same narcotics trade is managed by different ethnic criminal networks. For example, cocaine is distributed by outlawed motorcycle gangs, Vietnamese, Samoan, Tongan, Mexican, African-American, and White-American networks. There is more diversity among criminal networks than most people can imagine.

Although the Federal Government assists local jurisdictions and state governments to cover the cost of incarceration for illegal immigrants through the *State Criminal Alien Assistance Program* (SCAAP), the money provided does not cover more than about 25 percent of the cost, which is estimated to be between $800 million and $1 billion dollars annually.[453] There are thousands of illegal immigrants in jail simply because they were deported but dared to re-enter again. Others land in jail for DOI and other driving violations. Since it has been increasingly difficult for them to obtain drivers licenses since 9/11/2001, many are arrested for driving without a license and without insurance. There is evidence of an increasing number of non-violent offenders being incarcerated, in part because of their immigration status, which provides private companies operating prisons an additional source of revenue.

Behind the scenes, there are lots of companies that profit from the chaotic situation. The agricultural business community profits from cheap illegal immigrant workers. The agro-industrial sector profits from low wage illegal immigrant workforce. Packing houses all over the country operate with these workers. Visit any meat and chicken processing and packaging plant anywhere in the U.S. and see who is working there! Periodically the headlines cover a scandal here and there at these agro-industrial plants, but before long, everything goes back to normal and nothing happens.[454] The profit motive keeps the problem alive. Keep in mind that the U.S. Chamber of Commerce, representing business interests, claims that there are not enough Americans willing to take low-paying and low-skill jobs, and support immigration reform that will continue to maintain loopholes associated with uncontrolled borders.

Apprehending and massively deporting illegal immigrants is not necessarily a good idea, without considering the unintended consequences. For example, deportations of males arrested for non-violent violations trigger numerous social and economic problems. The spouses and unmarried partners are left behind in the U.S. to care of U.S.-born children, who more-often-than-not will become welfare recipients. Single-parent households and unwed mothers living in poverty can be a source of serious problems ahead. Not always – some mothers work very hard to help their children so that they can have a better future – but statistically these types of households do not have a good track record.[455] Chronic welfare households develop a dependency which is hard to shake. Future criminals are created by the disintegration of the family structure. Statistically, when fathers are absent families end up in poverty and children have a higher propensity to become violent criminals. Thus, deportations can have very serious unintended consequences.

One example illustrates how complicated the situation has become. Two immigrant grandmothers decided to call police to protect their grandchildren from an abusive and dangerous situation. One of the "*abuelas*" has a son in his twenties serving time in jail for drug violations and theft to support his drug abuse. His partner and mother of their two-year-old toddler is hooked on crack cocaine. She is physically abusive with the child. She has another five-year-old child resulting from a previous relationship with another partner. Her own mother reported her perception of child abuse to the paternal grandmother and they jointly decided to ask for a police investigation and for the Department of Social Services of the state to rescue the two children and take away custody from the mother for their protection. These two elderly women will probably end up raising their grandkids with the help of welfare programs. Both parents were born in the U.S. of illegal immigrant parents and were raised in poverty in trailer parks. Now their children will endure a similar fate. Where does it end?

The first generation entered the country illegally, their offspring were born in the U.S. and joined the American *counterculture*, leading to the birth of the second generation of U.S.-born children who will grow up in poverty, dependent on welfare, and exposed to the worst of the worst of the *counterculture*, particularly drugs. The chance that these children will grow up into a life of crime is high, regardless of the valiant efforts of their grandparents. How can immigration reform deal with numerous situations like this? What is the answer? For sure the guilty parties are the policymakers that failed to properly apply the *Immigration Reform and Control Act of 1986* (PL 99-603). These are the unintended consequences of the failure to enforce the letter of the law.

Immigration reform needs to be cut up into smaller pieces that require careful study, such as cleaning up the entire legal system, and the potential unintended consequences. Any new legislation should be homogenized, pasteurized and condensed to no more than 25-to-30 pages, stripped of heifer dust, and with mandatory provisions so that anybody involved in the application of the law would be faced with stiff penalties for dereliction of duty. If the goal is to secure the border, then whoever is in charge of applying the legislation should be held accountable, otherwise NOTHING will be done to really make the border impenetrable.

Utter Confusion and Disorder

The number of non-citizens arrested and processed for federal crimes increased an average of 10 per cent annually between 1984 and 1994. About 45 percent of these immigrants were in the country without a legal status. The numbers do not address racial characteristics or the type of violations of law. By the mid-1990s numerous foreign criminal gangs were operating all over the country. They continue to be active in all kinds of criminal activity, from fraud, violations of copyright and patents, to armed robbery, muggings, murder, and drug dealing. Without a definite number of illegal immigrants it is impossible to determine what percentage engaged in criminal activity. However, most of the people who come are not criminals, although by definition anybody who violates immigration laws is *de facto* a law violator, in the absence of a universally accepted definition.

The largest number of foreign-born prisoners are Latin Americans, but they are not the only source of crime. It is not only the traditional Italian organized crime linked to the Sicilian Mafia, the Camorra, and the Ndrangheta, now we have to deal with very violent and sophisticated organized crime from Russia and several of the old Soviet Republics, and former Communist countries in Eastern Europe. For example, two Russian organized crime figures were arrested and charged by the U.S. Attorney for the Eastern District of New York in 2006 for their participation in a plot to murder two Kiev-based businessmen. In February 2011, a large number of the so-called Armenian Power (AP) criminal organization were arrested in Southern California and charged with numerous crimes, including identity theft and credit card fraud.[456] Common activities for AP include kidnapping, extortion, bank fraud, aggravated identity theft, credit card fraud, marijuana distribution, illegal gambling, firearms offenses, and health care fraud taking advantage of programs like MEDICARE.[457]

While the U.S. is undergoing a dramatic crisis in the healthcare sector, foreigners are responsible for most of the fraud against MEDICARE, including Cuban-born criminals in Florida (many of them from Santa Clara). At least forty have escaped back to Cuba with millions of dollars fraudulently obtained from the MEDICARE program. The ultimate conspiracy to defraud taxpayers involved a group of Russian diplomats in New York City.[458] A group of about 49 Russian consular officials and diplomats assigned to the UN had been swindling MEDICAID for pregnancies, births, and postnatal care. Due to their diplomatic immunity they could not be arrested and prosecuted unless the Russian Government waived the immunity protection and turned them over for prosecution. Immigrants from the former Soviet Union living in Brighton Beach, Brooklyn, and New York City have one of the highest rates of healthcare fraud in the nation.

Chinese illegal immigrants have been arriving in large numbers since the 1980s and are engaging in multiple criminal enterprises, starting with human trafficking. For example, in March 2006, Chinese alien smuggler Cheng Chui Ping, better known as "*Sister Ping*," was sentenced to 35 years in prison for her role in leading an international alien smuggling organization that smuggled more than 1000 aliens into the country. According to information released during the trial, Sister Ping hired armed thugs from the *Fuk Ching*, a vicious gang in New York's Chinatown, to transport her customers and ensure they paid their smuggling fees. There have been problems with immigrant criminal activity since the 19th century and just about every nationality and ethnic group has been linked.

Despite promises by President Obama to push for immigration reform during the 2008 election campaign, as of November 2015, he had not sent a draft bill to Congress and no reform had been enacted. The legal process to deport an immigrant is cumbersome and the number of judges is not sufficient to handle expeditiously the backlog of over 300,000 cases. Nevertheless, close to two million immigrants were deported by ICE between 2008 and 2013. Considering that there are at least 12 million illegal aliens in the country, if policymakers were serious about deportations, there would not be a backlog of cases in the courts and there would not be a considerable number of vacancies among immigration judges.

The government prevailed in Immigration Court in about 52 percent of the cases, obtaining approval for deportations. The government success ratio in deportation cases has not been the same across the country. In states that have traditionally been more receptive to immigrants, including California, New York, Washington, and Oregon, immigrants facing deportation have been more successful in winning their cases. In less friendly states to immigrants, including Georgia, Louisiana and Utah, immigration judges have been more prone to order deportations. The figures support the notion that the entire process is not uniform. If the policymakers were serious about enforcing the law, and the process were equitable, geographic location would not have any bearing on the results.

Deportation efforts in 2013 were centered on deporting criminal elements, as well as identifying potential terrorists and preventing them from entering the country.[459] Of the 133,551 people deported in FY2013, about 59 percent were criminal offenders previously convicted of a crime. Another 235,093 people were arrested along the borders while attempting unlawful entry and were "deported," but these people never made it in. Are these truly deportees? Of the deportees who were apprehended within the boundaries of the U.S., about 48 percent (52,935) had been convicted of aggravated felonies. Of all the deportees, 30,977 had previously been deported but had managed to re-enter, of which 10,358 were repeat immigration violators. Anybody hell-bent on breeching the walls can eventually get in. Without a doubt, convicted felons should be expeditiously shipped back to where they came from.

Most of the people who arrived from Central America, particularly, El Salvador, wanted to escape war and earn a living. A large number of them ended up in poor neighborhoods in California, particularly in Los Angeles, where their children were often victimized by Mexican and Afro-American gangs. The parents worked, and the children were left unattended at home. There was no money to pay babysitters and no grandparents to help with the children. Before long, the Central American kids set up their own gangs for self-protection. They outdid rivals in violence and successfully gained turf. Such gangs as *Mara Salvatrucha* (MS-13), grew out of these battles, and became national gangs, as they spread to other cities with large concentrations of Central Americans. Because there was a failure of law enforcement, the new immigrants had to take the law into their hands for self-protection, and thus another Frankenstein monster was created due to the failure of "the system" to combat criminal gangs.[460]

PARTIAL ILLEGAL IMMIGRATION STATISTICS 2000-2013

COUNTRY OF ORIGIN	NUMBER OF UNDOCUMENTED IMMIGRANTS BY HOME COUNTRY 2010	INCREASE IN UNDOCUMENTED IMMIGRANTS FROM 2000 TO 2010	REMOVALS / DEPORTATIONS IN FY 2013
Mexico	7,030,000	50%	241,493
El Salvador	570,000	33%	21,602
Dominican Rep.	Legal and illegal in 2000: 908,531	~1.6 million increase	2,462
Guatemala	430,000	48%	47,769
Ecuador	n/a	n/a	1,616
Philippines	300,000	50%	?
Honduras	300,000	88%	37,049
Korea	240,000	33%	?
China	220,000	16%	?
Brazil	180,000	80%	1,500
India	160,000	33%	?

The total number of illegal immigrants as of 2014 is estimated to be above 12 million, but nobody has a clear handle on the real numbers.

As the gang problem spread many members were arrested and deported back to Central America. The gangs – previously unknown in Central America– became a nasty American cultural export that de-stabilized further the region. With few jobs, and unable to blend in back home in their countries, they reconstituted and expanded their gangs with local recruits. These gangsters had grown up in the U.S. and had even lost their Spanish language skills, speaking a type of *patois* or *Pidgin* Spanish or *Pidgin* English, commonly known as *"gangspeak."* They terrorized their countrymen, which in turn, created conditions that led more people to try to leave and head towards the U.S. to escape poverty and crime. The vicious cycle continues…

Participation in Welfare Programs

There is Anarchy in the management of welfare programs, and it extends to the coverage provided to legal and illegal immigrants and their American-born children. The impact of illegal immigration on welfare programs at the local, state, and Federal level is higher than most people would expect. I did not believe that people in the country illegally could be receiving welfare assistance unless there were extenuating circumstances, as for example, people involved in an accident, or children that suddenly became orphans, or school children participating in school lunch programs. The reality is very different. There are huge differences in coverage from one state to the next, depending on local politics.

In a study conducted by the GAO in 1997, and reported to Congressional Committees, it was found that in Arizona, California, New York, and Texas benefits were being provided to households with an illegal alien parent receiving benefits for U.S.-born children. Considerable fraud and misrepresentations were detected, but national statistics on the extent of the problem were not available.[461] Few cases were prosecuted for welfare fraud, in part because the process is "time-consuming and labor-intensive." In general, information collected on the immigration status of people receiving benefits is not transmitted to Federal authorities. Policymakers are generally flying blind and pontificating on immigration without facts.

Immigrants are a very heterogeneous population, even if only populations arriving from Latin America are considered. As of the 2010 official census, 308.7 million people lived in the U.S. at the time, of which 50.5 million or 16 percent were classified as *Hispanic* or *Latino*, representing an increase of 13 percent since 2000. A total of 26.7 million of these Spanish-surnamed people described themselves as *white* (however that is defined). A substantial percentage of this population are descendants of populations that have been in America for many generations, including people who have been in North America long before the American Revolution and some before the 102 Mayflower Pilgrims arrived in 1620, and long before the war with Mexico in 1848.[462] By the U.S. Bureau of the Census definition, *Hispanic* or *Latino* refers to people of Cuban, Mexican, Puerto Rican, South or Central American or other Spanish culture or origin *regardless of race*. (In other words, *Hispanic* or *Latino*, is not a race!)

Contrary to popular belief, many of the so-called *Hispanic* or *Latino* do not have a drop of Spanish blood and their only link to Spain is that they happen to have a Spanish surname. A total of 1.24 million "*Hispanic*" or "*Latino*" described themselves as Black or African-American, 685,150 as million as American Indian and Alaska Native, 209,000 as Asian, 58,437 as Native Hawaiian and other Pacific Islander, and 18,503 as some other race, and 3.04 million as belonging to two or more races.[463] Why is this important to understand the link between welfare programs and immigration? Because to understand the complications associated with dealing with the immigration problem is vital. For example, many immigrants from Mexico and Central America have a very poor educational background, and incorporating them into the American economy and culture will be extremely difficult without specific steps to deal with their peculiar circumstances. Many of these immigrants are Native Americans (Indians) who have been victims of discrimination in their home countries and have little or no education. They are illiterate, which makes it difficult and costly to address their needs.[464]

Principal Welfare Programs

- Aid to Families With Dependent Children (AFDC)
- Food Stamp Program (SNAP)
- Supplemental Security Income (SSI)
- Department of Housing and Urban Development (HUD) Rental Housing Assistance
- Medicaid/Affordable Care Act (Obamacare)

Estimates of welfare costs associated with illegal aliens range from $14 to $22 billion, but these figures are very speculative.

For example, in Mexico there are at least 62 distinct Native American tribes or sub-tribes with their own language and culture. A fairly large number of Mexican agricultural workers that cross the border into the U.S. come from these rural populations, who often do not have a complete command of Spanish, and have a high incidence of illiteracy.[465] For them learning English is a very difficult task because they lack education and may have a limited command of Spanish. These agricultural workers often arrive as family units, and both men and women work in agriculture planting and harvesting crops. By the very nature of agricultural work, the sector has seasonal employment, which means that in winter, they do not have a way of earning an income, and end up depending on welfare programs, particularly food stamps.[466] Operating a large-scale agricultural workforce composed of temporary immigrants that would come and go annually would be costly and impractical. By making it more difficult to enter the U.S. that keeps them here all year, whereas in the past, they went back and forth to Mexico.

An undetermined percentage of these families of agricultural workers, which may or may not be officially married, have babies born in the United States, who by their birth-right, according to the Constitution, are American citizens and entitled to receive assistance. Many children are born to unwed mothers, and fathers, who frequently abandon them. Single mothers exist in large numbers among these populations of illegal immigrants. Mothers with children from multiple fathers are not uncommon.[467] Welfare programs often restrict assistance to only U.S.-born children. However undocumented aliens are not left to die of hunger and be left untreated if they need medical care. Practically all states and local jurisdictions provide assistance regardless of immigration status, with some exceptions.

The challenges faced by Mexican illegal immigrants is vast. For example, a Mexican mother of three crossed the border with her three children and her partner. Once in the U.S., the couple obtained work, planting or picking crops, or doing other agricultural work. She never attended school as a child in Mexico and is illiterate. She had two more children in the U.S., who are American citizens. Somehow, after residing in the U.S. for several years, and being the mother of two U.S. citizens, she managed to legalize her immigration status. However, her partner went back to Mexico to visit an ailing parent, and never came back, unable or unwilling to return to the U.S. to take care of his family. The mother became the *de facto* new "*head of household*" with five children attending school. She applied for food stamps and cash through welfare programs, and is issued about $350.00 in food stamps monthly. They are granted medical care, first through the MEDICAID program, and more recently through Obamacare (The *Affordable Care Act*). The state helps them pay rent through access or referrals to HUD programs for the needy.

The local community through property taxes and some help from the state government provide education for the children, who also participate in the school lunch program funded through USDA.[468] The mother and five children have no idea as to what happened or if their father will ever get back to their home in the U.S. How can an illiterate single mother of five with little or no English survive? This family will be dependent on welfare programs for at least the next 15 to 20 years until the children grow up and find employment. This situation is real, only the names and location have been protected. There are thousands of similar situations all over the country, particularly in the South West and along the West Coast states.

In another instance, an illiterate Native American from Mexico is trying to renew her food stamps support for her American children. She needs to go to the welfare office in a rural area with long distances between towns and villages every six months to be recertified. She has a very difficult task understanding instructions, because she does not speak English. Being illiterate, understanding instructions is difficult, as she cannot read road signs or written instructions. She has to take her American-born 12-year-old child from school periodically so that kid can accompany her to reapply for food stamps. The kid has been educated in the U.S. and can read and write in English, but her knowledge of Spanish is limited to a *Pidgin Spanish* mixed with some Native language and *Pidgin English* spoken at home. The child has a very difficult time interpreting for her mother at the welfare office, so an interpreter has to be provided by the state. They live in a dilapidated trailer in a trailer park, constantly exposed to criminal activity. They can barely pay for electricity during the winter due to the high cost of heating. The former partner and father of the child was deported after a raid in a meat packing plant and has not been able to get back to the family. After this "very smart" move, American taxpayers will take care of the American citizen children for a very long time.

Medical insurance coverage for illegal immigrants living in extreme poverty includes costly support programs. For example, a first-time mother in January 2014 was having serious complications during childbirth, after she was admitted to a small regional clinic in one of the western states. She was transported by ambulance to the regional airport and flown to a larger hospital in the state capital, where she was again transported to a hospital by ambulance. The baby was born and a little over a week later mother and baby were transported by ambulance back to the airport to be flown home. A social worker at the state capital provided assistance, including interpreters, to assist mother and baby through the ordeal, all at taxpayer expense. The baby's father had been unemployed for about two months, due to the end of the harvest, with no possibility of employment until the spring. In other words, from November 2013 until March 2014, the family would be totally dependent on welfare programs and the local, state and federal levels. Taxpayers covered the costs, but a new American citizen was born and treated humanely. Without a doubt the baby will be dependent on welfare for the next 18 years or more. What could the jurisdictions involved in this case do other than what they did? Could they have allowed mother and baby to die without medical care? That would never happen. It would be contrary to everything that the U.S. stands for.

Contrary to the mythology associated with the immigration dilemma, not all legal and illegal immigrants are eager to sign up for welfare. For example, the divorced father of two American-born boys threatened his former wife of withholding child support payments if she applied for food stamps or other types of welfare because he fears that when the boys grow up the U.S. Government would force them to join the military against their will. Nothing like that is accurate! At age 18, like everybody else living in the US, citizens and legal residents, have to sign up for the Selective Service, but we have over thirty years of operating a volunteer military and nobody has been drafted against their will for a very long time.[469]

In summary, the costs associated with providing access to welfare programs – particularly the Supplemental Nutrition Assistance Program (SNAP), known as the "*food stamps program*" and healthcare – to an estimated 12 million illegal immigrants is unknown.[470] Just the cost of providing welfare coverage to American-born children of illegal immigrants is staggering, but as American citizens, they are entitled to coverage.[471] Their illegal immigrant parents are not entitled to coverage. The annual cost of participation in the food stamps program for illegal immigrants is a considerable portion of the $80 billion plus program, which generally operates with little oversight and contributes to the enhancement of a climate of dependency.[472] Nevertheless, Americans enjoy cheaper food because we have a large underclass of agricultural workers who live in extreme poverty. The bottom line is that the impact of legal and illegal immigration on welfare programs is considerable, but there are no reliable facts.

Consequences of the 14th Amendment

One of the principal sources of legal and illegal immigration from the Caribbean is the Dominican Republic (DR). Dominican immigration presents a different but similar set of challenges than immigrants from Mexico and Central America, both in the ethnic composition, cultural background, and because their own country is faced with illegal immigration from Haiti. The way that Dominicans address their own illegal immigration challenge would be totally unacceptable in the U.S. except by the most extreme chauvinists and xenophobes.

The Dominican Republic is an overpopulated country of approximately 10 million people, mostly of mixed race (White, Black, and some Native American stock), with Spanish surnames. Despite their African roots, Dominicans tend not to identify with non-Dominican Blacks, particularly Haitians, due to a very convoluted past. The two countries share the island of *Española*, but one is Francophone and in the other Spanish is spoken. One is almost 100% African, and the other has a very mixed population. One is dirt poor, and the other is a developing country, which despite high unemployment and poverty, is a magnet for Haitians who cross the border illegally to earn a living. Dominican Blacks claim to be "Indios," and discriminate against "Haitian Blacks."

As in the U.S. when a foreigner – *regardless or immigration status* – had a baby in the Dominican Republic, the newborn was granted Dominican citizenship automatically. The Dominican Congress enacted new legislation and obtained a Constitutional Court decision in September 2013 to *retroactively* deny citizenship to children born in the Dominican Republic of parents illegally in the country. All Dominicans born of illegal alien parents since 1929 were *stripped of their citizenship!* Just discussing a similar decision in the U.S. would trigger a huge international outcry! Nevertheless, some people support Draconian actions.

Under the 14th Amendment of the Constitution, anyone born in the U.S. is automatically an American citizen, *regardless of the immigration status of the parents*, just as in most countries around the world, including the Dominican Republic until they enacted legislation in 2013 to change the rules. The 14th Amendment to the Constitution was enacted during the Republican Administration of President Lincoln and has been in place for over 150 years. Despite the abuse, the chances of enacting legislation to make a change to the 14th Amendment are extremely limited. Draconian measures will not be supported by the American electorate.

It is estimated that as many as 35,000 pregnant women come with legal visas and pay as much as $50,000 in related costs to have their babies with no intention necessarily of illegally remaining in the U.S. The vast majority return home with their baby and a U.S. passport as a form of insurance in the event that they even have to leave their country as a result of some political upheaval. The real problem is that millions of illegal immigrants have settled in the country and have procreated. That is the real challenge. Coming up with a rational way to address the problem in line with American traditions will not be easy.

Illogical Contradictions

The best way I can illustrate numerous contradictions in the immigration picture is to relate some of my own experiences in a typical day. I worked at a secret government facility. Around 8:00 A.M. I would take off my badge and walk to a cafeteria on the ground level of the building for a cup of coffee. By then, the Korean-born owner and a crew of about five or six Koreans, without a doubt, legally in the country, are busy at work preparing for the lunch rush. I normally completed my work day by about 2:00 P.M. On this particular day, I went to see my 104 year-old mother, who was at a nursing home in Arlington, Va. My mother was attended by several African-born nurses who work on a 24-hour schedule at this facility.[473] Her physician was born in Iran. The cleaning and maintenance crew is almost one hundred (100%) percent made up of Central American immigrants. About the only few American-born employees are in administration. The physician and the nurses are well paid, above the median wage in the country for the type of work they perform. Why is it that we cannot put more Americans through nursing school to take care of the elderly as the baby boom generation enters retirement age starting in 2012?

After visiting my mother, I had to take care of a couple of problems. My wife told me the day before that she had found a water leak under the kitchen sink. I had to call a plumber, and it turns out that the repairs were made by a handyman from Honduras. It cost me $100.00 for less than one hour of work. I own a rental property, which happened to be occupied by an FBI agent and his family. He had called me the night before to tell me that there was something wrong with the heat pump and the air conditioning unit was not working. I called a reputable HVAC company in Northern Virginia with whom I have a service contract. I had to go over to receive the repairman, who turned out to be from Malaysia. The type of technical work he performs is compensated very well. The repair and renewal of the maintenance contract cost me $540.00. Obviously, he was not earning minimum wages.

On the way home I stopped by the U.S. Postal Service branch in McLean, fairly close to CIA headquarters. There were three people behind the counter and all three were Vietnamese-Americans. The lady that sold me a book of stamps had heavily accented English. These USPS workers spoke to each other in Vietnamese. About 6:00 P.M. I went to pick up my wife at the law firm where she works in downtown Washington, D. C. We decided to go out for dinner at a fast food establishment on the way home. All the people working behind the counter and in the kitchen were from Latin America.

When we arrived home, I reflected on my day and my multiple encounters with different people. It happened to be Friday, and I heard in the news that, once again, over 400,000 people had filed for unemployment compensation, that the unemployment rate continued at 9.1 percent, and that over 14 million people were unemployed. Something was very wrong with that picture. I remembered that back in the 1960s, most of the handymen in the D.C. Metro area were from West Virginia and Pennsylvania, whereas now, they all seem to be immigrants from Latin America. What do all of those people from West Virginia and Pennsylvania do for a living now? Did all the children and grandchildren of the handymen back in the 1960s go to college? We know they are not working at factories, since most of the few factories in their home turf closed and the production was shifted overseas. With a substantial Afro-American presence in the region, why is it that I hardly see any of them working as repairmen and handymen? If I go to the Home Depot at the 7 Corners shopping center, there are always between 20 and 30 illegal immigrants from Central America – seldom from Mexico – hanging around for someone to pick them up as day laborers.

Invariably, there are about a dozen trucks owned by immigrants who work as handymen and construction contractors picking up supplies parked at the Home Depot. The Home Depot staff is made up of immigrants, from Africa, the Middle East, and Asian countries, with a sprinkling of "natives." If I go to pick up hardware or software for my computer at Micro Center, Best Buy, or other electronic stores, more-often-than not I end up interacting with staff from some Asian country. When I go shopping for groceries I always see about ten illegal immigrants from Central America standing near the front of the store waiting for someone to pick them up as day laborers. Inside the store, the checkout clerks, and behind the meat and seafood counters, all include people from Brazil, Morocco, Vietnam, Peru, Ecuador, Chile, Turkey and other countries. In the pharmacy area, several of the people with degrees in pharmacology are mostly from Vietnam.[474] These are legal immigrants, who are not any different from previous waves of immigrants doing honest work.

With 14 million people unemployed, why were practically all the people I had to deal with during a normal day right around the Nation's Capital immigrants? Is it that Americans -of *all* races- do not want to work and prefer to collect unemployment? Why? *The system is blinking red! The American Afro-American community is being left behind- but who is at fault?*

NATIONAL BACKGROUND OF HISPANIC/LATINO POPULATIONS IN THE United States C. 2000 (U.S. Bureau of the Census 2000 Summary File)

ORIGIN	COMMENT	SIZE
Puerto Rico	U.S. Citizens by birth	4.6 million
Cuban	Political and economic refugees	1.8 million
Mexican	A large percentage are U.S. citizens by birth	31.8 million
Dominican	**This population grew from 765,000 in 2000 to 1.4 million in 2010. These figures are probably low.**	1.4 million
Central America	This category includes people who reported they were from Central America Indian groups, Canal Zone, and Central American countries. (Belize, Costa Rica, Guatemala, Honduras, Nicaragua, and El Salvador.)	3.98 million
South America	This category includes people who reported to be from South American Indian groups and South Americans	2.76 million
Spain	European	635,000
Other	This category includes people who reported Hispanic or Latino and other general terms. Many of them are from the Philippines, and only have a Spanish last name. They are no more Spanish or Hispanic, or Latino than a Black-Afro-American named Washington or Jefferson are European because they were given that name by the former slave owners of their ancestors.	4.45 million

DMV Cantina

And now, for one of my most infuriating experiences… a visit to the Virginia Department of Motor Vehicles (DMV) in Fairfax County, to renew my driver's license. The place reminded me of the bar scene (*Chalmun's Cantina* in the pirate city of *Mos Eisley*) in the first Star Wars movie released in 1977. When you walk in, you are directed to a booth where everyone is asked the reason for their visit before they are given a ticket with a number. I said that I had to renew my driver's license. I was asked if I had my passport with me. I told the lady – who had a rather strong foreign accent – that I did not have my passport with me, and I asked her why I had to have a passport to renew a Virginia Driver's License. She told me that I had to have either my birth certificate, a passport, or "green card." I told her that birth certificates do not have pictures, or fingerprints, or any other information that could be used to identify an individual. All they say is that a person was born on a given date, the location, and the name that was given to the person, and who the parents and possibly grandparents were. I was told… *we need to see one… or the passport*, or a "*green card*" or valid residency permit.

I asked why a passport would be needed, when most people in the U.S. are born, live, work, and die within a fifty mile area of where they were born, and never go overseas or get a passport. (Only about 21 percent of the population get a passport, and that has only recently increased to that number because they are now required to cross into Canada or take a cruise ship to the Caribbean and return home.)[475] Less than ten percent of Americans ever go overseas! I showed the receptionist at the DMV that I had several U.S. Government issued IDs, including a badge to enter the Pentagon, a badge to enter intelligence facilities, a government contractor ID, another ID as an authorization as a "courier" that allowed me to transport secret documents… another ID showing that I am a retired U.S. Foreign Service officer, and obviously, I had to be an American citizen with a government security clearance not available to non-citizens. None were acceptable.

The fact that I had a previously issued Virginia License did not have any meaning. Was I asked to produce an ID to show that I was legally in country because I have a slight accent? Was I a victim of discrimination, stupidity, or both? I asked to speak to a supervisor at the main counter, and was given a number and allowed to wait for about an hour until my turn came up. I did not let out that I had my passport in my pocket, plus my old cancelled black diplomatic passport. I was on the warpath by then, particularly knowing that in numerous other states they issue licenses to illegal aliens. When my number was called, the lady behind the counter was wearing a head scarf and was without a doubt an immigrant from a Muslim country. Again I was asked for a birth certificate or passport. I asked to speak to her supervisor. Finally, a person who seemed to be a "native" came over and explained that now the state requires proof of citizenship or legal status in the country, and that all my U.S. Government identifications were not considered valid.

That was obviously ridiculous, since my identifications were issued by the Federal Government, had my picture, name, partial Social Security number, level of security clearance, and phone numbers that could be called to verify the information with a security office, as compared with birth certificates that do not have any of these verifiable data points. Finally, I pulled my passports out and completed the transaction. I wrote to the Governor and to my Congressman about this incident, which I considered to be discriminatory and stupid. I received apologies, mixed with *gobbledygook*, which has become increasingly frequent in the culture of "political correctness."

The National ID Debate

Without a National Identity Card (NIC), it is impossible to verify who is legally in the country. The enactment of the *Real ID Act of 2005*, which was part of the *Emergency Supplemental Appropriations Act for Defense, the Global War on Terror, and Tsunami Relief, of 2005 (PL 109-13, 119 Statute 231),* was regarded as the first step in creating a NIC for the first time in American history. The *Act* established national standards for state-issued driver's licenses and "voluntary" identification cards for non-drivers, however that is defined. It also tightened the application and interpretation of existing laws regarding political asylum and the deportation of aliens. Several state legislatures objected, because there are constituencies that object to the creation of a NIC with the assumption that such a requirement would not be constitutional.

Lawmakers in Maine, Georgia, Montana, Wyoming, Vermont, New Mexico and Washington either adopted resolutions declining to comply with the *Real ID Act of 2005*, either because it is costly to implement, or simply because they oppose the creation of a NIC. Privacy is a big issue for Americans. However, the European Union (EU) has much tighter personal privacy protection legislation than the U.S. and *all EU members have national identity cards*. There is nothing in the Constitution that would preclude a NIC system. The enactment of legislation to create it is overdue. There is no way to control our borders or protect the country against potential terrorism if law enforcement lacks this vital tool. There is nothing intrinsically wrong with the concept. Without a NIC, American citizens become victims of the excesses and misdirected efforts to control the dual problem of illegal immigration, criminal activity, and potential terrorism. Racial and ethnic profiling can easily result in native born and naturalized American citizens being harassed by law enforcement because there is no ID card to prove beyond all doubts a legal presence in the country.

So-What?

America lacks direction in immigration policy. The situation is totally psychotic and based on a distorted sense of reality. Policymakers wait until they can figure out which way the wind is blowing, and few want to expose themselves by deciding which way to vote on immigration reform. Border fencing, double-fencing, video surveillance, unmanned aircraft, helicopters, and watercraft – have not worked. More border patrol agents (CBP) and Immigration and Customs Enforcement agents (ICE) have not improved the situation. The E-Verify system failed. The will to solve the problem simply does not exist.

X – CONCLUSIONS

> **To make no mistakes is not in the power of man; but from their errors and mistakes, the wise, and good learn wisdom for the future.**
>
> **Plutarch**

The United States of America is what its citizens make of it. There is no complex electromagnetic or cosmic force that can be blamed for creating the dysfunctions that affect the nation. There are multiple points of failure. The challenges of today are the cumulative result of mismanagement by policymakers of both political parties. Democrats and Republicans share the blame, but so do religious leaders, teachers, news media pundits, the Hollywood crowd, and the citizens who let them mismanage the country. This author does not claim to be gifted with prophetic powers, but has come to the conclusion that America has to overcome a bad case of allergy to logic. It is imperative to grab the rudder and a compass and figure out in which direction to move America. There is a saying that *people with goals succeed because they know where they are going… Only God knows where we are headed!*

As a society we need an adaptable and dynamic thinking mindset to address challenges and vulnerabilities in a constantly changing environment. History is what it is. It cannot be changed retroactively, even if every generation tries to reinterpret the past. American culture back in the 1950s was not perfect, however "perfect" is defined, but it represented historical events, shared traditions, expectations, rules of etiquette, and learned human behavior patterns. Since then, the predominant culture of the country was slowly taken over by a "*toxic counterculture*" that has destroyed a couple of generations of young people already. There is nothing wrong with progressive ideas, tolerance and pluralism, except when excesses lead to the creation of *freaks, mutants,* and *oddities* that do not belong in polite society.

Since independence, Americans developed a unique culture based on the principles outlined in the *Declaration of Independence* and the *Constitution*, incorporating new concepts and ideas, refining, taming, humanizing, and improving education, health, the economy, the democratic process, and governance. Foreign and domestic enemies surfaced periodically, but "*the system*" was able to overcome them. Common sense generally prevailed, until the antithesis of what the nation stood for emerged during the 1960s through the introduction of radical "*Progressive*" ideas, and the result has not been pretty. This hijacking of the country is to a great extent due to limited knowledge of the past by the average American, widespread ignorance, and the failure of the educational system to teach civics, i.e. *the practical and theoretical aspects of citizenship, ethical traditions, and their rights and duties.*

As on the eve of 9/11/2001, we have now numerous signs that we have vulnerabilities that could produce serious consequences if we fail to pay attention and take action. It is critical to understand who and what presents a threat to national security, internally and externally. We are faced with many nefarious actors, including domestic political extremists, transnational organized criminals, violent Islamic fundamentalists and unreconstructed Communists that should have been strangled at the cradle.[476] A sound intelligence and counterintelligence system – *free of heifer dust* - is vital to protect the nation from all of these enemies, each with their own bag of tricks.

We are past 4th generation into 5th generation warfare, with hybrid fronts deep into the homeland behind our national borders. Unconventional warfare tactics target civilians, as well as people in uniform. Under the "*new reality*" *we* need multiple alternative capabilities, but more than ever before we need good intelligence, i.e. *accurate, objective, usable, relevant, ready and timely.*[477] Intelligence analysts and their senior leaders cannot be put in the role of Cassandras, never to be believed, because policymakers refuse to accept their strategic assessments. Intelligence analysis that incorporates "Utopian political schemes" that do not reflect reality are garbage. Republican and Democratic leaders, Conservatives and Liberals, have disregarded intelligence reports because they do not support their illogical preconceived ideas that do not reflect reality, i.e. *the state of things as they actually exist.*[478] That is how we get into avoidable conflicts, and fail to act on unavoidable wars.

Nefarious actors are encouraged when they see numerous examples of American fumbling and blundering all over the place. These are some examples: Despite assurances of territorial integrity given to the Ukraine in the *Memorandum of Budapest* in 1994, Russia crossed the border and seized the Crimea in 2014, and continued to assist militarily pro-Russian separatists without a truly effective American and European response to undeniable armed aggression. How can other American allies believe assurances of assistance and mutual defense treaties when we fail to adhere to promises made in these documents? America's friends are losing trust, and the enemies are pressing the envelope to see how far they can get, because there is no obvious strategy or concept of what the endgame would look like.

We live with the background of failed and failing states and tinderboxes 'round the world. We have both, serious traditional peer-to-peer and asymmetric challenges. We have no choice but to prepare for all types of potential encounters. Most of the 57 Muslim majority countries present conditions that will continue to feed extremists into the future. We have a long conflict ahead, and the first step in winning is to recognize who the enemies are, and that it will take time to overcome the challenge.

We cannot defeat jihadists without addressing the causal chain of events. That is basic methodology for successful counterinsurgency (COIN). This type of conflict cannot be won militarily without addressing its' root causes. The problem is not terrorism; the problem is *insurgency* against perceptions of what Western Culture represents. The problem is a world-wide *Islamic extremist insurgency.* Terrorism is simply a tool of insurgency. Addressing misconceptions and myths about the U.S. would go a long way to defeat Islamic extremists. The images and metaphors used since 2001 do not adequately explain what the current security challenge is all about. There is considerable distortion of the true nature of the enemy; and in part, *the enemy is us.*

We are faced with a war of ideas and religious convictions, not a traditional peer-to-peer war against a nation state. The diagnosis of the problem, i.e. *terrorism*, is totally wrong. We are fighting the symptoms instead of the disease. As a result, our adversaries are able to exploit our weaknesses, i.e. our internal cultural war between *Traditionalists, Progressives,* and *lunatics.* The enemies are Muslim fundamentalists hell-bent on creating Islamic caliphates and eliminating Christians, Jews, members of other religious faiths, and secularist governments like the People's Republic of China and Russia. We have to use brute force, but wisely. At the same time we need an introspective look to determine why we are causing the rejection of American culture in the first place.

We are between four and five centuries past the religious conflicts in Europe associated with the Reformation that started around 1525. Since the Second Vatican Council (1962-1965), and the advent of Ecumenism (*Unitatis Redintegration*), Christians have made efforts to achieve some degree of unity, reconciliation, and fraternal harmony. The dialogue has expanded to create a community of people of faith particularly Western monotheistic religions (Jews, Christians, and Muslims). Since the Soviet invasion of Afghanistan in 1979, a resurgence of violent Islamic fundamentalists unwilling to accept any innovations since the seventh century and unwilling to coexist peacefully with other religions. They are convinced of their moral probity above everyone else, and that their violent psychopathy is supported by their interpretation of the Qur'an, Hadith, Sunnah and traditions. They have declared a holy war against everyone that does not share their views.

Jihadists are totally at odds with anything that resembles Ecumenism, Western ideas of human rights, freedom of speech, religion, and thought. The *Islamic State of Iraq and the Levant* (ISIL, also known as IS and ISIS), led by Abu Bakr al-Baghgdadi, claims authority over all Muslims in the world. The organization is a derivative of al-Qai'da but notoriously more intransigent, and has expanded its tactics to include more violations of human rights, war crimes, and genocide. Crucifixions, beheadings, burning captured enemies alive, mass executions, slavery, abductions, rape, and other atrocities carry their operational signature. Yet, little is done about it.

President George W. Bush and President Barrack Obama repeatedly said that *"not all Muslims are extremists..."* However, there are 2 billion Muslims in the world, or about 28.26 percent (28.26%) of the world's population. If only one percent (1%) are violent extremists that means that there are at least two (2) million violent Muslim extremists gunning for people who do not agree with their views, and that is an unrealistic small estimate.[3] The point here is that we are facing a really serious problem, and it is foolish to think otherwise. In other words, we do not even know the size of the problem we are facing, and cannot construct a viable response. We are moving without direction...

Even small cells of Islamic extremists can act independently and stage successful terrorist attacks. Examples grow every day. The way to fight this global insurgency – like any other insurgency – is to *reduce the elements that create conditions that drive populations to join the enemy*, and successful surgical military operations to wipe out the leadership. This realization brings us back to the challenge of reducing elements of the *1960s counterculture* that have created the adverse reactions to our excesses. Not everyone is willing to tolerate our excesses, and Muslims extremists are taking advantage of American and European vulnerabilities.

The widespread level of amorality and decay associated with the *counterculture* is linked to many aspects of personal insecurity, widespread violence, uncertainty about national security, and the convoluted way of handling foreign policy. The "logical" cannot be muted by deviant and bizarre monsters that originated the *counterculture*. I do not want to *Paint the Lily* or Throw *Perfume on the Violent*, but this is serious stuff. Are we going back to the *law of the jungle* where only the ruthless and strongest survive? Are traditional family patterns overtaken by irrational and unstoppable "revolutionary" new forces leading to almost 50% of American babies born outside marriage? All the *modernity* associated with the *counterculture* is a blasted mess! Where are we going with this?

---

3 Some polls show that about 27% of Muslims, or well over 220 million of them, support the goals of Jihad. A Pew Study estimated that over 350 million Muslims support violent Jihad. See: http://moralcompassblog.com/2013/05/03/pew/

Practically the entire American society is in need of psychotherapy to clean up behavior that leads to social disorganization, drug use, and unemployment, crime, packed jails, considerable suffering, and exposure to domestic and foreign enemies. Behavior correction cannot be done overnight. Traditionalists cannot become voiceless when faced with the conundrum of illogical idiocy. The *counterculture* is going to have to learn to put up with people who refuse to tolerate irrational behavior. *Traditionalists* have to speak out and take back the reigns of the country, or we will end up like the Titanic. Law and order has to be enforced across the board and the criminal justice system has to be overhauled. It may seem like an attempt to *boil the ocean* to destroy an infection, but when there is a will there is a way. Sure, there are law enforcement personnel that go rogue, but they are society's first line of defense, and the overwhelming majority of them are good people that deserve the support of the population.

The nation belongs to all its citizens, and in a perfect world, there should be unity of purpose and solidarity, i.e. *the elements that bind people together as one*. The early Christian theologian Saint Augustin of Hippo (354-430) pointed out that a political society should be guided by *truth*. Another influential Christian theologian, Saint Thomas Aquinas (1225-1274), pointed out that *the truth* is available to all people through their human nature and powers of reason. In this case, *truth* means *fidelity* to the original standards and *ideals* of the founders of the country. Human dignity, i.e. *inherent, inalienable rights-* is not negotiable. Dignity is what people keep when they preserve their pride and self-respect. The entire American system of government, starting with the Declaration of Independence, is based on this premise of inalienable rights:

> *We hold these truths to be self-evident, that all men are created equal, that they are endowed by their Creator with certain inalienable Rights - that among these are Life, Liberty and the pursuit of Happiness. That to secure these rights, Governments are instituted among Men, deriving their just Powers from the consent of the governed, — That whenever any Form of Government becomes destructive of these ends, it is the Right of the People to alter or to abolish it, and to institute new Government, laying its foundation on such principles and organizing its powers in such form, as to them shall seem most likely to affect their Safety and Happiness.*

Nothing will change unless public opinion truly and actively demands change. The permissive environment, the climate of impunity, and the abuse of entrusted power has to be brought under control. How? *Effective suffrage!* Democracy offers citizens the opportunity to vote on rational candidates for public office and significant changes in public policy. The Constitution provides the citizenry control of the decision-making process, assuming they are willing to exercise the power of the vote to improve governance. The American electorate seems to be unconcerned about the future, based on low participation in the electoral process. The average voter turnout in the general elections of 2000, 2004, 2008 and 2012, was about 55.1% of the electorate.[479] In the general elections held in November 2014, the voter turnout was the lowest since WW II. *Only 36.4 percent of the registered voters cast a vote!* We get what we elect. When citizens do not participate in the electoral process they allow a subset of society to make important decisions. For example, in the 2014 elections, about 18.3 percent of the total electorate prevailed, because that was all that was needed to win when only about 36.4% voted, not 50 percent plus one vote to achieve a majority. *A minority of about 18.3 percent is imposing its views masquerading as a majority!*[4]

A subset of "Evolutionary Anthropology" studies how the human family mingled, and how our ancestors might have varied or evolved from one generation to the next. The oldest member of the evolutionary lineage of man may date to about 2.3 million years ago, according to human fossil records. And then, there is the complex and more controversial "evolution" of ethics, morality, human behavior, psychology, values, and even sexuality. Deciding on transcendental ethical and moral issues of our time through plebiscites, or any other electoral process is dangerous. Moral evils result when deviating from the natural order and ignoring values, traditions, ethics, and beliefs that bind a society together.

---

[4] This is simple math… if only 36.4 percent of the electorate voted, half of them plus one, or about 18.3 percent of the electorate won the elections, placing their people in elected positions and deciding on every referendum around the country, from tax increases to moral issues.

Separation of church and state, as stated in the Constitution, does not mean that society should deviate from a basic bond resulting from universal values that are central to Western Culture. The government should not force religious communities to accept rules that are contrary to their basic moral values and religious convictions. By the same token, religious communities cannot force the rest of society to adhere to their religious views either. They cannot impose on non-believers codes of conduct based on religious views. The Constitution provides citizens *the freedom to choose* whether they want to believe in a Supreme Being or be atheist. However, there are basic values that should serve as moral guides for everyone, regardless of religious convictions.[480] Americans and other Westerners are tinkering with basic universal values as if evolution could be accomplished in a few decades, when anthropology and history points to very long processes to accomplish meaningful change. Introducing cultural aberrations as if they were morally acceptable, is derived from the growing culture of evil since the 1960s.

The economic system is dysfunctional because the political landscape is filled with *one-trick ponies* from both parties. They are the architects of *freakonomics,* with their inability to focus outside very narrow emotional parameters and lack viable ideas to improve governance. They try to fix things and end up causing havoc by undermining the entire economic system with great intentions that lack common sense. They are responsible for implementing ideas without careful study so as to avoid *unintended consequences* that place in danger the entire financial system. At best, the good intentions, populism and social engineering have been a partial failure. The people who have been most affected have been the poor in general. Poor governance did not come about accidentally. All the money in the world and all the well-intentioned programs will not work if we continue to mismanage them.

By playing around with *political correctness,* class warfare, and redistribution of wealth, "*Progressives*" are only wasting time that should be spent in a bipartisan effort to deal with the real problems of the economy. It is self-evident that the Utopian ideas and the legislation enacted since the 1930s need to be revised and refocused upon based on real numbers, actuarial data, and other relevant factors. The challenge is to *create wealth* by allowing the free flow of ideas and the freedom for entrepreneurs to invest in new businesses. It will be impossible to balance budgets, pay down the debt, and address the problem of unfunded liabilities without stimulating the economy through entrepreneurial creativity. *This is not rocket science!*

The current level of instability that has reached Europe results from huge unfunded liabilities stemming from bankrupt Socialist policies and uncontrolled immigration. Austerity measures designed to rescue the economies of these countries are far from achieving the desired results, but are triggering protests by people who were made Utopian promises that cannot be kept. All of these challenges have not produced a rational policy to address a very complex set of problems. Americans should learn lessons from what has happened in Western Europe. Some of the same symptoms resulting from improperly funded social programs and Utopian promises to the masses have resulted in trillions of dollars in unfunded liabilities, in addition to a national debt of at least $18 trillion.[481]

The *Achilles heel of the American economy* is the increasing number of regulations without scrupulous analysis of their impact on the basic dynamics of the economic system. The increase in the number of poor Americans clearly shows that *change is needed.* Considering that the percentage of poor people in the country has not changed since 1965, it should be obvious that all the resources invested did not produce the desired results. The median income has been declining since 1973. Serious cost/benefit analysis has to be carried out instead of continuing on a path that has not reduced poverty. All the good intentions are not enough to overcome mismanagement. It is irrational to think that if we continue making the same mistakes the results will somehow be different.

Despite all the smoke and mirrors used to describe the economy, it is unrealistic to call it anything but *pathetic.* Median income is down. Rising income inequality is a fact. More companies are going under than the number of new companies created. Young people graduating from college have a very difficult time finding jobs. There are homeless people, including veterans all over, even in the DC Metro Area, which has some of the wealthiest counties in the country. It is unrealistic to portray the recovery and all-time high levels of the stock market and decline in unemployment to about half of where it was in 2009, as a signal that the economy has recovered. In 2015 people are really suffering and for many there is no hope of recovery any time soon.

The principal problem that has emerged since the 1950s is the deterioration in governance through general mismanagement. These are not necessarily constitutional issues. These are *management issues*. Yes, it is possible to run a country without deficit spending and it is possible to reintroduce appropriate management to re-energize the economy. It is not a question of introducing austerity, but of *improving management*. America has the good fortune of having vast natural resources and a creative and entrepreneurial population that has managed to overcome even the most difficult challenges. The country is very resilient. Short of suicidal policies, Americans can recover from neglect and mismanagement, but they need the government to get out of the way of progress.

There are many co-conspirators that participate in the immigration mess. The only way to have a chance of putting an end to the problem is to create a *National ID Card*. It is not a Draconian measure, it is a sensible measure. There is no other fair way to figure out who belongs, and who does not belong in the country, and who can and cannot vote. Once a national ID is in place, different options could be explored for rational immigration. A NIC would serve as a key tool to make it more difficult for terrorists from staging another significant attack on the homeland. Everyone regardless of sex, creed, race, or national origin and political affiliation would have to get one. We have to do away with the conditions that allow people to breach our borders and dig in. Most of them may have good intentions and are only trying to survive, but we have plenty of Americans in need that should not have to face unfair competition from overseas. This is not a demonization of immigrants, but simply stating the facts. Most of them may be honest hard-working people that could contribute to our country, but any self-respecting country has to protect its borders! We arrived at the present situation through dereliction of duty, mismanagement, and corruption.

Greek philosophers over 2,000 years ago warned about the importance of learning lessons from the past. It is illogical that, despite the substantial per capita investment in educating American children, there is *widespread ignorance*. Aristotle (384–322 BCE), pointed out that *"the fate of empires depends on the education of youth..."* Research studies since 1990 reveal that American students could not place the Civil War, Watergate, the end of the Cold War, and other important historical events within the correct half-century. Civics lessons went in one ear and out the other with little knowledge retained, leading to a state of *collective amnesia*. The rights, privileges, duties, obligations and responsibilities and the role of citizens in the government are ignored.

When a large percentage of the population doesn't even know if the earth revolves around the sun or the other way around... any debate *about global warming*, for example, is a waste of time. When the average American has a limited knowledge of geography and history, policymakers enjoy the power to confuse and bamboozle the public into wrong policies. Informed citizen participation is vital for a democracy to survive. We have to clean up our schools of leftist agitators disguised as educators, as well as incompetent teachers, regardless of their political views. Citizens are ultimately responsible for the direction of the country. *The United States of America is what its' citizens make of it.*

My objective in writing this book has been to increase knowledge, with the hope of changing attitudes and strengthening "core values," defined as a combination of ethics and morals. History is full of examples of how a society's system of values can be hijacked by manipulative people. A historian normally shies away from writing about events that are less than 35 years old in order to allow enough time for analysis to be conducted without the heat of the moment. In some cases, I have waited over 50 years to write about my experiences. As I pointed out in the *Preface*, the United States of America is in the middle of a *Category 5 Heifer Dust storm*! I have come to the conclusion that America has lost its' compass and needs to find *True North* as soon as possible. The future of the country depends on it. *C'est ça qui est en jeu! Eso es lo que está en juego... That is in our hands, the cards were are playing. The game is for keeps.*

BIBLIOGRAPHY

Baer, John. *The Pledge of Allegiance: A Revised History and Analysis,* 1892-2007. Annapolis, MD: 2007.

Balko, Radley. *Rise of the Warrior Cop: The Militarization of America's Police Forces.* Kindle Edition, 2014.

Basler, ed. Roy P. *Abraham Lincoln: His Speeches and Writings.* Cleveland, Ohio: Da Capo Press, 1990.

Black, Conrad. *Richard M. Nixon: A Life in Full.* New York: McClelland & Stewart, Ltd. 2007.

Bryce, James. *The American Commonwealth* 2 V. London: MacMillan and Company, 1888.

Buchanan, Patrick J. *Suicide of a Superpower: Will America Survive to 2015.* NY: St. Martin's Press, 2011.

Bouza, Anthony. *The Police Mystique: An Insider's Look at Cops, Crime, and the Criminal Justice System*, New York: Perseus Publishing, 1990.

Cassidy, Robert. *Counterinsurgency and the Global War on Terror: Military Culture and Irregular War.* Westport, CT: Praeger Security International, 2011.

Chamberlain, Samuel. *My Confession: Recollections of a Rogue (Atrocities During the Mexican/American War)*, 2009. (Note: The original is at the West Point Museum at the U.S. Military Academy.)

Chumley, Cheryl K. *Police State USA: How Orwell's Nightmare is Becoming our Reality.* Kindle Edition, 2014.

Cohen, Ariel. *The Threat of Islamism in Central Asia and the North Caucasus*, Testimony before the Europe, Eurasia, and Emerging Threats; and the Terrorism, Nonproliferation and Trade Subcommittees, House Committee on Foreign Affairs, US Congress, 27 February, 2013.

Coyote, Charles Edmund. Iraq War 2003: What really happened behind the Political Scenes. New York: Barnes & Noble, Online books, 2013.

de Tocqueville, Alexis. *Democracy in America*. (Translated by Harvey C. Mansfield and Delba Winthrop). Chicago: University of Chicago Press, 2002.

Douglas, Lloyd G. *The Pledge of Allegiance, Welcome Books: American Symbols*. NY: Rosen Book Works, 2003.

Dreyfuss, Robert. *Devil's Game: How the United States Helped Unleash Fundamentalist Islam*. (New York: Metropolitan Books, Henry Holt and Company, LLC, 2005).

Eisenhower, President Dwight. *Farewell Speech*, 17 January 1961.

Ellis, Joseph J. *His Excellency: George Washington*. New York: Vintage Books Edition, 2005.

Engle, Eloise and Arnold S. Lott. *America's Maritime Heritage*. Annapolis, Maryland: Naval Institute Press, 1975;

Fisher, Louis. *The Mexican War and Lincoln's "Spot Resolutions."* The Law Library of Congress. James Madison Memorial Building, 2009.

Franklin, Benjamin. *The Works of Benjamin Franklin*. New York: G. P. Putnam's Sons, The Knickerbocker Press, 1904.

Gates, Robert. *Duty: Memoirs of a Secretary at War*. New York, Knopf, 2014.

Goffman, Alice. *On the Run: Fugitive Life in an American City*, Chicago: University of Chicago Press, 2014.

Gombert, David C. RAND Corporation National Defense Research Institute, *Heads We Win: The Cognitive Side of Counterinsurgency (COIN)*, 2007.

Greeley, Father Andrew M. "*A Stupid, Unjust and Criminal War: Iraq 2001-2007*. New York: Orbis Books, Maryknoll, 2007.

Greenberg, Amy S. *A Wicked War: Polk, Clay, Lincoln, and the 1846 U.S. Invasion of Mexico*. NY: Alfred A. Knopf, 2012.

Hahn, Harlan and Judson L. Jeffries, *Urban America and its Police: From the Postcolonial Era through the Turbulent 1960's*. Boulder: University of Colorado Press, 2003.

Hartung, William D. *Prophets of War: Lockheed Martin and the Making of the Military-Industrial Complex.* New York: Nation Books, A Member of the Perseus Books Group, 2011;

Hume, David. *An Enquiry Concerning the Principles of Morals* (1751). The text of an 1898 edition of the book is available on the Internet.

Kennedy, John F. *Profiles in Courage*. New York: Harper & Brothers, 1955.

Koper, Christopher S. *Updated Assessment of the Federal Assault Weapons Ban: Impacts on Gun Markets and Gun Violence, 1994-2003*. Jerry Lee Center for Criminology, University of Pennsylvania; Study conducted with funds from the US Department of Justice, July 2004.

Linden, Col. John H. *Surrender of the Dachau Concentration Camp 29 April 1945*. NY: Sycamore Press Ltd, 1997.

Madison, James. *Speech*, House of Representatives, 10 January 1794.

Ketcham, Ralph. *James Madison: A Biography*. Charlottesville, VA: The University Press of Virginia, 1990.

Mahan, Alfred Thayer. *The Influence of Sea Power Upon History: 1660-1783.* Cambridge: John Wilson and Son, 2012.

Marx, Karl and Friedrich Engles. T*he Communist Manifesto*. The original was published in 1848. NY: CreateSpace Independent Publishing Platform, 2010.

More, Saint Thomas. *Utopia*, first published in 1516. NY: Simon & Brown, 2012.

Nixon, President Richard M. *Statements on Social Security*, 25 September 1969, Social Security. Onlinehttp://www.ssa.gov/history/nixstmts.html#969

Nixon, Richard Milhous. *The Memoirs of Richard Nixon*. New York: Simon & Schuster, 1978.

Rickover, Hayman G. *How the Battleship Maine Was Destroyed*, (Washington: Dept. of the Navy, Naval History Division, 1976).

Redman, Ben Ray (Editor). *The Portable Voltaire*. New York: Penguin Group, 1949.

Sanchez, Lt. Gen. Ricardo with Donald T. Phillips, op. cit. *Wiser in Battle: A Soldier's Story*. NY: Harper Collins, 2008.

Seigenthaler, John. *James K. Polk*, NY: Henry Holt and Company, Times Books, 2003.

Leonard, Thomas M. *James K. Polk: A clear and unquestionable destiny*. NY: SR Books, 2008.

Smith, Adam. *An Inquiry into the Nature and Causes of the Wealth of Nations*. (1776). (An Electronic Classics Series Publication.)

John Petrie. *Collection of Benjamin Franklin Quotes*. http://jpetrie.myweb.uga.edu/poor_richard.html

Voltaire, O*uvres complètes de Voltaire*, Voltaire, éd. Paris: Moland, 1875.

Rabasa, Angel and Lesley Anne Warner, Peter Chalk, Ivan Khilko, Paraag Shukla, RAND Corporation National Defense Research Institute,

Money in the Bank: Lessons Learned from Past Counterinsurgency (COIN) Operations, 2007.RANDCounterinsurgency Study Paper #4).

The 9/11 Commission Report: *Final Report of the National Commission on Terrorist Attacks Upon the United States*; http://www.9-11commission.gov/report/911Report_Exec.pdf

Vila, Bryan and Cynthia Morris. *The Role of Police in American Society: A Documentary History*. NY: Greenwood Press, 1999.

Von Clausewitz, Carl. *Vom Kriege (On War)*. NJ: Princeton University Press, 1976).

Voltaire, Arouet François-Marie. *Le fanatisme, ou Mahomet le Prophète*, 1741, (*Mahomet the Prophet or Fanaticism: A Tragedy in Five Acts*, translation by Robert L Myers.) New York: Frederick Ungar, 1964.

Voltaire, Arouet François-Marie. Complete Works of Voltaire 77A: Oeuvres de 1775 (Complete Works of Voltaire) 1914.

Washington, President George. *Message to the House of Representatives. 1793.*

Whitehead, John. *A Government of Wolves: The Emerging American Police State*, Kindle Edition, 2014.

Wilbur, C. Keith. *Pirates & Patriots of the Revolution: An Illustrated Encyclopedia of Colonial Seamanship*, Old Saybrook. Connecticut: The Globe Pequot Press, 1973.

Wilson, Admiral Thomas R. Director of DIA, Statement to the Senate Armed Services Committee on *Global Threats and Challenges Through 2015*. 8 March 2001.

Wilson, James Q. *Varieties of Police Behavior: The Management of Law and Order in Eight Communities*, New York: Perseus Books, 1978.

Woodward, Bob. *Plan of Attack*. NY: Simon & Schuster, 2004.

INDEX

This Index was generated by software. It is created based on the way names appear on the manuscript in alpha-numerical order. Thus, people are listed as they appear in the text by their first name instead of their last name.

END NOTES

1 Gerry T. Grimaldi (1928-2009), was a Special Agent (SA) of the Federal Bureau of Investigation (FBI), assigned to the Washington Field Office (WFO), Squad 7 COINTELPRO-New Left Coordinator, and later supervisor of Squad 5 (1972-1974), Legal Attaché in Bolivia, Legal Attaché in Spain, and Inspector until his retirement.

2 Lawton Mainor Chiles, Jr. (1930-1998) was a Korean War veteran, former member of the Florida House of Representatives, State Senator, U.S. Senator 1970-1989, and Governor of Florida 1990-1998. I worked directly for Senator Chiles in 1971-1972, teaching him Spanish and on other duties as assigned.

3 Ambassador Terrence A. Todman (1926-2014). Despite institutionalized racism, Ambassador Todman rose to the highest diplomatic rank of Career Ambassador, in the U.S. Foreign Service, equivalent to the military's four-star general. He served as U.S. Ambassador to Chad, Guinea, Costa Rica, Spain, Denmark, and Argentina. I learned a lot working for Ambassador Todman, both by watching him operate, as well as by listening to his counseling.

4 V. Manuel Rocha was sworn in as U.S. Ambassador to Bolivia in July 2000. Previously, he served as Charge D'affaires at the U.S. Embassy in Argentina, and as Deputy Chief of Mission. He served as Deputy Principal Officer at the U.S. Interests Section in Cuba, and at the U.S. Security Council. We served together in U.S. Embassies in the Dominican Republic and Mexico early in our careers. He is a graduate of Yale, Harvard, and Georgetown Universities.

5 Since 1959 there have been at least 17,000 documented executions by firing squad in Cuba, a country that had at the time roughly eight million people. That would be equivalent to executing 680,000 people in the U.S. with a population of 320 million people.

6 In Greek mythology, Sisyphus (Σίσυφος), was sent to Hell where he was forced to push a Boulder up a hill, but before he could reach the top of the hill, the boulder would always roll back down, and he had to start all over again.

7 Tami Luhby, The American Dream is out of reach, *CNN Money*, 4 June 2014.

8 Not far from Washington, D. C., at the Chesapeake Beach in Maryland, there were signs posted that read "*no dogs, no Puerto Ricans, no Cubans*," until the early 1960s.

9 It took another twenty years before U.S. Attorney and later Mayor of New York City (1994-2001) Rudy Giuliani in the late 1980s truly declared war on organized

crime successfully using *the Racketeer Influenced and Corrupt Organizations* Act (RICO) to put the principal Italian Mob bosses in jail.

10 Joseph Raymond "Joe" McCarthy (1908-1957), was elected to the U.S. Senate from Wisconsin on the Republican ticket in 1957.

11 In January 1954, Senator McCarthy had a 50% favorable opinion in the country. By November his favorable opinion had dropped to 35%, with 46% of the population holding an unfavorable opinion of his tactics.

12 Soviet Major General Oleg Kalugin, a KGB officer, who was briefly the KGB Chief of Station at the Soviet embassy in Washington in 1968, has published details of how his mission included subversion across the board to weaken the United States.

13 The National Science Foundation released the result of this poll on 14 February 2014, confirming the findings of another poll taken by Gallop in 1999. See Steve Crabtree, New Poll Gauges Americans' General Knowledge Levels: Four-fifths know earth revolves around the sun, *Gallup News Service*, 6 July 1999; John Johnson, 1 in 4 Americans don't know Earth Circles the Sun, *Newser*, 15 February 2014; Another blind telephone survey of over 1000 Americans carried out by the McCormick Tribune Freedom Museum found only one person in 1,000 could identify the rights granted by the First Amendment of the US Constitution – freedom of religion, free speech, free press, freedom of association, and the ability to petition the government. See: Harry Alsop, Americans surveyed: misunderstood, misrepresented or ignorant, *The Telegraph*, 16 February 2014.

14 Salvador Rodriguez, 1 in 10 Americans think HTML is an STD, study finds, *Los Angeles Times*, 4 March 2014.

15 Molly Greenberg, AU Students Can't Name a Single U.S. Senator, *InTheCapital*, 26 March 2014.

16 Justin Gray, Orlando TSA agent who stopped DC man didn't know where 'District of Columbia' was, *My FOXdc.com*, 15 July 2014. After the incident, the TSA supervisor reportedly showed all the agents at the Orlando airport a picture of a District of Columbia driver's license.

17 Montesquieu was the most quoted author by the Founding Fathers, particularly James Madison, and is considered one of the most influential philosophers of the American Revolution. Richard Price is known to have received visits from Benjamin Franklin, Thomas Jefferson, and Thomas Paine. John Locke is credited with significantly influencing the views of Alexander Hamilton, James Madison, Thomas Jefferson, and the spirit of the Declaration of Independence and the Constitution. Franklin was particularly influenced by the ideas of Adam Smith. Hume influenced Madison, but Jefferson banned his writings at the University of Virginia.

[18] David Hume, *An Enquiry Concerning the Principles of Morals* (1751). The text of an 1898 edition is available on the Internet.

[19] Somewhere between 65,000 and 70,000 people loyal to the British monarchy elected to leave the U.S. after independence. There were about 500,000 loyalists in the colonies, but only around 18 percent left after independence. Peaceful reconciliation prevailed.

[20] There was no way of assuring that the electorate would vote people into office that would exercise "*good governance*," only a hope that they would do so.

[21] There are plenty of historical examples of nefarious characters who stir up the masses with promises and giveaways. Examples: Lenin, Hitler, Mao, Castro, and Chavez.

[22] The secessionist Texas Nationalist Movement (TNM), has been around for some time but obtained news media headlines after the 2012 general elections.

[23] After the Civil War, some of the old concepts, like property requirements and poll taxes, were resurrected as tools to deny African-Americans the right to vote.

[24] Statistics on Civil War casualties are not well established, particularly Confederate losses, because many of the records were lost during the war.

[25] In the First Battle of Bull Run in July 1861, the Confederate Army was successful. At the Battle of Shiloh in Tennessee in April 1862, the Confederate Army initially defeated the Union Army under General Ulysses S. Grant, but the battle ended with heavy losses for both sides. During June and July 1862, the Union Army tried to capture Richmond, but was defeated and forced to retreat by General Robert E. Lee. At the Battle of Antietam it became evident to international observers that the Union would eventually prevail, despite another Confederate victory in December 1862 at the Battle of Fredericksburg.

[26] After a Union Navy ship intercepted a couple of Confederate emissaries on board a British ship in Cuban waters headed to Europe, the British sent troops to Canada and put their fleet on alert for a possible war with the U.S. The British came close to recognizing the Confederacy as an independent country.

[27] As early as 1808, the British Parliament had enacted the Slave Trade Act, which not only banned the slave trade, but also set up a British Navy squadron to intercept ships carrying slaves out of Africa.

[28] Under the Tax Act of 1862, taxes of 3% were levied on income earners above $600 annually (equivalent to about $12,742 in 2009 dollars), and 5% on income above $10,000 (equivalent to about $212,369 in 2009 dollars).

[29] Lord Bryce was appointed British Ambassador to the United States in 1907 and served until 1913. He was a historian, and Liberal British politician, who had traveled extensively in the United States before publishing the two-volume book

The American Commonwealth in 1888, considered to be one of the most insightful studies of American society.

[30] Egalitarian policies are based on the theory that all people should have the same economic, social, racial, political, and civil rights, as well as access to education and health care. Multiple political and economic philosophies, often contradictory to each other, share certain egalitarian principles, as for example, Socialists, National Socialists, Communists, Anarchists, Fascists, Libertarians, Progressives, and certain Christian philosophers and sects, such as the Amish and Mennonites.

[31] The American Revolution predates the writings of philosophers who proposed class warfare, revolution, and the establishment of Socialism and Communism. George Wilhelm Friedrich Hegel was born in 1770, and his first books did not get published until after 1812. Karl Marx was born in 1818. Friedrich Engels was born in 1820. His book *The Condition of the Working Class in England,* was published in 1845. *The Communist Manifesto*, co-authored with Karl Marx, was published in 1848. Welsh social reformer Robert Owen was born in 1771. He did not start advocating Socialism until about 1813. French Socialist philosopher Pierre-Joseph Proudhon was born in 1809. He did not call private property theft until his book *Qu'est-ce que la propriété? Recherche sur le principe du droit et du gouvernement (What is Property? Or, an Inquiry into the Principle of Right and Government)* was published in 1840. British Liberal / Socialist philosopher John Stuart Mill was born in 1806. His publications did not start until after 1822. His book *Essays on Some Unsettled Questions of Political Economy* was published in 1844. In other words, the advent of Socialist ideology did not truly start until the 19th century.

[32] The original legislation was amended, and the maximum EITC was expanded with the enactment of the Deficit Reduction Act of 1984, the Tax Reform Act of 1986, the Budget Reconciliation Act of 1990, the Omnibus Budget Reconciliation Act of 1993, and the American Recovery and Reinvestment Act of 2009.

[33] Qualifying low income tax filers are required to submit Form 8862 to the Internal Revenue Service (IRS) to obtain benefits under EITC or EIC. A substantial number of wage earners in the military, including soldiers earning combat pay (which is non-taxable), qualify to receive benefits under EITC. Low income wage earners whose families qualify to receive benefits under the program receive a federal income tax refund.

[34] Phil Izzo, "Number of the Week: Half of U.S. Lives in Household Getting Benefits," *The Wall Street Journal*, 26 May 2012.

[35] Employers contribute through payroll taxes funds to cover workers during periods of unemployment. General tax revenues were not initially to be used to pay for temporary unemployment compensation. Medicaid and Medicare are funded through payroll taxes on the totality of earned income, without any cap, as compared to Social Security taxes.

36 William Drayton quotes, see: http://thinkexist.com/quotes/william_drayton/

37 Madison to Edmund Pendleton, letter written in 1792. Madison covered the subject in a speech to the Virginia Ratifying Convention on 6 June 1788: *"[T]he powers of the federal government are enumerated; it can only operate in certain cases; it has legislative powers on defined and limited objects, beyond which it cannot extend its' jurisdiction."*

38 Speech, House of Representatives, 10 January 1794.

39 John Petrie's Collection of Benjamin Franklin Quotes, http://jpetrie.myweb.uga.edu/poor_richard.html

40 The website of the Office of the Chaplain of the U.S. House of Representatives on 21 December 2012, featured a diverse list of religious gatherings and study groups, including a Catholic Rosary Group, a Latter Day Saints Staffer Scripture Study group meeting, a Senate Bible Study group, a Muslim Congressional *Jummah* Prayer Service, a non-denominational, non-partisan, diverse Christian Bible study open to staffers, interns, as well as Members of Congress, and other fellowship activities.

41 Quakers have strong pacifist convictions, even when war was necessary to gain independence from British rule. The seven Quakers among the Founding Fathers ran into conflict with their fellow Quakers, and were forced to choose between supporting the revolution or leaving their congregations.

42 Most people, including ultra-patriotic right-wing activists are not aware that the author of the original Pledge of Alliance, Francis Bellamy was a Utopian Socialist and Baptist Minister from Boston who promoted the idea of a planned economy with the goal of reaching social and economic equality for all, resembling Marxist/Communist goals and objectives. As a member and Chairman of the National Education Association he proposed that school children recite the Pledge. For more details, see John Baer, *The Pledge of Allegiance: A Revised History and Analysis*, 1892-2007, (Annapolis, MD, 2007), and Lloyd G. Douglas, The Pledge of Allegiance, Welcome Books: American Symbols, 2003, ISBN 0-516-27876-2.

43 George Washington in his farewell speech delivered on 19 September 1796, said: *'It is impossible to govern the world without God and the Bible. Of all the dispositions and habits that lead to political prosperity, our religion and morality are the indispensable supporters. Let us with caution indulge the supposition that morality can be maintained without religion. Reason and experience both forbid us to expect that our national morality can prevail in exclusion of religious principle."*

44 The Alien Registration Act of 1940 is also known as the Smith Act, after Representative Howard Smith of Virginia, who was the prime sponsor of the legislation.

45 See District of Columbia v. Heller, 554 U.S. 570 (2008), and McDonald v. Chicago, 561 U.S. 3025 (2010), for more information.

46 Ted Nugent, "NUGENT: Ten years of gratitude Americans must stand with our military until the long war is won," *The Washington Times*, 9 September 2011.

47 Islamic insurgents seeking to create an Islamic "emirate" in the Caucasus have attacked Russian schools, theaters, public transportation infrastructure, and other civilian targets since 1991. For example, on 24 January 2011, they carried out a terrorist attack at the Domodedovo International Airport in Moscow that killed at least 37 people and injured some 180 more.

48 For example, on 1 August 2011, a series of terrorist attacks in Xinjiang caused at least 19 dead and dozens of wounded civilians. In 2009, riots in the region by Urumqi Islamic extremists caused over 200 deaths. These insurgents are linked to Islamic insurgents in Pakistan, Turkmenistan, and the al-Qai'da network of Islamic jihadists.

49 At the time of the 1992 attack against the Israeli Embassy in Buenos Aires occurred, I was assigned as Counselor of Embassy for Commercial Affairs at the American Embassy in Argentina. About three days after the bombing I visited the area and witnessed the damage to nearby buildings, including schools, and a colonial Catholic Church several centuries old. Investigators linked the attack to a group called Islamic Jihad Organization, with suspected ties to Hezbollah and the Iranian Islamic government.

50 An area between 14th Street N.W. to about 14th Street N.W. from east to west, and about 30 blocks north of K Street was affected. Over 16,000 soldiers and Marines in addition to the D.C. National Guard and local police were mobilized. It took four days to get control of the situation, after at least 12 people had been killed, over 1000 injured, and over 6,000 arrested. At least 1200 buildings had been burned, including numerous small stores.

51 The visits to Cuba to receive training in terrorism were conducted under the cover of participating in the so-called *Venceremos Brigades*, which allegedly went to Cuba to help with the sugar cane harvest. Julian Torres-Rizo (born in 1944) was a key covert operative of the Cuban intelligence services assigned to the Americas Department of the Cuban Communist Party, and the Cuban intelligence station at the UN in New York City in 1968; in 1968, He was the principal recruiter of members of the *Venceremos Brigades* to work for the DGI. During this assignment he met and married Gail Reed, one of the Americans from Chicago who participated in the brigades, and a graduate of Emory University.

52 Bernardine Dohrn (Ohrnstein), born in 1942, married Bill Ayers. After spending several years in the FBI Most Wanted list, she surfaced again and was not prosecuted due to prosecutorial misconduct. She eventually became a Professor

of Law at Northwestern University and at the University of Illinois in Chicago. Only in America!

53 I was never involved with any wiretaps or any other stupid decision made within the FBI to track terrorists.

54 City of Brazoria, TX, Public Information Archives, "A bomb threat was called into the Brazoria County Courthouse, located at 111 East Locust…"

55 Timesfreepress. Com; http://www.timesfreepress.com/news/2012/aug/22/man-charged-in-alleged-terrorism-plot/?news

56 Alley Rojas, "investigation at Dodge City library complete, man arrested," *KWCH*, 23 August 2012.

57 "Bomb Squad Evacuates SF Apartment Building, Closes Streets Over Suspicious Items," *CBS News*, 24 August 2012.

58 Jerry Demarco, "Police: Nothing to Paramus Park bomb threat," Clieffview Pilot. com, 25 August 2012.

59 "Man allegedly threatened bank with Trident missile," *New Iberia Forum,* 27 August 2012.

60 James Bennet, "ICE agents find 6 grenades in Rio Rico home," Tucson News KOLD/KMSB, 25 August 2012;

61 "Hollywood gunfire leads to arrests, evacuations," *Contra Costa Times*, 27 August 2012.

62 "Bomb squad sent to PetSmart in Torrance to check suspicious package," Dailybreeze.com, 28 August 2012.

63 "St. Charles police: fired worker threatened to blow up office building," *St. Louis Post-Dispatch*, 29 August 2012.

64 Chelsea Karnash, "Absecon Woman Arrested For Bomb Threats Against Atlantic Cape Community College," *CBS Philadelphia*, 6 September 2012.

65 Travis Hudson, "Hoax report of explosive liquid aboard sends Dallas-bound plane back to Philly," *Dallas News,* 6 September 2012.

66 Dave Phillips, "Car bombing reported in Holly," *The Macomb Daily*, 6 September 2012.

67 D. S. Woodfill, "Authorities release photos of suspected Glendale serial bomber," *AZcentral.com/ Arizona Republic*, 6 September 2012.

68 In the period between 1 July 2013 and 30 June 2014, there were 841 recorded IED incidents in the U.S., of which 54 resulted in explosions, causing 16 casualties.

69 Republicans and Tea Party activists want limited government, defend free market forces, and want people to be personally responsible for their actions. They accept

separation of church and state, but do not believe that all references to God or to religion should be taken out of public buildings or that government should act without respecting Western cultural traditions. Conservatives come in all shades, colors, and ethnic groups.

70 On 17 October 2011 multiple press reports indicated that both, the American Nazi Party and the Communist Party USA issued statements supporting the Occupy Wall Street demonstrators: See Jim Hoft, "Nazi Party and Communist Party Support Occupy Wall Street," Human Events, 15 October 2011. Fox News, "American Nazi Party Declares Its' Full Support for Occupy Wall Street Protests," 15 October 2011.

71 I have serious doubts that people who use the term have any ideas of what *Caucasoid*, *Europid*, or *Europoid* mean.

72 Federal Bureau of Investigation, Famous Cases & Criminals, "Bonnie and Clyde;" According to the FBI description of the case, Clyde C Barrow and Bonnie Parker were shot dead by officers near Sailes, Louisiana, on 23 May 1934, after an spectacular manhunt.

73 The Youth International Party (Yippies), led by Abbot Howard "Abbie" Hoffman (1936-1989), participated in numerous violent confrontations with police all over the country, including the riot at the 1968 Democratic National Convention in Chicago.

74 The UAW/MF was an Anarchist street gang based in the Lower East Side of New York City, closely linked with the Yippies, and later with the SDS terrorists that formed the Weather Underground. Among their leaders were Abbie Hoffman, Ben Morea, Tom Neumann, and Alan Hoffman. Among their claims to fame was their participation in trashing Columbia University in 1968. Anarchism is a political doctrine that advocates the abolition of all governments as immoral, generally oppose all authority, and advocate for the creation of stateless societies. Among the principal theoreticians is Russian-born revolutionary theoretician and criminal Mikhail Alexandrovich Bakunin (1814-1876), who opposed Marxist and their goal of creating proletarian dictatorship. Insurrectionary Anarchists in the 1960s included Karl Hess, Murray Rothbard, and Abbie Hoffman. Trotskyism was a brand of orthodox Marxism advocated by Lev Davidovich Bronstein, aka, *Leon Trotsky*, a Ukrainian Jew and Russian Communist leader, second to Lenin, who competed for power with Joseph Stalin, in the Soviet Union, and was forced into exile in 1929. Among the different organizations that claimed to follow Trotsky in the U.S. were the Socialist Workers Party (SWP), International Socialists (IS), and the Revolutionary Socialist League (RSL). Around 1968 Maoism became one of the radical ideologies that sprung up in the U.S. clustered around the Progressive Labor Party (PLP), one of the sub-groups of the Students for a Democratic Society (SDS) and the anti-Vietnam War movement. It was a splinter group of the

Communist Party USA. Most of the PLP members were students at Harvard and Yale, not part of the so-called "working class," but claimed inspiration from the Great Proletarian Cultural Revolution in the PRC. They were very hostile to the different Anarchists groups, and constituted the principal internal opposition to the so-called Central Collective clustered around the Chicago headquarters of the SDS, which became the seed for the Weather Underground. As the PLP collapsed around 1970, some members drifted into the Revolutionary Union (RU) around San Francisco, and the October League (OL).

75 Bob Dylan, Columbia Records, single *Subterranean Homesick Blues*, 1965.

76 A foreign government must request "*agreement*," through a diplomatic note from the embassy of the country in Washington to the Department of State, or from the Ministry of Foreign Affairs of the country to the American embassy, and await approval for an individual to be accepted as Ambassador to the United States. The *agreement* can be taken back if the ambassador is declared a *persona non grata*, and requested to leave.

77 This incident has similarities with the terrorist attacks carried out on 9/11/2001, because in both cases there was intelligence that should have alerted authorities. However, the intelligence community did not connect the dots.

78 Three people, including an eight-year-old boy were killed, and over 150 people were wounded, at least seventeen of them critically, with several of them losing limbs

79 This incident had some similarities with another incident in Spain that was prevented due to the arrest in July 2012 of two terrorists from the N. Caucasus and a Turkish associate. Two former Russian Special Forces soldiers and veteran Chechen Islamic separatists, who had spent time in Pakistan, Eldar Magomedov and Muhammad Adamou, together with Turkish Islamic activist Cengiz Yalcin, had been planning to attack a crowd watching the London Olympics at a shopping mall in the British enclave in Gibraltar. Spanish news media published considerable details about the plot. However, in April 2013, the Spanish court dropped charges due to insufficient evidence, or perhaps because intelligence organizations were not willing to disclose to the court information about tactics, techniques and procedures (TTPs) used to prevent the terrorist attack. See: Nathan Toohey, "Russians reportedly arrested in Spain over terror plans," *The Moscow News*, 2 August 2012.

80 Stephen J. Blank, *Russia's Homegrown Insurgency: Jihad in the North Caucasus*, U.S. Army War College, Strategic Studies Institute, October 2012; Ariel Cohen, *The Threat of Islamism in Central Asia and the North Caucasus*, Testimony before the Europe, Eurasia, and Emerging Threats; and the Terrorism, Nonproliferation and Trade Subcommittees, House Committee on Foreign Affairs, U.S. Congress, 27 February, 2013.

81 Ellen Nakashima and Julie Tate, "Prosecutors say Manning collaborated with WikiLeaks' Assange in stealing secret documents," *The Washington Post*, 22 December 2011.

82 David Leigh, "how 250,000 U.S. Embassy cables were leaked – from a fake Lady Gaga CD to a thumb drive that is a pocket-sized bombshell 0 the biggest intelligence leak in history," *Guardian.co.uk*, 28 November 2010.

83 Charley Keyes, "Investigator: Manning's Computer Had Downloaded Secret Documents," *CNN* and *The Los Angeles Independent*, 18 December 2011.

84 Daniel Cooney, "Computer drives stolen at U.S. base up for sale," Associated Press, 15 April 2006; "The *Los Angeles Times* reported that some thumb drives had classified military secrets, including maps, charts and intelligence reports that appeared to detail how Taliban and al-Qaeda leaders have been using southwestern Pakistan as a planning and training base for attacks in Afghanistan."

85 FBI, "Chinese National Charged with Economic Espionage Involving Theft of Trade Secrets from Leading Agricultural Company Based in Indianapolis," *U.S. Department of Justice, Public Affairs*, 31 August 2011.

86 King David was betrayed by his son Absolum. See 2 Samuel, 15th chapter.

87 See Psalm 41:9; Matthew 10:4; Zechariah 11:12; Mark 14:50; and Matthew 26:15.

88 See Rose Mary Sheldon, *Spies of the Bible: Espionage in Israel from the Exodus to the Bar Kohhba Revolt*. Greenhill Books, 2007. The Israelites frequently used spies against their adversaries, starting with Moses.

89 Contrary to the way the uninformed press describes CIA employees, they are not agents. The FBI has *special agents*, but the CIA does not use the term "agent" for its employees. For the CIA an *agent* is a spy that has been recruited to work for the U.S. betraying his or her own country.

90 FBI. *A Review of FBI Security Programs*, March 2002. (This document is also known as the *Webster Report.)*

91 The indictment against Velázquez, who is also known as "Marta Rita Kviele" and as "Bárbara," was returned by a grand jury in the District of Columbia on 5 February 2004. Velazquez has continuously remained outside the U.S. since 2002. Velázquez was born in Puerto Rico in 1957. She graduated from Princeton University in 1979 with a BA in political science and Latin American studies, and later obtained a law degree from Georgetown University Law Center in 1982 and a Master's Degree from Johns Hopkins University School of Advanced International Studies (SAIS) in 1984. She joined the State Department's U.S. Agency for International Development (USAID) as a legal officer with responsibilities encompassing Central America.

[92] In December 2012, President Obama announced that he was ending the embargo that had been placed on Cuba by President Kennedy, and that an agreement had been reached for an exchange of prisoners. One mystery spy that was traded with Cuba turned out to be Rolando Sarraff, who a lieutenant in the Cuban DGI, who was covertly working for the CIA in the late 1990s, and turned over Cuban codes, which allowed the U.S. Government to identify Ana Belén Montes as a Cuban spy.

[93] Ana Belén Montes was the daughter of a U.S. Army physician posted in West Germany where she was born in 1957. Her parents were born in Puerto Rico. Montes had earned a BA in Foreign Affairs from the University of Virginia, and a MA from the Johns Hopkins School of Advanced International Studies. She initially worked for the U.S. Department of Justice before taking a job with the DIA in 1985. A brother and a sister were employed by the FBI, and one of them had actively participated in the investigation leading to the arrest of an important Cuban spy ring in Florida known as the *Wasp Network.*

[94] The true story of what happened as a result of Pollard spying may never come out. Israeli intelligence had been penetrated by the Soviets. As many as forty agents working for American intelligence were *blown out of the water*, arrested and executed. According to one version, Israel willingly provided information stolen by Pollard to the Soviets in exchange for exit permits for Russian Jews. See *John Loftus: The Truth about Jonathan Pollard*, IMRA Newsletter, 24 May 2003,; "Shabtai Kalmanovich: Death of a Double Agent – Former Israeli double agent shot dead near Putin's office," *Jewish Russian Telegraph*, 9 November 2009; Sam Vkruin, "Analysis: Russian Roulette – The Military," *UPI*, 23 January 2002.

[95] The 9/11 Commission Report: *Final Report of the National Commission on Terrorist Attacks Upon the United States*; http://www.9-11commission.gov/report/911Report_Exec.pdf

[96] Public Law No. 95-511, 92 Stat. 1783, was enacted on 25 October 1978. Cosponsors of the bill included Senators Birch Bayh, Frank Church, James Eastland, Jake Garn, Walter Huddleston, Daniel Inouye, Charles Mathias, John McClellan, Gaylord Nelson, and Strom Thurmond.

[97] The Marxist People's Democratic Party of Afghanistan (PDPA) killed President Mohammed Daoud Khan and his family and took power in April 1978. PDPA leader Nur Muhammad Taraki became the new President of the Democratic Republic of Afghanistan (DRA). In September 1979, Taraki was murdered by order of Hafizullah Amin, who had served as his Prime Minister. Amin had attended Graduate School at Columbia University in New York. Upon his return to Afghanistan, he became a prominent Marxist affiliated with the PDPA, but due to his U.S. link perhaps, Amin was not trusted by the Russians. Apparently the Soviets were particularly concerned because Amin was holding secret meetings with the American *chargé d'affaires* (acting ambassador) J. Bruce Amstutz after

the assassination of the ambassador earlier in the year. Babrak Karmal, who had served as Deputy Prime Minister under Taraki, and had been forced into exile, was returned to Afghanistan by the Russians and made President in December 1979, after KGB operatives assassinated Amin. All of these Communist rulers brutally repressed the population, zeroing in on Islamic leaders and orthodox followers of Islam. Entire villages were destroyed and all the residents killed. Thousands of Afghanis fled to Pakistan and Iran.

98 A PDD is a type of executive order issued by the President of the United States (POTUS) with the advice and consent of the National Security Council (NSC), with the full force and effect of a law. Most PDDs are classified.

99 For more details see: Robert Dreyfuss, *Devil's Game: How the United States Helped Unleash Fundamentalist Islam*, (New York: Metropolitan Books, 2005).

100 The northern part of the Afghanistan was under the control of fighters under Ahmed Shah Massoud, who had a long-term relationship with the CIA, and another area in the south was under the control of Gulbuddin Hekmyar with his own *Hezbi Islami* fighters. Massoud was given assistance by Russia and Iran, to continue fighting the Taliban, but was assassinated on 9 September 2001.

101 Craig Whitlock, "Analysis: To Gates, Taliban a 'cancer' but part of Afghan political fabric," *The Washington Post*, (23 January 2010).

102 The Commission was funded by the Intelligence Authorization Act for Fiscal Year 1995 (P.L. 103-359) and the report was issued on 1 March 1996. The Commission's report was given the title: *An Appraisal of U.S. Intelligence.*

103 Ibid.

104 The PRC has announced that is spending over $132 billion annually in defense, which is the second highest in the world after the estimated $600 billion spent annually by the U.S.

105 A few years before, around 1998, when Adm. Wilson was the J2 at Joint Staff, he was chastised by a political appointee for mentioning a growing potential conflict in Afghanistan during the morning briefings to OSD. He was told that the U.S. did not have any national interests in Afghanistan and should not be reporting on things OSD did not care about.

106 *"Islamic State of Iraq and the Levant (ISIL)," "Islamic State," Al-Qai'da in Lands of the Islamic Maghreb (AQIM), Islamic Revolutionary Guards Corps-Quds Force (IRGC-QF)," "Islamic Republic of Iran,"* and "*Islamic Institutions.*"

107 Do not confuse this statement about Communist intentions to dominate the world and establish a one-world government with conspiracy theory that claims that the United Nations, the Vatican, Masons, the Tri-Lateral Commission, elite

businessmen and politicians are trying to set up some kind of supra national government or "New World Order."

108 In 1979, the Soviets could not even handle successfully their invasion of Afghanistan, where they could just roll their tanks across the common border. They did not have forces to successfully deploy to Egypt against the British and the French in 1956, and they would not have engaged in a nuclear engagement with the West for the sake of the Egyptians.

109 Secretary Dulles described brinkmanship as: *"The ability to get to the verge without getting into the war is the necessary art."*

110 Migration of Jews to Israel started as far back as the 1880s with the emergence of the Zionist Movement. Several distinct waves of immigrants totaling about 140,000 arrived mostly from Romania, Poland, and Russia (the Soviet Union), before 1932. As persecution of Jews intensified under the Nazis, another 200,000 immigrants arrived between 1932 and 1939. From Argentina alone, over 250,000 Jews went to live in Israel. During WWII, another 70,000 arrived from Central and Eastern Europe, as well as from Nazi occupied territories. After WWI, the Ottoman Empire lost control of Palestine, which came under a British mandate. Despite British efforts to stop Jewish immigration, the flow of immigrants continued. In 1947, the UN proposed the creation of two states in Palestine, leading to the first Arab-Israeli war and the creation of Israel, resulting in Palestinian refugee settlements in part of the West Bank of the Jordan River, and in the Gaza Strip, both under Jordanian rule. After 1948, over 600,000 additional immigrants arrived. Another wave of Ukrainian and Russian Jews totaling over 1.3 million arrived after 1990.

111 They claim that Israel has bulldozed or blown up the homes of Palestinians and destroyed ancient orchards as an integral part of an aggressive expansionist policy, in addition to expanding Israeli borders through military conquests since 1947. They neglect to consider land purchases by Jews, or territory awarded to Israel by the UN in 1947, and other factors that provide a more complete picture of how the current state of affairs came about.

112 Convicted spy Jonathan Pollard was released from jail in November 2015, after serving a 30-year sentence. He has been ordered to wear an electronic ankle bracelet with a GPS system. He was granted parole from the initial life sentence imposed in 1987.

113 A Caliphate is a Muslim spiritual community – or theocratic state run under sharia law - led by a political and supreme Muslim religious leader.

114 *Show me just what Muhammad brought that was new, and there you will find things only evil and inhuman, such as his command to spread by the sword the faith he preached...* Byzantine Emperor Manuel II Paleologus (1391 – 1425)

115 فَتَعَـٰلَى ٱللَّهُ ٱلْمَلِكُ ٱلْحَقُّ وَلَا تَعْجَلْ بِٱلْقُرْءَانِ مِن قَبْلِ أَن يُقْضَىٰٓ إِلَيْكَ وَحْيُهُۥ وَقُل رَّبِّ زِدْنِى عِلْمًا (١١٤)

116 *Rationalism*: The term is used: (1) in an exact sense, to designate a particular moment in the development of Protestant thought in Germany; (2) in a broader, and more usual, sense to cover the view (in relation to which many schools may be classed as rationalistic) that the human reason, or understanding, is the sole source and final test of all truth. It has further: (3) occasionally been applied to the method of treating revealed truth theologically, by casting it into a reasoned form, and employing philosophical Categories in its' elaboration. Source: *Catholic Encyclopedia. Secularism*: The word secular means *"of this world"* in Latin and is the opposite of religious. As a doctrine, *secularism* is usually used in reference any philosophy which forms its' ethics without reference to religious dogmas and which promotes the development of human art and science.

117 The Ottoman Empire came about after the conquest of Constantinople in 1453 by Mehmed II, and reached its peak around 1590, when the borders of the Empire reached Africa, Europe, and Asia. After WWI, in 1922, the Turkish monarchy was abolished, and the Ottoman Empire came to an end.

118 The tomb and shrine of Hussain ibn Ali was destroyed in 850-851 by Umayyad and Abbasid caliphs, but they were rebuilt and expanded in 979-80 in Karbala and Najaf, and became pilgrimage sites for Shi'a Muslims. After the Wahhabis damaged the shrine in 1801 it was rebuilt in 1817. Additional repairs were made in 1866, 1939, and 1941.

119 Saeed Shah, "Pakistani Taliban call girl's shooting 'obligatory,' saying she spread secular ideas," McClatchy Newspapers/ Kansas City Star, 10 October 2012; Saud Mehsud, "Pakistani girl shot by Taliban defied threats for years," Reuters, 10 October 2012; Kamila Shamsie, "What has Malala Youdafzai done to the Taliban?" The Guardian, 10 October 2012.

120 Mathew Lee, "Clinton condemns attack on Pakistan teen activist," *Associated Press*, 10 October 2012.

121 Jon Boone, "Taliban poison attack or mass hysteria? Chaos hits another Kabul girls' school," *The Guardian*, 25 August 2010.

122 Rahim Faiez and Heidi Vogt, "Taliban Poisoned School Girls, Say Afghanistan Officials," *Huff Post World*, 16 June 2012.

123 Seed Kamali Dehghan, "Iran executes three men on homosexuality charges," *The Guardian* (UK), 7 September 2011.

124 According to Shia Muslims, women who die as virgins are allowed into Heaven, and to prevent that, they are raped before they are executed. "Women and the death penalty in modern Iran," http://www.capitalpunishmentuk.org/iranfem.html

[125] Austin Cline, "Iran: Gay Teens Executed by Hanging," *About.com Guide*, 25 July 2005.

[126] "Belgian honor killing: Pakistani family sentenced to prison," *The International Herald Tribune*, 13 December 2011.

[127] Vasudevan Shridharan, Iran: Top Court Orders Man's Eyes to be Gouged Out and Ears Chopped for Pouting Acid on Girl, *International Business Times*, 3 March 2014

[128] Michelle Faul, 4 accused gays whipped in north Nigerian court, *Associated Press*, 6 March 2014.

[129] Salma Abdelaziz, Death and desecration in Syria: Jihadist group 'crucifies' bodies to send message, CNN, 2 May 2014.

[130] Mitt Romney, Third Presidential Debate, Boca Raton, Florida, 22 October 2012.

[131] Lyrics by Jude Anthony Cole and Jason Michael Wade.

[132] Robert Wilson Lynd was an Irish essayist and nationalist.

[133] Oxford English Dictionary, and possibly first printed in the Army Weekly on 7 January 1944. In the 1998 film *Saving Private Ryan*, the term is used to describe the mission given to Captain Miller's squad to find Private Ryan and deliver him to a higher headquarters.

[134] Josh Rogin, After $200 Million, Afghan Soldiers Still Can't Read, *The Daily Beast*, 28 January 2014.

[135] I worked at the U.S. European Command (EUCOM) from 2004 to 2007, when General Jones was the Commander of EUCOM, as well as NATO Supreme Allied Commander.

[136] Robert Gates, The Quiet Fury of Robert Gates: Bush and Obama's secretary of defense had to wage war in Iraq, Afghanistan – and today's Washington, *The Wall Street Journal*, 7 January 2014. (Robert Gates served as Secretary of Defense from 2006 to 2011).

[137] In the case of Vietnam it took the U.S. five years to develop the CORDS program. See: Dale Andrade, "Three Lessons From Vietnam," *The Washington Post*, 29 December 2005.

[138] John Heilprin, Associated Press, "1999 war games foresaw problems in Iraq," 6 November 2006;

[139] Robb S. Todd, "War Games in '99 Predicted Iraq Problems," CBS News (4 November 2006). George Washington University obtained documents related to the military exercise under a FOIA request. The CIA held the exercise in September 2002, and a result, it became clear in the mind of participants that the regime in Iraq would not go away easily, because even if Saddam Hussein went

away, there were many people who supported the views of the Baath Party. It was not clear what would replace the Baath Party.

140 U.S. Senate, Select Committee on Intelligence, "Report on Prewar Intelligence Assessments about Postwar Iraq," 25 May 2007.

141 Ibid.

142 I travelled to Tampa, and worked on a project in preparation for the invasion of Iraq during January 2003. In 2008, I deployed to Iraq with the Army Human Terrain program. In hind sight, and after examining the facts, I have come to the conclusion that the decision to invade was faulty, and bordering on criminal intent. The decision to withdraw troops from Iraq by President Obama was just as dumb.

143 Michael R. Gordon and Bernard E. Trainor, "Dash to Baghdad Left Top U.S. Generals Divided," *The New York Times*, 13 March 2006.

144 Ibid.

145 Ibid. Gen. Keane later told National Public Radio that V Corps was not prepared or staffed to run civil affairs or peacekeeping operations. He also warned that an insurgency was in its infancy.

146 So many unsubstantiated estimates were made by senior military and civilian officials that it is impossible to get a clear handle on how many foreign fighters actually arrived.

147 Collaborator: defined as *cooperating treasonably, as with an enemy occupation in one's country*. The connotation (Arabic for connotation: مو ﻫﻔـم) of the word created problems for Iraqis who wanted to help with the transition.

148 George Tenet with Bill Harlow, At the Center of the Storm: op. cit, p. 418.

149 NSC Advisor Condoleezza Rice was not happy with the reporting. George Tenet, *At the Center of the Storm*, op. cit, p. 422-423.

150 James A. Baker, III, Lee H. Hamilton, Co-Chairs, The Iraq Study Group Report (New York: Vintage Books, 2006).

151 The ISG was created by a bipartisan group of Members of Congress to assess the situation, and selected as co-chairs the former chairman of the House International Relations Committee Lee Hamilton (D-NY) former Secretary of State James A. Baker, III (R), who in turn selected the rest of the team. They did not have a background on analyzing insurgencies.

152 Ibid.

153 The Iraq Study Group made multiple suggestions but did not say how to accomplish them.

[154] For example, Gen. Casey, Commander of MNF-I in July 2005, during a visit to Baghdad by Secretary Rumsfeld said that he believed that a "*fairly substantial*" pull-out of American troops could take place by mid-2006. Again in July 2006 during a press conference Gen. Casey again said that: "*We've certainly have delayed our, our thoughts of drawing down this year. It's been delayed. Now, it is not, it's definite that we won't draw down this year but it's probably less likely.*" Op. cit.

[155] Lt. Gen. Ricardo Sanchez with Donald T. Phillips, op. cit. *Wiser in Battle: A Soldier's* Story. NY: Harper Collins, 2008, p. 198.

[156] Gen. James Mattis coined the term "*command and feedback.*" "*War is time sensitive, the general says. Noncommissioned officers and officers must be able to use initiative and take advantages of opportunity. Subordinates must exercise initiative to carry out commanders' intent, he said. The general added that commanders' intent also accepts the reality that the enemy is thinking and active rather than passive and reactive. Another important aspect of command and feedback is that it is fast and keeps the enemy off balance by being unpredictable. He notes that in war, the enemy will always create fog and friction.*" Henry Kenyon, 19 August 2009, "Land War Net Show Daily," http://www.afcea.org/signal/signalscape/index.php/2009/08/show-daily-wednesday/

[157] The concept is borrowed from engineering, which uses the term "dynamic positioning" (DP), through the use of back-up redundant systems to sense failure and use standby systems to take over and perform required operations and avoid catastrophes such as explosions, fire or flooding.

[158] Comment attributed to Yogi Berra. An extension of the remark is credited to Red Raiders of Texas Tech sports information director Ralph Carpenter, who said "*the opera ain't over until the fat lady sings.*" Thus the new "*It ain't over 'til it's over and the fat lady sings*" was born.

[159] Angel Rabasa, Lesley Anne Warner, Peter Chalk, Ivan Khilko, Paraag Shukla, RAND Corporation National Defense Research Institute, *Money in the Bank: Lessons Learned from Past Counterinsurgency (COIN) Operations*, 2007. RAND Counterinsurgency Study Paper #4).

[160] David C. Gombert, RAND Corporation National Defense Research Institute, *Heads We Win: The Cognitive Side of Counterinsurgency (COIN)*, 2007.

[161] Ibid.

[162] *Quds Force*, which is a special unit of the *Revolutionary Guards*.

[163] T.S. Eliot (1888-1965) was a playwright, essayist, and poet, who was awarded the Nobel Prize for Literature winner in 1948. He was born in the U.S., but later became a naturalized British citizen.

[164] By *Cassandras* I mean – like the Cassandra in Greek Classical Mythology, whose prophecies were never believed – that intelligence analysts are regarded as prophets of doom, whose warnings of impending disaster are ignored by policymakers.

[165] T. S. Eliot, essay Christianity and Communism, *The Listener*, 1932.

[166] President Clinton instructed the armed forces to start a bombing campaign in Kosovo in 1999, without evidence of a need to repel an attack against the U.S. The Constitution authorizes the President as Commander-in-Chief under Article II, Section 2, to repel an attack using the military without first requesting authority from Congress.

[167] There is no clear definition of "*Nation Building*," and the concept has morphed over time. A key reason for failure of the concept is that the same elements that bind together one nation are not necessarily *exportable* to another country with different historical experience, cultural and religious traditions.

[168] The Whig Party, forerunner of the Republican Party, created by Henry Clay around 1832 in opposition to President Andrew Jackson's policies, generally opposed Manifest Destiny. President Jackson, who was instrumental in the creation of the Democratic Party from what had formerly been named Republican-Democratic Party, was an early supporter of Manifest Destiny. Jackson gained a reputation as national hero for defeating the British in New Orleans during the War of 1812, but in violation of orders, while the country was not at war, invaded Spanish Florida and created an international incident, which resulted in calls for his censure, but produced the *Adams-Onis Treaty* by which Spain sold Florida to the U.S., and established an official boundary between New Spain (now Mexico) in 1819.

[169] Despite the glorification of James "Jim" Bowie, he was a smuggler, slave trader, and violent frontiersman who had killed lawmen in Louisiana, and not fit to enter the American pantheon of folk heroes. He had moved to Texas and become a Mexican citizen around 1830. David Crockett was born in East Tennessee in 1786, and had earned a reputation as a frontiersman, scout, hunter, and Indian fighter before entering politics in Tennessee. He was elected to the U.S. House of Representatives in 1827, 1829, and 1833. In 1835 Crocket moved to Texas and joined the revolutionaries. He had achieved notoriety with an assortment of real and fictitious eccentricities published in the 1830s.

[170] Under the *Missouri Compromise* of 1820 between pro-slavery and anti-slavery Members of Congress, a balance would be maintained as new states were admitted into the Union. The annexation of Texas reopened the battle which eventually led to the Civil War in 1861.

[171] In 1846, during a visit to his plantation, Polk was confronted with the challenge of runaway slaves. He had two recently recaptured slaved whipped as punishment. He claimed that opposition to slavery was wicked, and possibly leading to

dissolving the Union. See: John Seigenthaler, *James K. Polk*, NY: Henry Holt and Company, Times Books, 2003; Thomas M. Leonard, James K. Polk: A clear and unquestionable destiny, NY: SR Books, 2008.

172 Louis Fisher, The Mexican War and Lincoln's "Spot Resolutions", The Law Library of Congress, James Madison Memorial Building, 2009.

173 See resolution passed on 22 December 1847 in the House of Representatives.

174 Louis Fisher, The Mexican War, op. cit. p.5. After a new Congress took over with a Whig Party majority, an effort was made to stop the war, and on 7 December 1847 an amendment was passed by a vote of 85 to 81, censuring President Polk and calling the war unnecessary and unconstitutional

175 Gabbert, Ann R. "'They Die Like Dogs': Disease Mortality Among U.S. Forces during the U.S.-Mexican War." *Military History of the West*, 31/1 (Spring 2001); McCaffrey, James M. "Santa Anna's Greatest Weapon: The Effect of Disease on the American Soldier During the Mexican War" *Military History of the West* 24/1 (Fall 1994).

176 Although this percentage of desertion was high, it was less than the approximately 12 percent desertion rate during the War of 1812, and the approximately 14 percent during peace time in the first half of the 19th century. What was different was that several hundred defected to the enemy.

177 The costs of the war with Mexico continue to the present. There are over 750 American soldiers buried near Mexico City, all casualties of the war. When this author was stationed at the American Embassy in Mexico from 1984 to 1989, there was a representative of the *Battle Monuments Commission* stationed at the embassy. That person was in charge of policing the military cemetery and placing an American flags by each grave on Veterans Day, just as it is done at Arlington and other national cemeteries. American taxpayers continue to pay – as they should – to honor the fallen.

178 Owen Thomas Edgar (1831-1929) according to the Department of Veterans Affairs enlisted in the U.S. Navy in 1846 and was discharged in August 1849.

179 Louis Fisher, *The Mexican War"*, op. cit.

180 Roy P. Basler, ed. *Abraham Lincoln: His Speeches and Writings*, Cleveland, Ohio: Da Capo Press, 1990, cited in Louis Fisher, *The Mexican War"*, op. cit. p.8.

181 *Yellow journalism* is defined as *an unscrupulous and sensationalistic reporting of the news, with practically no legitimate due research and facts to support news coverage.* William Randolph Hearst was one of the most influential yellow journalists in American History. Joseph Pulitzer was a contemporary of Hearst and significant producer of yellow journalism who engaged in a private war with Hearst to see who

could outdo each other with sensationalist reporting, but eventually gravitated to reporting the news based on facts.

182 Alfred Thayer Mahan, particularly his book *The Influence of Sea Power Upon History: 1660-1783*, Cambridge: John Wilson and Son, 2012.

183 For example, the investigation claimed that the ship was blown up by an underwater mine. However, all the metal was blown out, which clearly indicated that the source of the explosion had been internal, not external.

184 The amendment was passed by the Senate on a vote of 42 to 35 and the House approved it by a voter of 311 to 6 on 19 April. The war lasted three months, and all Spanish troops departed by December 1898. Cuba became independent in 1902, but the U.S. took over Puerto Rico, the Philippines, Guam, and other small islands in the Pacific. Senator Teller had investments in domestic production of sugar, and the annexation of Cuba would have cut his profit margin, as domestic producers were be protected by high import tariffs.

185 This information is based on an account by H. H. Kohlsaat, Editor of the Chicago-Times Herald, who was a personal confidant of President McKinley. See H. H. Kohlsaat, *From McKinley to Harding: Personal Recollections of Our Presidents*, New York: Charles Scribner's Sons, 1923.

186 General Frederick N. Funston (1865-1917), son of a U.S. Congressman from Kansas became a General Officer in the Cuban Army fighting for independence from Spain. He participated in at least 22 battles, had 17 horses shot from under him, and was wounded multiple times. Other Americans reached the rank of General in the Cuban Army, but Funston is the most interesting. He returned to the U.S. for medical treatment, and was serving as a Colonel of the Kansas National Guard in 1998 when the Spanish-American War started. After the Spanish defeat, Funston was sent to the Philippines, where he was awarded the Congressional Medal of Honor for heroism in action fighting insurgents, and promoted to brevet Major General. He is credited with designing a successful covert plan to capture Aguinaldo, which earned him a reputation as a national hero in 1901. During the border conflict with Mexico in 1914, General Funston landed in Veracruz in command of a combined Navy, Marine, and Army force totaling over 5,000 men, which was recorded as a first of its kind. When the U.S. entered WWI, Funston was favored to command American Expeditionary Forces, but he died of a heart attack, and was replaced by General John J. Pershing.

187 Assistant Secretary of State William R. Day ran day-to day management of the Department of State, assisted by Alvey A. Adee. John Sherman had served as Secretary of the Treasury and had been instrumental in the enactment of important legislation, including the Sherman Anti-Trust Act in 1890. However, by the time he was appointed Secretary of State he was in ill health and of advanced age.

Sherman resigned his position on 25 April 1898, and was replaced by William R. Day.

188 Hostilities started on 24 February 1895. Spain had about 20,000 regular troops supported by an additional 60,000 volunteer militia composed of Spanish residents and Cubans who did not support independence. Within months, the number of regular Spanish troops increased to over 98,000, supported by at least 63,000 volunteer militiamen. By the end of 1897, regular troops had increased to over 240,000, considerably outnumbering the Cuban Army. However, using a combination of guerrilla and regular tactics, the insurgents had checked the Spanish. Foreign volunteers, including Americans, and a steady number of expeditionary landings supplied the Cubans with weapons and additional manpower. Nevertheless, several of the principal Cuban leaders had been killed in combat. Spanish tactics included forcing the rural population into internment camps to prevent the insurgents from receiving food and other assistance from farmers. The internees suffered from poor sanitation and hunger. However, as the Spanish officials recognized, they only controlled the land in which their soldiers were standing and no more. Despite negotiations with the U.S. to find a solution to the conflict, the Spanish were determined to fight to the end to keep Cuba as a colony.

189 Admiral Hyman G. Rickover (1900-1986), directed the original development of naval nuclear propulsion, and is known as the *Father of the Nuclear Navy*. He served for a record of 63 years on active duty. His reputation indicates that the study he carried out of the sinking of the USS Maine was thorough.

190 See Hayman G. Rickover, How the Battleship Maine Was Destroyed, 1976.

191 In the case of Iraq, policymakers and senior military leaders came up with an impressive list of descriptors for the insurgency that characterized the situation in multiple ways, except what the insurgency was all about. Examples: Saddam loyalists, Bath Party operatives, criminal elements, outsiders, professional terrorists, anti-Iraqi elements, bitter-enders, remnants of the old regime, jihadists, and insurgents for hire.

192 Paul says in Romans 13 [:4] that *it is the duty of the sword to protect and punish, to protect the good in peace and to punish the wicked with war. God tolerates no injustice and he has so ordered things that warmongers must be defeated in war.*

193 On 8 March 2001, Vice Admiral Thomas R. Wilson presented to the Senate Armed Services Committee a statement on *Global Threats and Challenges Through 2015*. Wilson stated that after 1990 the U.S. had faced new security paradigms and challenges, and he expected these to continue during the next 10 to 15 years. As a manager of intelligence resources, he told the Committee that he was concerned that the country's intelligence capabilities were being stretched *"a mile wide and an inch deep."* Admiral Thomas R. Wilson, Director of DIA, Statement to the Senate

Armed Services Committee on *Global Threats and Challenges Through 2015*, 8 March 2001.

194 Several hundred HUMVEEs had been produced and sent to American forces in Kosovo in the mid-1990s, but they were still needed there. Sure, one has to fight wars with what is available, not with the stuff you wished you had, but the need for armored HUMVEEs was predictable.

195 Bosnia and Herzegovina, is home principally to three ethnic groups, Bosnians, Serbs, and Croats, and was a province of the Socialist Federal Republic of Yugoslavia from WWII until it gained its' independence as a result of the Yugoslavian Wars in the 1990s. Like other areas of the Balkans, the territory was taken through military conquest by the Ottoman Empire, which ruled the region from 1463 to 1878, which resulted in forced religious conversion to Islam. The region came under Austro-Hungarian rule from 1878 to 1918. Local ethnic tensions led to the assassination of Archduke Franz Ferdinand in June 1914, which became the spark that started WWI. From the end of WWII in 1945 to 1992, the territory was part of Yugoslavia under Communist rule. As Yugoslavia broke up, the three principal ethnic groups fought over joining Serbia, or becoming independent. Serb forces attacked the other ethnic groups and engaged in ethnic cleansing, ransacking and burning down villages and homes of Bosnians and Croatians, resulting in the displacement of over 2.2 million people. In addition to the ethnic conflicts, the region was also divided by religion, with Muslims being targeted by Serbian Christians, culminating on a massacre of Muslims at Srebrenica in 1995. See Bedrudin Brijavac, "Bosnia – between ethnic-nationalism and Europeanization," *Transconflict*, 17 January 2012.

196 Joint and Coalition Operational Analysis (JCOA), Joint Staff (J7), *Decade of War, Volume 1, Enduring Lessons from the Past Decade of Operations*, 15 June 2013. (Unclassified)

197 Ibid.

198 Eloise Engle and Arnold S. Lott, *America's Maritime Heritage*, Annapolis, Maryland: Naval Institute Press, 1975; C. Keith Wilbur, *Pirates & Patriots of the Revolution: An Illustrated Encyclopedia of Colonial Seamanship*, Old Saybrook, Connecticut: The Globe Pequot Press, 1973, 1984

199 Michael S. Schmidt, Flexing Muscle, Baghdad Detains U.S. Contractors, The *New York Times*, 15 January 2012; Civilian contractor casualty counts have never been totaled up or officially disclosed. However, based on published information, at least 300 were killed in Iraq during 2012 alone. As of 16 July 2006, there were 192 death claims filed at the U.S. Department of Labor for civilian contractors. According to DOL, at least 103 death claims were filed against an uninsured employer who had U.S. Government contracts and were providing personnel in Iraq. As of December 2011 it is estimated that at least 3,258 contractors had been

killed, and at least 89,182 contractors had been wounded in Afghanistan and Iraq, based on Defense Base Act claims filed for civilian contractors with DOL. These contractors are called the "*Disposable Army*."

200 The U.N. General Assembly passed resolution 44/34 on 4 December 1989, known as the International Convention against the Recruitment, Use, Financing and Training of Mercenaries, which went into force on 20 October 2001, and is known as the UN Mercenary Convention. This Convention predates the 9/11/2001 terrorist attacks, as well as the interventions in Afghanistan and Iraq; "In Place of Fear: Is Obama giving American private security contractors immunity from prosecution just like Bush did – Who will protect Iraqi civilians from them?" *In Place of Fear Blog*, 15 December 2011, http://inplaceoffear.blogspot.com/2011/12/is-obama-giving-american-private.html; Jeremy Scahill, "Blackwater Busted," *The Nation*, 1 December 2008; Tom Bowman, "No U.S. Troops, but An Army of Contractors In Iraq," *National Public Radio*, 27 December 2011; James Glanz, "Report on Iraq Security Lists 310 Contractors," *The New York Times*, 28 October 2008.

201 Eleven soldiers were convicted by military court martial in trials that were held between 2004 and 2006.

202 On 4 May 2004, Secretary of Defense Donald H. Rumsfeld, described the abuses at Abu Ghraib as "an exceptional, isolated" case. In a nationally televised address on May 24, President George W. Bush spoke of "disgraceful conduct by a few American troops who dishonored our country and disregarded our values."

203 Michael A. Fuoco, Ed Blazina and Cindi Lash, "Suspect in prisoner abuse has a history of troubles; Whitehall native had checkered work record, stormy marriage," Pittsburgh Post-Gazette, 08 May 2004. "*Graner served as a corrections officer from May 20, 1996, until he was called to active military duty. He was disciplined six times for problems at work: two written reprimands, a one-day suspension, two five-day suspensions and a dismissal that was reduced to a three-day suspension by an arbitrator.*"

204 Nicholas de B. Katzenback and John Gibbons, *VERA Institute of Justice, Commission on Safety and Abuse in American's Prisons*, June 2006.

205

206 "Jon Boone, "Photos show U.S. soldiers in Afghanistan posing with dead civilians," The Guardian, 21 March 2011.

207 Raf Sanchez and Dean Nelson, "U.S. Defense Secretary Leon Panetta condemns 'utterly deplorable' behavior of U.S. Marine 'urination' video," *The Telegraph* (London), 12 January 2012.

208 U.S. Department of the Army, Marlow, Hair, Gazzetti, and Blanks testimony, Trial Proper, Compton Court-Martial, 27-34, 15-6, 35, 7-9.

[209] Col. John H. Linden. *Surrender of the Dachau Concentration Camp 29 April 1945.* Sycamore Press Ltd, 1997, ISBN-13-9780966515107. None of the American soldiers who shot and killed the unarmed German soldiers who had surrendered was prosecuted. Zarusky, Jürgen, "'that is not the American Way of Fighting:' The Shooting of Captured SS-Men during the Liberation of Dachau". 2002.

[210] Max Hastings, "The unspeakable war and the savage Japanese soldiers who would never surrender," *The Daily Mail* (London), 14 September 2007;

[211] Harrison, Simon (2006). "Skull trophies of the Pacific War: Transgressive objects of remembrance". *Journal of the Royal Anthropological Institute* 12 (4): 817–36.

[212] Second Lieutenant William Calley, a platoon leader of Charlie Company was convicted of killing 22 villagers, and originally given a life sentence, but only served less than four years of house arrest. "Atrocities During the Vietnam War," Olive-drab.com, http://olive-drab.com/od_history_vietnam_atrocities.php; "The My Lay Massacre," Public Broadcasting Service (PBS), http://www.pbs.org/wgbh/amex/vietnam/trenches/my_lai.html; Department of the Army, *Report of the Department of the Army Review of the Preliminary investigations into the May Lay Incident, Vol. 1-111.*

[213] Seth Ackerman, "Digging Too Deep at No Gun Ri," *Associated Press,* September 1999. The AP published an investigative story documenting the massacre, including eyewitness stories, including American veterans of the war. Over 100 civilians were shot during this incident that took place in 1950. Multiple American newspapers ran stories on the subject, including the *Washington Post, The New York Times,* and the *Chicago Tribune.*

[214] The vessel was built under the cover story of deep-sea mining to recover manganese nodules from the ocean floor, for Global Marine Development, a Howard Hughes company. The ship had a massive claw designed to pick up the submarine and raise it to the surface using a massive hoisting mechanism hidden under the ship.

[215] A fairly large number of generals were punished for misconduct between 2010 and 1013. For example, Brig. Gen. Jeffrey A. Sinclair faced a court-martial on sodomy charges and sexual misconduct. Army Maj. Gen. Ralph O. Baker, commander of troops in the Horn of Africa was fired on 28 March 2013 for sexual misconduct. Lt. Gen. David H. Huntoon, Jr. Superintendent of West Point, and Lt. Gen. Joseph F. Fil Jr., former Commander of troops in Iraq and Korea, were sanctioned for misconduct. Lt. Gen. Patrick J. O'Reilly, commander of the Missile Defense Agency, was sanctioned for creating a toxic atmosphere and mistreating his staff. Gen. William E. "Kip" Ward, chief of AFRICOM was demoted and ordered to reimburse $82,000 to the government for unauthorized expenses. Gen. Stanley A. McChrystal, Commander of American troops in Afghanistan was removed from his assignment as a result of statements allegedly made for an article in Rolling

Stone. CIA Director and retired Gen. David Petraeus resigned due to sexual misconduct.

[216] Richard Lardner, Sexual Assaults in Military Rose to Over 26,000 in 2012: Pentagon Survey, *Huff Post*, 7 May 2013.

[217] Rowan Scarborough, Victims of sex assaults in military are mostly men: women are more likely to speak up, *The Washington Times*, 20 May 2013.

[218] Assuming that a wounded soldier between 20 and 30 years of age will live to somewhere between age 70 and 80 years, in line with current actuarial data for life expectancy, future costs will be huge. Remember that the last veteran of the war with Mexico ending in 1848 lived to 1929, future costs could be huge as the population continues to live longer.

[219] James Madison (1751- 1836) was the 4th President of the United States, one of the framers if the Bill of Rights and the Constitution, and the first President to ask Congress to declare war, as the British Navy seized American ships, cargo, and impressed American sailors into serving their military.

[220] Who is considered poor in the U.S.? In 2011, a single person under 65 years of age living with an income of less than $11,702, or a couple with two children with an income under $22,811. The most recent data available is from 2011. About 25 % of all jobs pay less than $23,000, and about 50% of all jobs pay less than $34,000 annually. See: U.S. Bureau of the Census, *Income, Poverty and Health Insurance Coverage in the United States: 2012*, released 17 Sept. 2013.

[221] United States Census Burau, Median Income of Households Using Three-Year Moving Averages 1999-2011.

[222] Terence P. Jeffrey, "54 months: Record Stretch of 7.5%+ Unemployment Continues," *CNSNews.com*, 6 July 2013. The situation improved slightly by mid-2014, but for lower-wage labor earning less than $15 per hour.

[223] Jeane Sahadi, 1 in 3 U.S. adults have 'debt in collections,' CNN Money, 29 July 2014.

[224] Asma Ghribi, Why It's Worrying That U.S. Companies Are Getting Older, *The Wall Street Journal*, 4 August 2014

[225] U.S. Conference of Mayors, August 2014: Income and Wage Gaps Across the US.

[226] Blake Ellis, Student homelessness hits another record high, *CNN*, 22 September 2014.

[227] According to published statistics, there are about 633,000 chronically homeless people on any given night in the US. Veterans are overrepresented among the homeless population. Source: National Alliance to End Homelessness. Incredible as it may seem, there are more people on welfare than gainfully employed in eleven

states, namely Alabama, California, Illinois, Kentucky, Maine, Mississippi, New Mexico, New York, Ohio, and S. Carolina.

228 American Society of Civil Engineers, 2013 Report Card for America's Infrastructure: "*Now the 2013 Report Card grades are in, and America's cumulative GPA for infrastructure rose slightly to a D+. The grades in 2013 ranged from a high of B- for solid waste to a low of D- for inland waterways and levees. Solid waste, drinking water, wastewater, roads, and bridges all saw incremental improvements, and rail jumped from a C- to a C+... Bridges: Over two hundred million trips are taken daily across deficient bridges in the nation's 102 largest metropolitan regions. In total, one in nine of the nation's bridges are rated as structurally deficient, while the average age of the nation's 607,380 bridges is currently 42 years. The Federal Highway Administration (FHWA) estimates that to eliminate the nation's bridge backlog by 2028, we would need to invest $20.5 billion annually, while only $12.8 billion is being spent currently.*"

229 During the Trayvon Martin / George Zimmerman trial, one of the witnesses, Rachel Jeantel, 19, said *"I don't read cursive."* This was a clear case of failure of Florida educators, who should be put on trial themselves. How can teachers and administrators at Miami Norland High School explain that a senior at the school approaching graduation could not read cursive? The Miami-Dade County entire public education structure should have resigned in shame for malpractice. James Marshall Crotty, "Rachel Jeantel, Star Witness in Trayvon Martin Murder trial Cannot Read Her Own Letter – Now, Whose Fault Is That? *The Huffington Post*, 28 June 2013.

230 Michael Nutter, Mayor of Philadelphia made the following statement: TO THE BLACK YOUTHS OF PHILADELPHIA: *Take those God-darn hoodies down... Pull your pants up and buy a belt, 'cause no one wants to see your underwear or the crack of your butt... You walk into somebody's office with your hair uncombed and a pick in the back and your shoes untied and your pants half down, tattoos up and down your arms and on your neck, and you wonder why somebody won't hire you? They don't hire you 'cause you look like you're crazy.* 9 August 2011.

231 Marcus Tullius Cicero (106 –43 BC) was a Roman lawyer, orator, philosopher, consul, and political theorist, who is widely considered to have been one of greatest Roman orators and writers. His ideas influenced 18th century thinkers including David Hume, John Locke, and Montesquieu, who in turn influenced American revolutionaries.

232 Standard and Poor's (S&P) is one of the three principal financial services companies. The other two principal companies are Moody's Financial Services and Fitch ratings. S&P evaluates and publishes financial research and analysis on stocks and bonds, including sovereign debt paper.

[233] Gross public debt at the end of FY 91 was $3.598 trillion, and the Federal deficit was $269.2 billion. Total spending was $2.230 trillion. Defense spending was $320.4 billion. Health care spending by the Federal, state, and local governments was estimated at $250.3 billion. GDP was $5,992.1 billion.

[234] The strong demand for workers triggered a considerable increase in legal and illegal immigration. In some parts of the country unemployment went down to around 2 percent.

[235] BBC, *Business: The Economy U.S. to buy back national debt*, 4 August 1999.

[236] At the end of FY 2000, the budget surplus was $236.2 billion. The national debt was $5.628 trillion. Total gross public debt, adding Federal, State, and local debt was about $7.080 trillion. Defense spending was $358.6 billion. Health care costs (Federal, State, and local governments) were estimated at $508.7 billion. The Federal budget was $1.789 trillion.

[237] The real culprits have names: Vice President Richard B. Chaney is on record dismissing the importance of budget deficits; Secretary of Defense Donald Rumsfeld downplayed the cost of military operations and thought that it was possible to fight wars on the cheap; CIA Director George K. Tenet, under whose leadership the IC failed to prevent the 9/11/01 terrorist attacks, and then failed to properly *speak truth to power* about the real conditions in Iraq; and finally, President George W. Bush, who bought the story that war could be fought on the cheap.

[238] Among the Conservative elements that promised that the best way to balance the budget and pay down the debt was the Heritage Foundation. The organization, together with other Conservatives pointed to the so-called *Laffer Curve*, which proposed that tax cuts would pay for themselves and generate additional income due to the stimulus that the cuts would provide to economic growth. The *Laffer Curve* is based on theories proposed by British economist John Maynard Keynes (1883-1946), which were later partially debunked by University of Chicago Professor Milton Friedman (1912-2006). Friedman was a key economic adviser to President Ronald Reagan.

[239] President George Washington, *Message to the House of Representatives, 1793.*

[240] U.S. Federal Debt As Percentage of GDP, U.S. from FY1792 to FY2010. Data Sources for 1792: *GDP: Measuring Worth - U.S. GDP*; Federal*: Bicentennial Edition: Historical Statistics of the U.S., Colonial Times to 1970 State and Local:* not available Data Sources for 2010: *GDP: Measuring Worth - U.S. GDP*; *Federal: Fed. Budget: Hist. Tables 3.2, 5.1, 7.1; State and Local: State and Local Gov. Finances; "Guesstimated*" by projecting the latest change in reported spending forward to future years.

241 Robert Schroeder, U.S. Debt now about 73% of GDP, CBO says, *Marketwatch*, 17 September 2013.

242 The federal budget deficit was $1.4 trillion in 2009.

243 The first known version of this nursery rhyme was published in 1797 by Samuel Arnold's *Juvenile Amusements*. A revised version was published in 1803, and again in 1810. The current version dates to James William Elliott's *National Nursery Rhymes and Nursery Sons*, London, 1970.

244 Fannie Mae is the Federal National Mortgage Association (FNMA). It was created in 1938 as a government-sponsored enterprise, to expand home ownership through an expansion of the secondary market for mortgages, by creating pools of mortgages that could be sold as mortgaged-backed securities. In 1954, Fannie Mae became a "mixed-ownership" corporation, in which the Federal Government holds preferred stock and private investors hold common stock, but in 1968, it became once again a privately held corporation, as part of the Housing and Urban Development Act of 1968. The Act also created the Government National Mortgage Association or "Ginnie Mae," which is the only home-loan agency backed by the U.S. Government, together with home mortgages issued by the Veterans Administration and the Farmers Home Administration. Freddie Mac is the Federal Home Loan Mortgage Corporation (FHLMC), which functions as a government-sponsored organization. It was created in 1970 to increase the secondary market for mortgages, by creating "pools" which are then resold as mortgage-backed securities to investors. In September 2008, the Federal Housing Finance Agency put both, Fannie Mae and Freddie Mac under a "protectorship" or "conservatorship" to keep them from going under.

245 The list of business failures since 2008 include Aloha Airlines, Circuit City Stores, Frontier Airlines, Levitz Furniture, Ritz Camera Centers, Borders Group, AMR (American Airlines), Hostess Brands, Washington Mutual, Colonial Bank, Guaranty Bank, Downey Savings and Loan, Bank United, Am Trust Bank, United Commercial Bank, California National Bank, Conus Bank, Franklin Bank, Silverton Bank, Imperial Capital Bank, La Jolla Bank, Frontier Bank, First National Bank of Nevada, Midwest Bank and Trust Company, ANB Financial, Georgia Bank, New Frontier Bank, Georgia Bank, and about 20 additional banks with smaller assets at time of failure.

246 The largest recipients of government funds were Fannie Mae, Freddie Mac, the insurance company AIG, General Motors, Bank of America, Citigroup, JP Morgan Chase, Wells Fargo, GMAC/Ally Financial, Chrysler, Goldman Sachs, Morgan Stanley, PNC Financial Services, U.S. Bankcorp, Sun Trust, and Capital One Financial.

247 John Cassidy, "Taxing," *The New Yorker*, 26 January 2004. This is the type of strange mentality associated with the George W. Bush Administration, departs from traditional Conservative views regarding balanced budgets.

248 James Madison, Speech, House of Representatives, 10 January 1794.

249 By "Egalitarian" ideas I mean that the Founding Fathers believed in the principle that all people are equal and deserve equal rights and opportunities. The term "Judeo-Christian" did not surface until 1821, when it was first recorded in a letter. The Founding Fathers were aware of multiple passages in the Old and New Testament about helping the poor, orphans, widows, the sick, and the needy. (From the Old Testament: Leviticus 23:22; Deuteronomy 10:18, 15:7 and 24:19-21; Job 29:12; Psalm 12:5, 68:5 and 68:10; Proverbs 13:23 and 28:3; Isaiah 10:2; From the New Testament: *"Jesus answered, if you want to be perfect, go, sell your possessions and give to the poor, and you will have treasure in heaven. Then come, follow me;" Mathew 19:21; "For I was hungry and you gave me something to eat, I was thirsty and you gave me something to drink, I was a stranger and you invited me in."* Mathew 25:35; *"If anyone has material possessions and sees his brother in need but has no pity on him, how can the love of God be in him? Dear children, let us not love with words or tongue but with actions and in truth."* 1 John 3:17-18). The Founding Fathers, who were not necessarily religious, did empathize on ethical grounds through logic and reason a sense of moral responsibility to ensure that everyone acts with ethical principles of justice and universal morality. Immanuel Kant (1724-1804) ideas and secular ethical principles, including a fundamental moral disposition in human nature, influenced the writers of the U.S. Constitution.

250 The start of *sequestration* was delayed until 1 March 2013, by the American Taxpayer Relief Act of 2012, in the hope that an agreement for reducing government spending could be reached. Under sequestration many government programs and the Department of Defense were dramatically and dangerously cut.

251 Under *sequestration* cuts were evenly split between defense and non-defense programs, but entitlement programs like Social Security, Medicare, Medicaid, and federal civilian and military pensions were exempted.

252 President Richard M. Nixon's Statements on Social Security, 25 September 1969, Social Security Onlinehttp://www.ssa.gov/history/nixstmts.html#969

253 Ibid.

254 See: Eric Sprott and Etienne Bordeleau, The Detroit Template, 1 August 2013. http://news.goldseek.com/GoldSeek/1375387260.php

255 Social Security is officially called the Old-Age, Survivors, and Disability Insurance (OASDI). Ryan Kierman, Social Security Faces $9.6T in Unfunded Liabilities - $83,894 Per Household, CNSNews.com, 4 June 2013.

256 Government Accountability Office, *Sustained Improvements in Federal Financial Management is Crucial to Addressing Our Nation's Financial Condition and Long-Tem Fiscal Imbalance*, 1 March 2006.

257 Long before the warning made by President Eisenhower in January 1960, Gen Smedley Butler had provided a similar warning in 1935 in his book *War is a Racket*; Defense Secretary Rumsfeld admitted on CBS News on 29 January 2002 that DOD could not track $2.3 trillion in transactions!

258 DOD report prepared for Senator Bernie Sanders, Fraudulent Defense Contractors Paid $1 Trillion, 20 October 2011.

259 William D. Hartung, *Prophets of War: Lockheed Martin and the Making of the Military-Industrial Complex,* New York: Nation Books, A Member of the Perseus Books Group, 2011; Lockheed Martin: First in Federal Funding, First in Government Fraud, 25 November 2011, http://corporategreedchronicles.com/2011/11/25/lockheed-martin-first-in-federal-funding-first-in-government-fraud/

260 So much for patriotism as interpreted by the top defense contractor!

261 Lawrence Wittner, Lockheed Martin at the Trough, *Huff Post Business*, 21 March 2013.

262 DOD Report to Senator Sanders, 20 October 2011, op. cit.

263 Nick Schwellenbach, Fraud cases fell while Pentagon contracts surged: procurement experts say more investigators are required, *Center for Public Integrity*, 24 March 2011. Author's note: I was employed by Northrop Grumman between August 2004 and August 2005. I was again employed by the company in June 2014.

264 The ICCTF was staffed with personnel from the DOD Criminal Investigative Service; Army Criminal Investigation Command; Department of State Office of Inspector General; U.S. Agency for International Development Office of Inspector General; Air Force Office of Special Investigations; Naval Criminal Investigative Service; Special Inspector General for Afghanistan Reconstruction, and FBI agents.

265 Ibid.

266 Jill R. Aitoro, As much as $60 billion wasted in Iraq, Afghanistan, report says, *The Washington Journal*, 31 August 2011.

267 Hong Kong is part of the PRC, but enjoys a special status. It shares the top ranking with Singapore.

268 Index of Economic Freedom 2013, The Heritage Foundation and The Wall Street Journal.

269 James Gwartney, Robert Lawson, and Joshua Hall, *Economic Freedom of the World: 2013 Annual Report*, (Vancouver: The Fraser Institute, 2013).

270 President Ulysses S. Grant's Secretary of War resigned just before he was impeached by the House of Representatives for bribery in 1876. William Lorimer (R-IL) was expelled from the Senate in 1912 for accepting bribes. Albert Fall, Secretary of the Interior under President Warren G. Harding (R-OH) was convicted and sentenced to two years in prison in 1922 for bribery linked to the Teapot Dome scandal. In 1950 a Justice Department investigation led to the firing of 166 IRS employees for corruption. Senator Thomas J. Dodd (D-CT) was censured by the Senate for financial misconduct in 1967. Vice President Spiro Agnew was convicted of tax fraud and bribery and forced to resign in 1973. Congressman Charles Diggs (D-MI) was convicted of mail fraud and participating in a kickback scheme with members of his staff and sentenced to 3 years in 1978. Congressman James Traficant (D-OH) was convicted of felony, bribery, and racketeering and sentenced to 8 years in prison in 2002. Six Members of Congress were convicted in 1980 in as a result of the *Abscam* FBI sting for bribery and conspiracy. Michael Deaver, who was Deputy Chief of Staff to President Ronald Reagan pleaded guilty to perjury related to lobbying and was sentenced to 3 years' probation and fined $100,000. Speaker of the House Jim Wright (D-TX) resigned after an ethics investigation related to improperly accepting gifts in 1989. Catalina Vasquez Villalpando, Treasurer of the United States under George H. W. Bush was sent to prison for tax evasion and obstruction of justice in 1992. Congressman Dan Rostenkowski (D-IL) was sentenced to 18 months in prison in 1995.

271 Transparency International is a non-governmental organization headquartered in Berlin, Germany. European Commission, Institute for the Protection and Security of the Citizen, European Commission, *Corruption Perceptions Index 2012.*

272 Heritage Foundation and the *Wall Street Journal, 2014 Index of Economic Freedom*, 14 January 2014.

273 The OECD was established in 1948 to manage the Marshall Plan funded by the U.S. to reconstruct Europe after WWII. The Organization for Economic Co-operation and Development (OECD) was officially born on 30 September 1961. Today, 34 OECD member countries worldwide regularly turn to one another to identify problems, discuss, analyze, and promote policies to solve them. The New America Foundation is a nonprofit and nonpartisan public policy institute created in 1999.

274 Małgorzata Kuczera and Simon Field, OECD, Reviews of Vocational Education and Training, *A Skills Beyond School Review of the United States*, July 2013.

275 Jean-Baptiste Colbert (1619-1683), who served as Minister of Finance and Minister of Commerce under King Louis XIV of France, was a prime proponent of the need to support a positive trade balance.

[276] The limited language in support of hydraulic fracturing was blamed on Vice President Cheney, because of his previous position as CEO of Halliburton, a key player in fracking.

[277] Oil and Gas Journal Editors, WoodMac: Unconventional production changing energy trade patterns, *Oil and Gas Journal*, 26 September 2012.

[278] Maybe it isn't China, *The Economist*, 23 August 2010.

[279] The manufacturing sector consists of these subsectors: Food, beverage and tobacco products, textile mills, textile product mills, apparel manufacturing, leather and allied products manufacturing, wood product manufacturing, paper, printing and related activities, petroleum and coal products manufacturing, chemical manufacturing, plastics and rubber products manufacturing, non-metallic mineral product manufacturing, machinery manufacturing, computer and electronic product manufacturing, electrical equipment, appliance, and component manufacturing, transportation equipment manufacturing, furniture and related product manufacturing, and miscellaneous manufacturing.

[280] Black Feet, Cheyenne, Arapahoe, Delaware, Cree, Mohican, Shawnee, Apaches, Navajo, Kiowa-Apache, Creek, Seminole, Pawnee, Pueblo, Hope, Comanche, Sioux, and other tribes had their own distinct cotton fabrics long before the Arrival of European settlers.

[281] The garment industry was famous for paying low wages, employing children, as well as causing multiple ailments resulting from dust accumulation, long hours of work, and other abuses, which led to the creation of the United Tailoresses of New York, in the 1820s, leading to the eventual creation of the Textile Workers Union.

[282] Unless the American electorate paints the White House blue and prays in the hope of welcoming a baby boy with elephant-size gonads, or alternatively, a female with the courage of a Joan of Arc willing to truly protect American workers and the American economy.

[283] Ralph Nader, a left-wing activist, and Harvard Law School graduate published in 1965 *Unsafe at Any Speed*, an analysis of how American auto manufacturers, particularly GM, were making cars that were unsafe. Nader should be given credit for making the U.S. automotive industry improve car design, which ultimately rendered them more competitive.

[284] Chrysler survived and came up with new models, including the popular minivan, but in 1998, it entered into a partnership with German-based Daimler-Benz AG. Later on, Daimler bought controlling shares of Chrysler, and a new company emerged under the name DaimlerChrysler Motors Company LLC. In 2007, DaimlerChrysler announced the sale of 80.1% of the operating subsidiary in the U.S. to American investors trading under the name Cerberus Capital

Management. The German company Daimler continued to hold about a 20 % share of Chrysler. In 2009 Daimler AG agreed to give up its' share of Chrysler to the Cerberus Capital Management, and paid a debt of around $600 million owed to the union's retirement fund. The U.S. and Canadian governments provided around $7 billion in financing to Chrysler, which was operating under Chapter 11 bankruptcy. Many dealerships and plants were closed as part of the restructuring of the company, and surprisingly, in May 2011, the company paid back the over $7 billion loan by the U.S. and Canadian governments.

285 See Michael V. Seitzinger, *Foreign Investment in the United States: Major Federal Statutory Restrictions*, Congressional Research Service, 17 June 2013.

286 The Asheville area is a tourist destination, with such attractions as the Biltmore Estate built by George W. Vanderbilt and National Parks. Cleaning hotel rooms, waiting on tables in restaurants and other low-paying service jobs were prevalent in an area not-known for economic affluence. On the Tennessee side of the border, around Knoxville, the situation was a little better, due to the presence of the University of Tennessee, the Tennessee Valley Authority, and the Oak Ridge National Lab. Nevertheless, the textile and manufacturing industries had been destroyed by foreign competition and had shut down in the 1960s and 1970s, sending many blue collar workers to the unemployment lines. The difference in popular attitudes in the east and west ends of Tennessee were remarkable.

287 While in the Netherlands I frequently visited *Delfshaven*, from where the *Speedwell* carrying Pilgrims from a congregation of British religious exiles in Leiden sailed to Plymouth in the UK in 1620, to meet with other Pilgrims that were to board the *Mayflower*. The two ships sailed together, but when the *Speedwell* developed problems, all 104 Pilgrims on board moved to the *Mayflower*. I visited the Pilgrim Fathers Church, (*Oude Kerk* or *Pelgrimskerk*). A Memorial Plaque in *Delfshaven* marks the site from where they sailed to America. The Pilgrims were part of a British colony of dissenters that had fled the UK to find religious tolerance in the Netherlands, before deciding to travel to America seeking religious freedom, which is a central constant in U.S. culture. In Leiden I visited the area around *Pieterskerk*, where they lived and worked as best they could as religious exiles. In Holland they picked up elements of Dutch culture, particularly their children. I learned more "on-site" about this period of early American history and the immigrant culture that most people learned about in superficial elementary, middle, and high school history classes in in most parts of the U.S.

288 The Port of Rotterdam in the Netherlands is the second largest port in the world and one of the main ports of Europe, with a throughput of about 430 million tons. Over 34,000 sea-going vessels and over 100,000 inland (river) vessels call at the port annually.

289 Scott Harris, "Bradley Says Racism Stirs Foreign Investors' Critics," *Los Angeles Times*, 17 February 1089; Peter T. Kilborn, "Economic Nationalism Shapes Democratic Campaign Debate," *The New York Times*, 22 March 1988.

290 This type of stupid actions are the sort of thing that can lead to tragedies like the 1982 incident in Detroit, in which two unemployed auto workers beat to death a young Chinese-American because they thought he was Japanese and somehow responsible for their unemployment. To compound the incident, a judge, noting the stress that Japanese imports had caused the men, gave them each three years' probation and a $3,700 fine. Source: David Boaz, "Yellow Peril Re-infests America," *Wall Street Journal*, 7 April 1989.

291 Kaiser Motors (failed in 1955), Packard (failed in 1958), Studebaker (shut down in 1963 in the U.S. and in 1966 in Canada), Nash and Hudson consolidated under American Motors (taken over by Renault in 1980, and absorbed by Chrysler Corporation in 1987). General Motors shut down the Oldsmobile Division and Chrysler shut down the Plymouth Division.

292 There were an estimated six million companies in the U.S. as of 2013. Thousands go under and thousands are created every year by entrepreneurs. Only a small fraction are able to survive over 30 years. About 50 percent of the American workforce is employed by small companies. Most of these companies are too small to have viable pension plans.

293 AT&TY operated local franchises as Bell Operating Companies in cities throughout North America. AT&T Long Lines provided long distance interconnectivity, Bell Labs carried out R&D for the conglomerate, and Western Electric produced the equipment.

294 According to PBGC, "The total number of participants in the Plan as of the Plan's Jan. 1, 2011, valuation date was 616,131. Of this number, 237,353 were active participants, 252,608 were retired or separated from service and receiving benefits, and 126,170 were retired or separated from service and entitled to future benefits.

295 Telecommunications line installers and repairers earn a median income of $29.84, equipment installers and repairers earned a median income of $27.55. Radio, cellular and tower equipment installers and repairers earn a median income of $22.27. Communications equipment operators earned a median income of $16.21. These wages compare fairly well with the median hourly wages for all occupations in 2012, which was $27.66.

296 The U.S. produces about 5% of iron output worldwide and consumes about 7% or all the iron ore produced in the world. Iron is the most used metal, which is transformed into steel for structural engineering use, automotive industry, shipping, and all ties of industrial machinery. The U.S. has been a traditional producer of aluminum, cement, coal, copper, gold, iron, lad, molybdenum,

phosphates, potash, salt, sulfur, uranium, and zinc. As with the development of domestic energy resources, environmental groups have blocked additional development in mining. For example, a political battle has been underway in Wisconsin over the approval of a $1.5 billion investment in a new iron ore mine in N.W. Wisconsin, which would be the largest in N. America, and would create an estimated 700 new mining jobs and over 3,000 construction jobs.

[297] *Liberal* values defined as supporting free markets, civil liberties, and the ideals of the American Revolution and the Constitution– *not far-left politics*!

[298] James Bryce's book is considered one of the three basic studies of the United States system of government, the others being *The Federalist Papers*, consisting in a series of 85 essays published between 1787 and 1788 by James Madison, Alexander Hamilton, and John Jay, outlining how they perceive that the new government would function under the U.S. Constitution; and Alexis de Tocqueville's *Democracy in America.* Born in France in 1805, de Tocqueville was a historian and political thinker who traveled to the United States and wrote about his experiences and observations of life in the young nation. The book was published in two volumes in 1835 and 1840. He wrote highly of the U.S. Constitution, and applied many of his observations later on in France, when he participated in writing a new Constitution for the Second Republic in 1848. One of de Tocqueville's most important observations was: "*there is no country in the whole world in which the Christian religion retains a greater influence over the souls of men than in America, and there can be no greater proof of its' utility, and of its conformity to human nature, than that its' influence is most powerfully felt over the most enlightened and free nation of the earth.*" If he were writing about the U.S. in 2014, would de Tocqueville be able to make the same observation?

[299] During the 3rd century AD, the Roman Empire suffered military defeats, plagues, civil wars, Barbarian invasions, corruption, abuse of power, insecurity, economic decline, religious discord, unrestrained immigration, government confiscation of private assets, famine, and the inability to recruit and maintain an effective military, and finally Rome fell and was sacked in 410 AD.

[300] These race statistics are misleading, as the so-called "*Hispanics*" or people with a Spanish surname could be White, Native American, of African descent, or a combination of several races.

[301] U.S. Bureau of the Census, *The 2012 Statistical Abstract – The National Data* book.

[302] U.S. Bureau of the Census, *Op. cit.*

[303] *Violence against Teachers*, American Psychological Association, http://www.apa.org/ed/schools/cpse/activities/violence-against.aspx

[304] Public Schools: New Violence Against Teachers, *Time Magazine*, 14 November 1969. And to compound the problem, after the December 2012 massacre at the

Newtown, CN elementary school, some mentally challenged individuals have proposed as a solution to have teachers carrying guns on school grounds.

305 The song was composed by Sascha Konietzko, Gunter Schultz, and En Esch. Konietzko was the frontman of the band KMFDM. The song was not only posted on the website of Eric Harris, one of the perpetrators of the Columbine school massacre, but also on YouTube by Pekka-Eric Auvinen, perpetrator of the Jokela High School shooting in Finland in 1989. Prior to the shooting, Auvinen had posted a description of what he was going to do with the *Stray Bullet* song playing in the background. He apparently was fascinated by the Columbine massacre and the Waco Siege in 1993, and David Koresh, cult leader of the Branch Davidians.

306 The exception to the rule were John Muhammad and Lee Malvo, two Black men who randomly killed people of practically all races and ages with a sniper rifle in the Capital area (D. C. Metro, including the suburban areas in Maryland and Northern Virginia.

307 The British contributed to the rock scene with Gerry and The Pacemakers, The Searchers, Freddie and the Dreamers, Herman's Hermits, The Hollies, The Animals, and the famous Beatles and The Rolling Stones. In my opinion they also contributed to introducing many distortions to the culture.

308 20 percent of Americans are mentally disturbed, 19 January 2012, http://rt.com/usa/disturbed-mental-illness-study-225/; U.S. Census Bureau, POPClock Projection, 29 December 2012; See National Institute of Mental Health's National Comorbidity Survey, and Substance Abuse and Mental Health Services Administration's National Survey of Drug Abuse and Health (NSDUH).

309 E. Fuller Torrey, M.D., Sheriff Aaron D. Kennard, MPAA, Sheriff Don Eslinger, Richard Lamb, M. D. and James Pavle, *More Mentally Ill Persons in Jails and Prisons Than Hospitals: A Survey of States*. National Sheriffs' Association and Treatment Advocacy Center, May 2010.

310 Wade Michael Page, the perpetrator of the attack on the Sikh Temple committed suicide after being shot by a responding police officer. Page had been tied to White supremacist groups and had a history of alcoholism, according to press reports.

311 William Spangler, 62, committed suicide after setting a house on fire to lure the firefighters to the location. Dawn Nguyen, a 24-year-old neighbor had purchased the guns in June 2010 for Spangler was arrested on 28 December and charged with violating federal firearms legislation. Associated Press, *Rochester woman who acted as straw buyer of guns used by William Spangler in Webster Shooting is busted for lying about who would own the weapons*, 28 December 2012.

312 Cynthia Johnston, Killers of Las Vegas cops harbored anti-government ideology, *Reuters*, 9 June 2014; Nicole Hensley, Las Vegas police officers gunned down at pizza restaurant, one civilian killed, *New York Daily News*, 9 June 2014.

[313] Robin Sax, *The Complete Idiot's Guide to the Criminal Justice System*, New York: Alpha Books, Penguin Group, 2009; Jerome G. Miller, *Search and Destroy: African-American Males in the Criminal Justice System*, Cambridge: Cambridge University Press, 1996; Larry J. Siegel and Joseph J. Senna, *Essentials of Criminal Justice*, New York: Wadsworth CENGAGE Learning, 2009.

[314] Roger Woolhouse, *Locke: A Biography*, Cambridge: Cambridge University Press, 2007; Graham Faiella, *John Locke: Champion of Modern Democracy*, New York, Rosen Publication Group, 2005.

[315] Canada, with a similar culture, is ranked 123rd in the world with 117 prisoners per 100,000 inhabitants, and the PRC, a dictatorial Communist regime has about 120 prisoners per 100,000 inhabitants. As of 2009, the U.S. was holding an average of 754 prisoners per 100,000 inhabitants, totaling about 2.3 million prisoners; however, due to the large number of jurisdictions holding prisoners it is impossible to obtain an accurate number on any given day.

[316] Kimberly Kindy, and reported by Julie Tate, Jennifer Jenkins, Steven Rich, Keith L. Alexander, and Wesley Lowery, Fatal police shootings in 2015 approaching 400 nationwide, The Washington Post, 30 May 2015.

[317] Legislation enacted since 1968 that has resulted in a considerable increase in the prison population include: *Omnibus Crime Control and Safe Streets Act of 1968*, (Public Law 90-351 – June 19, 1968); *The Comprehensive Drug Abuse Prevention and Control Act of 1970*, (Public Law 91-513, Oct. 27, 1970); *The Anti-Drug Abuse Act of 1986* (Public Law 99-570 – Oct. 27 1986); *The Violent Crime Control and Law Enforcement Act of 1994* (Public Law 103-322 – Sept. 13, 1994)

[318] This quote is attributed to Mahatma Gandhi (1869-1948).

[319] Peter Hermann, Ed. O'Keefe, and David A. Fahrenthold, Driver killed after car chase from White House to Capitol, *The Washington Post*, 3 October 2013. Six months later, in April 2014, new revelations came. Miriam Carey was not under the influence of controlled substances, prescription medications or alcohol. She was not armed. Apparently, she was not mentally unbalanced. But she was shot multiple times, including once in the back of the head. She had not crashed a security gate or barrier as was originally reported. But, she was chased by the Secret Service, Capitol Police, and DC Police and shot to death with her infant in the car. Police actions violated police policy against shooting into a moving car.

[320] N.M. police fire on minivan filled with kids and their mom, *CBS This Morning*, 18 November 2013; New Mexico state officers under investigation after firing at minivan with children inside, *Associated Press*, 18 November 2013.

[321] Nick Chiles, Jonathan Ferrell, 14, Gunned Down by Charlotte Police While Seeking Help After Car Crash, *Atlanta Blackstar*, 16 September 2013.

[322] Joshua Rubin, Catholic college police officer kills student after struggle, university says, *CNN,* 10 December 2013.

[323] Kevin Sheehan, Cops bloody old man – for jaywalking, *New York Post,* 19 January 2014; Sanders, Elderly man hurt in jaywalking dispute with police on Upper West Side, Metro NY, 20 January 2014; Daily Mail Reporter, Man left beaten and bloodied for jaywalking is 85-year-old who doesn't understand much English. *The Daily Mail,* 20 January 2014; John Marzulli, Manhattan man, 84, ticketed for jaywalking to file $5 million lawsuit against city, *The Daily News,* 27 January 2014.

[324] Ian Urbina and Sean D. Hamill, Judges Plead Guilty in Scheme to Jail Youths for Profit, *The New York Times,* 12 February 2012. The two judges were Mark A. Ciavarella, Jr. and Michael T. Conahan. They pleaded guilty to wire fraud and income tax fraud for kickbacks totaling over $2.6 million. As many as 5,000 juveniles may have victimized by the two judges.

[325] Verdict tossed in Culpeper '96 death, *Richmond Times Dispatch,* 3 January 2012; U.S. judge overturns 2001 Culpeper capital murder conviction, *Richmond Times Dispatch,* 29 February 2012.

[326] Debbie Denmon, Miles set free in Dallas court after exoneration, *Dallas WFAA-TV,* 22 February 2012.

[327] AP, Ex-prosecutor released from jail after 4 days, *ABC 13 Eyewitness News – KTRK-TV Houston,* 15 November 2013; Alexa Ura, Ken Anderson to Serve 9 Days in Jail, *The Texas Tribune,* 8 November 2013.

[328] Bianca Facchinei, Montana Judge Sentences Rapist to 30-Day Sentence, says Victim was "In Control of Situation," *HNGN,* 29 August 2013; Dana Ford, 30-day rape sentence may be illegal, says Montana judge at center of controversy, *CNN,* 3 September 2013.

[329] Associated Press, Montana Judge reconsiders controversial 30-day rape sentence, *Associated Press,* 4 September 2013.

[330] Matthew Strout, A Fundamental Problem with Judicial Elections: Low Voter Turnout, *Judges on Merit,* 10 June 2013.

[331] Lincoln Caplan, The problem with judicial elections, *Constitution Daily,* November 2013.

[332] Dorian Johnson had a criminal background, including an arrest in Jefferson City, MS in 2011 for theft and a false report to police. He had an active arrest warrant for failing to appear in court.

[333] Ferguson Police Department report of strong-arm robbery, #14-12388, video of incident is exceptionally clear. 8/09/2014.

[334] Tim Molloy, Ferguson Police: Michael Brown Stole Cigars Before Shooting (Photos), *TheWrap.com*, 15 August 2014. Was it the first time he acted that way? The news media apparently was not interested in finding the answer.

[335] Violent crime in Ferguson, Missouri, since 2007 was higher than the U.S. average; Property crime rate has also been higher than the U.S. average since 2000.

[336] There is a recording of the police dispatcher and questions by a police officer who is asking for more details. The policeman was informed about the strong-arm robbery carried out about 15 minutes earlier.

[337] Officer Wilson apparently was verbally abusive himself right from the start, when he told the two youths to get the F… off the street and move to the sidewalk.

[338] YouTube videos made right after the police shooting of Michael Brown. https://bay173.mail.live.com/default.aspx?fid=flinbox#tid=cmGs-fMyMn5BGcFwAhWtcTDg2&fid=flinbox

https://www.youtube.com/watch?v=9_icVWKO4_o

[339] Jesse Jackson: There's a 'Ferguson' near you, *USA Today*, 13 August, 2014; Steve Straub, Here's What Happened When Jesse Jackson Asked A Crowd In Ferguson For Money, *The Federalistpepers.org*, 17 August 2014; In Ferguson, Jesse Jackson Reportedly Booed After Asking Crowd for Donations, *FoxNews.com*, 17 August 2014.

[340] Al Sharpton: Ferguson Shooting Is 'Defining Moment,' Huffington Post, 17 August 2014 (Updated 18 August 2014); Erik Badia and Corky Siemaszko, Rev. Al Sharpton accuses Ferguson, Mo.; police chief of 'smear campaign' against Michael Brown, *New York Daily News*, 16 August 2014.

[341] Farrakhan Attacks Arab, Chinese, Koreans, Indians, Whites in Ferguson Rant, *BreibartTV*, 25 August 2014.

[342] Farrakhan In His Own Words, *Anti-Defamation League*, 30 April 2014.

[343] Danielle Cadet, Louis Farrakhan Critiques Obama's Gay Marriage Endorsement, *The Huffington Post*, 29 May 2012. As covered by this article, Farrakhan attacked President Obama for being *"the first president that sanctioned what the scriptures forbid."*

[344] Ed Payne and Ana Cabrera, Tensions ease in Ferguson after scuffle breaks out near police chief, CNN, 26 September 2014.

[345] Outside contributing factors were a decision by a Grand Jury in Ohio not to convict two police officers for shooting a young Afro-American at a Walmart store on the same day that Michael Brown was shot (see next section Beavercreek Ohio Vignette), the broadcasting of another police officer in South Carolina shooting another Afro-American for no valid reason. In that case the policeman was fired immediately from his job. Jason Hanna, Martin Savidge, and John Murgatroyd,

Video shows trooper shooting unarmed man, South Carolina police say, *CNN*, 26 September 2014.

346 According to a Rasmussen Reports national telephone survey taken during the rioting in Ferguson found that 23% of all American Adults believe the police officer who shot and killed Michael Brown in Ferguson, should be found guilty of murder. Twenty-six percent (26%) thought that he was acting in self-defense. Fifty-one percent (51%) were undecided. Fifty-seven percent (57%) of black adults, however, thought that police officer Darren Wilson should be found guilty of murder, compared to just 17% of whites and 24% of other minority Americans. Most whites (56%) and a plurality (49%) of other minorities were undecided. See: A Tale of Two Cities? Blacks, Whites Sharply Disagree About Ferguson, Rasmussen Reports, 18 August 2014. Darren Wilson was not indicted.

347 Jon Swaine, Ferguson protest leaders: 'We'll take our anger out on people who failed us', *TheGuardian.com*, 8 October 2014. Report: Missouri Authorities Planning for Riots if Ferguson Officer Not Indicted, *CBSNewsSt.Louis*, 8 October 2014.

348 Ferguson witness accounts of the Brown shooting differ from story on street, *Fox News*, 25 November 2014; Marc Fisher and Wesley Lowery, Ferguson violence broke the mold in three ways — one of which is just unfolding now, *The Washington Post*, 25 November 2014; Chico Harlan, Wesley Lowery and Kimberly Kindy, After a night of violence in Ferguson, Nixon moves to prevent more destruction, *The Washington Post*, 25 November 2014; AP, Ferguson Mayor: National Guard deployment delayed, *Associated Press*, 25 November 2014; Report: Body Found Shot to Death, Set Fire Near Apartment Complex Where Michael Brown Died, *CBS St. Louis/ AP*, 25 November 2014.

349 Louis Head served at least two terms for five and seven years for felony convictions.

350 The movie Super Fly, classified as a *Blaxploitation film*, came out in 1972, featuring an African American cocaine dealer and catchy lyrics by Curtis Mayfield and starring Ron O'Neal. This genre of films was made for urban Black audiences with funk and soul music and glorifying anti-hero stereotype roles and elements of the growing counterculture. The NAACP and other Afro-American organizations fought a losing battle against these counterculture efforts to exploit the poor and the uneducated while promoting wrong role models for young people.

351 The members of the UN committee as of November 2014 represent Chile, China, Denmark, Georgia, Italy, Mauritius, Morocco, Nepal. Senegal, and the United States of America.

352 A misdemeanor is a "lesser" criminal offense and generally punished less severely than felonies, normally with fines instead of jail time.

[353] Resisting arrest is by itself a criminal violation, without regard to what is involved, including verbally or physically resisting when a police officer tries to execute an arrest.

[354] A horticulturist works in the branch of agriculture that engages in plant cultivation, including plant conservation, park restoration, and landscapes.

[355] Sleep Apnea can cause mental illness, according to some medial studies, particularly because it causes a reduction in the flow of oxygen to the brain, and may cause mood swings.

[356] J. David Goodman, Man Who Filmed Fatal Police Chokehold Is Arrested on Weapons Charges, *The New York Times*, 3 August 2014; Victoria Cavaliere, Ramsey Orta, Man Who Filmed Eric Garner's Chokehold Death, Arrested on Weapons Charges, *Huffington Post*, 4 August 2014; Eric Garner's Killer Wasn't Indicted, But The Man Who Filmed Him Was, Refinery 29, December 2014; Michael Stevens, Ramsey Orta Filmed Indicted: Man Who Filmed Eric Garner's Death Indicted, *Twitter*,4 December 2014.

[357] Wesley Cook, AKA Mumia Abu-Jamal, is currently serving his sentence at Mahanoy State Correctional Institution in Frackville, Pennsylvania.

[358] Goddard College taps man who killed police officer to speak at commencement, *Rutland Herald*, 01 October 2014. The graduating class numbers 23 students.

[359] Goddard College is an accredited – but experimental - private coed educational institution founded in 1938, with about 700 students, located in Plainfield, VT. At this "experimental" school students are allowed to design and self-direct their studies, with an intensive low-residency model. A new branch of the school was stablished in Seattle, WA in 2005.

[360] Rudolph fled to the Appalachian Mountains and lived in the wilderness as a fugitive for five years, becoming a hero to extremist anti-abortion and anti-homosexual organizations, until his arrest in 2003.

[361] Overland Park Shooting Suspect Has Long White Supremacist History, *ADL Blog*, 14 April 2014.

[362] Michael Rubinkam, Police say sniper suspect wanted revolution, *Associated Press*, 14 November 2014.

[363] In the first seven months of the Fiscal Year 2013, the top ten traffic cameras in the capital issued $29.5 million in speeding tickets, making the system an important income resource for the city. The most profitable camera is the one placed in the eastbound direction under Washington Circle, as the Whitehurst Freeway merges into K Street. There are no side streets or intersections, making it practically impossible to have an accident, yet the camera issues the largest number of traffic fines where it hardly justified to have such a device. The prior history of accidents

at that location is practically non-existent. D.C. Speed Cameras: $29.5 Million in Tickets Issued Since October, *Huffington Post*, 28 May 2013.

364 Anjani Trivedi, How the American Privatized Prison Is Spreading Overseas, *Time*, 23 August 2013; Angelo Young, Top Private Prison Operators GEO, Corrections Corp of America Worry About Fewer Illegal Immigrants in Jail Because It's Good For Business, *International Business Times*, 21 March 2013; Associated Press, Private Prison Companies Make Big Money Off Detaining Undocumented Immigrants, *Huff Post*, 01 October 2012. ADI News Services, Attorney General called to investigate for-profit private prison operators, *Arizona Daily Independent*, 10 August 2012.

365 Max Ehrenfreund, Mass incarceration is making the Federal Reserve's job harder, *The Washington Post*, 17 September 2014.

366 See Anthony Bouza's book *The Police Mystique: An Insider's Look at Cops, Crime, and the Criminal Justice System*, New York: Perseus Publishing, 1990, and James Q. Wilson, *Varieties of Police Behavior: The Management of Law and Order in Eight Communities*, New York: Perseus Books, 1978.

367 The expression has been around for some time, going back to around 1576. It was used, for example, around 1717 by English novelist Daniel Defoe in *Memoirs of the Church of Scotland.* Born Daniel Foe around 1660, Defoe is best known for his novel *Robinson Crusoe.*

368 Ray Sánchez, The Growing Number of Prosecutions for Videotaping the Police, *ABC News*, 19 July 2010; Dan Goodin, Police Cuff US Citizen for Videotaping Arrests, *Broadband/DSLReports.com*, 12 January 2010; Matt Sledge, Rochester Woman Arrested After Videotaping Police From Her Own Front Yard, *Huffington Post*, 22 June 2011; Fall River Man Arrested For Videotaping Police Officer, *CBS Boston*, 7 March 2014; Navy vet arrested after taping police on cell phone, 10 News (Tampa Bay Sarasota *www.WTSP.com*), 22 July 2011; Adam Cohen, A New First Amendment Right: Videotaping the Police, *Time*, 21 May 2012; Man Arrested After Taping Arrest With Cell Phone, *CBS Miami*, 28 April 2014.

369 Rodney King was no saint. He had prior convictions for assault, battery and robbery, and had been drinking, which was a violation of his parole terms. Nevertheless, police officers had no excuse for subjecting him to a beating, even if he had initially resisted arrest.

370 Marisa Taylor, Rodney King Case Changed Perceptions of Police Brutality, *Los Angeles Times*, 17 June 2012. (The Afro-American community in Los Angeles reacted angrily. The trial was followed by rioting in South Central Los Angeles, which spread to other parts of the city in April, 1992. Looting, arson, and assaults resulted in at least 53 deaths, over 2,000 injured, and an estimated $1 billion in property damage. Over 6,300 people were arrested. The Governor had to mobilize

the California Army National Guard and the President had to send in the Army 7th Infantry Division and the 1st Marine Division to assist police in restoring peace. The public outcry led to the Justice Department's indicting of the police officers on civil rights charges. The trial in Federal District Court on 16 April 1993 resulted in the finding of guilt for two of the officers, who were sent to prison, and the acquittal of two of the other officers.)

[371] Alan Wang, Witnesses upset over Antioch arrest, police confiscating cellphones, *ABC 7 News (San Francisco, Oakland, and San Jose)*, 8 August 2014.

[372] For example, the U.S. Court of Appeals for the First Circuit in Boston ruled that police violated the First Amendment rights of Simon Glik by arresting him for making a cell-phone video of a police arrest, and Glik was awarded $170,000 in damages and legal fees. Adam Cohen, A New First Amendment Right: Videotaping the Police, *Time*, 21 May 2012.

[373] Spencer Ackerman, NSA surveillance: Narrow Defeat for Amendment to Restrict Data Collection, *The Guardian*, 24 July 2013.

[374] Ken Dilanian, Secret Surveillance Court Judges Oppose Reform Ideas, *Los Angeles Times*, 14 January 2014.

[375] Abu Ghraib Photos May be Released by Judge Order, *Reuters*, 27 August 2014;

[376] July K. Brown, For allegedly brutal prison guard, day of reckoning arrives, *The Miami Herald*, 20 September 2014.

[377] Cristopher Graveline, *The Secrets of Abu Ghraib Revealed,* Dulles, VA: Potomac Books, Inc. 2010; Karen Greenberg, Abu Ghraib: A Torture Story Without a Hero or an Ending, *The Nation,* 28 April 2014; Iraq Prison Abuse Scandal Fast Facts, *CNN Library,* updated 30 October 2013; David Dishneau, Charles Graner Released: Abu Ghraib Abuse Ringleader Set Free From Kansas Prison, *The Huffington Post*, 6 August 2011;

[378] Jeff Garis, Executive Director, Pennsylvania Abolitionists United Against the Death Penalty.

[379] http://www.kersplebedeb.com/mystuff/nwo/paguard.html (Last accessed on 29 September 2012).

[380] Liz Fields, Half of Sexual Abuse Claims in American Prisons Involved Guards, Study Says, *The Huffington Post*, 26 January 2014.

[381] Allen J. Beck, Ramona R. Rantala and Jessica Rexroat, Sexual Victimization Reported by Adult Correctional Authorities, 2009-11, U.S. Department of Justice, Office of Justice Programs, Bureau of Justice Statistics.

[382] Ryan J. Reilly, ACLU Report Reveals Immigrant Abuse In 'Shadow' Private Prisons, *The Huffington Post*, 11 June 2014.

[383] Allen J. Beck, Ramona R. Rantala and Jessica Rexroat, Sexual Victimization, Op. Cit.

[384] Vicki Brown, Man Dies in Police Raid on Wrong House, *ABC News*; http://abcnews.go.com/US/story?id=95475&page=1; Time to Curb Rise in Deadly Paramilitary Police Raids, *CATO Institute*, 17 July 2006; Shaila K. Dewan, City to Pay $1.6 Million in Fatal, Mistaken Raid, *The New York Times*, 29 October 2003; Family of Michigan Girl Killed in Police Raid Files Lawsuit, *CNN*, 18 May 2010; Melissa Melton, This Is Why They Should Knock First: Multiple Cops Shot, One Killed in No Knock Raid, *The Daily Sheeple*, 13 May 2014; Tim King, American Police and the *'No Knock Raid,"* Salem-News.com, 18 June 2011; 80,000 SWAT Raids Against the General Public Every Year, *EconomicCollapse@CollapseReport on Twitter*, 30 March 2013; Jonathan Turley, Texas Jury Refuses To Indict Man Who Shot and Killed Officer During "No Knock" Raid, http://jonathanturley.org/2014/07/14/Texas-Jury-Refuses-to-Indict-Man-Who-Shot-and-Killed-Officer-During-No-Knock-Raid/ (last accessed on 16 September 2014; Andy Kravetz, Peoria Man Files Suit Over Mistaken 2012 Police Raid, http://www.pjstar.com/x1343095199, (Last accessed on 16 September 2014)

[385] Rick Nelson, Adam Isles, The First DHS Bottoms-up Review, *Center for Strategic and International Studies (CSIS)*, 31 August 2010.

[386] Government Accounting Office, Department of Homeland Security: Opportunities Exist to Strengthen Efficiency and Effectiveness, Achieve Cost Savings, and Improve Management Functions, GAO-13-547T, 26 April 2013.

[387] Cheryl K. Chumley. *Police State USA: How Orwell's Nightmare is Becoming our Reality*. Kindle Edition, 2014; John Whitehead. *A Government of Wolves: The Emerging American Police State*, Kindle Edition, 2014; Radley Balko. *Rise of the Warrior Cop: The Militarization of America's Police Forces*. Kindle Edition, 2014; Harlan Hahn, Judson L. Jeffries, *Urban America and its Police: From the Postcolonial Era through the Turbulent 1960s*. Boulder: University of Colorado Press, 2003; Bryan Vila, Cynthia Morris. *The Role of Police in American Society: A Documentary History*. NY: Greenwood Press, 1999. Alice Goffman, *On the Run: Fugitive Life in an American City*, Chicago: University of Chicago Press, 2014.

[388] Asset seizures fuel millions in police spending: Part 1: Motorists' cash seized, Part 2: A police intel network, Part 3: A fight to get money back, The Washington Post, 12 October 2014.

[389] James M. Farrell, The Writs of Assistance and Public Memory: John Adams and the Legacy of James Otis, *New England Quarterly, 2006*; John Clark Ridpath, Charles K. Edmunds, and G. Mercer Adam. James Otis, the Pre-Revolutionist (Available on line as eBook); James Otis Jr. [Internet]. 2014. The Biography.com

website. Available from: http://www.biography.com/people/james-otis-9430449 [Accessed 12 Oct 2014].

[390] Editorial Board, Forfeiture without due process, *The Washington Post*, 2 January 2012; A Virginia State Police officer stopped a car in which two Hispanic males were travelling on I-95, near Emporia, close to the N. Carolina border, without any violation of traffic laws. Police seized the collections from the *Nuevo Renacer* Christian church, which were to be used to purchase a trailer. The FBI and ICE were called into the case, but the FBI refused to participate. After the incident hit the news, the police officer claimed that they car had been driven above the speed limit, but no such ticket for a law violation was issued.

[391] Among the companies organized to profit from the program set up to seize assets are: 4:20 Group, Caltraps, Diamondback Training, Desert Snow, Global-Smuggling Training Consultants, and Hitz.

[392] Stop and seize, *The Washington Post*, 6 September 2014.

[393] Ian Urbina, It's a Fork, It's a Spoon, It's a... Weapon? *The New York Times*, 11 October 2009.

[394] Un profesor denuncia a una niña por llevar una tarta y un cuchillo para cortarla, *ABC Spain*, 24 de Marzo de 2014.

[395] This statement is based on active political leaders since 2000, including Barbara Boxer, Hilary Clinton, John Conyers, Russ Feingold, Tom Harkin, Steny Hoyer, John Kerry, Dennis Kucinich, Barbara Lee, Jim McDermott, Barrack Obama, Nancy Pelosi, Harry Reid, Bernie Sanders, Kshama Sawant, and Elizabeth Warren,

[396] These comments should not be misinterpreted as an endorsement of homosexual behavior. Persecution of people for their sexual orientation of for any other reason beyond their control is unacceptable.

[397] Associated Press, Pastor with AIDS sued after revelation of multiple affairs, *Fox News*, 15 October 2014.

[398] While right-wing religious extremists like to point out the story of Sodom and Gomorrah in relation to *sexual depravities*, they forget that the story also points out the *humiliation of strangers*, inhospitality, lack of compassion for the poor and the needy. They probably find it "*inconvenient*" that the lesson contradicts their anti-immigrant views and lack of compassion for the needy.

[399] Jim Hoft, ISIS Celebrates Gay Love by Tossing 4 Gays from Roof of Building, GP, 26 June 20115. http://www.thegatewaypundit.com/2015/06/isis-celebrates-lovewins-by-tossing-4-gays-from-roof-of-building/

[400] Hillary Rodham Clinton (1947-) was First Lady between 1993 and 2001, and was elected U.S. Senator for New York in 2001. She ran for President in 2008, and was nominated to be Secretary of State by President Obama in January 2009, and

served in the position until 2013. In March 2013 Hilary Clinton endorsed same-sex marriage in a video recording posted on Internet by the advocacy organization Human Rights Campaign. Her husband, former President Bill Clinton, who signed into law the Defense of Marriage Act in 1996, urged the U.S. Supreme Court to strike down the law.

401 *Lumen Fidei* (The Light of Faith), 5 July 2013. In an unusual way, the encyclical represented the work of both, Pope Emeritus Benedict XVI, and Pope Francis.

402 The *Iliad* is a Greek epic poem set during the Trojan War attributed to Homer. It is considered a sequel to the *Odyssey*, also attributed to Homer. Both works dated around the 8th century BC is one of the oldest works in Western literature.

403 With the rise of fundamentalist Islam, particularly Wahhabism, since the 1980s, polygamy has been slowly decriminalized in some Muslim countries, as for example, Tajikistan, Kyrgyzstan, Bosnia and Herzegovina, Pakistan, and even in secularist Turkey.

404 "Man Charged With Sexually Abusing Animals," *10TV News and 10TV.com*, Ohio; 17 June 2011.

405 Peter Jamison, "A Clearwater man Arrested for Bestiality Worked at Humane Society of Pinellas, Florida," *Tampa Bay Times*, 3 May 2012.

406 "Florida Man Arrested For Having Sex With Miniature Donkey." *The Inquisitor*, 19 September 2012.

407 Stephen J. Hucker, *Professor, Division of Forensic Psychiatry, University of Toronto* Necrophilia, Forensic Psychiatry.CA, http://www.forensicpsychiatry.ca/

408 David Schoetz, Cops: Man Caught in Hospital Necrophilia Act, ABC News, 30 October 2007.

409 James Howard Patton Likes 'em Cold, *The Deamin'Demon Real Life Horror*, 6 October 2009.

410 Daily Mail Reporter, "I didn't know she was dead" claims man, 55, charged with necrophilia, *MailOnline*, 14 January 2011.

411 Lawrence J. Clement, Funeral home employee arraigned for sexually abusing corpse, *Examiner*, 23 March 2012; Greg Noble, Associated Press, Kenneth Douglas: Sex-with-corpses lawsuit against Hamilton County can go to trial, court rules, WCP) Cincinnati, 15 August 2014.

412 Cindy Adams, Male nurse in California accused of necrophilia for sex acts with dead woman, Examiner, 22 January 2013.

413 Katherine Ramsland, Abuse of Corpse: Some people prefer the company of the dead, *Psychology Today*, 27 November 2012

[414] For more information, see Anil Aggrawal, *Necrophilia: Forensic and Medico-Legal Aspects.* CRC Press, ISBN 978-1-4200-8912-7

[415] Neanderthals either interbred with anatomically modern humans, or shared ancestry, which points to interbreeding or a common ancestor about 500,000 years ago; there is evidence that peaceful cross-breeding took place between early humans and Neanderthals.

[416] "Neanderthals and human lived side by side in Middle Eastern Caves and even interbred, research finds," Daily *Mail online*, 29 September 2012; Alan Boyle, "Did humans and Neanderthals 'do it'? Some experts doubt it," *NBCNews.Com*, 13 August 2012.

[417] Deuteronomy 7:3-5; Deuteronomy 23:2; Joshua 23:12-13; Hosea 5:6-7; Exodus 33:16; Nehemiah 13:23; Malachi 2:11.

[418] Galatians 3:28; Acts 17:26: *And he made from one man every nation or mankind to live on all the face of the earth, having determined allotted periods and the boundaries of their dwelling place...; Leviticus 19:18: You shall not take vengeance or bear a grudge against the sons of your own people, but you shall love your neighbor as yourself: I am the Lord.*

[419] The Apostle Saint Paul (Saul of Tarsus) (C. AD 5 – c AD 67), one of the most influential Christian missionaries, preached throughout the Roman Empire and Asian Minor to anybody would listen. He is credited with the initial Christian practice of preaching mostly to Jews who converted to Christianity.

[420] Friedrich Wilhelm von Steuben (1730-1794), a former Prussian officer, assisted General George Washington to train the Continental Army, and as his Chief of Staff. He is credited with rebuilding the Army during the Revolutionary War in essential discipline, manual of arms, and tactics. According to historical records, Benjamin Franklin was aware that von Steuben was homosexual, but dismissed it when he introduced him to George Washington as a person who could help reform the Continental Army. Tolerance is not a new phenomenon.

[421] Michelle Bauman, African American Leaders blast NAACP's 'gay marriage' support, *Free Republic*, 23 May 2012. When the NAACP endorsed same sex marriage in May 2012, prominent Afro-American leaders objected, and according to a poll taken at the time by the Pew Research Center, only 39% of African Americans favored redefining marriage. *"Dr. Alveda C. King, niece of Dr. Martin Luther King, Jr., said that neither her grandfather nor her uncle "embraced the homosexual agenda that the current NAACP is attempting to label as a civil rights agenda." "We who marched with Rev. King did not march one inch or one mile to promote same-sex marriage," agreed Rev. William Owens, founder and president of the Coalition of African American Pastors.*

[422] Associated Press, Former President George H. W. Bush serves as witness at friends' Maine same-sex wedding, *The Washington Post*, 26 September 2013.

[423] Devin Dwyer, Barbara Bush Campaigns for Same-Sex Marriage Rights, *ABC News*, 1 February 2011.

[424] David Badash, Watch: George W. Bush Uses Bible to Say People Shouldn't Judge Same-Sex Marriage, *Marriage News, Politics, Religion*, 7 July 2013.

[425] David Remnick, Annals of the Presidency: Going the Distance On and off the road with Barack Obama, *The New Yorker* Magazine, 27 January 2014.

[426] Legalization of Illicit Drugs: Impact and Feasibility (A Review of Recent Hearings) Report of The Select Committee On Narcotics Abuse And Control, One Hundred First Congress, First Session. 1989.

[427] In 2007 I published *The Next Phase of Jihad: A War with Islamic Narco-Terrorists*, in which I predicted that there would be an increase in heroin trafficking from Afghanistan into Russia, Western Europe, and eventually into the U.S. Cocaine, amphetamines, and marijuana became the drugs of choice since the 1960s, to be partially replaced by the misuse of ethical drugs (Prescription medications), particularly opioids such as OxyContin (Vicodin).

[428] Tony Dokoupil, Treatment or Jail: Patrick Kennedy Wages Fierce Anti-Pot Crusade, *NBCNews*, 17 February 2014.

[429] St. Thomas Aquinas was a Dominican priest, philosopher, theologian, and one of the most influential thinkers of medieval Scholasticism.

[430] One of the first signs of the growth of a new culture was the 1962 decision of the Supreme Court in Engel v Vitale (370 US 421), which declared unconstitutional for states to compose an official school prayer, even non-denominational prayers, and allowed students to excuse themselves from participation.

[431] Rebecca Barnes and Lindy Lowry, 7 Startling Facts: An Up Close Look at Church Attendance in America. http://www.churchleaders.com/pastors/pastor-articles/139575-7-startling-facts-an-up-close-look-at-church-attendance-in-america.html

[432] Frank Newport, In U.S., Four in 10 Report Attending Church in Last Week, Gallup Politics, 24 December 2013.

[433] Jones had been arrested on 13 December 1973 in Los Angeles for soliciting a man for sex in a movie theater. He abused male members of his congregation, and engaged in sexual relations with males and females.

[434] Jim Jones, Jamestown Audiotape Primary Project: Transcript, Recovered tape by the FBI Q 1053.

[435] Brian Ross and Rehab El-Buri, Obama's Pastor: God Damn America, US to Blame for 9/11, *ABC News,*13 March 2008.

[436] These are some examples: James O. Bakker, Jimmy Swaggart, Jim Whittington, and Ted Haggard.

[437] For example, PPACA (Obamacare) requires employer-provided health insurance to cover contraceptives, even for employers who happen to be religious institutions that do not approve, such as the Catholic Church and religious orders, in direct contradiction to the First Amendment. The reputable Little Sisters of the Poor filed a lawsuit. If the government prevails, the institutions staffed by the nuns that take care of the poor and the elderly will have to close these centers. Many Protestant denominations share similar views with Catholics, particularly their opposition to abortion.

[438] This was the Immigration and Nationality Act of 1965 (Public Law 236 of the 89th Congress, also known as the Hart-Celler Act or the INS Act of 1965). The new law abolished the national-origin quotas that had been in place in the United States since the Immigration Act of 1924.

[439] U.S. Bureau of the Census. About 13% of illegal immigrants in the country were from Asia, about 6% from Europe and Canada, about 3% from Africa and the rest of the world. The vast majority – about 57% -is from Mexico, and about 21% from other Latin American countries.

[440] I worked at the American Embassy in the Netherlands between 1993 and 1996, and my observations are based on personal eyewitness experience.

[441] Ayaan Hirsi Ali later moved to the U.S. and became an American citizen. Part of the reason for her moving to the U.S. was to escape numerous threats against her in the Netherlands by Islamic extremists.

[442] The French national motto has been *Liberté, Egalité, and Fraternité* since about 1791 during the French Revolution, although it became more popular in the early 19th century.

[443] In November 2005 I was working at the U.S. European Command in Stuttgart, Germany. I had taken time off from work and had driven to Paris. I drove into Paris from the East, and I entered the *Périphérique*, or "beltway" around the city, I happened to find myself in a mostly poor Muslim area of the city in the middle of the riots by Arab, North African (mainly Algerian), and African youths. They were burning cars and attacking public buildings and Catholic churches. Parliament had declared a state of emergency days before, on 16 November. Thousands of rioters were arrested. Riots also took place in Lyon, Grenoble, Marseille, Dijon, Rouen, Strasbourg, Nice, and about 274 French towns and cities. One thing is to read about it in newspapers or watch it on television, and another to be in

close proximity to the rioting. Close to 9,000 cars were burned, and at least 126 policemen and firefighters were hurt.

444 Exact numbers are not available because France's Constitution prohibits the collection of data related to race, religion or the ethnicity of prisoners.

445 Merah was born of Algerian parents, who divorced when he was five years old, and was raised by a single mother. He had a history of petty crimes and violence.

446 I have been to London several times and visited an area of Hyde Park where on Saturday Islamic extremists jump on their soap box and using British freedoms speak out in support of al-Qai'da and in favor of destruction of Western culture, the U.S. and Great Britain.

447 The situation in Spain is very similar. On 11 March 2004, several commuter trains were bombed by Islamic extremists in Madrid, killing 191 civilians and wounding another 1,800. The terrorist attacks were carried out by immigrants from Morocco, Tunisia, and Syria, and had been assisted by Pakistani shopkeepers. The victims were from 17 countries: 142 Spanish, 16 Romanians, 6 Ecuadorians, 4 Poles, 4 Bulgarians, 3 Peruvians, 2 Dominicans, 2 Colombians, 2 Moroccans, 2 Ukrainians, 2 Hondurans, 1 Senegalese, 1 Cuban, 1 Chilean, 1 Brazilian, 1 French, and 1 Filipino. Spain has been very receptive to immigrants, but friction with Moroccan immigrants is considerable. Just as the US allows Mexican agricultural workers to cross the border to pick crops, Spain allows thousands of Moroccan agricultural workers to cross over annually to pick up crops in Andalucía and other parts of Spain. Spanish jails are packed with a large number of criminal elements from N. Africa, particularly Morocco, who are guilty of most crimes, particularly theft. I served at the American Embassy in Madrid from 1996 to 2000. I remember driving north from Madrid towards Burgos, and as I drove into a small town along the way about one hour north of Madrid to get a cup of coffee, I witnessed a huge billboard painted on the side of a large building right at the entrance of the town. It read: *Africans back to Africa – We do not want Moors here!*

448 The members of the "Gang of Eight" are Senators Michael Bennet (D-CO), Richard J. Durbin (D-IL), Jeff Flake (R-AZ), Lindsey Graham (R-SC), John McCain (R-AZ), Bob Menendez (D-NJ), Marco Rubio (R-FL), and Chuck Schumer (D-NY)

449 I am using the term Spanish-surnamed instead of Hispanic or Latino, because these terms are a misnomer, as they could be White, African, Asian, Native American, Pilipino, or of mixed race. Spanish-surnamed prisoners can be native-born or nationalized American citizens, legal or illegal immigrants.

450 As already explained, the terminology used fails to properly identify citizenship, race, and legal status. Having a Spanish name does really describe the individual.

451 At least we try to track prison populations. In Europe for the sake of protecting privacy, it is illegal to keep track of nationality, place of birth, ethnic or religious affiliation of prison populations.

452 There are many causes for the high rate of recidivism, which has increased since the 2008 economic crisis, which resulted in high rate of joblessness, poverty, welfare dependency, poor educational attainment, and increasing drug trafficking. Mexican Cartels recruit incarcerated Mexicans for their distribution systems once they get out of prison, which contributes to a higher rate of recidivism. Among these Mexican gangs are *Barrio Azteca, Hermanos Pistoleros Latinos, La Eme, Mexicles, Mexikanemi, Mexican Mafia, Nuestra Familia, Pura Vida, Raza Unida, and Texas Chicano Brotherhood*

453 U.S. Drug Enforcement Administration, *Drug Trafficking in the United States*, September 2001.

454 George Skelton, Illegal immigrants are a factor in the budget gap math, *Los Angeles Times*, 2 February 2009.

455 Tysons Foods Inc. was involved in a scandal in 2001 at their meat packaging plant in Kansas City, which was packed with illegal immigrants. Some Tyson executives were fired and others arrested and prosecuted, but that did not change industrial practices. In 2006, there were similar raids at six Swift packing plants in Colorado, Iowa, Minnesota, Nebraska, Texas and Utah, but nothing changed. Instead, there was an outcry because the breadwinners were arrested and deported, leaving behind American-born children and their mothers, who became dependent on welfare. In 2008, there were raids at chicken processing plants in Monroe Union County in North Carolina, where illegal immigrants were employed at low wages and horrible working conditions. In March 2013 there were similar raids at chicken processing plants.

456 While the number of single-parent families increased since the early 1990s, crime rates have been declining. There is no direct correlation between the two. However, there is an absence of reliable data on the family background of the huge prison population, or predictive statistics for juvenile incarceration. There is a large body of literature that shows that children of single mothers are more likely to commit crimes. See Kay Hymowitz, The Real, Complex Connection Between Single-Parent Families and Crime, *The Atlantic*, 3 December 2012; Patrick F. Fagan, The Real Root Causes of Violent Crime: The Breakdown of Marriage, Family, and Community, *The Heritage Foundation*, 17 March 1995.

457 Department of Justice, "More Than 100 Members and Associates of Transnational Organized Crime Groups Charged with Offenses Including Bank Fraud, Kidnapping, Racketeering and Health Care Fraud: Six Indictments Returned in Los Angeles-area, Miami and Denver Allege Widespread Criminal Conduct by

Members of Armenian Power and Other Transnational Groups," February 16, 2011.

[458] U.S. Department of Justice, "Two Russian organized crime figures charged in plot to murder businessmen," March 24, 2006.

[459] Benjamin Weiser, U.S. Says Diplomats Defraud Medicaid, *The New York Times*, 5 December 2013. According to the U.S. Attorney in Manhattan, it is estimated that the Russian diplomats had defrauded the Medicaid program for at least $1.5 million.

[460] During fiscal years 2009 and 2010, ICE special agents initiated 1,133 criminal investigations related to terrorism. During that same period, ICE agents made 534 arrests and conducted thousands of seizures of money, arms, contraband and other assets related to illegal schemes. There is no information in the public domain about the nationality of terrorists and potential terrorists identified, investigated, and arrested by ICE, and there is no published information of similar information for fiscal years 2011, 2012, and 2013. Source: ICE.

[461] Black gangs included the Crips and the Bloods, the Black Panther Party and the Brown Berets, which had steadily increased since the late 1960s after the Watts riots in 1965 and had become well-established by 1980. By 1982 there were at least 155 Black gangs in Los Angeles with links to other gangs all over the country. Mexican gangs, including *Sureños* were operating since the early 1970s in southern California, with ties to the Mexican Mafia (La Eme). By the time the Central Americans arrived in the second half of the 1980s, the Black and Mexican gangs were dedicated to criminal activity and control of territory.

[462] Illegal Aliens: Extent of Welfare Benefits Received on Behalf of U.S. Citizen Children, GAO/HEHS-98-30, U.S. Government Accounting Office (GAO), November 1997.

[463] About 400 Spanish conquistadores arrived in Mexico in 1519 under the command of Hernan Cortes. The best colony-wide census taken during the Spanish colonial period covering Mexico and the former Spanish/Mexican territory in present day Texas, New Mexico, Colorado, Utah, California, Washington and Oregon was carried out under the order issued by Viceroy Count de Revillagigedo (1789-93), and later census carried out by Alexander von Humboldt around 1803. There were Spanish families living in Florida way before the American War of Independence that started in 1776.

[464] For example, there are many people from the Philippines that have Spanish surnames, as the Islands are a former Spanish colony. Technically, they are Pacific Islanders, and may not have any Spanish blood or ancestry.

[465] I wrestled with the term *American Native* because it can be confusing to some people. These are aborigines or native populations of the Western Hemisphere,

i.e. the Americas. Although some people may misunderstand the term American, it does not cover uniquely people from the United States of America. Mexico's official name is United States of Mexico, and it happens to be in North America. Venezuela, officially, is the United States of Venezuela, and it happens to be in South America. The term Indian or "*indio*" could have been used, but it is the product of Spaniards who arrived with Cristopher Columbus in 1492, who did not have any idea of where they were and assumed they had reached India.

[466] Left-wing Anthropologists are partly to blame for the extreme poverty of Native American populations. For example, in Mexico, after the Mexican Revolution, there was a serious concern about the native populations, and an interest in educating and assisting them to move out of the Stone Age. However, as usually happen with leftist extremists, they began to suggest that the native cultures should be protected and left intact without subverting them with European imported culture. The end result has been that the natives where left to live in poverty *for their own good*, to protect their cultures.

[467] The price of food in the U.S. is kept relatively low as a result of the low wages paid to this floating population of agricultural workers. In their absence, food prices would skyrocket.

[468] There is insufficient data to compare this subset of the entire population in such areas as the incidence of unwanted pregnancies, children born out of wedlock, or children abandoned by their fathers, and fathers not paying for child support.

[469] The U.S. has funded a national school lunch program since 1946. The program has been expanded over the years to include a School Breakfast Program. Denmark, Finland, France, Japan, Norway, South Korea, Sweden, and the UK have school meals for children. Other countries, as for example, Canada, do not sponsor school lunch programs.

[470] Many legal and illegal immigrants, as well as U.S. Citizens with Spanish surnames volunteer every year to join the military. Hundreds were killed and wounded in Afghanistan and Iraq. If you question this fact, simply do a "Google search" for lists of casualties and take a look at the pictures and the surnames of casualties in both conflicts.

[471] The estimate of the number of illegal immigrants was made by the U.S. Bureau of the Census.

[472] According to Los Angeles County Supervisor Michael Antonovich, the cost of providing welfare to American-born children of illegal immigrants in the county surpassed $600 in 2010. These costs did not include the cost of providing education in public schools, which would add several hundred million dollars. The total cost of providing welfare coverage to illegal immigrants in California alone is estimated to cost at least $21.8 billion. See: Welfare Tab for Children of

Illegal Immigrants Estimated at $600 M in L.A. County, *Fox News*, 19 January 2011.

473 The cost of the food stamps program over the next ten year period is expected to surpass $630 billion. The Federal Government, namely USDA, through state governments promote through documents in Spanish participation of legal and illegal immigrants in the "food stamps" program. Although legal immigrants are supposed to have to wait at least five years from their arrival to have access to food stamps, unless they are 60 years old or less than 18 years old, or handicapped, the issue of legality is ignored. Applicants do not need to disclose their status to obtain benefits for their children, regardless of where they were born. If the legal immigrant obtained their visa through a sponsor, the sponsor is supposed to be responsible for the cost for five years, but this technicality is ignored, and the technicality does not apply to children anyway.

474 During a visit with my mother in June 2013, I decided to ask several of nurses at my mother's nursing home where they were from. One told me that she was from Sierra Leone, three told me they were from Ghana, and two told me that they were from Kenya.

475 There is a large Vietnamese colony in Northern Virginia. Thousands of refugees fleeing the Communist takeover in Vietnam in 1975 settled in the Washington Metropolitan Area, particularly in Northern Virginia.

476 According to the Profile of U.S. Resident Travelers Visiting Overseas Destinations: 2009 Outbound, International Trade Administration, U.S. Department of Commerce, 39% of the travelers were from the Middle Atlantic, 19% from South Atlantic, Pacific 14%, 8% from New England, 7% from East North Central, West South Central 5% and only 2% from West North Central and East South Central. The average household income was $109,200, and the median income was $99,600. According to the U.S. Bureau of the Census, the median household income in 2009 was $50,221. The median household income in Virginia in 2009 was $59,330, which although higher than the national median, was well below the median household income of Americans who travelled overseas. Most Americans never obtain a passport, and do not travel overseas. Requiring passports to get a driver's license is *ridiculous*, and requiring as an alternative a birth certificate, which do not have fingerprints or pictures, is even more stupid.

477 This author agrees with Sir Winston Churchill's remark that *Communists (Bolshevism) should have been strangled at the cradle.*

478 Captain William S. Brei (USAF). *Getting Intelligence Right: The Power of Logical Procedure.* Occasional Paper Number Two. Washington, DC: Joint Military Intelligence College, 1996. The so-called Six Fundamental Principles of Intelligence are derived from William F. Brei's book.

479 Examples include a refusal to accept that an insurgency was building in Afghanistan, confusing GWOT with a COIN, going into Iraq ignoring critical intelligence reports, and a refusal to accept that the enemy is composed of Islamic extremists, not Martians newly arrived from outer space, and calling the "Islamic State," or ISIS the "JV team."

480 In the UK, voter turnout in general elections between 1945 and 2010 was on average above 70% of the electorate. In Canada the lowest voter turnout on record was in 2008, when 58.8% cast their vote, but on average about 70% of Canadians vote. In Ireland, historically, over 65% of the electorate vote. In Spain, over 70% of the electorate vote. Unusually, only 63.26% of the electorate voted in 2011. In Argentina, on average, close to 80% of the electorate cast their vote in general elections.

481 Most of the Ten Commandments apply regardless of religious convictions: *4th - Honor thy father and thy mother; 5th - Thou shall not kill; 6th - Thou shall not commit adultery; 7th – Thou shall not steal; 8th – Thou shall not bear false witness against thy neighbor; 9th – Thou shall not covet thy neighbor's wife; 10th – Thou shall not covet thy neighbor's goods.* There is nothing illogical about these commandments separate and apart from religion.

Estimated unfunded liabilities as of 14 February 2015: Medicare $36 trillion, Social Security $6 trillion, other liabilities, including military and civil service retirements $13 trillion, for a total of at least $56 trillion.

Printed in the United States
By Bookmasters